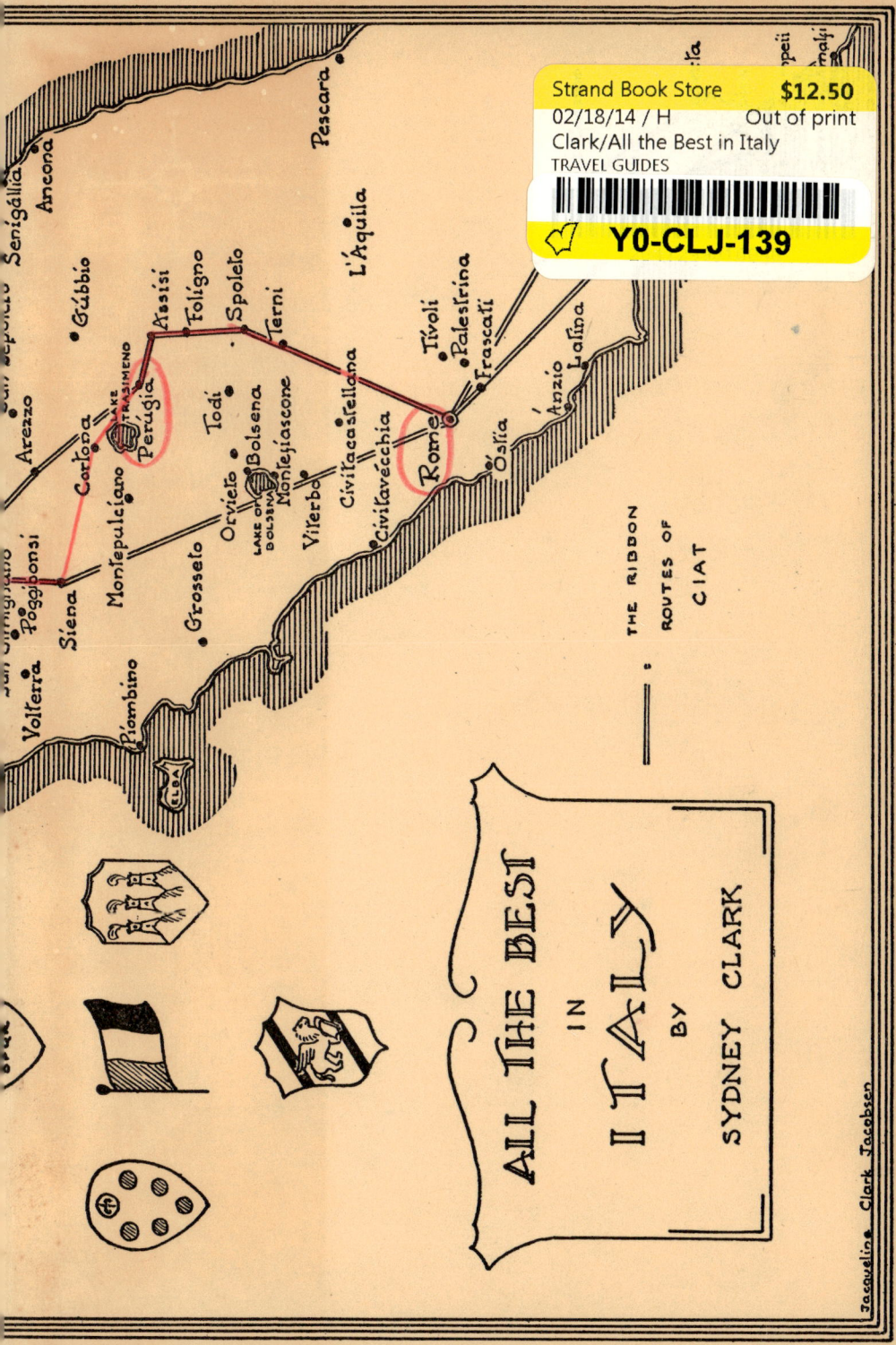

All the Best in Italy

BOOKS BY SYDNEY CLARK

ALL THE BEST IN CENTRAL AMERICA
ALL THE BEST IN CUBA
ALL THE BEST IN SOUTH AMERICA—WEST COAST
ALL THE BEST IN SOUTH AMERICA—EAST COAST
ALL THE BEST IN FRANCE
ALL THE BEST IN THE CARIBBEAN
ALL THE BEST IN ENGLAND
ALL THE BEST IN SCANDINAVIA
ALL THE BEST IN MEXICO
ALL THE BEST IN HAWAII
ALL THE BEST IN HOLLAND
ALL THE BEST IN SWITZERLAND
ALL THE BEST IN THE MEDITERRANEAN
ALL THE BEST IN ITALY

SYDNEY CLARK

All the Best in
Italy

With Illustrations and Maps

DODD, MEAD & COMPANY
NEW YORK   1953

COPYRIGHT, 1953,
By SYDNEY CLARK

ALL RIGHTS RESERVED
NO PART OF THIS BOOK MAY BE REPRODUCED IN ANY FORM
WITHOUT PERMISSION IN WRITING FROM THE PUBLISHER

Second Printing

PRINTED IN THE UNITED STATES OF AMERICA

Library of Congress Catalog Card No.—52-14194

CONTENTS

Illustrations follow pages 148 and 276.

THE FOREGROUND OF THE PICTURE

CHAPTER		PAGE
I	THE ROADS THAT LEAD TO ROME	3

    Through the Air
    Across the Sea
    On Rails from Northern Capitals
    By the Ribbons of CIAT
    By Car, with You at the Wheel

II WHAT'S IN A NAME?   16

    This *Name Has Everything*
    From Art to Scenery and Back Again
    Let the Map Explain
    War Damage Disappears
    A Tale of Ten Cities
    And of Towns That Perch on Hills

III FIRST FACTS OF TRAVEL   27

    See ENIT *Before You Go*
    See CIT *Here, There and Everywhere*
    The Pozzo Brothers on Railways
    Homemade Tours for the First-Timer
    Counsel in Rome and the Provinces
    Guidance in Print
    What to Know About Money

IV HOTELS AND THEIR PRICES   44

    Annuario Alberghi d'Italia
    Your Bill—Before You Get It
    Tips on Tipping
    Suggestions—Between You and Me
    Your Anchor in Rome

CONTENTS

CHAPTER		PAGE
V	ITALIAN FOOD, ITS FASCINATION AND ITS FAULTS	52

    Meals of the Traveler's Day
    A Blackboard Talk on Pasta
    Exploring the Menu
    Regional Favorites
    Wine—Red, White and Chianti
    Don't Be Surprised
    Eating Under the Sky
    Cafés and Bars—Italian Style

VI	ALL SORTS OF THINGS TO KNOW	68

    About Shopper's Fever
    About Your Mail, Both Ways
    About Tobacco
    About Luggage, Laundry and the Self-Ironing Fabrics
    About Coathangers—They're Important
    About the Midday Closing Hours
    About Transportation in the Cities
    About Gypping of Tourists; Does This Happen?
    About the Wonderful "Day Hotels"
    About Music, for All Brows
    About Special Festivals and Their Dates
    About Evenings in the Cities
    About Sports of Summer and Winter

VII	ITALIAN IN TEN MINUTES WITHOUT A MASTER	86

    Pronunciation
    Stress
    Essentials of Speech

THE BACKGROUND OF THE PICTURE

VIII	THIRTY CENTURIES ON A THUMBNAIL	95

    Races That Made a Race
    Thirty Dates on Call
    Today's Republic

IX	GREAT NAMES ON ITALY'S SCROLLS	110

    In Saintly Life and Influence
    In Patriotism, Politics, Adventure

CONTENTS

In Science and Letters
In Music
In Contacts with Visiting VIP's
Above All, in the Arts

YOURSELF IN THE PICTURE OF ROME

X THE ROME YOU ENTER NOW — 145
Approaching and Settling
Problems of Orientation
Simplicities of the Fixed Tours
But Finding *Is Keeping*
The Restaurants of Rome
Bright Nights and Dim Ones

XI FIVE ROMES IN A CITY'S FABRIC — 159
Preliminary Thoughts
Roman Rome, with a Word About Il Duce
Church Rome
Città Vaticana: *A Small State Within a Large City*
Today's Rome, New and Newer
The Subway to Tomorrow—EUR

XII PERSONAL ZIGZAGS IN ROME — 178
A Fountain Tour, Self-Conducted
Beloved Corners in the Sun
A Kit of Facts, with Some Surprises

XIII THE RING OF WONDERS — 187
The Appian Way to the Catacombs
A Papal Palace and the Mother of Rome
Castelli Romani, *Hill Towns of Wine*
Tivoli for Temples and Scenery
Villa d'Este and Its Fifteen Hundred Fountains
Latina, a Wonder of Reclamation
Ánzio and Nettuno for Memorials of '44
Óstia for Relaxation

CONTENTS

YOURSELF IN THE PICTURE OF ITALY

CHAPTER		PAGE
XIV	TO NAPLES AND ITS FABULOUS BAY	199

    Fórmia or Cassino on the Way
    Settling at Santa Lucia
    Sights and Scenes of Napoli
    Tourist Geography of the Bay
    The Fields of Vulcan and the Lake of Hell
    Herculaneum, Pompeii and Their Mountain of Murder
    Beauty in Crescendo: Amalfi, Sorrento, Capri
    Essentials of Capri, from Tiberius to Axel Munthe
    Forgotten Íschia
    Tangents to Heel and Toe

XV	THE SPECIAL WORLD OF SICILY	225

    How to Go and Where to Stay
    Palermo, Where Saracens and Normans Met
    Rolling Out the Golden Ribbon
    Three Towns of Trinacria

XVI	CITIES THAT "CANNOT BE HID"	235

    Two Hill Routes to Florence
    Orvieto on an Upthrust Fist
    Siena's Sleepy Splendors and Its Seething Palio
    Sortie to San Gimignano—Which Can't Be True
    Halts on the Central Route
    Assisi and Its Famous Poverello
    Perúgia, the Grand Balcony of Umbria

XVII	THE HILL COUNTRY BY FIAT	260
XVIII	FLORENCE, STRONG LOADSTONE OF TRAVEL	270

    Your Shelter in a Much-Sought City
    Florentine Facts and Tourist Pleasures
    Letting Florence Seep into Your System
    Selection versus Surfeit

XIX	PISA AND ITS NEIGHBORS	285

    Lucca as Foretaste
    Pisa's Marbled Meadow
    The Game of the Bridge and the Night of Lights
    Tuscan Neighbors, South and North

CONTENTS

CHAPTER		PAGE
XX	PASSES TO THE ADRIATIC	294

    Rival Highways to Ferrara
    Ravenna, Abandoned by the Adriatic
    Ferrara, the Este Citadel
    High Points of the Northerly Route
    Bologna at the Crossroads

XXI	TO SAN MARINO, POCKET REPUBLIC ON THE SKYLINE	305

    The Town of Faïence on the Way
    Rímini, Port of the Republic
    The Strange Case of San Marino—Postwar
    Climbing into the Republic
    Romance on Three Levels
    Summits of Contrast
    Winter Sport and a Summer Fete

XXII	A CONSTELLATION OF CENTRAL STARS	316

    Módena for Its Exclamation Point
    Parma for Correggio and the Farnesi
    Piacenza for Its Civic Palace
    Cremona for a Favorite Square—and Violins
    Mantua for Mantegna
    Montagnana for Its Surprising Self

XXIII	VENEZIA	324

    No Other "Venice" Can Touch It
    Facts for Your Arrival
    Hotels, Pensions and Restaurants
    St. Mark's Square, the Nucleus of Romance
    Venice by Excursion—with Supplements
    How to Get Lost—and Like It
    The Siren Lido
    Venice Under Moon and Lanterns

XXIV	FOUR TOWNS ON THE ROAD TO MILAN	343

    Halts of the Motor Coach Route
    Great Padua, Neighbor to Venice
    Vicenza of Palládio
    Verona of Can Grande
    Brescia, the Lioness

CONTENTS

CHAPTER		PAGE
XXV	LAKE GARDA AND THE DOLOMITES	354

    Is This the Finest Lake?
    Bolzano as a Scenery Center
    Merano for Orchards Amid Snow Peaks
    Merano's Heights; the Avelengo Climax
    The Cheerful Spokes of SAD
    The Dolomite Road
    Cortina d'Ampezzo, a Favorite in Two Roles

| XXVI | MILAN, METROPOLIS OF LOMBARDY | 374 |

    Lodging and Living in the Great City
    The Cathedral and La Scala
    From the Ridiculous to the Sublime

| XXVII | THE LUSTROUS ORBIT OF MILAN | 381 |

    Il Giro dei Laghi
    Lake Como on Two Legs
    Lake Lugano and Its Enclave of Chance
    Maggiore's Shores and Famous Isles
    Lake Orta, the Big Lake's Shining Satellite
    Bérgamo in Three Layers
    Certosa di Pavia for Secluded Splendors

| XXVIII | PIEDMONT, WITH AUTONOMOUS AOSTA | 392 |

    Discovering Turin
    The Fiat Colossus at Home
    The Valley of Aosta and the White Roof of Europe

| XXIX | GREAT GENOA AND ITS TANDEM RIVIERA | 405 |

    The Crescent of the Centuries
    Today's Genoa, Its Amenities and Luxuries
    The City Circuit—Predigested
    Via Garibaldi, Italy's Finest Street of Palaces
    Electric Ladders to the Heights
    Riviera of the Rising Sun
    Riviera of the Setting Sun

| XXX | MEANDERINGS OF MEMORY | 418 |
| | INDEX | 425 |

A FOREWORD ABOUT ACCENT

THE Italian language has only one form of written accent in common use, the *grave* accent on certain concluding vowels, as *città* (city) and *bontà* (goodness). This helps us in the pronunciation of those few words and place names (e.g. Forlì) where it appears. It does *not* help us to cope with the scores of words and names whose proper stress puzzles us because the correct placing of the tonic (unwritten accent) is difficult to guess.

In the majority of cases, the tonic is on the penult, that is, the next to the last syllable, but there are many important exceptions, where it is on the antepenult, or second from the last. This book, trying to aid the reader, will follow the example of the Italian Touring Club by inserting an *acute* accent, non-existent in actual Italian practice, on place names where the stress is on the antepenult. Three typical cases, by way of illustration, are Módena, Táranto, Ádige, each of which is often wrongly stressed by American travelers on the penult. When no such mark appears on a place name, and likewise no grave accent on the final vowel, it means that the stress is invariably on the penult. In this category, the name Pavia is typical. Since no accent at all is on it, either real (grave) or invented (acute), the *i* of the penult is to be stressed. Most travelers wrongly stress the first *a*.

One special word may be in order about the most frequently mispronounced name on Italy's entire map. The glamor island of Naples Bay has no accent mark on it. Therefore the *first* syllable of CApri should be stressed rather than the final one.

* * *

On a quite unrelated subject, it should be stated here that a few paragraphs of Chapter 15, about Sicily, are substantially repeated, with latest up-datings, from the author's recent book *All the Best in the Mediterranean.*

THE FOREGROUND OF THE PICTURE

CHAPTER 1

THE ROADS THAT LEAD TO ROME

Through the Air

THE roads that lead to Rome have multiplied almost beyond counting and a few dozen of them have now been built through the air, including that smooth layer above clouds and storms called stratosphere. To dramatize this modern tapestry of travel, all of the scheduled transatlantic air lines introduced, in May 1952, a completely new program (on North Atlantic routes) of all-year tourist flights at rates averaging one-fourth to one-third less than the all-year first-class fares. This was a revolutionary idea, drastic reductions even in the peak season of tourism (May to November), with still further cuts offered during off-peak months. It brought distant lands within the holiday means of countless Americans whose brief vacation forbade consideration of steamers.

Most of the world's large systems of international air transport now make Rome a major knot in their networks, a major goal of attraction in their spreading patterns. For them a fine air terminal has been installed in Rome's colossal new railway station. Among the networks serving Rome are the two great American systems, Pan American World Airways (PAWA) and Trans World Airline (TWA), flying from New York by several routes, these giants, especially PAWA, having instigated and brought to fruition the economical tourist-rate program. Of course Italy's own international lines need mention, LAI (for Linee Aeree Italiane), with a service from New York to Rome and various scheduled flights within Italy, and Alitalia (for Aerolinee Italiane Internazionali), which ties South America to Rome. Conspicuous also are other great world systems with home base in Europe, such as Air France, British Overseas Airways (BOAC), with its affiliate British European Airways (BEA), and KLM-Royal Dutch

Airlines, all flying their huge and comfortable ships of the air from New York and offering the inducement of a stopover, if desired, in the capitals of the home countries concerned. And every plane includes—by axiom nowadays—a personable host or, more often, a pretty little hostess who makes pretty little speeches in several languages to inform and charm the traveler.

Air France was the system I elected to use in visiting Italy for the final preparation of this book, partly—I may as well admit it—because I wanted a stopover both ways in familiar Paris, a travel beacon whose glow never fades, and partly—I admit this too—because I had experienced the system's food up aloft and knew it for the very finest in the air. It is offered frankly and sumptuously as an advertisement of the country that *invented* modern epicurean dining.

The lure of good food is not insignificant in a transocean flight. You have a dozen hours or so in the air, not counting the plane's possible halts for refueling at Gander or Shannon (but "The Parisian Special," at a little extra fare, makes no halts at all), and you cannot read or sleep all the time. Two of the hours spent dallying with a hot dinner that is a French chef's masterpiece, liquefied most lavishly and all "for free," can *make* a trip that would otherwise be merely a quick method of getting to Europe. The west-to-east meals, for which the food is procured in New York, may be merely excellent and lavish. The east-to-west meals, for which the food is bought in Paris, are a gourmet's dream.

To document this statement I cannot resist submitting here the menu I enjoyed on this latest Paris-New York flight, adding nothing from my imagination, changing nothing by way of enhancement. I kept the printed card and it reads exactly as follows:

Apéritif—being a choice of Cinzano, Dubonnet, San Raphaël
Terrine de Caneton Nantaise, a mouth-watering duckling paté
Médaillon de Langouste en Bellevue, a fancy circle of lobster meat with a superb sauce
Tournedos Sauté Grand'mère, a hot tenderloin like the genuine fillet mignon that it was
(At this point there was a choice of several château wines)
Epinards Frais au Beurre—and this buttered spinach even Junior would eat with relish

Fromage, a cheese of France, the country of cheese connoisseurs
Napolitain, a slice of multi-flavored ice cream tagged with the name of Naples
Fruits de Saison, which turned out to be a dish of fresh strawberries
Champagne—an individual bottle of the Charles Heidsieck product of Reims
Café
Cognac Hine V.S.O.P. ou Liqueur Royal Combier

Then came cigarettes, on the house, followed by an hour's general hubbub of plane chatter, and so—lights down and to sleep, either in a berth or in one's reclining chair. That was an evening in France Aloft, zooming through the stratosphere in a pressurized cabin at a speed of several miles a minute.

The air road to Rome from Paris leads over the lesser Alps, skirting Mont Blanc and the other highest points, to pass almost or quite over Genoa, Pisa and Leghorn en route to the Eternal City, reached in three and a half hours. Some flights go by way of Nice, where a stopover may be made. Still others make Milan a halting point.

From London, Brussels, Amsterdam, Zurich, Lisbon, Madrid, Barcelona and other centers of Europe frequent planes follow their respective roads to Rome, and most of the capitals of Europe may be elective stopovers for the passenger from America, to enrich his trip. Plane travel gets better, faster, smoother, more luxurious year by year, even month by month. The novelty of transocean flights yields to the advancing times but the speed, comfort and exhilaration of them yield to nothing. Air travel, to trumpet the obvious, has opened Italy, as all Europe, to the vacationist who has but a week or two at his disposal.

The "man that hath no travel in him" may find the long, smooth hours in the stratosphere something to pull through the best he can, but he is crossing the ocean only by compulsion, at the call of business. The traveler for travel's sake will be stirred, even on repeated flights, by this modern miracle that dissolves one civilization before his eyes and replaces it with another, and then another. At Shannon, if his plane stops there, he will encounter the red hair, the red faces, the red coats, of the airport personnel, and the rich, authentic Irish talk, straight out of Limerick, which is but a few miles distant. He will recall, with wonder, that he has just "stepped out of New York." At Orly, the overseas airport of Paris, three hours or so beyond Shannon, he will meet the faces and voices of France, as utterly different from those of Shannon as *they* are different from those of Manhattan.

If he continues directly on to Rome, three or four hours will find him at that capital's Ciampino Airport, good-naturedly filling in reams of printed forms that seem to have no particular importance to anybody. He may grumble, if he likes, and josh the officials about all this useless home work. It's a free country, Italy, and his heated words will probably evoke some good Italian smiles of sympathy, which are just about the best smiles in the world. As he rides to town in the company bus, he is immediately in an atmosphere so Roman that no schoolboy could mistake it. He is actually on the New Appian Way, and the old one is close by. The arches of classic aqueducts, Aqua Claudia and then Aqua Felix, march in a column across green fields, and the dome of St. Peter's looms ahead. Yet "just now" the traveler was in Paris, in Shannon, in New York or Boston.

This dissertation will close with a special tip to travelers: It's a wonderful age we live in.

Across the Sea

Ships are fun, always have been and always will be. If you are so amply provided with holiday time that you can devote from sixteen to twenty-four days of it to the round-trip passage to and from Italy, you will be rewarded by that many days of sheer delight, and the journey will probably be enlivened by at least one or two exciting halts en route. Roll through your mind such names as Ponta Delgada in the Azores, Lisbon, Gibraltar, Algiers, Barcelona, Cannes, Palermo, and let them wreck your resistance. Perhaps you will find those days that you thought did not exist.

Ships from New York to Genoa and Naples come chiefly under three heads, so far as passenger travel is concerned, *American Export Lines*, with the four familiar "Ex" ships (e.g. *Excambion*) and those two superb American giants of 29,500 tons, the *Independence* and the *Constitution;* *Home Lines*, an economy service with business home in Genoa; and the *Italian Line*, whose big gleaming *Saturnia, Vulcania* and *Conte Biancamano* are now supplemented by the fine new *Andrea Doria.*

Venturesome and impecunious travelers will look up the freighters and perhaps will be astonished at what they find. Many modern freighters provide luxurious quarters, and the passengers are considered first-class passengers, though the fares correspond to those of cabin or tourist class. Free-and-easy is freighter life, as I know from having tried it. There's no keeping up with Lizzie, as on the big, sleek "whitehounds" of the Mediterranean. The only real hitch is that accommodations, at least eastbound, are usually limited by law to a meager twelve and it is not easy to get a booking. One has to be very forehanded. A pamphlet-compendium of freighter information is *Travel Routes Around the World*, published by that tireless issuer of travel literature, Harian Publications, Greenlawn, New York. The same house publishes *Freighter Life* and countless other pocket pamphlets of thrift travel, including the annual with a long but significant name, *Seeing Europe Today Without Red Tape As Nearly as Possible on a Shoestring*, by Frederic E. Tyarks. I do not know this author nor any of the Harian people but I am impressed by the down-to-earth liveliness of the prose and the multitude of practicalities corraled within the paper covers.

While on the subject of thrift, I must emphasize the important economies that can be effected by crossing the ocean in one of the ships of Home Lines. The two at present in the Mediterranean service, to Lisbon, Gibraltar, Barcelona, Genoa, Naples (Palermo, Piraeus), are the *Homeland* and the *Argentina*, of about 11,500 tons each. The former I know from personal enjoyment of it. I found its food excellent, its service courteous, its standards of maintenance meticulously high, yet the cost of the passage was a good third less than that of luxury vessels on competing lines. Its rates for first class, which I chose, were substantially less than cabin class on the larger, faster ships, and indeed not much above tourist class on those ships.

The time consumed on the crossing is considerably greater, perhaps eleven or twelve days each way instead of eight or nine. For those with limited time, this is a matter of some concern, but those who are not pressed by dates or deadlines will likely find the leisurely pace a further advantage of the economy ships. An extra week, all told, of good sea travel in balmy latitudes, fortified by good meals and snacks between meals, all figured into the low fares, is economy upon economy. Ship life, much of it on deck, burgeons marvelously in Mediterranean latitudes, and the more days of it one has, at a given fare, the greater the bargain. Only that little problem of where to find those needed extra days remains to plague many planners whose vacation time must be strictly measured.

The passenger lists on low-fare ships that serve four meridional countries directly and many more indirectly, will be, of course, very diversified in nature. There will be fewer American vacationists, more people going back to their motherland for a visit; and in the case of westbound sailings, more that are coming to the New World for the first time. Some of the passengers, especially westbound, will speak no English at all, others will speak it haltingly, with a strong foreign accent. This can be very interesting indeed to the traveler whose spirit is open and exploratory. We can talk with our own kind, our own friends and neighbors, any time. A slow crossing of the ocean in the company of a widely mixed group may prove fascinating. One feels oneself to be at a floating session of the United Nations!

On Rails from Northern Capitals

The Great European Expresses—one sees this title in large metal letters in various languages on many a Pullman car, sleeping car (wagon-lit) and diner all over western Europe—are aristocrats of the rails. They are also ambassadors of travel and would seem to deserve some sort of recognition from the U.N. They push through all barriers of international red tape, waiting at frontiers only for the minimum demands of protocol. They even penetrate the iron curtain, pushing through to Prague, Warsaw, Budapest, Bucharest, Istanbul and—since the spring of 1951—through Belgrade to Athens. They plunge through the Alps at unslackened pace, or hurdle them through the lower passes. They pay practically no attention to weather, as planes still must. They may be one's home on wheels, in *free Europe*, for as long as fifty-six hours of high speed.

To be specific, we may list a round dozen of the chief trains that concern the Romeward traveler. Services alter and improve, but these may at least serve as present samples.

From London's Victoria Station to Dover; then cross-channel on the ferry to Calais, whence direct sleepers proceed to Rome by way of Paris, Modane, Turin, Genoa, Pisa.

From London (Liverpool Street Station) to Harwich; then cross-channel to Hook of Holland, whence direct cars proceed to Genoa; or one may change in Eindhoven, Holland, for direct car to Rome.

From Paris (Gare de Lyon) sleepers to Rome by the Modane-Genoa route; sleepers to Milan, Venice (through cars to Florence, Rome) by way of Lausanne and the Simplon Tunnel, world's longest. This is part of the famous Simplon-Orient route.

From Geneva to Rome, through sleepers by the Simplon route.

From Berne to Rome—similarly by the Simplon route.

From Brussels via Luxembourg, Strasbourg, Basle, Milan, Florence to Rome—through sleepers.

From Amsterdam—through cars by the St. Gotthard route to Milan, Genoa, Rome.

From Stockholm to Copenhagen to Frankfurt to Rome (by the St. Gotthard)—through sleepers in three nights and two days, about fifty-six hours. This is the Scandinavian-Swiss-Italian Express.

From Zurich to Milan (St. Gotthard), Venice, Genoa, Rome—through cars.

From Munich via Innsbruck and the Brenner Pass to Verona, Florence, Rome—through sleepers.

From Vienna (Südbahnhof) via Semmering Pass to Klagenfurt, then by the San Cándido route to Venice, Bologna, Florence, Rome —through sleepers.

Madrid (Atocha Station) via Barcelona to the French frontier where passengers must change because of Spain's wide-gauge tracks; direct cars from this frontier via Marseille and Nice to Rome; direct sleepers available from Nice. (From Lisbon there are fast trains via Madrid, San Sebastian, to the French frontier at Hendaye, where change is made to direct cars to Rome via Toulouse, Marseille, Nice.)

All such international rides by train should be booked through some travel agency, whose coupon tickets have much longer validity than those arduously bought at station ticket windows. Europe's better sleeping cars of today are excellent, with separate compartments or staterooms that are equipped with all conveniences. Europe's dining cars are good, though hardly to be called excellent by American standards. A surprising thing to know about them is that their table d'hôte meals—again good but hardly excellent—are priced very moderately. You pay substantially less than in most Continental restaurants of similar quality. They are courteously served and strictly controlled as to price. A service charge, to the exact franc or lira, is invariably added to the bill. Beverages and the concluding coffee are always extra.

The arrival at Rome's Termini Station provides one of the major thrills of rail travel, for this colossal terminal is indeed a postwar wonder. Begun in 1938 and fully finished, with copious aid from Marshall Plan funds, only in 1951, it is, beyond question, the biggest, finest, most modern railway station in Europe. It handles about 120,000 passengers a day, a figure exceeded no doubt by various stations of Paris and London, but its massive and luxurious modernities put all rivals in the shade. Its architecture, exhibiting a severe, striated façade and a curious bulging roof over its lower, forward portion that "juts" into Piazza dei Cinquecento, makes architects argue and laymen gasp. The structure's courteous self-effacement in deleting fifty yards of itself, on the far side, to avoid disturbing a section of the brown brick wall of Emperor Servius Tullius is the most Roman thing about it. Intrusions of ancient Rome upon the modern city are seen in all parts of the metropolis and they add undeniably to its charm.

The Stazione Termini is a spectacle of Rome in its own right and if you are too quickly whisked away in a taxi to your hotel be sure to come back and take another look, or perhaps a tea or a meal in one of its restaurants.

By the Ribbons of CIAT

CIAT (pronounced Chee-aht) stands for *Compagnia Italiana Autoservizi Turistici* and the words translate themselves. They tell you, and perhaps the news has previously reached your ears or eyes, of public bus services unsurpassed anywhere and rarely equaled on either side of the Atlantic. CIAT has revolutionized Italian tourism since the end of the Second World War. It has quite overturned the traditional conception of travel in Italy.

This book will have plenty more to tell of CIAT services when it starts to roll through Italy in Chapter 14 et seq., but the elementary facts may be set forth here. Foreseeing that Italy's war-battered and overworked railways would make rail travel a crowded, scrambling business for some years to come, a group of powerful interests set themselves to open the highways to mass travel in comfort and luxury. One hears that the State Railways, along with the Fiat Motor Company and several large banks, organized and now own CIAT, but it doesn't much matter who owns it. Results are what interest us and the results are no less than spectacular.

Throughout tourist Italy and Sicily roll frequent de luxe Fiat Motor coaches seating thirty persons. Each coach is mechanically operated by a uniformed chauffeur and mechanic, socially operated by a multi-lingual young hostess who acts as courier, guide, counseler, nurse, companion-in-kidding and barmaid. Oh, yes, there is a refrigerator with cold drinks—only soft ones—in the front of the coach. The drinks are wonderfully welcome on hot days. The hostess, who promptly instructs the passengers to call her by her first name, Maria, Hebe, Giuliana or whatnot, is welcome on any kind of a day. She has an appealing personality and lots of education or she would not have landed the job.

The coaches are as comfortable as any I know and I am no stranger to busses in America or Europe. The seats are called in burbling folders, "divans," and the word is fair. In front of each seat is a little table that will fold down from the back of the seat in front, over the passenger's knees. Overhead is an individual night light in case of post-sunset hours, though the coaches do not make actual night trips. In the front of the bus is a radio which is mercifully turned off much of the time, though it will occasionally regale passengers with such gems of song as "Old MacDonald Had a Farm"—done in Italian! As comfort insurance Fiat even installed, in the rear of the newer coaches, a toilet room, but rest stops make this feature unnecessary. It's a good sales point anyway! Luggage is not stowed in the busses but in a trailer, or sometimes on top.

The Ribbons of CIAT are highway routes. The most popular summer ribbons (they lose their colors and part of their service in winter) are the Pink Ribbon (*Nastro Rosa*) and Blue Ribbon (*Nastro Azzurro*), of which much more will be told later in this book. They cover the heart of tourist Italy from Naples to Lombardy and Piedmont. The Sicily Circuit is the Gold Ribbon (*Nastro d'Oro*), offering a marvelous CIAT week, to be discussed in Chapter 15.

A ribbon that concerns us upon *entering* Italy is the international *Nastro dei Fiori*, or Flower Ribbon, which unrolls from Nice (a long tangent operates even from Paris) to Monte Carlo and the frontier, then along the Riviera di Ponente to Genoa—and along the Riviera di Levante to Pisa, and so to Florence and Rome. It is marvelous, this Double Riviera Road, skirting the sea for two hundred miles, and should be given careful thought by the planner. The planner should also know that *Europabus*, a relatively new international motor-coach system owned by the Railways of Europe, now ties Nice to Stresa, via Savona; Montreux to Milan, via the Simplon Pass; Innsbruck to Venice, via Bolzano and Cortina d'Ampezzo.

To tidy up this bus subject as it concerns peninsular travel, CIAT is the motor arm of CIT (pronounced Chit), which stands for *Compagnia Italiana Turismo*. This vast and energetic travel agency, semi-official in Italy, has its main central office (and hence that of CIAT) at 68 Piazza Esedra in Rome, under the crescent arcade, and a conspicuous branch office in every tourist city of Italy and many abroad. Its Nice office, for local inquiry about the Flower Ribbon, is at 16 Avenue de Verdun; its Genoa office at 16 Via XXV Aprile; its New York office at 11 West 42nd Street. We shall look into CIT's general activities in Chapter 3.

By Car, with You at the Wheel

To see Italy by car, your own car or one rented in Italy, is THE way, beyond all question, to get the feel of the country, to sponge up its infinite variety of delights, to savor its multitude of special treats, scenic, artistic, historical. In no other way can you be master of your plans and personal wishes to anything like the same degree. To polish the self-evident, you go where you want, when you want, and this means finding a thousand *little* wonders that public transportation cannot or does not find. The roads of Italy are *good*, the main ones excellent. Every ten kilometers, on state highways, lives a roadbuilder, in a pleasant red house, and it is his job to be responsible for the upkeep of his stretch.

I happen to know rather a lot about motoring in Italy because now, while writing in many interludes, I am actually driving, with my wife, a little rented Fiat throughout the country. It is my dozenth seeing of Italy, my first prying into its lovely hidden corners. I am ecstatic; but more presently on the rented car idea.

If you plan to bring your own familiar car abroad you'll find that Italy encourages you with a tasty bit of bait. It gives you gasoline coupons that provide you with about 8 gallons a day at approximately 35 per cent reduction. Since gas in Italy, all imported, now costs about 20 cents a liter, which is more than 70 cents an American gallon, this reduction is something to note with interest. High test gas costs about 8 per cent more than the regular.

I, having always a tender regard for my budget, am something of a fanatic on *small-car* driving in fuel-costly Italy. A further and very great advantage is that the small car will thread almost any narrow *vicolo*—and there are thousands of them in a thousand towns and villages—that the average American car would have to forgo completely. It will also U-turn and wriggle around tight corners almost like a bicycle, and in crowded streets and before hotels it will poke into an amazingly tiny "aperture," for parking.

The rented car we are driving is a Fiat 500 Berlina Belvedere station wagon, one form of the famous *Topolino* (meaning Mickey Mouse), 11 feet long by 4 feet 3 inches wide by 4 feet 7 inches high. We call it—her—Tina, for Fiatina, and if that is "cute," well, so is she! Her engine, with four speeds forward, has the power of eight horses, but the horses must certainly be like the muscular beer-van horses of Munich's Oktoberfest, for they pull us up any hill of any hill town. In the folded-down rear (a double seat that can be folded into a large, flat luggage compartment) we have four good-sized bags, a portable typewriter and an array of loose books and bundles. The maximum speed of the 500 is stated in the English language instruction book to be 56 miles (90 kilometers) per hour, but anyone who wants to push along through the changing glories of Italy at more than even 40 or 50 miles an hour simply isn't bent on pleasure.

Gasoline consumption? I trust I have your full attention now. On our first day, driving through Rome traffic and using the lower speeds far too much, till we got used to the car's ways, then heading straight for the hill roads of Latium and Umbria, we did 265 kilometers on exactly 15 liters of ordinary gas. An American gallon is approximately 3¾ liters. An "American mile" is 1⅗ kilometers. By my arithmetic, which I invite you to correct, we averaged 41.64 miles to the gallon on that first experimental day. Since then we have traversed *high* mountain passes, one after another, but have continued to do almost as well on mileage.

As a performer on mountain roads, the little 500 deserves a special accolade. My experience of it has amounted to some four thousand miles, fully half of which has been in the Apennines and high Alps, including the Dolomites, where dizzy passes seem to form an endless chain. Not once has the car faltered, not once has its engine boiled. At least thirty times, and I mean this literally, I have passed big American cars standing and steaming, their hoods up. They have vastly more power, of course, but they are not built specifically for mountain climbing, as Italian cars have to be. On these occasions I have put on my finest expression of commiseration, striving valiantly not to look *too* smug, and have kept on rolling along. Very often I've been in third or second speed, occasionally in toiling first on steep turns, but never once have I had to stop out of mercy to my motor.

Fiat has a name to maintain and Tina is certainly doing what she can to maintain it. Our midget car is about the smallest possible item in the company's huge output of motor products for land, sea and air. Fiat made the famous royal train for ex-King Farouk and his bride, the most sumptuous train ever to roll on tracks. It makes planes too, yet finds time to turn out electric refrigerators and other household gadgets. It is the General Motors of Italy, with 65,000 employees in Italy alone, other thousands throughout the world.

I rented our station wagon from the Rome branch at 67 Viale Manzoni, but one may do the trick quite as easily in any city of Italy *and* even in twenty or more cities in other European countries, at varying supplementary costs. The car need not be turned in in the same city where it is taken.

The daily rental (*noleggio*) tariff for the 500 is at present $9, but a used car less than a year old may be had at $7. After each period of thirty days, the rental is reduced by 10 per cent. Larger and more powerful new cars than the 500 are to be had at $13 a day (the 1100-E) and $17 (the 1400). A chauffeur may be "rented" with the car, but of course this comes a bit high; and anyway who wants a chauffeur? With little or no knowledge of the Italian language, you may drive anywhere with ease. Here again, I know!

Insurance costs, now $1 a day, are on the client, but—this next is very comforting—*maintenance costs are on the company*. A booklet of coupons entitles the client to a complete check-up every 1000 kilometers and to changes of oil as needed, all this being scot free. Only the gasoline costs are on the car's user.

A special thing to watch out for when driving is the sign ZONA DEL SILENCIO at the entrance to many cities and resorts. It means that you may not sound your horn in that Silent Zone (often, as in Florence, the entire city) under penalty of a substantial fine. Foreigners driving foreign cars are generally let off with a warning, but foreigners in an Italian car, a Fiat for instance, may not fare so well with the traffic police.

Tina will roll again in Chapter 17, when this book reaches the Hill Country, but it may suffice to say here that you haven't felt the saturating wonder of Italy, from very old to very new, until you have seen it from behind the wheel of a car you drive yourself.

CHAPTER 2

WHAT'S IN A NAME?

This *Name Has Everything*

THE five letters that spell Italy contain, I think, more promise of *variety* in travel pleasures than any other five, or fifteen, that spell a country's name. The only serious challenger to this contention would be the six letters of France, which also spell infinite variety, but France, with all its wonders, lacks one thing, lakes. It has only little Lake Annecy, the negligible Lac du Bourget and about a third of the shoreline of Lake Geneva. Italy has Lake Como, most of Lake Maggiore, part of Lake Lugano, all of Lake Garda and half a dozen smaller lakes, little known to tourism, each of which is a jewel worth crossing the ocean to find.

Italy has a complete alphabet of marvels. One could go around a circle of assorted friends of both sexes, all ages, all tastes—try it sometime—asking, "What do you like best about vacation travel? What do you chiefly want to see and do when you're abroad? Tell it straight, no answers barred." Whatever the response of each one, Italy has it, in abundant measure, unless perhaps some hunter expresses a yearning for big game.

Is it art? Italy has the most and the best.

Is it scenery? There's a whole continent of it, of every conceivable type, in this long peninsula and its adjacent islands.

Is it good food? The food of Italy is lavish and well cooked, even if you don't go for the *pasta* items, which are supreme. (Every little *trattoria* can handle spaghetti and its culinary colleagues with the skill of a three-star chef in most lands.)

Is it fine wines? Italy is, pre-eminently, a wine country though admittedly not another France. It has a considerable number of fine wines that are all its own and its popular wines are as popular with tourists as with natives. (We shall have a look at the subject under the heading, "Wines—Red, White and Chianti" in Chapter 5.)

Is it pretty girls? Wait till you see them, in the big cities, in the remote hamlets of the hills, in the cabarets of Rome, on the multitude of beaches, where you see a *lot* of them, quite literally!

Is it music? You know that Italy and music have been interchangeable terms for centuries. The best violins and the best operatic throats came from here. So did Toscanini. In Italy you can hear the very best, and see it too, in such settings as Milan's La Scala and (outdoors) in the flood-lighted ruins of Rome's Basilica of Emperor Maxentius.

Is it sport? Italy offers all kinds, from skiing to swimming.

Is it the patina of the past? Rome, Florence, Venice, Genoa, Palermo, Agrigento and a hundred other places are fairly bathed in the colors of a brilliant past.

Is it the present and the future? Italy is born again with each great upheaval, and there have been many. It is a democracy now, springing up as if by magic. This has been based solidly on the wishes of Italy's voters and it has been spurred by Marshall-Plan dollars, yours and mine, paid the hard way, so we have a right to *see* what our payments have done to support Italian energies.

Is it great churches, or the pageantry of ritualistic religion? Nothing in this field surpasses the vast ecclesiastical structures, the cathedrals, churches, convents of Italy, or the outpourings of faith in any major event of the Roman Catholic calendar. Whatever your faith, or lack of it, you cannot see the Vatican in action, before half a million people in and just outside St. Peter's, without being awed by the emotional electricity of the mighty spectacle. Vatican City itself is a specialty of travel, to state it in lay terms, quite without rival.

Is it pageantry of the *people* that calls you? In Siena, Florence, Arezzo, Pisa, Gúbbio, a dozen other towns, folk festivals of infinite variety in costume and significance are staged annually on dates announced in a specially printed annual *Calendar of Italian Events* and also in *Tourist News*, a monthly magazine published by the Italian State Tourist Office. Some of these events are thrilling spectacles of sport from an earlier age. Some are compellingly beautiful.

Is it drama in special settings that you like? Each year, on several dates in the spring, the National Institute of Ancient Drama presents in the Greek Theater of Syracuse, dating from about 480 B.C., such plays as "The Bacchantes," by Euripides, and "The Persians," by Aeschylus. The theater is one of the greatest and most stirring relics of Hellenic Sicily. The view of Syracuse and its harbor *from* the theater is magnificent. It wouldn't seem to matter too much whether or not you understand Greek drama done in Italian. The program tells you, anyway, in English, what is happening on the stage and one can follow much of it.

Our list of personal likings grows long and shall come to an abrupt halt, though it is by no means a complete catalog of Italy's offerings. Perhaps it tells enough to prove our point that *whatever* you like best is there awaiting you.

From Art to Scenery and Back Again

Italian art and Italian scenery need a little amplification even in so modest an "appetizer" as is this chapter.

Art in Italy is a world in itself. Virtually every little town has some few masterpieces that would *make* a town of similar size in most lands, and the great art centers, notably Rome and Florence, have such a wealth of artistic treasure that the layman often feels discouraged and passes up the whole subject, leaving the matter generally in the hands of his own competent laywoman. This is a defensible attitude, since every visitor should concentrate on the things he honestly likes best. It is defensible, but the man who adopts it robs himself of pleasure that could surprise him by its potency. A single painting or statue understood, a single artist or sculptor known as a person, with a person's virtues and faults, becomes comprehensible and all of a sudden exciting to the most art-blind visitor. Perhaps a dozen such selections, instead of a hundred or a thousand, can transform him into an astonished "fan," and his capacity will grow as art familiarity grows.

In Chapter 9 this present layman will offer a roster of the great in art, done in the simplest, swiftest terms, and throughout the other chapters the book will try to make the art and artists of Italy easy to take, since that is the candid level on which I have learned to love the subject. A few easy-to-take background books will be suggested.

The specialist, the art student, the eager beaver, already has at his or her elbow a library of erudite books that explore and develop this inexhaustible field.

The "continent of scenery" in Italy is as overwhelming as the continent of art but it takes no learning for anybody and everybody to enjoy it. Consider the things that this leg and foot and football of a country has for us to look at. To cope with such ramifying munificence of nature I shall have to fall back on the *list* approach, working down from north to south. Here are a few of the peninsula's features.

The *Valley of Aosta*, paradise of Alpinists, is in the lee of Europe's loftiest Alps, including Mont Blanc, the Matterhorn and Monte Rosa. This superb valley, whose villages bear French names, is surprisingly little known to Americans in general. It was virtually unknown to me, despite very much traveling in Italy, until I saw, in a gallery in Washington, a painting of Courmayeur, one of the valley's resort villages. Then I could hardly wait to start personal explorations.

The *mountain fringe of western Piedmont*, an utterly neglected wonderland. This shrank infinitesimally after the Second World War when the peace treaty awarded to France the two hamlets of Tenda and Briga, angering Maestro Toscanini so much that he promptly canceled a concert in Paris which he was to have conducted. The treaty did not shrink Piedmontese grandeurs.

The *Double Riviera* of Genoa, from Ventimíglia and San Remo on the Riviera di Ponente (meaning Westward) to Rapallo, La Spézia and Viaréggio on the Riviera di Levante (meaning Eastward). The well-known place names tell their own story.

The *Italian lakes*, already mentioned. They match, glory for glory, the lakes of Switzerland.

The *Dolomites*, a bizarre specialty of nature, with the sharpest, weirdest, most utterly improbable mountain peaks in all Europe. Roads and rails play hide and seek amid these miracles of mountainry.

The *Lido* and the *Romagna Riviera* along the Adriatic, from Rimini down, with wide, hard beaches, mile upon mile, good waves, sea breezes.

The *Apennines*, extending the entire length of Italy, from the borders of France to Calabria and on through Sicily. In mountain scenery they are less grand than the Alps, less tempestuous than the Dolomites, but this immensely long range is the mise en scène for scores of dramatically lovely hill towns and hundreds of equally lovely hill villages.

The *Bay of Naples*. I need not gild the lily by saying anything about it here.

The foot of the leg of Italy, *Calabria* being the toes, *Basilicata* the instep, *Apulia* the heel. In almost any part of this foot the scenery is striking, and if you go there you will have it to yourself. You'll lose yourself in Untouched Italy and you'll love being lost.

Sicily—and again the name's enough.

The *Islands of Italy* not counting the Sicily classic. They include large, primitive *Sardinia*, reached by plane or steamer; *Elba*, reached easily by steamer from Piombino; *Capri* and *Ischia*, the deservedly famous stars of the tourist heavens in Naples Bay; and the seven *Lípari*, or *Aeolian*, *Islands*, with *Vulcano* and *Strómboli*. The latter, brought to the world's attention in 1949 by Ingrid Bergman and Roberto Rossellini, is reached by steamer from Milazzo, Sicily. Its cone erupts every hour or two, month in and month out. Scenery is axiomatic to islands and all those named above have it in abundance.

Let the Map Explain

Italy without a map is ever so much worse off than pie without cheese. It simply demands cartography and gets it in full measure. Every guidebook has a map, or maps, as does this, the endpapers herein having been specially drawn by the author's daughter.

Italy, like Norway and like Chile, is a long, lean affair, geographically, and issues sharp challenge to the mapmaker. Any map of this country needs a stout set of hinges so that it can be folded over, but there are various other devices in use.

The map in the *Orario Generale* of the Italian State Railways splits into two independent sections, a northern one and a southern one, and even so it has to telescope Italy's long leg into a fat and dumpy limb, an unfortunate distortion in a land of graceful young figures. The magnificent general map of the Touring Club (see below) puts northern Italy on one side, southern Italy on the reverse. CIT's busways map, a good one for the bus rider but not for the motorist, frankly gives up and amputates the whole foot, chopping it off just below Naples on the lower shinbone. It arbitrarily plants Sicily out in the blue opposite Rome. Without going to that extent I too have found certain surgical operations necessary for this book's endpaper maps. The Istituto Geografico Visceglia (7 Via Boezio, Rome) publishes a road map, with English explanations, that actually manages, and not too clumsily, to get the whole of Italy on a single surface, without distortion.

The *Touring Club Italiano,* with its publishing office in Milan (10 Corso Italia), is the master of masters when it comes to mapping Italy and I cannot too highly recommend its cartography. This active and meticulous organization, which incidentally compiles and copyrights the Italy guidebooks published in English under the Guide Bleu aegis (*Editions Nagel*) in Paris, puts out an exhaustive collection of great and greater road maps. The one mentioned above is but a single example of its many offerings. It publishes also a 2-sheet map, a 13-sheet map, a 30-sheet map and a 62-sheet map. The 30-sheet affair is ideal for the motorist. On a scale of 1 in 200,000, it presents every conceivable detail with as much loving care as Michelin devotes to its maps of France and one cannot say more. For every traveler, motorist or not, I recommend with enthusiasm the general, all-Italy map (1 in 800,000) called *Carta Stradale d'Italia.* For him who drives the roads, some sheets of the 30-sheet affair would seem essential. They are exciting just to look at—with mountains and their altitudes, lakes, rivers, glaciers, passes, resorts, castles, notable monuments, isolated inns and *campi di golf.* They also indicate cemeteries, but you are unlikely to need one if your car follows the map's beautifully clear instructions.

War Damage Disappears

War damage in Italy was, of course, severe, but it is surprising how these few years of peace have effaced or at least softened it. As to the great churches and monuments of art, Allied fliers were carefully and sternly briefed to *miss* them with their bombs and even the Nazis showed some respect for them. Most of the best of them, throughout the land, are largely or wholly undamaged.

For the traveler's information we may give here a brief report on where and to what extent war damage is still to be noticed by the average traveler.

Rome, respected by both sides, came through almost without a scratch, the exception being the basilica of San Lorenzo fuori le Mura which was badly hurt but has now been restored.

Naples suffered heavily in its port section, which is now being extensively rebuilt and developed. Its central post office, destroyed in a bomb tragedy that left many civilians dead and wounded, has been replaced by an oval-front structure of monumental proportions. The chief tourist sections of the city, such as Via Partenope and Santa Lucia, were little damaged.

Salerno, south of Naples, and *Ánzio* south of Rome, where heroic American troops rushed the beaches in hails of Nazi fire, were left grotesque ruins and there is still plenty of evidence of the violent fighting.

Sicily suffered considerably but one does not greatly notice it now.

Cassino, between Naples and Rome, was left a fantastic wreck, as many a familiar photograph has shown, but even this is being laboriously restored, though it may be decades before the battered Benedictine monastery on the mountain above is fully restored, if ever.

Florence was terribly lacerated by artillery on both sides of the Arno but its central portions and most of its greatest monuments are intact. The Uffizi Gallery has long since been fairly thoroughly restored and its art works have been brought back to their familiar walls from their hiding places in Italy and from Germany, where they were taken by Nazi "collectors" like Göring. The bridges over the Arno were all knocked out except the famous Ponte Vecchio, which still stands.

Pisa got rather a beating and there are still some very minor evidences of damage even to the celebrated cathedral and baptistery, though not noticeably to the Leaning Tower. The *camposanto* (cemetery), adjacent to the cathedral, was, and is, terribly mangled from an Allied artillery bombardment.

San Marino, capital of the tiny republic of that name embedded in Italy, near Rimini, had one black day of Allied bombardment in 1944 that did much damage, but the most conspicuous wounds, like that to the Palace of the Public, have been healed by energetic measures.

Ravenna, a veritable museum of Byzantine art, was terribly lacerated by the war and has not recovered quite as fast as other cities, but it is still wonderful.

Venice was practically untouched by bombs and shells except in its shipyard sections, seldom visited by tourists.

The *Ádige Valley*, pathway of the Brenner Pass railway line from Munich and Innsbruck, caught it pretty hard and some scars are still evident, but they are not too grim now.

Milan and *Turin* also caught it hard and there are still plenty of signs of wreckage, but these thriving industrial cities are rebuilding at a tremendous clip. The Milan Cathedral was damaged very little. Its west front was scarred, but repairs have been pushed with energy.

Genoa took a terrible punishing in its commercial harbor and its chief industrial sections but in viewing the portions that tourists chiefly know and love one would hardly realize, today, that there had been a war.

All in all, physical recuperation of Italy's cities and towns and railways and roads, in so few years seems absolutely amazing. Italian muscle and brains deserve vast credit but American visitors may also take time out to be proud of the well-known "enlightened self-interest" that played so great a part in this recovery through the contribution of dollars in the European Recovery Program, replaced in 1952 by the Mutual Security Agency. Few tourists will say, as a well-padded American lady said to me in a luxury hotel of Milan, "Why, this country doesn't need help. Just look at it. I've been tightening my belt all these years to pay out good money for countries like this!" As I looked at *her* I thought it would do her no harm to tighten her belt a bit more.

A Tale of Ten Cities

Italy, the name that has everything, is outstandingly rich in its suggestion of *special cities*, not including its special capital, and not including any of its hill cities, which are like a separate tribe in travel interest. I would say that in this department only Spain, with such charming rarities as Granada, Seville, Toledo, Segovia, Palma de Mallorca, Ronda, could issue a mild challenge for a place of parity with Italy.

This tale of ten cities shall catalog, by way of proof, a mere ten of the odd, appetite-whetting specialties of Italy.

Venice is so great and wonderful an oddity that it has been flattered by almost every country on earth claiming that this or that community, with a few canals, is the Venice of its country or region. I have visited at least twenty of these imitation Venices, as well as that country whose very name is Little Venice (Venezuela), and not even the best of them is the smallest patch on the real thing.

Bérgamo is a three-story city of Lombardy, many of its businessmen and business girls going to and from work by funicular. Its "ground floor," Bérgamo Bassa, is an important city of industry. Its second floor, Bérgamo Alta, is replete with wonderful buildings of a storied past. Its attic, San Vigílio, offers a glorious panorama of the two "lower floors" and of the Orobian Alps and the Lombardy plain.

Genoa is one of my personal passions and this book, being a very personal one, shall have plenty to say about it. Clinging by its eyelashes to an amphitheater of hills above its curving harbor, Genoa has more *hidden* glamors to the square meter than almost any other city of Italy. I think it is inadequately and even wrongly shown by most guides and agencies and I shall "speak my piece" on the subject —in Chapter 29.

Pisa should bring suit against Neptune for desertion. It was once the brilliant bride of the Ligurian Sea but now it is an inland city. The whole world knows its Leaning Tower but Pisa is very much more than a city with a tower.

Ravenna was similarly deserted by the Adriatic Sea, which is now seven miles away, but its great eras, three of them (see Chapter 20), left a wealth of mosaics hardly rivaled in lustrous beauty except by those in Palermo. Ravenna, almost alone, kept civilization alive in a world that was elsewhere sinking into a long, ignoble coma.

Florence is an Italian specialty of such world appeal that nothing save its name need be set down here.

Naples, in its utterly different way, is quite as special, quite as important to tourism, as Florence.

Palermo, capital of Sicily, is made of magic. It has had more lives than a cat, ten to be specific, and each life left its mark, the Saracens and the Normans leaving the brightest mark. The city's location, its curving contours, its golden mosaics, its ultra-Sicilian atmosphere—these are some facets of its specialness.

Syracuse was once the largest *Greek* city in the world and its Greek heritage is of supreme interest today. The city fills to the brim the classic little island of Ortygia, against which big surf pounds on windy days, and spreads across a causeway to extensive areas on the main shore of Sicily.

Agrigento, clinging to a slope of southern Sicily high above the sea, looks down like a mother hen, upon its brood of six Greek temples. Even those travelers who are "fed up on ruins" go mildly wild over the insistent beauty of this much-templed city.

And of Towns That Perch on Hills

The hill towns of Tuscany, Umbria, Latium, the Marches and, for that matter, almost every region of Italy, including Sicily, are so numerous, so redolent of romance, so perfect as pictures, that they have been attacked by tireless pens and lenses for decades past. Nobody can do them justice, though many have tried. These ancient otherworldly communities are too elusive ever to be trapped by words or even by films. They climbed the hills to get away from enemies, and having climbed they stayed up aloft, as they do today, however awkward the location may be in matters of transportation and commerce. *Requiescant in Pace* seems to be Italy's motto for them. They rest in peace because the scurrying world of progress has no time to climb and find out what they are doing. Only tourists have the time and the will, and by some strange freak of luck tourists have never yet succeeded in spoiling them. "Those falcon nests," says one comment, "are restful because they are not striving for anything. They are charming because they are not concerned with their charm."

Perúgia alone, the chief city of Umbria, exhibits an unorthodox animation for a place so very loftily situated, and *Siena*, at the times of the Palio festival, goes plumb crazy with excitement, but in general all is quiet on the sky front.

This book will attempt a practical hill program in Chapter 16. The present introductory mention, like all the foregoing discussions, is meant only as a relish, an offering of *antipasto*, before spreading the dinner intended to nourish your own experience of Italy.

Some names rush in, to stem my garrulous talk: *Assisi,* where Francis, most appealing of all saints, was born; *Orvieto,* with a church and a type of wine you won't easily forget; *San Gimignano,* with Italy's most fantastic group of towers; *Viterbo,* once a stronghold of the Popes; *Urbino,* home of Raphael; *L'Áquila,* which means The Eagle; *Montefalco,* the Falcon Mountain; *Gúbbio, Arezzo, Volterra, Spoleto, Trevi, Cortone, Montefiasco, Caprarola, Civitacastellana;* and if you would like the name of the most impossibly inaccessible hill village in all Italy, in all the world of hill communities, it is *San Marco d'Alúnzio.* This roc's retreat, which I cannot find listed in any guidebook, is a hamlet attached to the dome of heaven some six miles (I am told) by mule track above the village of Torrenova (near Sant'Agata di Militello) on Sicily's north coast. I have never visited it but I have seen it, with amazement, several times from the windows of the Messina-Palermo train. Refusing to believe that a mule could ever make the grade, I am sometime going to fit myself out with mountain gear, pickax, rope and everything, and attempt it. If you get there before I do, and if it proves to be an actual village, not a mirage, please let me know how life is lived up there.

CHAPTER 3

FIRST FACTS OF TRAVEL

See ENIT *Before You Go*

ENIT stands for *Ente Nazionale Industrie Turistiche*, which stands for National Organization for Tourist Industries. Wherever the organization has an office in English-speaking countries it labels it Italian State Tourist Office. Its New York office is at 21 East 51st Street; its London office at 201 Regent Street; its Paris office at 23 rue de la Paix.

The New York office, in attractive modern quarters, is one that any American planning a trip to Italy may visit with travel profit and personal pleasure. It does not sell tickets or arrange itineraries but it does tell you anything and everything you need to know. It gives you free and enticingly illustrated literature. It tells you where and how to make contacts for the detailed planning of your trip and for pursuing it or altering it on the other side of the sea. It answers your questions about what to do when you first arrive in Italy. If you have any special goal in Italy, any purpose beyond pleasure travel, it opens doors for you and writes or secures letters of introduction. ENIT is your friend in court and, even more important, a friend before you go to "court."

In Rome the central office of ENIT is at 2 Via Marghera, just beyond the far side of the enormous Termini Station. This office, in handsome, newly rebuilt quarters, has taken on a new lease of life since I first became acquainted with it a few years ago. It is sparked by an easily accessible person named Dr. Annunziata and staffed by energetic people who understand tourism and serve it with courtesy. Its functions, however, are more of the top-level administrative type and the average tourist will hardly need to hunt it up, since various travel agencies, more centrally located, will give all the practical aids needed and will sell tickets and services as well. ENIT in Rome is the central executive organ of the government's Tourist Commission, concerned chiefly with tourist legislation and publicity. In New York —and London and Paris—it is your ready friend, quick with answers to your queries.

See CIT Here, There and Everywhere

CIT, under the direction of its able and imaginative director, Comm. Enrico Linzi, has effected a revolution in Italian travel, largely through the development of its luxury coach services (CIAT), as stated earlier. These services have established road travel as *the* thing for tourists, bringing town and village Italy to the ken of thousands who formerly saw only the chief cities and resorts by means of train travel. It used, for instance, to be a formidable job to visit even such essential hill towns as Perúgia, Siena and Assisi. Now there is nothing to it. Your tourist chariot rolls right to the center of each community and it rolls through hundreds of lovely, unsung villages that tourists rarely saw before the Second World War.

CIAT covers most of Italy, but is supplemented in the northern part of the country by two other good bus systems, SATI (*Società Autoservizi Turistici Italiani*), specializing on the Genoese Riviera region, and SAD (*Società Automobilistica Dolomiti*), covering the whole Dolomite region and penetrating also into Switzerland's Engadine. One SAD line, associated with the *Europabus* system and the Swiss postal coaches, even cuts *through* Switzerland, from Bolzano to Lugano, giving its passengers an overnight stop in St. Mortiz. In Piedmont another notable purveyor of regular and special tourist pullman coaches is SADEM, owned outright by the Fiat colossus. It provides services that fan out in every direction from Turin, the capital of Piedmont and the "capital of Fiat."

CIAT is the very big brother to the other systems and CIT is the father of CIAT. The parent organization is a full-sized, many-sided travel agency, specializing, of course, in Italian travel. Its New York office, at 11 West 42nd Street, has been previously mentioned, and there is one also in Los Angeles, at 523 West 6th Street. In London, Paris and some fifteen other cities it maintains prominent offices, as also in forty or more Italian cities and resorts. It sells tickets of every kind and books reservations of every kind. It keeps uniformed welcomers at the principal points of entry into Italy and at the chief metropolitan railway stations. It furnishes private automobiles, chauffeurs, licensed guides, interpreters, porters. It maps out tours by the hundred, fixed or to order, and in addition to its national highway tours it operates many local excursions in and around the chief centers. These include full coverage of Rome and its environs, of course with guides who speak good English, and similarly full coverage of Naples and its bay, Florence, Genoa, Milan, the Italian lakes and even Venice. In that city it forgets about wheels and offers a variety of tours by gondola.

Other agencies of travel provide most or all of the services that CIT offers but usually they are general practitioners rather than specialists and those that do make a specialty of travel in Italy seem to me far less broad in scope.

CIT even publishes its own English-language guidebook, an easy-to-use one of less than Baedeker bulk but livelier prose, with picture maps of each province, with many city plans and with scores of color plates. The authorship is not revealed but whoever wrote it knew what travelers want. The book includes all sorts of things not generally stressed in this type of compendium, for instance ten pages on Italian gastronomy and wines, a full calendar of folk festivals, a chapter on the great theaters and concert halls and one on sports. If you secure this guide in advance it will halve the problems of your itinerary—and double them too, for you will find all sorts of unsuspected musts in the book's three hundred spirited pages.

For guidance of a more personal sort, those with special travel problems and those engaged in any kind of tourist research seek out CIT's Giovanni Galleni, chief of the company's Foreign Travel Agents Department. Known to hundreds of Americans as "John," he is one of Italian tourism's assets, quick and definite in giving help, just as quick in repartee. When it comes to "joshing," he can take it and he can dish it out.

The Pozzo Brothers on Railways

In the Second World War the railways of Italy took a more severe and prolonged beating than did even the railways of France and that is saying plenty. The whole system was fearfully disrupted and thousands of miles of line were put out of commission or destroyed outright. Nearly *all* bridges and marshaling yards were wiped out. Stations by the hundreds were razed and rolling stock was very largely depleted by direct war action and removal. Today the whole vast intricate network is in full use, as it has been for several years, and it is definitely *better* than it was in 1939.

For this swift transformation my hat is off to Ing. di Raimondi, the general manager of the Italian State Railways, whose ability and drive have largely wrought this modern miracle, aided, of course, immeasurably by Marshall-Plan funds. No American, remembering his own tax returns for the Marshall-Plan years, need feel a bit bashful about this latter acknowledgment, but on the other hand, voluble boasting of our aid, and too many tourists are guilty of this, is about the worst performance we can put on in Italy. We did what we did, to state the oft-forgotten obvious, not from philanthropy but so that the Russian bear could not gobble prostrate Italy at one bite. We needed her for a partner in freedom and she has become an invaluable one. In some of the general timetables of Italy, at various railway construction and repair operations, and in such newly built stations as the huge Termini of Rome I occasionally saw placards giving tribute to the aid of ERP, when this was functioning strongly. Such tributes, far from fulsome, were richly deserved, but it should not be forgotten that essentially the skills and infinite labor of Italians did the trick.

Pozzo Brothers of Turin have been publishing Italy's official *Orario Generale*, or General Timetable, for as long as my experience of Italy extends into the past, and that is several decades. The familiar buff-colored tome has grown impressively in bulk and cost and now sells, at all railroad newsstands, for about a dollar. It is a noble work and contains every possible detail about Italian trains, together with chief itineraries of planes, coastwise and island steamers, lake boats and some inter-city tram lines. Bus routes are covered in a separate Pozzo volume, *Orario Generale degli Autoservizi* and there is a colossal combination volume, quite impractical because of its bulk and costing about $2.50, that combines *all* information on *all* transportation. The ordinary dollar Pozzo is the thing to get. Its *Indice*

Grafico shows what table one must look up to find the facts on any rail line in Italy and its islands.

There are, in addition to this general timetable, numerous small sectional ones which are certainly *much* handier to carry, but if you travel in several parts of Italy, you no sooner become familiar with one than you must discard it and buy another, whereas stout Pozzo becomes a permanent friend, tried and true.

What does Pozzo teach us about Italian trains, their categories, speeds, classes, and prices? He explains that the trains are divided into four main classes as follows:

1. *Elettrotreni* (1st class only) and *rapidi* (1st and 2nd class). These are the nobility and call for moderate supplementary fares.
2. *Direttissimi* and *diretti*, a numerous company of expresses, the mainstay of general travel.
3. *Elettromotrice* and *Automotrice* (Diesels) are one-car affairs similar to the *autorails* familiar to all who have traveled in France.
4. *Accelerati*, *omnibus* and *misti*, the humble crawlers which are likely to get there if you give them time enough. Do not be misled by that word accelerati. Even a snail can accelerate his pace, but he is never a whippet.

The tariff, both for fast and slow trains, is too complicated to quote in full. Pozzo devotes twenty-two packed pages to setting forth the whole story, but we are very little interested. For the occasions when we may wish to buy regular tickets the following is enough to know. Tickets valid on all trains (except the nobility) average approximately $3\frac{1}{2}$ cents per mile 1st class; $2\frac{1}{2}$ cents 2nd class; $1\frac{1}{2}$ cents 3rd class.

Return tickets (Andata e Ritorno), issued only for distances up to 250 kilometers (155 miles) and also for journeys between chief provincial towns, give the purchaser a 20 per cent reduction, but the period of validity is meager, being only three days.

Italian stations are not too well signed. Sometimes the hours of departure and the tracks of departure are not conveniently posted, and it becomes necessary for the traveler to do a bit of inquiring, but there is one phrase—just one—that saves a multitude of troubles: *Quale binario?* Which track? If you can ask that and murmur your destination you are safe, provided, of course, that you can understand the answer. Learning to count at least to twenty in cardinals and ten in ordinals is perhaps the prime essential in any language.

Buying your ticket in railway stations (for short trips) is something of an ordeal, needlessly so it seems, for the ticket windows frequently do not open until a very few minutes before the train is due to start, though *twenty* minutes is the legal minimum, and there is often a long queue waiting. As some special tickets take a long time to prepare, those persons farthest from the window grow more and more nervous as train time draws near, teetering back and forth and peering over the shoulders of those in front. And the last-minute scramble is always a fearsome thing for those caught in it.

I remember one occasion, at the Assisi station, when I happened to be the only person waiting to buy a ticket. I arrived fifteen minutes before train time but the window was not flung open until my train was actually in sight up the track. Breathlessly I made my demand and the ticket clerk started figuring the price, whipping out this tariff and that for confirmation. The train came to a stop. *"In vettura,"* (All aboard!) bawled the guard presently, but the clerk was still figuring. Finally the train *started*. I snatched up my ticket and then the change he was counting out and galloped through the barrier. Too late! But no, with a grind of brakes the train was halted and I was taken aboard. At Foligno, the next station, a railway policeman, hat peak-tilted, came running along the platform calling for the person who had boarded the train at Assisi. I pleaded guilty and he said, "Ah, signore, I have a telegram. It seems the clerk at Assisi made an error in figuring your ticket. I shall have to ask you for a small further payment." Just what clerks do during the lean hours when no trains are leaving is a point on which I am uninformed, but they must be exceedingly busy, for it is only by the grace of God that they are enabled to find the irreducible minimum of time to transact their main business.

Do not take the above too hard, I beg. The chances of your actually missing a train through the ticket clerk's fault are probably not one in a hundred, and you can usually remove even this element of risk by buying your ticket ahead of time in the CIT office or some other agency.

Circular tour tickets for fixed itineraries bought from CIT or any agency *abroad* offer a comfortable solution to all problems of ticket purchase. If the Italian portion of the itinerary starts at the frontier the ticket has a 60-day validity and stopovers are unlimited. Similar circular tour tickets with but 30-day validity and unlimited stopovers may be purchased inside Italy. At the frontier, or initial station, and at each station of stopover the ticket must be validated with a rubber stamp. *Vidimazione* is the word to murmur, with rising inflection, but often a CIT office will be in or near the station and most of the CIT staff speak English.

First or second class, which shall we take in Italy? First is 50 per cent more costly and on many trains 50 per cent less crowded. The load carried by Italian rails is terrific and it sometimes seems that *every* Italian is going somewhere every day. This is a thing to keep always in mind. If standing up in a train is torture to you, the extra cost of first class, still only matching our day-coach fares, will seem negligible. In any case, even with a first-class ticket, get your advance reservation, for any long trip, or else be ready to enter your train as soon as it is made up, or as soon as it *enters* the station, regardless of the fact that it may mean a half-hour wait.

Second class is comfortably upholstered and *sometimes* it is not crowded. There are eight places in each compartment as against six in first, but usually all eight are occupied before the train starts.

And what about Italian third? Third class is certainly endurable, especially by men and especially in the north. An American woman traveling third south of Rome might feel uncomfortably conspicuous, and she might not relish the appearance of her traveling companions. There is leather upholstery on the fast trains, as in French third, and the slope of the benches is good. One *can* get used to this mode of travel. I know because I have done some thousands of kilometers of it. The saving in fares is impressive, third being not much over half as much as even second. Nevertheless I would say again that Italian tariffs are so moderate that they make third-class travel unnecessary except for the very frugal budgeter.

Lake boats have only first and second class. The latter has its advantage (being at the bow of the boat) in fine weather, and one will scarcely wish to sail the lakes in any weather that is not at least reasonably fine, but of course first is far more comfortable and roomy. It is the class of tourism.

A caution about luggage. Go light in Italy. Together with my family I once traversed the country with three trunks, a monstrous Gladstone and several suitcases. I lived through it, but my pocketbook almost did not. It was expensive, frightfully expensive, at every move. The travel leaflets, and Pozzo, state very firmly that only twenty kilos (44 lbs.) of luggage can be taken free into the carriages, but there must be, I think, an extremely liberal interpretation of what constitutes 44 lbs. Certainly I have never once been challenged at the gate and sometimes my bags have weighed—plenty.

Very often you will wish to leave your bag at a station while spending a few hours in some small town. The phrase you want on this occasion is *Deposito di Bagagli;* and *dove* (which can only be phonetically spelled *dough-vay*) means "where." It costs little to leave luggage 'in pawn." Umbrellas may be slid under the straps of suitcases, thus getting in free.

And now this dry-as-sawdust chapter shall close with a cheerful note of railway news. Or is it not news? Do you know that pleasant institution the *cestino di viaggio?* It means "travel basket" and can be bought (sometimes hot, oftener cold) at important railway stations or junctions in Italy for about a dollar. It takes over the whole burden of providing convenient travel "eats" and is so simple and handy that one wonders why, and why again, other countries do not adopt it. The *carrozze ristorante* (dining cars) of Italy are cheerful and they serve a good meal at only about $1.50, but on many trains there is none, and when such a car is carried it may often be jampacked.

The *cestino caldo* (hot), when procurable, contains a good-sized portion of chicken or hot meat, often a veal cutlet, sometimes with potato and a vegetable; a casserole of hot macaroni; bread, cheese and a small bottle of wine; perhaps a piece of sweet chocolate and certainly one or two oranges. All this, together with a rude fork (but no knife), enclosed in a neat paper container rigged with strings to insure easy carrying, makes a tasty meal, though eating it may be a bit un-dainty. Compare it, I beg, with the ordinary station scramble to secure a dry ham sandwich, hard as nails, a little bottle of pop or beer, and some fruit at fully as much money and infinitely more inconvenience. Crossing the border from Italy to any other land you will sigh for that really agreeable companion of travel, the cestino di viaggio.

Homemade Tours for the First-Timer

For the traveler to whom Europe is a Dream Continent, quite unknown and maybe unreal, to whom foreign languages, moneys, customs, are restless interludes in the dream, there is solid comfort, blissful relaxation, in letting some skilled purveyor of fixed tours "can" the whole thing. The customer tells the expert what country or countries he wants to see and lets the expert fit him into one of the tours that is prearranged, to the minutest detail. The thing is all set down in black and white on a neat folder and the customer need do virtually nothing except sign a check and procure his passport.

After I had made at least twenty long trips to Europe on my own and had lived for a total of six or seven years in various countries of the Continent, including Italy, curiosity finally overcame me and I actually did join a canned group tour. The agency that ran it was the Metropolitan Travel Service of Boston, whose director, a Swiss-American named Ernest Ruegg, I knew as a man who speaks fluent Italian, one of the three languages of his native Switzerland, and who has long specialized in this type of travel. The tour, his Italy Fall Special, conducted by himself and his wife, was the first of four trips I have undertaken to get material for the present book. The other three I engineered for myself.

I have often proclaimed, and I do again, the delights of making one's own way, all minor troubles and annoyances included, but I must candidly admit that I loved also that predigested tour. I felt like a teacher attending the lecture of another teacher. I didn't have a care in the world. Details of itinerary? I didn't have to give them a thought. Hotels? At each stop we were taken to the selected hotel and assigned rooms. Luggage? I only followed instructions, leaving my bags for collection outside the bedroom door at whatever hour the daily bulletin said to do so. It was really an experience, perhaps more exciting for the dyed-in-the-wool, professional traveler than even for the first-timer. We traveled from place to place by a big rented bus. We had the best local guides everywhere. We travelers, about twenty-eight of us, engaged in an enormous lot of banter, and at every halt there was a minimum of fussing, a maximum of relaxation and bonhomie. The trip will be further viewed "from the inside" in Chapter 16. Various agencies, including, of course, the American Express Company and Cook, offer fully-arranged group tours, but I think the large agencies are able to put less heart into it, and less personality, than do the smaller specialists.

Counsel in Rome and the Provinces

The *American Express Company's* offices are the club rooms of American travel in Italy. In all of them one is certain to find, at almost any hour, a group ranging from three or four to a throng. They are cashing checks, calling for letters, booking tours, making reservations and more especially they are just *talking* with each other.

The Rome office is at 39 Piazza di Spagna, just below the Spanish Steps. The new Naples office is in the new Hotel Vesuvio, on Via Partenope. The Genoa office is in Piazza Acquaverde, adjacent to Hotel Savoia and Majestic, opposite Hotel Colombia. The Venice office is a few steps from Piazza San Marco, as one leaves this nuclear square at the opposite end from the cathedral. The natural popularity of these offices with nostalgic Americans makes the doing of business tough. I have waited in line as long as twenty minutes to cash a check, as long as forty to ask a question about travel, but the waiting is almost always "conversational." You talk with the person in front and the person behind, making new friends if you wish to.

Cook's Rome offices are at 11 Via Veneto and 93 Piazza San Silvestro, both very central and conspicuous. Cook owns the Wagons-Lits system throughout Europe. This ramifying world firm of Britain has been in active business virtually since the Year One.

CIT has its main Rome office at 64-68 Piazza Esedra, others at 193 Piazza Colonna, 7 Via Barberini and in the Termini Station.

Pier Busseti and *Oltremare* are two other travel agencies prominent in Italy and there are many more, but we need not confuse ourselves by knowing who they are. "Enough are enough."

* * *

Ente Provinciale per il Turismo is a phrase extremely well worth knowing. It designates a provincial office of ENIT and such offices exist in the chief cities of all Italian provinces. In my opinion they are excellent, sometimes even wonderful. They get to the grass roots of local tourism and are definitely helpful to travelers. They fill your hands with brochures and local maps. They give you the most direct counsel about what you want to do *now*. Often the manager himself is in sight, not hidden in some sumptuous third-floor office. Learn to know the *Enti Provinciali*—that's the plural. Each one is a separate entity—no pun intended—eager to let you know about the glories of its own city and region. Each is sparked by some one man and the brightness of the spark varies according to his capacity and personality. The Ente office for the city of Rome is at 47 Via Barberini, with branches in the Termini Station and the Ciampino Airport.

In many cities and nearly all tourist resorts and spas there is to be found a good tourist-booster organization with the heavy name *Azienda di Cura, Soggiorno e Turismo;* and in tiny places with big attractions a *Pro Loco* will be found. All of these offices are more or less helpful but the Enti generally rouse my enthusiasm.

Guidance in Print

Books about Italy are like the sands of the sea for number. More than a dozen new ones were brought out almost simultaneously in early 1950 to cope with the travel demands of Holy Year. I shall not offer any general bibliography but only a partial listing of some of the books that I have found practical in tourist guidance.

The Guide Bleu now entitled *Nagel's Italy* seems to me absolutely essential. It is the Baedeker of today, five hundred compact pages in small and smaller print (but clear), with innumerable maps and city plans and a text that is replete with meticulous detail. The book is surprisingly small in bulk and light in weight. It will slide into a topcoat pocket. There is also an up-to-date Nagel for *Rome and its Environs*.

The CIT guide has been mentioned earlier. It is not quite a substitute for such a "total" handbook as *Nagel's Italy* but it is an excellent supplement to it for the reasons mentioned (food and wine;

festivals; theaters and concerts; sport) and because it puts its place information into abridged and readable form.

The well-known Clara Laughlin guide *So You're Going to Italy*, formerly in two volumes, was accordioned into one in 1950 by Betty Laughlin Sweeney.

Gordon Cooper, an English travel writer with a simple, straightforward approach, wrote *Your Holiday in Italy* for the 1950 rush and it was republished in New York. This small volume is long on sensible practicalities and ABC advice.

Horace Sutton's *Footloose in Italy* is one of the volumes in his successful "Footloose" series of practical, lively guides. He is the widely known travel editor of *The Saturday Review of Literature*.

Doré Ogrizek's *Italy*, with its many alluring color sketches, is one of the eye-catching volumes in the series called, "The World in Color."

Sean O'Faolain's *A Summer in Italy* stood out, in the large 1950 crop of books, as a work of literature. It did not, of course, pretend to be a guidebook, but it revealed the Italy that its gifted author saw.

Agnes Rothery's *Rome Today*, another item in the 1950 avalanche, was written with the sympathetic and expert touch of this very satisfactory author. Aimed especially at the 1950 pilgrims, it remains useful.

Eleanor Clark's more recent (1952) book *Rome and a Villa* is decidedly readable in all its sparkling and very personal pages. (The author is no relative of this author.)

Parenthetically—for *current* information about what to see and do in Rome, and the how and when of it, consult the lively columns and advertisements of *The Daily American;* also the lists in *La Settimana a Roma* (This Week in Rome), appearing each Friday.

Rome, in the *Medici Art Series,* edited by Giuseppe Fattorusso, is at the opposite end of the guidebook spectrum from the light weekly just mentioned. It is a superlative guide to the city's myriad works of art and boasts more than a thousand illustrations.

And, speaking of illustrations, the Medici book on all Italy, entitled *Wonders of Italy,* has 3265 of them, plus six full-page plates in color and some charts. *Wonders of Italy* is really a wonder of book making. It is brought out in Italian, French and English in two editions, one with cloth binding, the other in de luxe tooled leather. It weighs well over three pounds and is thus a problem for the traveler who would like to use it while moving from place to place, but as a book to enjoy "before and after" and to possess for life and show to all who enter your home it is perhaps without parallel in the catalog of books on Italy. Actually it is a one-volume encyclopedia of that country's art and architecture, an impressive tome that makes an interesting gift. Its editor is the same Giuseppe Fattorusso who compiled the volume on Rome. The book, in its English de luxe edition, now costs about $12.50 in Italy.

A place where visitors, along with many Italians, may browse contentedly among the forenamed books and countless others on Italy is the library of the *United States Information Service* (USIS) at 62 Via Véneto. Its large, cheerful reading room, seen directly from the street, is one of the most inviting retreats of its kind in Europe. It makes any American proud of the way our country is *offering* information—in this capital and some ten other Italian cities, as well as throughout Free Europe—in a fine, attractive, honest way as against totalitarian methods of stuffing tortuous propaganda down the throats of all whom it can reach. The *Mutual Security Agency* (MSA), replacing the former Economic Cooperation Administration (ECA), has its Rome office on the upper floors of the same building and is doing a magnificent job of fanning the flames of freedom in Italy.

What to Know About Money

At the official rate of exchange prevailing now—approximately 625 lire to the dollar—Italy is *by no means* one of the cheap countries of Europe, like Spain and, to a lesser degree, Portugal and Austria, nor is it, to be fair in comparisons, expensive by American standards. Tourist Italy, the peninsula and the Sicily of the beaten track, can cost *plenty* if you stay only in the luxury and first-class hotels and eat only in the restaurants of such hotels, but it costs "more than plenty," as we know too well, if travelers live and eat in hotels of similar type in our own country.

I will submit here a brief primer about Italian money, with apologies to those who know all these elementary facts. Paper notes range from the tiny ones of 1 lira, hardly bigger than large postage stamps and worth less than one-sixth of a cent, to the normal-sized 500-lire and 1000-lire notes and on up to the outsize 5000-lire and 10,000-lire notes, though many of those in circulation in the larger denominations are still the odd, temporary ones shaped like elongated checks. They'll buy just as much as the handsomer and newer notes. Below the 500-lire bills the ones you will use are of the denominations 100, 50, 10, 5. The 2 and 1 affairs are very rarely seen nowadays and are quite useless except as souvenirs. It takes a fist-full of them to buy a newspaper. Aluminum-weight coins of 5 and 10 lire exist, as they have existed for several years but even now you do not too often see them. The disappearance of these coins has deeply puzzled Italian fiscal authorities, the accepted theory being that the peasants, not having seen or *felt* coins for many previous years, have been hoarding them as treasures. Another theory, a bit fantastic I think, is that Swiss traders buy them up solely for their metal content.

Italian money is among Europe's awkward currencies to use. The 1000-lire and 500-lire notes, which are worth about $1.60 and 80 cents respectively and which melt away from you like snow in a warm rain, are of standard size and usually of fairly good quality. The 100's and 50's are smaller, raggeder things, the 10's and 5's still smaller and still more ragged. When they are old, and most of them are, they resist folding but seem to welcome tearing. Very many have been patched with paper or Scotch tape by previous users. In general these small bills, including the 100's (worth 16 cents), tend to become a *wad* of paper in your pocket or pocketbook, with high relative humidity in hot weather. I look forward with earnest hope to the day when coins up to a hundred lire will be in general use.

There is a solution, more or less, to the present crumpled-money problem. The larger bills of 5000 and 10,000 lire may be folded twice and kept with respect like any money of value in wallet or pocketbook. The 1000- and 500-lire notes may be folded once and kept (by men) in a separate pocket or (by women) in a separate compartment of the pocketbook. Hundred and fifties, still worth something, may likewise be worthy of folding and stowing in some separate place. The 10's and 5's, in the class of pennies, may be wadded into a big clip or merely left to shift for themselves. Detach a few of them from the wad for use when you want to buy a paper or take a local tram or bus ride.

Much more important than the appearance of the money is its value to you. At present the traveler is allowed to bring into Italy an unlimited amount of lire, but in notes of no higher value than 1000 lire. If he declares the amount upon entry he may legally take out up to 30,000, but nobody ever wants to do this, as the sale value of lire outside Italy is poor. It *does* pay to buy a stock of at least 20,000 before coming to Italy, for use on the first few days. The free-market rate abroad is generally a few per cent more favorable to dollars than the established rate in Italy. A reputable and convenient foreign exchange office in New York is that of Perera and Company on the ground floor of 636 Fifth Avenue, in Rockefeller Center.

Ten-dollar bills are wonderful things to take with you, supplementing your regular supply of travelers checks. At the cambio dens, being exchange offices conspicuous in every city, ten-dollar bills will command a nice premium. I have usually received at least thirty lire more per dollar in this way than through cashing American Express checks at the office of that company. The cambio dens, in Rome at least, will also cash travelers checks at a rate somewhat lower than that for ten-dollar bills but well above the official rate of the banks and the American Express offices. Five-dollar bills are less desired than tens, and one-dollar bills are very dimly viewed by the cambio men, who will give fewer lire for them than even the established rate. But a few ones are always desirable for settlement of small bills that pop into view just as you are leaving the country. In any case never let yourself get stuck, at the last moment, with only fifty-dollar travelers checks, or even twenties. You will have to take an awful exchange beating when you sell the balance of your lire outside Italy.

Beware of sidewalk brokers who offer you Italian money at fabulous rates of exchange. The more they offer, the more likely they are to be crooks. Some are honest, in their mildly illegal way. Some are outright thieves, especially in Naples, where there is a scandalous money racket. If you trade with these people examine each note of any size to see if the watermark (a human head) is visible in the white circle. And make *sure* that the packet of money the man hands you is what it seems to be. I have met tourists who had just bought what they could plainly see was twenty, or fifty, of the 1000-lire notes. They "actually counted them." On pretense of courteously changing one or two dirty and ragged notes for clean ones the broker-thief has managed to substitute a different packet containing pieces of newspaper folded neatly within a single 1000-lire note! Or perhaps he has whispered in agitation, "Hurry, sir! Polizia." The customer has looked up for a second to see if a policeman is coming and the swindler has seized that second to change the packet. Then he runs away "to avoid being caught." Travelers who stick to the banks, the American Express offices and the openly tolerated cambio dens will almost never receive false money or any less than the proper amount.

The required declaration, upon arrival, of all the moneys and travelers checks you carry is one of the oddities of the present Italian system. The declaration looks *so* formidable. You must put down everything "in figures and in letters." You are sternly warned in four languages that every exchange transaction must be recorded by the seller on the back of the paper, that the declaration must be saved and shown upon leaving the country, that you must prove that any articles bought in Italy were bought with money thus legally exchanged and recorded. What actually happens? The exchange offices, including the American Express, simply don't record any transactions on your paper. If you ask them to do so they smile indulgently, recognizing you for a first-timer, and say, "Forget it. Keep your declaration as a souvenir." And a souvenir it is. I have *all* of mine. Not once, in at least eight exits from the country, in the last three years, has any customs officer even hinted that he would like to have a look at it, much less collect it.

I suppose this pleasant tolerance is in part a mark of affection, financially speaking, for American tourists, who are highly desirable visitors (and spenders) all over Europe, and who have all contributed tax money to aid Europe's recovery. At all entrances and exits to or from any country, I make it a practice to keep my American passport always conspicuously in sight. It is a magic wand of travel. On half the occasions the custom folk have not asked me any questions at all, nor even shown any interest in my bags except to chalk them

FIRST FACTS OF TRAVEL 43

rapidly and wave me through the barrier. It makes the traveler humbly thankful to be the lucky possessor of so priceless a document. Virtually all free European countries, including Italy, welcome the bearer of an American passport and now require no consular visa in it—just as if we offered the same kind treatment when their nationals wish to enter our country!

CHAPTER 4

HOTELS AND THEIR PRICES

Annuario Alberghi d'Italia

THE *Annual of Hotels of Italy*, brought out by ENIT, tells in four languages practically everything, except the color of the walls in each room, that any traveler might wish to know about Italy's six thousand or more hotels. The fat little volume of 830 pages, rather heavy to carry about, may be procured from the Italian State Tourist Offices abroad (New York: 21 East 51st Street) or from the head office in Rome at 2 Via Marghera, north of the station. The tome is subdivided into many regional and city sections, published separately, and these are of no more than pamphlet size. The *local* annuals are procurable at the various Ente offices (in Rome at 47 Via Barberini) and may sometimes be found at travel offices, especially the semi-official one of CIT.

Italian hotels are sorted by law into fixed categories: Luxury, First, Second, Third, Fourth, with a residue of "Lower Class Hotels" presumably never patronized by tourists and not deemed worthy of listing. *Pensions* are officially considered—for tourist tax purposes— to be one class lower, all along the line, than hotels, a first-class pension, for instance, being taxed the same as a second-class hotel. Pension prices, at a reduced rate, *in* hotels, meaning the overall figure for room and three meals (no wines included), are usually not granted for stays of less than three days, but it is a wide-open secret that in periods of lean trade many *albergatori* are quite willing to bargain about this and establish reduced pension rates for a stay of one or two days.

The *Annuario* lists maximum and minimum prices for one-bed and two-bed rooms, with private bath and without, on the temporary basis and *en pension*. Where peak-season and off-season rates differ, as is the case in some cities and most resorts, it prints two sets of figures. For every locality it gives the altitude in meters (a meter is about 10 per cent more than a yard) and for every hotel it discusses, by conventional symbols, such vital matters as hotel bus service, elevator service, running water and telephone in the bedrooms, hotel banking facilities and central heating.

That last item, *riscaldamento* in Italian, rarely concerns travelers who visit balmy Italy between April and November. In winter it can provide an unpleasant shock, adding to your bill daily almost as much as the cost of breakfast. This charge and all others must, by law, be prominently posted, and though this is sometimes neglected, a great many hotels, of all categories, do set forth the whole story in detail on cards in every room.

Your Bill—Before You Get It

"The whole story" of Italian hotel charges is an involved one that often causes a sharp pain in the middle of one's budget *if* the traveler has not informed himself in advance about them. The *total* charge would not seem to Americans too high if all the minor charges were absorbed in it. The following paragraphs propose to ease this pain by careful explanation.

Here is a typical bill I once encountered and paid in a provincial city. It was for one night, in a bathless room, and breakfast in a first-class but not luxury hotel.

Appartamento, 1600. The appartamento was my room.

Riscaldamento, 300.

Prima colazione, 400. This was my Continental breakfast of coffee, rolls, butter, jam.

2% *Imposta generale, sull'entrata*, 50. This was the 2 per cent "Income Tax" levied on all hotel bills. It was reduced in 1950 from 3% to 2% and in 1952 to 1%. (The amount of my tax was strictly 46 lire, being 2% of 1600 plus 300 plus 400, but neither hotel nor guest can bother with such trifles as 4 lire.)

Imposta di Soggiorno, 50. This was the Sojourn Tax, applicable in most cities and all resorts of Italy. It is a fixed item, not a percentage, and varies from 60 lire in luxury hotels to 5 in those of lowest class.

15% *Servizio,* 345. The service charge is 15 per cent in most places, but 18 per cent in Rome, 20 per cent in Palermo.
Bollo di quietanza, 10. This was the "quittance stamp."
Totale da pagare, 2845 lire.

The total comes to about $4.50 or $4.00 without heat. The room had a pleasant balcony and a washroom alcove, with running water, but no bath. The breakfast, as I have said, was the very simple one customary in Europe. Certainly the bill was plenty, yet by no means exorbitant, since the hotel was a quality one. My point in presenting the above analysis is to forewarn the reader about *extras* and *more extras.* In the above account there are five of them, totaling $1.25. The *bollo* item at the end is but one cent and a half, yet there it is, invoking a mild frown from the guest. Personally I think it would be smart practice for Italy to work out a system whereby the *three* annoying little taxes, amounting above to but eighteen cents all told, could be absorbed and hidden in the main bill, leaving only the basic items and the service charge, but that is Italy's business. This being the case, the traveler may as well do the next best thing and understand his bill before he gets it. The total of service and taxes, even in Rome where the 18-per-cent service charge prevails, increases the account by only about one-fourth. If this is known in advance, and sportingly accepted, the guest will increase his own pleasure by more than a fourth instead of wasting half an hour each time in futile fuming.

Tips on Tipping

Hotel bills often carry the printed note: *Le Mance Sono Aboliti*—Tips Are Abolished—but travelers should not take this too seriously. The Nagel guide says very daintily, "Although tips have officially been abolished the habit has not yet died out." Not yet? It never will as long as maids are maids, waiters waiters and tourists tourists. I should say that the habit is even increasing. In strict theory there is no excuse for it when there is a substantial service charge, but servants would not be themselves if they were not magically present and officious when you are leaving a hotel; and tourists would not be themselves if they refrained from putting at least something into each willing hand. This too I think should be known and expected by the traveler.

There is no need of overdoing it and indeed the wealthy tourist who gives almost as much in tips as if there were no service charge is being most unkind to other travelers who are quite unable to "throw it around." *Little* tips will sweeten one's departure and leave smiles behind. A 100-lire note (16 cents) here and there, with substantially more to the head porter if he has helped you, as he nearly always does, leaves you in the clear with no sense of sneaking out of the place. The above is for first-class and luxury hotels. In modest establishments tips may be on a much lower scale, or omitted altogether. In restaurants 20 to 50 lire per person above the service charge is plenty unless the meal has been a big and de luxe dinner.

Tips in beauty shops and barber shops, for taxi men, for almost anybody who does you a service, are expected, but these minor disbursements do not amount to much in dollar cash. Even when you buy an *espresso* (coffee brewed "expressly" at your order) in any of the innumerable little stand-up cafés you are expected to leave 5 lire (less than a cent). You will see an eloquent saucer on the counter filled with 5-lire notes and a few generous 10's. The taxi tip may be a bit over 10 per cent of the fare, but you will hardly wish to give less than 50 lire for even the shortest haul.

Tipping, in all countries, is a problem that invites an inordinate amount of tourist worry and tourist talk, *sotto voce*. There is no clear answer to it, no one rule. In general, however, you will enjoy your travels more if you can handle the problem in a reasonably generous but *not* lavish way.

Suggestions—Between You and Me

Some personal thoughts, warnings and counsels about hotels may be at least worth their weight in paper and printer's ink. Here they are.

Watch out for breakfast. The charge for it, in first-class hotels, seems to me the one thing in Italian travel that is definitely way out of line. Of course it is the hotel's way of getting a little better price for its rooms, since not one tourist in twenty will ever go outside for breakfast, and possibly, from that angle, there is justification for it, since basic room costs *are* fairly moderate. The usual breakfast charge of 400 lire, which comes to nearly 500 with service and tax and a little tip, seems far too much for coffee, two rolls, butter and jam. If you order orange juice, cereal, eggs, the price soars like a rocket. One of the indoor sports of the seasoned traveler is to watch an American newcomer ordering the same breakfast he would eat at home and then watch his face, or hers, when the bill comes. In the land of oranges it is not unusual, for instance, for a hotel to charge 300 or 350 lire for a good-sized glass of orange juice. That means, at present rates, about 55 cents, plus another 15 cents for the extras. I hardly know—and hate to think—what breakfast eggs and cereal cost, since I never order them and there is never a morning menu. My counsel is this. If your pocketbook is not bulging, stick to the Continental breakfast. It is even permissible to go outside and get the rolls-and-coffee breakfast at half the price in a café or milk bar, but this is not usually very practical, nor does one feel quite comfortable to do it.

A financial item of minor importance but worth knowing about is the so-called income tax of 1 to 4 per cent on meals taken in any type of restaurant, including the dining room of any hotel *in which you are not lodging* (as against 1 per cent on overall hotel bills). In luxury restaurants and hotels it is 4 per cent. The same scale of taxes applies to all drinks and also to food ordered *à la carte* (first-class or luxury places) *even* if you are lodging in the hotel.

Prezzo globale is a good phrase to know. It means "inclusive price" and it is often possible, especially in slack seasons, to bargain for this overall figure, which should include—and be sure this is understood—the service charge and *all* taxes. Such bargaining implies a stay of at least several days. There is solid comfort in the arrangement.

Letto matrimoniale is another phrase to know, meaning "matrimonial bed," or, in less bold parlance, double bed. Italy is not like France, where the double bed is standard in small hotels, nor is it like Switzerland or Germany, where a double bed, in a hotel, is quite as rare as a white crow. The room with the double bed is bound to be cheaper than one with twin beds and it has other advantages. It leaves more space, if the room is small—and you may prefer it anyway. Period.

Monasteries and *convents* in some isolated places offer travelers extremely cheap room and board, perhaps two dollars a day or less for everything. Students occasionally avail themselves of this chance to save a lot of money. Inquiry may be made through the Ente offices. These places are not restricted to Roman Catholics.

In university towns, student hostels will also accommodate foreign students when the university is not in session.

Locanda means inn and one finds these small inns everywhere in village Italy. The lean of purse can stay in them *very* cheaply and without *too* much discomfort. Locande are not listed in the hotel annual.

Appartamento (or *Camera*) *Affittasi* (or *da affittare*) means "Room to Let," and one sees this sign in many a street of many a city. I have several times explored the quarters thus offered and twice I have thus found a satisfactory room and have stayed in it for two or three weeks at a time, foraging for all my meals, including breakfast. There is good fun in this super-footloose way of travel but it can be tiring after a time.

In general, the traveler without much money but with the courage born of eagerness can make out all right in Italy at a quarter or a fifth of the daily costs incurred by the average tourist. I shall have more to say about this when the text reaches the subject of food.

Your Anchor in Rome

My anchor in Rome, on recent trips, has usually been *Hotel Quirinale*, on Via Nazionale, a stone's throw from Piazza Esedra. It is in the first-class category as to price, but with public rooms and various facilities that place it very close to the luxury class. It shelters the booking office of British Overseas Airways and British European Airways, whose busses also arrive here from the airport and depart from here for the airport. (Nearly all the other systems use the new air terminal in the railway station.) The central offices of CIT and CIAT are only a few steps from the hotel, in Piazza Esedra; the railway station but five minutes' walk; the air-line booking offices, a whole nest of major ones, about five minutes' walk in the opposite direction, on Via Bissolati, an ultra-modern street which was cut through a crowded quarter a few years ago. The opera house is back to back with the Hotel Quirinale, the shopping district is at its doors and half of Rome's chief sights, including the Quirinal, the Capitoline, Santa Maria Maggiore and the Forum, are within easy walking distance.

Another hotel of first-class category where I have anchored with complete satisfaction is the *Continentale*, on Via Cavour at the corner of the huge, newly landscaped square on which the Termini Station fronts. This big, cheerful, well-run hotel is wonderfully handy for the transient. Not only is it adjacent to the station but also many of Rome's busses and trams start from the local terminal in the square, and the electric railways for Albano, Frascati, Castel Gandolfo and many other places in the Alban Hills start from their terminus on Via Amendola, a block from the Continentale's doors.

Among the luxury hotels, of which Rome has six at present, the only one where I have stayed is the Swiss-operated *Hassler-Villa Medici*, fronting on the Piazza Trinità dei Monti at the top of the Spanish Steps. The place has a quiet elegance and character all its own and the location is superb. Its dining room and terrace face a seemingly almost perpendicular lawn and one marvels that such even and velvety grass has been made to grow on it. There is also a roof dining room and terrace with a magnificent view of Rome.

Hotel Excelsior, on Via Véneto close to the American Embassy, is easily the best-known of Rome's luxury hotels, best-known, that is, to American tourists. It is almost an American hotel and you hear little in its lobby and public rooms except our various brands of English. Some come here for its sheer, luxurious comforts including partial air conditioning. Others undoubtedly come because they think it important to be seen in the right place with "the best people."

Among Rome's *pensioni*, four of recommendable quality that have happened to come within my ken are the *Bellavista-Milton*, at 16A Via Porta Pinciana near Via Véneto and the Pincian Gate; the *Dinesen*, at number 18 on the same street; the *Florida*, at 18 Via Gregoriana, a street leading from Piazza Trinità dei Monti; and *La Quiete*, at 26 Via Orazio, close to the Castel Sant'Angelo and not far from St. Peter's.

A *motel* type of hostelry giving more or less the effect of a displaced court from the sunnier side of the United States, is *The California*

Garden, near the Villa Corsini on the Lungotevere (meaning "Tiberside") Farnesina, close to the Ponte Sisto. In flowery English its folders welcome you to its cabin colony (with two hundred rooms), its garden restaurant, swimming pool and so on. I have never stopped here but this retreat of America-on-Tiber looks acceptable.

* * *

It seems almost absurd to pick out and name a half dozen anchors in Rome, where more than three hundred are listed in the annual, but I fall back on my usual defense, that this is a *personal* guide telling what I personally know and like. Gordon Cooper has a suggestion so sensible that I shall steal it, with thanks. He proposes that the traveler reserve his room for one night, with the right to extend the reservation if he wishes, rather than pay in advance, through the use of hotel coupons or otherwise, for the whole of his stay in Rome (or Florence or Venice or Naples). This permits him to do his own sleuthing and change to another place if he happens upon one that strongly tempts him. In times of peak trade this plan may encounter considerable resistance from the *albergatori* but often it seems to work rather easily. As a matter of fact I had followed it many times before I read the suggestion in Mr. Cooper's guide.

And here is an item from my own stock of gratuitous counsels. Remembering that the Italy trip is your own, don't let anybody dragoon you into putting it through in some manner that is not of your own choosing. If you like to bask in sybaritic luxuries and spend your leisure hours in café gardens or in shops, that is the way you'll get the most out of your sojourn. If you want to content yourself with modest rooms—lots of them have glorious outlooks—saving all your funds and energies for a campaign as demon shopper or demon sightseer, crowding in everything of Italy that you can possibly manage, don't be talked out of it. Tourists who can come to Europe every year for long stays like to speak condescendingly of those rushers-about who do Italy in two weeks, but such chatter may be ignored. "Travel and let travel" is as good a motto in the free world—and Italy, thank heaven, is a part of the free world—as "Live and let live."

CHAPTER 5

ITALIAN FOOD, ITS FASCINATION AND ITS FAULTS

Meals of the Traveler's Day

THE *prima colazione*, first meal of the tourist day, has been amply and a bit frowningly discussed. It is sometimes called the *piccola colazione* (small breakfast) and it is small indeed, small except in price. Its component parts, in Italian, are *caffè al latte* (coffee with milk), *pane e burro* (bread and butter) and *conserva* (jam) or *marmellata* (marmalade). Tea (*tè*) or chocolate (*cioccolata calda*) may be substituted for coffee.

Colazione is lunch and *pranzo* dinner. In these two meals, one hardly differing from the other as the menu reads, the distinctive cuisine of Italy manifests itself beyond question. *Antipasti*, Italy's popular version of hors d'oeuvres, always head the list and after them come the *Minestre*, being the great clan of soups and flour-based dishes, that is macaroni and its countless pleasant relatives, collectively called *pasta*. *Pesci* is the fish list and *Carne* is meat, though meat items and chicken are generally listed under the headings *Piatti del Giorno* (Dishes of the Day) and *Piatti da Farsi*, or *Piatti a Farsi* (Dishes to Order). *Legumi* means vegetables; *Insalate* salads; *Formaggi* cheeses; *Frutta* fruit; *Dolci e Gelati* sweets and ices.

Most restaurants, but by no means all, serve only à la carte meals, which almost invariably cost more, all over the world, than do fixed-price meals. If economy is of interest to your budget you may watch for the words *Prezzo Fisso*, with a price mark, on the menus posted in the windows of many restaurants in all cities. These will seldom be the smart places of tourism, but rather the ordinary lunchrooms of ordinary Romans, Neapolitans, Milanese, Venetians. An inexpensive lunchroom is more likely to be called *Trattoria* than *Ristorante* and places of still humbler order, specializing in pizza pie, are labeled

Pizzeria, while the lowest-bracket places, sometimes with standing room only, will be labeled *Rosticceria*, but almost all the establishments serve good food, for the elemental reason that Italians, of any bracket, expect good food when they eat out. I will have more to say on the subject of informed thrift in coping with Italian restaurant prices, but right now I feel a considerable digression coming on.

A Blackboard Talk on Pasta

The cuisine of Italy, even on its loftiest levels, lays remarkable stress on *pasta* in all its multitude of forms. The person who skips this "foundation paste" can still construct a full meal, and an Italian one, from the bill of fare but he will be missing the very soul of it, to my way of thinking.

If you do not like macaroni, possibly it is because you have never eaten it cooked right. It is almost always cooked right in Italy and very seldom in other countries. No, I will not plead guilty to exaggeration, for this is one of the established facts of life. Even the so-called Italian restaurants outside of Italy almost invariably overcook macaroni or spaghetti so that it becomes an uninteresting mess, but in Italy it is a prince among dishes, though a very democratic prince.

Under many names this noble nutritive food graces Italian menus. Here are a few of them: *maccheroni, spaghetti* (which means "little strings"), *vermicelli, tagliatelle, lasagne, cappelletti, canneloni, pappardelle, fettucine, tortellini*. There are plenty of others, but the foregoing are the more prominent ones. These dishes are served *al pomodoro* (with tomato sauce), *al sugo* (with meat sauce), or *al burro* (in butter). The whole family of them come under the heading of *minestra asciutta* (dry soup) and they are often called *pasta asciutta* (dry paste). *Ravioli* is, of course, little pillows of pasta with a meat and egg and spinach filling, as is its first cousin *agnolotti*.

Do not, I beg, confuse yourself with all these names unless you chance to find them entertaining. If you say to the waiter, "*Pasta*," adding *al pomodoro* or *al sugo*, your meal is sure to get away to a good start. But if dry soup simply does not call you, merely murmur, "Minestrone," as you would at home, and you will find the dish a definitely damp, thick vegetable soup. And if even this proves too semi-solid for your taste you may count on *minestra in brodo* to be *wet*. *Zuppa di verdura*, often with spinach, is also wet.

One special word about the fine art of eating spaghetti I must insert before drifting away from the subject. You will note that many Italians, at least in the less elegant restaurants, do not cut these "little strings." They take up a few strands on the fork, plant the tines of the fork securely in the bowl of a large spoon and twist (clockwise) until the spaghetti is wound up into a little ball of yarn, so to speak, then pop it in and start winding up the next mouthful. No, it is not dainty, and I am told by Italian Emily Posts that nowadays the "best people" are not doing it any more. Against this I must register my alien protest. It is impossible to be dainty with dry soup and your true connoisseur, I choose to maintain, has nothing but scorn for those who attempt it.

Another humble but delectable dish listed on menus under Minestre and often used as an opener of the Italian meal, is *risotto alla milanese*. It is stewed rice, and when made correctly—which it often is not—it is gorgeously spiced and tinted with saffron. *Risotto con funghi*, with mushrooms, is another pleasing variant.

Exploring the Menu

Italy has been so used to tourists for so long that its leading restaurants can always provide a meal of international type indistinguishable from its counterpart in any large European city, *but*—they have by no means mortgaged their souls to timid tourism. Except in a very few places, chiefly luxury hotels, they still stress and serve delicious *Italian* meals. May it always be so, for Italian cooking is among the greats of the epicurean world. International cooking is the cuisine without a country, descended vaguely from France.

I invade with apprehension the vast and various subject of Italian cookery, but from much experience of it, I can at least set forth a few elemental facts and foods, following this with a look at some regional specialties.

Pesce (plural *pesci*), pronounced *payshay*, is important in a country surrounded by seas on three sides and rich too in rivers and lakes. All sorts and varieties of finny folk, including the beloved eel (*anguilla*), which has no fins at all, have their places on the menu. You will often see the item sea fruit (*frutti di mare*), which means black mussels, an unfancy word being *muscoli*. Among fish items familiar to the visiting palate are *salmone* (salmon), *sogliola* (sole; plural *sogliole*), *orata* (gilthead), *dentice* (a cousin of mackerel), *triglia* (red mullet), *sgombro* (mackerel), *rombo* (turbot). *Ostriche* means oysters. In the crustacean clan, *aragosta* is lobster, *gamberi* means crayfish and *gamberetti* means a type of shrimps. *Scampi* is the more usual word for shrimps.

Meat (*carne*) is very good in Italy, especially veal (*vitello*), which seems to occupy the place of honor. You are likely to find that what you order "blind" turns out to be veal in one form or another. *Arrosto di vitello* is roast veal; *costoletta* (or *cotoletta*) *alla Milanese* is the popular *Wiener Schnitzel*, and proves that when a veal cutlet is well fried in bread crumbs it does not matter whether it is tagged with the name of the Austrian capital or, as in Belgium, with the name of Liége (*côtelette Liégeoise*).

Manzo lesso, or *manzo bollito*, is boiled beef, no better and no worse than it sounds.

Filetto al burro is beefsteak, but not quite Porterhouse.

Rosbif is—roast beef. (*Bue* is beef in various forms.)

Maiale is pork, but don't look for it in summer.

Prosciutto is ham.

Agnello is lamb; *abbacchio* is baby lamb.

Rognoni are kidneys.

Fegato (accent on first syllable) is liver.

Controfiletto is contrefilet (of beef).

Pollo is chicken; *tacchino* is turkey.

Fritto misto is a fried mixture, mostly of meats, being a popular blend of liver, artichokes, sweetbreads and other odd bits, left-overs possibly, but definitely good in good restaurants.

Remember these main types of preparation:

Arrosto means roast.

Lesso or *bollito* means boiled.

Ai ferri means grilled.

Al forno means baked.

Fritto means fried.

Ben cotto means well done.

All'inglese means rare (literally "English style").

Vegetables (*legumi* or, often, *contorni*, for "surroundings" of meat dishes) are not especially exciting in Italy. Broccoli, spinach (*spinace*) and potatoes (*patate*) are the mainstays, but one finds also:

Fagioli, diminutive *Fagiolini* (beans; not green or wax).
Piselli (peas).
Carciofi (artichokes).
Asparagi (asparagus).
Cavalfiore (cauliflower).
Funghi (mushrooms).

The words for green salad are *insalata verde*.

Dessert, in unpretentious restaurants, nearly always simmers down to *Frutta* and *Formaggio* (plural *Formaggi*), being fruit and cheese. The *Frutta* simmers down to *aranci* (oranges), *fichi* (figs) and *mele* (apples), though in spring months it is frequently abetted by *fragoli* (strawberries) or delicious *fragolini* (tiny wild "strawbs"). They usually swim in wine, and one may name one's preference. *Fragoli* (or *fragolini*) *in Marsala* is common and delectable. The *Formaggio* often simmers down to a ripe *Gorgonzola* (called also *Stracchino*) or *Bel Paese*, a delicious soft cheese.

You also occasionally encounter *finocchio* (fennel root) as a vegetable or even as a dessert, but if you can learn to like it you are a better man than I. As a boy, I grew finocchio on a summer farm and sold it to the summer neighbors, which troubles my conscience slightly, as I cannot believe that anyone bought it except to please an importunate youth.

Zuppa inglese is a more familiar *dolce*, or dessert, in places of some quality. An ancient Baedeker of mine calls it "a kind of trifle." Well done, Baedeker! Granting that "trifle" means to the British a sponge cake soaked in some pleasant liquid, the comment seems to damn this dish with faint praise. It is inconceivable that the Inglesi ever order it, despite the nationalistic tag. They have no need to do so, for delightful *gelati* (ice creams) and meringues and tarts (*torte*) are usually to be had. In the ice cream family, Italy has its own well-liked specialities, notably *spumoni* and *cassate*. The last-named (singular *cassata*) is a slice, or wedge, of ice cream, often multi-colored and multi-flavored, featuring candied fruits and spiked with some sort of sweet liqueur. It is frequently named *cassata alla siciliana*. A small black coffee (*espresso*), brewed in a pleasantly sputtering stainless steel machine, ordinarily concludes one's colazione or pranzo.

Regional Favorites

The different regions of Italy, like those of France, have specialties in food for which they are famous, and some of the best known of these will be listed briefly here, in the general geographical sequence of the chapters of this book. (A leaflet called *Eating the Italian Way*, published by ENIT, may serve as a convenient pocket guide of regional foods as well as a dictionary of food names in Italy.)

Rome, like Paris, offers all the specialties of all its country's regions but it has developed also certain masterpieces that are peculiarly its own. *Saltimbocca alla romana* is one of them, being thin slabs of veal, together with ham, seasoned with sage and doused with a copious sprinkling of wine. *Gnocchi alla romana*, a dumpling dish of semolina flavored in various ways, is another. *Abbacchio alla cacciatora* (meaning hunter's style) is fried baby lamb with anchovy sauce, while *agnello alla cacciatora* is less youthful lamb cooked in the same manner and always lusciously seasoned.

Naples and the South is the inner shrine of macaroni and spaghetti in many a marvelous style. Cuttlefish delicacies, and they *are* delicate beyond your probable belief, are listed on menus as *calamari* and also, rather more often, under the head of *polpi* (singular *polpo*). *Polpo alla luciana*, honoring Naples' Santa Lucia, is the special dish to ask for if you are in Lucullan mood. *Pizza napoletana* has gone to the ends of the culinary earth and I don't need to mention, but will anyway, that it is an open "pie," filled to its crisp gunwales with a mélange of oily anchovies, tomato sauce, mozzarella (soft, white cheese), mushrooms, seafood tidbits, *anything* that the cook's virtuosity deems suitable.

Sicily takes pride in *maccheroni in casciate*, being a marriage of pasta and well-seasoned eggplant, and also in elaborate salads called *caponatine*. The island's climate suggests fruit of many sorts and it is indeed abundant and superb. Cassata alla siciliana has been mentioned just above.

Florence and all Tuscany will seem to you like the very habitat of good food. "Everything is special," one enthusiast said to me, and I could not deny it. Unusual items of game, like roast boar and hare cooked "sweet and strong" (*dolce e forte*), as recipes always phrase it, are *not* unusual in Tuscany.

In *Genoa* and its region *ciupin* is a sort of Ligurian bouillabaisse held in great esteem and *buridda* is another popular fish dish with a taste-teasing sauce. Genoese ravioli, with a sauce called *pesto*, reaches the utmost pinnacle of good pasta eating. A local Easter cake which the people of Genoa talk of exuberantly (I have not yet had a chance at it) is called *torta pasqualina*.

Milan, the metropolis of Lombardy, has so many dishes named after it that its savory reputation is an axiom. *Cotoletta alla milanese*, the ever-popular breaded veal cutlet, and *risotto alla milanese* have been mentioned above in the category of "universal" dishes. *Ossobuco* is another Milanese favorite that is rather well known in America. The word means literally bone-hole and it is indeed a beef or veal bone with delicious marrow inside it and with a vast amount of succulent meat clinging to the bone's surface. A Milanese plum cake, of extraordinary lightness, is perhaps the general Italian favorite of all the specialties of Lombardy.

Turin, chief city of Piedmont, is known for its superior *agnolotti* (see above) and more especially for its widely relished *bollito variato*, a Piedmont boiled dinner that quite puts in the shade, I fear, the boiled dinner of my own New England. It is a complex mixture of flesh and fowl in a vegetable "setting." *Fonduta*, a cheese-and-butter-and-egg affair of the region, differs considerably from its cousin, Geneva's famous fondue. This dish of Turin goes in strongly for truffles, to give it a good fillip. *Grissini* are very light, crisp breadsticks, of Piedmont, so popular that they are shipped to many parts of Italy. I cannot resist recording an exact English quotation from the wrapper of some grissini once served to me in a Genoa hotel. Here it is: "These sticks of white bread of Turin are realizing the best friability, of long conservation, very good digest, energetic, opposite obesity, convenient also to the weak persons and the children. The sticks of white bread of Turin they send every day into a envelope with seal." This priceless prose has now been revised into "the queen's English."

The north-central cities are dominated, in the gastronomical sense, by *Bologna,* which has invented very much more than the Bologna sausage. This erudite university town has long been so partial to good food that it used to support the classic sobriquet *Grassa e Dotta,* meaning Fat and Learned. *Scaloppine,* a veal delicacy familiar in Italian restaurants of American cities, is a Bologna specialty, as are noodles in various shapes and forms. In the celebrated *Ristorante al Papagallo* (Parrot) I savored *lasagne verdi al forno* (baked green noodles), followed by a *filetto tacchino cardinale* which was a filet of turkey, the sacerdotal tag at the end of the name indicating truffles and very thin slices of cheese, the whole thing being doused with melted Emmenthaler and butter.

Venice offers *risi e bisi* as its most universal specialty, this being a minestra (soup) with rice, peas and maybe ham beloved by Venetians since the days of the doges. *Polenta,* a corn meal affair served with fish or meat, is another item familiar to Venetian tables and the city lends its glamorous name to *fegato alla veneziana,* the Venetian part being skill in frying the liver, along with onions.

Finally, the cooking in the *Trentino* and *Upper Ádige* regions, with the Dolomites, takes on a more Austrian taste, for Austria long held the area down to, and including, the northern portions of Lake Garda. Hearty soups and dumplings are good here, and hare is delicious. Certain valleys, especially that of Merano, provide wonderful fruit and abundant grapes.

Italy's roster of choice foods, prepared by thousands of dedicated chefs, is as long, it seems, as the physical form of the country itself.

Wine—Red, White and Chianti

Italian wines add up to almost as complex a subject as French wines and I make no claims to expertness, but a few signposts may be erected for the guidance of the uninitiated traveler.

Vino rosso is red wine, *vino bianco* is white wine and Chianti, which may be either red or white but is usually red as tourist tables see it, is considered by Italian connoisseurs the wine of Americans! That does not imply any contempt for Chianti, a long-celebrated product of the Tuscan hills, but merely emphasizes its popularity with overseas travelers. Chianti, always dry, whatever its color, and with alcoholic content of about 13 per cent, is known in all parts of America. It is standard and good. Its name is easy to pronounce, "Kee-ahntee." It is contained in charming little fat bottles often bearing the magic inscription *Poggibonsi*. That delightful name, not so easy to pronounce though sounding rather like baby talk, is borne by the rail junction town, south of Florence, used by travelers in reaching the tipsy-towered hill village of San Gimignano. Poggibonsi makes the bottles, nature grows the grapes, Tuscan vintners produce the wine and no American traveler can go wrong in ordering the Chianti that is already familiar to him. In countless restaurants all over Italy a *fiasco* (bottle; compare our word flask) of Chianti will be in evidence on the table when the traveler takes his seat. Among the well-known trade names are Brolio Chianti, Chianti Antinori and Chianti Ruffino.

A few wines that I have learned to know, from the scores of types available in Italy, will be listed here—with brief comment.

Rufina, not to be confused with the Chianti named above, is another popular wine of Tuscany, a dry red.

Barolo, a fairly strong, dry red wine, is from the vineyards of Piedmont.

Valpolicella is an exceedingly smooth dry wine, not too strong, of Venetia. Its color is rather more rosy than a full red.

Verdicchio (dei Castelli di Yesi), a white wine grown near Ancona, though I first learned of it in Perúgia, as it came from the Hotel Brufani's *cave*, is a delight to the taste, even suggesting champagne. It is put up in gracefully tapering green bottles.

Carmignano is a dry white wine popular in the Montecatini area, where it is grown.

Orvieto, one of the charming hill towns of Umbria, lends its name to two types of white wine of about 12 per cent alcoholic content. *Orvieto Secco* is dry and *Orvieto Abboccato* (or *Dolce*) is sweet. Both are widely and deservedly admired.

Montepulciano is a popular white wine of Tuscany.

Frascati is one of the *vini dei castelli romani* (literally, "wines of the Roman castles") from the Alban Hills. Like Chianti it is found ready and waiting on many a restaurant table. Other Alban wines of Rome are *Marino* and *Grottaferrata*.

Motarosso is a dry red wine of rather heady type (15 per cent alcohol).

Sorriso d'Ischia is a sweet, white-amber wine from the lovely island whose name graces it.

Salaparuta, both red and white, is from Sicily. Both have plenty of kick (15½ per cent).

Marsala (amber colored) and *Malvasia* (red) are dessert wines of Sicily and the second-named has quite a history. It originated in the Peloponnesus, was developed in Crete, where Malvasia vineyards still flourish, mile on mile. Henry the Navigator, a prince of Portugal, established it on the island of Madeira, where it became famous, under *English* development, as "Malmsey." It made its way, perhaps about the same time, to Sicily where it is widely grown, and favored, today.

Among special wines one must certainly mention the familiar *Asti Spumante* of Piedmont. Spumante means, of course, foaming or sparkling. In a restaurant in Venice I once saw a tourist who thought himself gifted in such techniques attempt to open a bottle of this wine, with the result that when he succeeded a pink-purple flood inundated himself, the table, even the floor. Italian waiters have more know-how.

Another wine of special character is oddly named *Est! Est!! Est!!!* and comes from vineyards of Montefiascone, a small hill village of striking profile near Viterbo, in Latium. The story goes that a certain medieval canon made it a practice, when traveling in Italy, to have a wine-wise servant ride on ahead to scout out inns with good wine, and when he came upon one that warranted special mention, as of a guidebook star, he chalked on the outside of the inn the Latin word EST, meaning "is" or "this is." On an inn in Montefiascone the servant enthusiastically wrote the word three times. The canon came, concurred with the lackey's judgment, lived out his remaining days (far fewer of them than if he had been more temperate) in vine-rich Montefiascone. The bibulous canon was named Johannes Fugger and he was of the famous Swabian banking family of Augsburg.

Italian apéritifs center around vermouths, those of Martini (& Rossi) and Cinzano being the best known. Their popularity is shared by a widely advertised *aperitivo* called *Sartisoda*. Of liqueurs perhaps the best and best known in Italy is the amber firewater called *Strega*, made in Benevento, east of Naples. Another favorite is *Aurum*, and the Campari factories have popularized both a *Bitter Campari* (apéritif) and a postprandial *Cordial Campari*.

Some budget-saving words of wine to know when ordering are: *vino del paese* (like *vin du pays* in France), meaning local wine, not of some expensive brand; *vino comune*, meaning "common wine" (*vin ordinaire*); or if you simply murmur to the waiter *mezzo litro bianco* or *quarto litro rosso* you will receive a half liter of ordinary white or a quarter liter of red, as your mood and thirst may dictate.

In case you do not like wine with your meals you can purchase *birra bionda* (or *chiara*), which is blond beer, or *birra scurra*, which is "obscure" and dark. *Bottiglia* is bottle; *bicchiere* is glass. There are many good mineral waters too (ask for *acqua minerale*) and even *acqua fresca* (plain drinking water) is nearly always good in the cities, though the waiter may look at you with disapproval if you restrict yourself to that. One may learn to endure the disapproval of waiters. They are a genuinely friendly lot in Italy and not too painfully mercenary, though there are plenty of exceptions to this last. Also an amazing truth has sunk into their collective consciousness in these days of universally heavy taxes. Not all travelers, nor even all American travelers, are presumed now to be disguised gold mines.

Don't Be Surprised

Don't be surprised by your restaurant bill. Indeed, you probably won't be surprised if you have read the analysis of Italian hotel bills in Chapter 4. Your restaurant bill too will display a distressing wealth of separate items and the total *will* surprise those who are not forewarned. To make it seem fair and honest, which it usually is, the traveler must accept, without reservation, the almost unique Italian system which "includes" virtually nothing with the meat order or with the meal itself. To secure your bill you request *"il conto,"* adding a polite *"per favore"* (please). It will probably contain eight or ten items.

Coperto e Pane is your cover-and-bread charge. Virtually every restaurant imposes a cover charge of from 50 to 250 lire, but this does include a good-sized cloth napkin. If the charge is not printed it is prudent to ask. Otherwise it will be the restaurant's "decision."

Then comes the charge for *vino,* your wine.

Minestra is your soup or your macaroni or noodle dish. (Note that I have not put down anything from the Antipasti section.)

A meat or fish or grill item will come next and *if* the menu says so, not otherwise, it may, in occasional instances, be garnished with a few *piselli* (peas) or some *spinaci* (spinach).

Patate, plural of potato, will almost invariably involve a separate item and this is the hardest one for the bill-gazer to "swallow."

From the *Contorni* or *Legumi* (vegetables) or *Insalate* (salads) section some item is presumably ordered, and it will cost about a third as much as the fish or meat order.

Formaggio (cheese) is supposed to follow.

Frutta follows the cheese.

Caffè espresso concludes the meal but not the bill.

Servizio ed I.G.E., or some similar printed legend, appears after the coffee. The service charge is (or should be) 10, 12, 15 or 18 per cent, depending upon the category of the place (3rd class, 2nd, 1st, de luxe) and the income tax proves so variable, from 1 to 4 per cent, that you may as well accept the item philosophically *if* it appears at all. I have found that some restaurants of undeniably second class become suddenly first class for purposes of bill-rendering! Similarly third-class places nimbly mount the ladder by one or two rungs.

A *bollo,* or stamp tax, has occasionally appeared on my restaurant bills, but I look with deep and definite suspicion on this as a waiter's personal invention, if the amount is more than a tiny, nominal sum, say 5 or 10 lire. A waiter in a Florence restaurant once added to my bill 50 lire for a bollo. It struck me as so absurd that I laughed aloud and merely pointed to the item. This proved to be sound strategy. The waiter withdrew, theoretically to discuss my complaint with the manager. Presently he was back, explaining that the charge was an unfortunate error!

The ten-story structure of the hypothetical bill outlined above can tot up to $1.50, or even $2.50, in a modest but clean place, $3.00 to $6.00 in a first-class or luxury place, these general levels hardly differing, despite the Ossa-on-Pelion method of reaching them, from those prevailing in most of Italy's neighbor countries and in America. As I have said in the hotel chapter, the traveler who studies his bills from an angle of comparative costs rather than from an angle of annoyance at the seemingly interminable number of items will find that he is doing fairly well in Italy. My personal feeling, if I may interject it again, is that Italy would make a smart move if it were to abolish the coperto in moderate-priced restaurants and include bread and potato with every meal, upping menu prices slightly on other items if necessary. Most other countries do it and thereby lessen customer consternation and the knitting of brows.

To de-knit the brows of this discussion I may state with some firmness two important facts of restaurant thrift.

First, the patron ordering à la carte need not be cowed in the slightest by the hovering waiter, whose job it is to make him feel ill at ease unless he orders the whole many-item meal. It is *quite permissible*—and the waiter be hanged—to order just the big, filling pasta and an orange, or one plate-of-the-day, with wine, and cheese. I have done this scores of times, generally leaving a nice extra tip to sweeten my reputation with the *cameriere*.

Second, many restaurants of modest standing offer, as I have mentioned, *prezzo fisso* meals. The fixed price is always a pleasure to the budget, which thus knows just where it stands. Many a restaurant of this type, eager for trade, announces *Compreso Coperto Pane e Vino* (Including Cover, Bread and Wine). Often, however, even in such establishments, an à la carte menu will be hopefully thrust into the patron's hands as soon as he is seated, but if a firm request is then made for the "Colazione [or Pranzo] a prezzo fisso" the fixed-meal menu, and meal, will certainly be forthcoming.

Eating Under the Sky

Italy does not match France in the number of sidewalk restaurants in the large cities—Via Véneto in Rome, for beverages and light refreshments, is a very notable exception—but I think it surpasses France and all other countries, in garden, lake-terrace and sea-quay restaurants. I think of numerous examples that come within every traveler's ken. Here are a few of them.

The *skyscraper terrace* of *Olimpo, in Genoa* (formerly well known as the *Capurro*), with the stars spread above, the city and bay below; and the *hillside restaurants* of the same city, reached by funiculars. *Rapallo* and many other Riviera resorts in both directions from Genoa are all dotted with competing restaurants that survey the Ligurian Sea.

The *skylight restaurants*, such as the sumptuous *Biffi*, under the lofty glass roof of the vast and towering Galleria Vittorio Emanuele in Milan.

The *lakeside restaurants*, in dozens, lining the shores of Lake Como, Lake Maggiore, Lake Garda and other blue heavens of northern Italy.

The *canal-side restaurants of Venice*, a double row of them, for instance, fronting on the Grand Canal, near the Rialto. Others are numerous on the lively Riva degli Schiavoni and even on the "quays nobody knows" in remoter parts of the city.

The abundance of restaurants on the famous chain of *sand-lands* from the Lido to Chioggia overlooking the Adriatic or the Venetian lagoon.

Restaurants up aloft at Fiesole, the picture hill town above Florence. They find their perches in the main square and on terraces that look down upon the city of the Medici.

The *hilltop and garden restaurants of Rome*, such as the spectacularly placed *Casina Valadier* in the Pincian Gardens, almost overhanging the center of the city, and the *Casina delle Rose* in the Borghese Gardens (called also Villa Borghese).

The *Santa Lucia restaurants of Naples*, beside the fishers' harbor, and the shore restaurants of Capri, Ischia, Sorrento, Amalfi in settings so beautiful that you can't keep your mind on mere food. To these must be added the "hanging restaurants" of Upper Naples, captained by *Le Arcate* and *D'Angelo*.

The *terrace and garden restaurants that look up at Etna*, and down at the Ionian Sea, from that treasure of tourism, the one and only *Taormina*.

I could go on. Indeed, the problem is to halt at any point, but I have done so—now.

Cafés and Bars—Italian Style

The *cafés* of Italy are a multitude surely beyond the scope of statistics. It sometimes seems that there is one for every three or four inhabitants. They fall into two main types or categories. The "loafing type" has tables and chairs on the sidewalk or under the arcades or in the great city gallerias, with orchestras in some of the more pretentious places. They are at the peak of their liveliness late in the afternoon and far into the evening. The get-on-with-it type is the workaday hole-in-the-wall, busy at many times of the day, including breakfast time. At these places, small but generally clean and shipshape, one stands at a counter while the man or girl behind it brews a spluttering espresso, very cheerful in sound and fragrant in smell. One sips the steaming coffee, downs a brioche or a couple of *biscotti* or maybe a small cake and is off in five minutes.

The loafing life of the sidewalk and arcade places is delightful, reaching its apogee in such places as the Piazza di San Marco of Venice and the Piazza della Repubblica of Florence. Perhaps, instead of the little black espresso, you order *caffè-latte* (coffee with milk) or a hot *cioccolata* or a fruit drink (*limonata, aranciata*). There are always excellent ices too. The earlier-mentioned *cassata alla siciliana* is perhaps the most popular, with *spumoni* as runner-up. A lazy hour in such a place, reading the paper, perhaps the *Daily American*, published in Rome, or plotting the next moves of travel, cannot fail to be the Hour of Charm.

The bars of Italy, except hotel bars, seldom resemble our instinctive picture of bars. In short, they are not brass-rail tippling places nor dimly lit flirtation retreats serving only alcoholic drinks. They are brightly lighted and have more the atmosphere of tearooms, and sometimes of milk bars. If vermouth is popular, it usually seems that fruit drinks, ices and coffee or chocolate with cakes are more so. There are usually a few tables inside, a few more on the sidewalk.

Some bars of Rome and other large cities have a somewhat American look, with startlingly American eats. A notable example is the *Bar Gelateria Esedra*, on Via Nazionale, near Piazza Esedra and the Hotel Quirinale. Big, bold signs announce Hot Dogs; Cheeseburgers; Banana

Splits; Malts; Real American Coffee. Most startling of all, these offerings actually do taste more or less like what the signs proclaim. I had been so often disappointed in Europe by "*un*reasonable facsimiles" that I was amazed at the success of my first samplings in the Bar Esedra.

CHAPTER 6

ALL SORTS OF THINGS TO KNOW

About Shopper's Fever

Italy is dangerous terrain for those of us, and that means all of us, who are subject to shopper's fever abroad. The windows tempt, the goods demolish resistance and the fever has claimed another victim.

Florence is the greatest "danger spot" and many a woman tourist, prepared to drink in that city's culture in great draughts, ends up by spending nearly all her time in the shops near the Duomo or along the Arno or on the Ponte Vecchio. Silk goods, table linens, embroidered blouses and lingerie, majolica, articles of Florentine silver, splendidly bound books, vast stocks of irresistible photographs, and of course art works, are the chief tempters here.

Venice is almost as dangerous as Florence. Its myriads of little shops in the arcades of Piazza di San Marco and on the tortuous Merceria add up to a mile or more of magnetism. Venetian glass, costume jewelry, items in tooled leather, delicate lace goods, novelties that are sometimes really novel, make this city a perpetual challenge to the resisting budget.

Rome offers, of course, the fine goods of the whole country. So, perhaps, in a less formidable way, does great Milan, whose central Galleria alone, with the adjacent arcades, contains enough temptation for any average city. Items of masculine appeal, such as Borsalinos and fine silk ties, are at their best in these large centers. (Borsalinos for women may also be had in unfinished form, for blocking, or as berets.)

Naples has its own specialties, chiefly cameos, tortoise-shell items, ornaments in coral and terra-cotta art works that are hard to take home.

Sicilian cities, notably led by the mere village of Taormina, a community that *lives* on tourism, offer innumerable items for feminine wear, exquisitely embroidered blouses and lingerie, angora wool sweaters, linen and silk temptations beyond naming or numbering.

And the *cost* of these things? Though a male of at least average immunity to shopper's fever, I have been drawn into the contagion on many occasions in many cities, chiefly in the purchase of things for feminine wear, destined to be brought back to my family, and I should say that these things cost less, even in inflation-plagued Italy, than their counterparts would cost in America. Of course such items as Venetian glass, Neapolitan cameos and Florentine works of art are things of Italy and to buy the same things in New York would cost at least twice as much. I have found that a way to make my own budget cope with the fever, retaining some chance to win the bout, is to set aside a fixed sum for purchases, personal and for gifts, *before entering Italy*. No, it doesn't always work. There are apt to be "contingencies." But at least the budget doesn't sink into a mortal illness.

About Your Mail, Both Ways

Receiving and dispatching home mail is a matter of supreme, and often surprising, importance to most travelers, including those who wanted nothing more earnestly than to get away from mail and phone calls. A letter that doesn't come, and *still* doesn't come, can ruin the most perfect summer day and the best-laid plans for it. A letter that may never have reached Jack or Barbara or Mother and Dad, or may have been long delayed in transit, can gnaw at pleasure and wreck relaxation.

I have tried virtually every means of receiving mail abroad. Having it come through American embassies and consulates is practical in the large centers, but this involves some delays, as on days when the offices are closed, and it is not applicable in small towns and pleasure resorts. Having it come through American Express, Cook or some other agency is a method employed by countless thousands of tourists every year, so many thousands, in fact, that duplication of names and consequent mixing of letters is an occasional and distressing flaw. If your name is Grant Gremlin or Violet Vigor there will be no duplication but if it is Williams or Curtis or Clark you may be in trouble. In any case the use of agencies involves your knowing their business hours and using valuable time to hunt them up, or else arranging for forwarding. If, however, you are using them anyway, for purchasing tickets or cashing checks, there is something to be said for this system.

Having your mail come by way of *Poste Restante*, called, in Italy, *Fermo in Posta*, the equivalent of our General Delivery, is surely the worst possible system. Mail clerks in the large cities seem always to be harried, cross, unaccommodating. Their work makes them so. Every eager person who presents himself at the window is sure the clerk is holding out on him, so the clerk becomes impervious to dark and baleful looks. He, or usually she, refuses sharply to "look again." It is far easier to say sternly, "Niente, signore" (Nothing, sir). Actually there may be something, or several things, especially in Italy, for *Italians customarily put the surname first*, in addressing an envelope. If you do use Poste Restante and receive no letters under your surname do not fail to inquire under the letter of your *given* name also. I once haunted Rome's central post office for days, fruitlessly demanding letters for Clark. "Niente, signore. Niente. Niente." Finally, when I had grown desperate, someone suggested to me to inquire under the name Sydney. I did so and got a good handful of letters, so I then knew that my name was Clark Sydney to Italian post offices.

The above negatives bring us to a positive. I think that the use of a few key hotels for mail addresses brings the best results. And if, upon arrival at each of these key hotels, you make the hall porter your friend, adequately "remembered" from time to time and especially when you leave, the chances are very good that he will take personal and meticulous care of your mail, including forwarding. Perhaps even a single hotel, in Rome, will be sufficient to mention to your home friends. For three months of travel in Italy I once used the Quirinale as my mail headquarters and I didn't lose a letter. I remembered the porters, two of them, and they remembered me.

Mailing letters from Italy to America calls, in these days, for the use of air mail, almost exclusively. It saves ten days or so and to most travelers is more than worth the difference, about ten cents per thin letter. Like other countries of Europe, Italy weighs its letters in grams, and *five* grams, meaning one thin sheet and thin envelope, is the standard minimum. For each five grams above this minimum there is a surcharge of about half the initial cost. An air mail post card calls for a little less postage than a five-gram letter. To state it in terms of *present* tariffs, always subject to revision, usually upwards, an air letter of five grams calls for 120 lire, ten grams 180 lire, fifteen grams 240 lire, etc., a post card by air being 95 lire. This seems a lot and it *is* a lot, but a letter by steamer (up to 20 grams) now costs 60 lire, which is, by current exchange, about ten cents. That too is decidedly a lot—twice the America-Italy eastbound postage. A post card by steamer is 35 lire, and if it has only a five-word greeting and your name 10 lire. (Surface postage to Europe is like steamer postage to America, except that *for France* the Italian internal tariff now applies, 25 lire for a letter, 20 lire for a post card.)

I have gone into this rather fully because it seems to me a point of major comfort to the traveler to understand mail and its costs. Very many travelers simply hand their letters for posting to the hotel porter and say, "Put it on the bill." During a long tour in Italy they never take two minutes out to learn what the tariff is. This gives no solid assurance that the letter will go by air mail, even though the guest may be charged air mail rates. Furthermore, it implies an almost indefensible helplessness, like always holding out a handful of money to a creditor and saying, "I can't get the hang of your funny money. Take what I owe you." (Some travelers persist in this practice even after many days in a new country.) If you wish to be wholly independent in the matter of stamps—*francobolli* is the word, singular *francobollo*—check up the current tariffs, not with the porter, who may give "approximate" figures, but at a post office or tobacco shop (*all tobacconists in Italy, as in France, sell postage stamps*) or at the mail department of American Express or Cook or in the rear pages of the Pozzo railway timetable. Then, by blowing in two or three thousand lire on stamps of various denominations that will make up any desired postage, you become master of your mail for a good while to come.

About Tobacco

A few years after the war, Italy suddenly liberalized her regulations on the importation of tobacco, though not as much as France did. She allows you to bring in free of duty 400 cigarettes or a quantity of cigars or pipe tobacco not exceeding 500 grams, this being about 1.1 pounds. Even travelers who do not smoke will do well to bring in their full legal allowance of duty-free cigarettes for they are highly prized in Italy, as all over Europe, and in any European country they cost, if obtainable at the tobacconists or from furtive black-marketeers, at least two or three times as much as at home. A pack of American weeds makes a superlative tip and never fails to win a grateful smile.

Tobacco is a government monopoly in Italy, as is salt (you see the sign *Sale e Tabacchi* on government shops all over the country), and this means that prices are high. They are, in fact, very high, and one wonders how Italians, without the benefit of foreign exchange, can afford to smoke at all. Many patrons will be seen in the shops buying five loose cigarettes, or even two. For a package of twenty, one of the least expensive smokable brands I have found bears the frivolous name *Sport*. These cost 200 lire (32 cents) a pack. *Macedonia* (pronounced Machedonia) is another cheap but (barely) smokable brand, the Macedonia Extra being a lift better and costlier. *Edelweis, Serraglio* and *Rosa d'Orient*, the last two suggesting Turkey and Egypt, are in the half-dollar class and *Due Palme* is still more expensive. If one is climbing into such brackets as these one might as well climb a trifle more, if necessary, and buy familiar American brands. With each cigarette costing three cents the smoker learns to show due deference to Lady Nicotine.

About Luggage, Laundry and the Self-Ironing Fabrics

Luggage and laundry are always interlocking topics in travel and even more so in this air age, when countless Americans equip themselves with self-ironing fabrics that can save so much in luggage weight before flying abroad. I personally take no more than half as much, in weight, as I used to before the age of overseas planes. First I provide myself with a couple of the modern featherweight suitcases—those of Daisy Products are "gooperfeatherweight"; my two have seen me through thirty thousand miles of going, some of it rugged—and these I fill with nylon, orlon, dacron articles of clothing, so far as practical. Tuxedo and evening shirts I take, reluctantly, only when steamer travel is involved. Not three times, in a average trip *in*

Europe, am I ever in any real need of such gear. Europe simply doesn't expect it from Americans, in an era of air travel.

Laundry in Europe was long a worrisome thing but is far less so nowadays. The hotels are the launderers to *turismo*. If they do not have their own laundries, as most big ones now do, they send the things out and one must allow the better part of a week for their return. When there is a laundry in the hotel, three to five days will be enough, and for a 50 per cent surcharge the job can usually be done in one or two days, especially if an appropriate *mancia* is slipped into the hand of the chambermaid who takes the bundle from your room.

The tourist laundry business languishes a bit in Europe since the coming of the new and newer fabrics. A surprising number of American men, in these days, particularly those who travel much by air, take only two or three shirts instead of a dozen as formerly, and wash one out every night. I have found that the firmer orlon, which is supposed to "breathe" better than most nylon fabrics, irons itself with amazing neatness. After a hundred wearings and washings—a conservative estimate—an orlon shirt will look almost as smart as on the first wearing, its disciplined collar taking its correct stance after each wetting down and two-hour drying. Pajamas, sox and underwear also are worn and washed by many traveling males. This system calls for a few minutes' chore every evening, saves fifteen to twenty pounds of luggage weight and many dollars in laundry charges —which are high in Europe's hotels. It may cost up to 35 cents when your hotel washes and irons a shirt, and up to 40 cents or a bit more for a pair of pajamas.

"Dacron travelers" like to speak of those who depend on nylon or orlon as living in the Paleonylon Age or the Neo-Orlon Age, but the less-new fabrics still have their multitudes of uses. Dacron summerweight *suits* (pioneer purveyor Witty Brothers, New York) have several extraordinary advantages. They need but *very* infrequent pressings, with a cool iron. Spots can be washed out with soap and lukewarm water and trousers may be dunked without even losing the sharpness of their crease, though dry cleaning is still preferable. Coats with shoulder pads cannot be safely washed. Ever newer wonder-textiles make one hesitate to record *any* advance lest it presently become old hat.

Feminine travelers go in for the easy-laundering materials quite as much as men. Dresses, blouses, nightgowns, "mentionables" (the "un" has long since vanished) are more often than not made of these remarkable modern goods, whose novelty has gone but whose practical worth grows ever more evident.

To sum this up, don't open a chain of tourist laundries in today's Europe unless you yearn for insolvency.

About Coathangers—They're Important

A seemingly small matter of amazing importance in Italy and throughout Europe is coathangers, or the lack of them. You'll find hardly a dozen hotels in all Italy, hardly thirty in all Europe, whose wardrobes have an adequate supply of them, and when you do find enough they will often not be of the type on which trousers can be hung, but big, clumsy affairs for coats only. Bring half a dozen at least, of the type you like and as light in weight as you can find. The little metal or plastic ones don't weigh much and though they *are* awkward to pack, the lack of them is several times as awkward. After you've strewn your clothes over bedroom chairs and suitcases for a few nights you'll know what I mean. The things can be bought in Italy, though you may not find very light ones. The word (in the plural) is *attaccapanni*.

About the Midday Closing Hours

Italy closes up shop—and offices and museums and everything else—daily for about three hours while the sun is high. The closing period, especially in summer, is usually from 1 o'clock till 4, sometimes 4:30. A lot of time and a lot of lacerated feelings can be saved if this is known, recognized, accepted, planned for. When shops do finally reopen they stay open until at least 7.

About Transportation in the Cities

Italy's *city taxis*, reasonably plentiful nowadays though often rather archaic in appearance, operate by meter and despite the very high cost of gasoline and oil (imported, though some fuel—actually a *gas*, called *metano*, of limited uses—has recently been discovered in northern Italy), the tariffs are moderate. Meters are usually easy for the customer to read and the Republic is endeavoring to keep this trade of transportation well disciplined. An important thing to know is that after ten o'clock in the evening fares are doubled.

The *horse-drawn cabs* are generally thought by tourists to be cheaper than taxis. I find it quite the other way and if I have a particular goal in mind I always make an advance bargain with the driver. If I am hiring the vehicle by the hour or the half day I bargain on that. If the cabby's price seems too high (the first proposal is always too high in Naples and generally in Sicily), I beat down my man and even walk away when his "final" terms do not suit me. Usually he shouts after me and resignedly accepts my figures, or at least a halfway point between his and mine, after making it clear that he is doing me a *very* special favor.

The open calèche, found frequently in Rome and some other cities, is marvelous on a warm summer afternoon or evening. For trips of pleasure it is unbeatable, since it rolls along slowly and is wide open to all the wonders and little eye-catching sights along the way.

City busses, trolleybusses and trams are excellent in many cities, notably in Rome, but there is one cumbersome rule that I have found they all have in common, except sometimes in Milan and frequently in lovable, sloppy, who-cares Naples. They require you to enter by the rear door and leave by the front, which sounds innocuous, even sensible. It no doubt appeared so to the bright young man who first thought up the rule, but in actual practice it is the most awkward and maddening thing imaginable. These conveyances are very often terribly crowded and unless you are going to the end of the line you must begin the moment you enter to fight your way forward. A seat may be available near the rear but you dare not occupy it lest your passage be blocked and you find yourself unable to get off at your stop. *Lasciate Libero il Passaggio per Passegieri in Procinto di Scendere!* (Leave the passage clear for passengers in process of getting off) is a familiar bus and tram sign but one that is hardly ever heeded. *Prepararsi in Tempo a Scendere* (Get ready in time for your descent) is another, and your whole trip is spoiled by trying to comply. To show exactly how bad this system can be I must report a personal anecdote, and I could add many others.

I was on the back platform of an extremely crowded Roman trolleybus and wished to get off near the Piazza Venezia. I even did so, from the back platform, but the conductor spied me and sternly bade me get on again. I must leave, he reminded me, by the *front* platform.

"But it is impossible," I said. "Nevertheless you will have to," he countered severely, and I knew he would call the police if I disobeyed. The bus started up and I fought to get through its aisle. Midway, I was absolutely blocked. I could not, it seemed, budge another inch. The bus was three, four, five, six blocks beyond the Piazza Venezia. Then I am afraid I lost my temper. Lashing out with fists, elbows, knees, I fought for each inch. All the passengers were interested in my plight and those whom I prodded so angrily were angry in their turn. At long last, a good *half mile* beyond the Piazza Venezia, I was able to get off that bus!

Well—the telling of this anecdote will not correct the situation, but at least it should put me in right with the taxi men and cabbies.

About Gypping of Tourists; Does This Happen?

Answering the above question as fairly as I can, with honest friendliness for Italy and honest concern for my readers, I must say that gypping of tourists does happen, and not infrequently. On the other hand it happens *far less frequently* than outraged victims imagine. It is very easy to generalize, especially when you're sore about something. If attempts have just been made to cheat you on two successive restaurant bills or taxi fares, it is humanly easy to assert, "They'll gyp you every time if you don't watch out." To put this in personal, anecdotal form, the last three times I used a taxi in Rome (I won't even mention Naples and Sicily) before writing this comment, deliberate and flagrant attempts were made to "do" me. Once the meter was hastily shut off in the hope that I hadn't read it (but I had), and twice the figure on the meter was blandly raised, by the driver's demand, two and three hundred lire respectively, in the hope that I hadn't noticed (but I had). These things were annoying, even infuriating, but I counted up—and this took self-discipline, for I was "mad"—the number of Roman taxi rides taken on this last visit when I was *not* gypped, when the driver pleasantly quoted the precise figure on the meter. There were eleven such occasions. Eleven out of fourteen isn't a wonderful score, but it isn't so terrible either.

I've been cheated in restaurants too, in cafés and bars, occasionally in cambio offices and shops, by short change, "mistakes" or otherwise, but *very much more often* I have not been done out of a single lire nor has any trickery whatever been attempted, even though I was obviously a tourist of tourists, with but the barest smattering of Italian at my command.

The tourist should bear in mind two things. First, when he thinks he is being cheated, there is at least a 50-50 chance that he actually *has* misunderstood; that there is a legitimate taxi surcharge not revealed by the meter; that there is a fair and honest item on the restaurant bill which he hastily assumed to be a fraud. Second, he should bear in mind the psychology of the taxi man, or waiter or shopkeeper. For many decades the Italian "little fellow" has been firmly convinced that most tourists and *all* Americans are rich. He looks upon us in somewhat the same light that we look upon billion-dollar corporations. He often thinks it quite fair and defensible that there should be two scales of charges, one for Italians, another—whatever the traffic will likely bear—for rich tourists. This attitude is not right. It does not generate goodwill for Italy. But it *is* understandable. Remembering that America too is honeycombed with faults, we should not be quick to cast stones at the Italian small fry who live on the tourist trade.

This doesn't mean that one should accept cheating as an "act of God" in *any* tourist land! Certainly not. One should make every effort to know what the proper charges are and when sure of one's ground, should insist upon correct tariffs and billing. This insistence can be managed with vigor and dignity, perhaps with a saving spot of humor now and then, avoiding all appearance of hot anger, which only invites counter-anger and weakens one's case. Such managing serves the interests of both countries, the one visited and the one from which the visitor hails.

Polonius has now finished his talk to Laertes.

About the Wonderful "Day Hotels"

Don't fail to discover that wonderful institution of Italian cities, the *Albergo Diurno*. An extensive chain of these "Day Hotels," founded by one Cleopatro Cobianchi, runs from Milan to Naples and beyond. Generally you find them underground in some central square or arcade, but wherever you find them they are useful and clean. And they are all things to all transients. Consider this list of the advertised services of the Milan *Albergo Diurno:*

- Baths of every sort
- Dressing and toilet rooms
- Hairdressing parlors
- Manicure and pedicure
- Luggage check room
- Public telephone (these are rare in Italy)
- Writing rooms
- Public stenographers
- Clothes pressed while you wait
- Umbrellas rented
- Exchange office
- Tickets of every sort
- Tourist service, guides, etc.
- Open timetables
- Canned music or radio (to cheer you while waiting for the clothes presser).

What a noble conglomeration of services; but why, I wish to know, does the Cleopatro Cobianchi "College" not teach you Italian and handle your investments? Anyway, it does what it does cheaply and well.

About Music, for All Brows

Grand opera is as much at home in Italy as name bands are in America. It reaches its peak, as every music lover in the world knows, in *La Scala* (officially *Teatro alla Scala*) in Milan. This shrine of opera, and of ballet, was heavily damaged by bombs in 1943, but since the war it has been faithfully restored in precisely the same form, even to the sumptuous royal box. La Scala is a magnificent sight in itself, a vast horeshoe with six tiers of boxes rising above it, the white and gold tone of the décor contrasting with the billowy sea of red plush seats. This auditorium, above all in the world, is intimately associated with Arturo Toscanini, who considered it "home" for many decades and who had much to do with its postwar restoration.

The Opera House (*Teatro dell'Opera*) of Rome is nowadays considered almost the equal in prestige of La Scala, as it is in the magnificence of the interior. I have heard and seen Verdi, for instance, in both houses and have been quite unable to make up my amateur mind which company I thought did the better job. Both seemed to me in the perfectionist class.

Another Roman opera "house" of unique and marvelous appeal is the *Baths of Caracalla*. Here, on summer evenings, grand opera reaches a wider audience than that found inside any theater. *Aïda* is one of the most successful and popular offerings in these prodigious ruins. I have not yet seen it here, but those who have, assert that "it's a question whether the opera was composed for this setting or the setting contrived for the opera."

Other Italian cities with opera houses of the first rank are the following: *Turin*, with the *Regio Theater*; *Venice*, with *La Fenice*, in whose constricted "water square" the gondolas have a dreadful time navigating; *Genoa*, with the *Carlo Felice Theater* (bombed, but now in use again); *Florence*, with its *Teatro Comunale*; *Bologna*, similarly with its *Teatro Comunale*; *Naples*, with its enormous and resplendent *San Carlo Theater*; and *Palermo*, with its *Massimo Theater*.

I must insert here a parenthetical complaint. On one occasion in Milan, two in Rome and two in Naples I secured moderate-priced, though not cheap-and-lofty seats in side boxes, but was unable, on any of these memorable and painful occasions, to glimpse more than a small corner of the stage without standing up and straining over the shoulders of the persons seated in the front row. Of one hundred and eighty-four boxes in the Rome opera house eighty-eight are so built that only two or three persons can conveniently see the production. Everywhere, throughout the theater, I noticed men in tuxedos standing up and decorously leaning over the heads and bare shoulders of their womenfolk in the effort to see as well as hear. The diamond horseshoe is magnificent, the crystal chandeliers glittering, but this fault of poor vision is common to nearly all the great historic opera houses of Europe, notably including those of Italy.

The city of Florence sounds a very special note with its *Maggio Musicale Fiorentino*. Since 1932, with the exception of the war years, this Musical May of Florence, extending sometimes halfway through June, has been an event of Europe, increasing steadily, of recent years, in prestige. Many orchestral, vocal and ballet features, including the Russian performances that made such a world sensation in 1951, have been presented in the Communal Theater, in the Pergola Theater and in the lovely Boboli Gardens.

The symphony orchestras of Italy, while not yet on a par with the best of certain other lands, including America, have become of much greater importance in recent years. Rome's *Academy of Santa Cecilia* gives distinguished concerts from October to May; and the capital's *Collegium Musicum Italicum* is an association of virtuosi. Florence, Venice, Milan, Naples and, in fact, all the large cities and some smaller ones, like Siena, maintain orchestras that are at least very good, if not superlative.

In summer, Rome's Academy of Santa Cecilia offers outdoor evening concerts in the *Basilica of Maxentius* and I think I have never had any musical experience surpassing in glamor these Basilica concerts in the Roman Forum. Among the flood-lighted sights on every side are the *Church of Santa Francesca Romana*, hoary with age and curious with architectural surprises, the *Capitol*, close by, and the vast *Colosseum*.

In *sacred music* Rome is, of course, supreme. Several of the famous chapels of famous churches have equally famous choirs, heard at their best during the church festivals, and the *Roman Polyphonic Society* is the recognized dean of the country's, and perhaps of Europe's, associations for sacred choral music.

In light summer music and general gaiety, Italy has a thousand settings that vie with each other in romantic appeal. Most of the entertainment in such settings accompanies dining, or at least drinking, and some of the most popular places have been given a quick listing in Chapter 5 ("Eating Under the Sky").

About Special Festivals and Their Dates

Italy is quite as rich as France or Spain in festivals and other events of special color and interest. Since a knowledge of these and their annual dates can have a most important bearing on your itinerary, it seems worth while to sketch in the main events in the Foreground of the Picture. I shall omit mention of such obvious high points of the calendar as Christmas, New Year's and the Carnival (in Riviera resorts), and I shall try to keep a stern checkrein on my report lest it bog down with the weight of numbers. Only the "utterly best," not *all* the best, shall be listed.

Holy Week sees colorful and sometimes very moving *Processions of Penitents* on Thursday and Friday in many a town and village, these processions reaching their exhibitionist peak in the more emotional southern communities. In *Rome*, the Pope's blessing, *Urbi et Orbi* (To the City and to the World), is given on Easter Sunday from the balcony of St. Peter's before an enormous multitude in the square. In *Florence* I have watched, with as much interest as the children all about me, the event of Saturday, when a fiery "dove" flies along a wire from the high altar of the Duomo (Cathedral) to reach and ignite a chariot of fireworks. The *Blowing Up of the Chariot* is but one more proof that excitement and religious expression are compatible in Italy, as in all Mediterranean lands.

First Saturday in May and September 19; Naples. The *Miracle of San Gennaro* gives impetus to processions and various celebrations centering around the cathedral. The saint's blood, in two sacred phials, is thought by the faithful to liquefy on these dates every year.

First Sunday in May and June 24; Florence. Il Giuoco [or *Gioco*] *del Calcio* is a medieval football game played in gay sixteenth-century costumes in the Piazza della Signoria.

The *Musical May* (and part of June) of *Florence*, mentioned just above, is an item to weigh heavily in the planning of your tour.

On the *first Sunday in June, Pisa* has a richly costumed pageant and *Giuoco* [or *Gioco*] *del Ponte* (Game of the Bridge) that attracts throngs of onlookers. There is also, on an evening in about mid-June, a glorious illumination of the banks of the Arno by thousands of oil lamps.

Mid-May Fortnight of Greek Drama; Syracuse. This series of plays, given in the natural setting of the ancient Greek Theater, constitutes a dramatic and cultural event of the first magnitude. The charm of the setting makes it a thing of interest to the middlebrow almost as much as to the highbrow.

May 15; Gúbbio. The *Feast of the Candles* makes this small medieval town of Umbria the cynosure of all eyes, for one day. In the climactic event, husky men of various competing guilds carry massive *ceri* (literally "candles") three times solemnly around the Piazza della Signoria and then *race* from a city gate to a local shrine.

July 2 and August 16; Siena. Il Palio is perhaps the most spectacular and colorful festival in the whole Italian calendar. I, at any rate, have seen nothing else to match it. After the long and brilliant medieval procession around the strange shell-shaped square called Il Campo there is a horse race circling the same square that pales into "Sunday School stuff" any race you've ever seen before. (For details see Chapter 16).

Third Sunday in June; Nola (near Naples). The *Feast of the Lilies* features a gay procession of huge artificial lilies.

July 11-15; Palermo. The *Feast of Santa Rosalia,* patroness of the Sicilian metropolis, culminates with an earnest and colorful pilgrimage to the saint's shrine on lofty Monte Pellegrino. The whole city is temporarily absorbed in its saint-with-the-lovely-name.

September 3; Viterbo. The Feast of Santa Rosa builds up to a torchlight procession in which muscular celebrants carry an enormous sixty-foot belfry on whose top is a figure of the saint. It takes at least sixty men, "one man to the foot," to carry the towering saint.

September 7; Naples. The *Piedigrotta Festival* is an explosion of fiery and musical joy, spurred by plenty of wine. For "life," nothing can beat this violently gay affair.

The *Calendar of Italian Events,* published by *Tourist News from Italy,* lists some three hundred annual events, with their dates, so the dozen-or-less above are a heroically reduced list. If your aim in travel is to *avoid* festival throngs, perhaps you can find this list of chief events, and throngs, useful in a warning way!

About Evenings in the Cities

Some comments about some evening delights in some cities have been given above but they chiefly concern music and outdoor cafés. As the traveler's evening wears on toward undeniable night, and then morning, there are still things in plenty to do. This was not always so, for cabarets and floor shows are less natural, less traditional, to Italy than to many countries, and during Mussolini's long era the government tended to frown on midnight goings-on as being too soft and effete for rugged fascism.

Rome has become, since the Second World War, one of the gay night cities of Europe, though it still is far from being another Paris. Because of its much milder climate than that of Paris this city can and does specialize on *outdoor* cabarets, which can count on five or six months of suitable weather for open-air shows. All-year night spots (*locali notturni*) are numerous enough, many of them calling themselves "Dancings" and stressing the "hostess" angle, with good-looking girls eager to hook their customers and ever ready to give companionship and whatever else the customer will pay for. I have been accosted, near the central post office, by a pretty young hostess who wished to escort me personally to the cabaret where she worked. There is nothing of the shrinking violet about these girls.

Of course there are also quality night clubs of genteel standing, often connected with the outstanding hotels, such as Rome's *Excelsior* and Naples' *Vesuvio*.

A feature of the night in several cities, especially Rome, is the cellars of song where strolling musicians and singers keep the atmosphere gay. Bottles often line the walls of these cellars from the floor clear to the ceiling, and some of the places have romantic or literary background, as for instance Rome's *Hostaria dell'Orso*, where Dante is said to have lived and where certainly Montaigne and Rabelais dined. Perhaps Dante turns in his tomb (in distant Ravenna) at the thought of what modern man has done to his Roman lodgings!

Red lights, of the official, fancy-house variety, are supposed to have vanished, or to be in process of vanishing, from Italian cities, following roll-call votes on the subject in the national parliament, this being in line with the action France took in 1947 (and now openly regrets), but in some cities, especially and eternally Naples, the lone male pedestrian is likely to be accosted on the sidewalk by a friendly youth who says cheerily, "Good evening, sir. Remember me? Waiter at your hotel?" You don't remember him, but all the same he *might* be your waiter, so you are polite to him. Thus encouraged, he quickly warms to his basic theme. "Like to see the Crystal Palace, sir? House of Mirrors? Very interesting, sir." If such choice sights are not on your evening agenda you can lead your "waiter" to embarrassed defeat by inquiring, "At what hotel, by the way, are you a waiter?" There are at least half a dozen very good tourist hotels in the city, so he has not better than a one-in-six chance to name where he has "served" you. If he doesn't guess right he has revealed himself as the professional pander or tout that he is.

About Sports of Summer and Winter

Sports, in the traditional sense, meaning golf, tennis, fishing, horse racing, have less chance in Italy than in most countries, of capturing even a tithe of tourist attention, for the land is simply too rich and varied in sights to yield much time for things that can be done anywhere. *Golf* is perhaps a partial exception, for some of the courses are amid such glorious settings that an eighteen-hole tempo in viewing the scenery seems admissible. Courses of eighteen holes exist, for instance, near Lake Como (the *Villa d'Este Club* and the *Menaggio Club*), at Rapallo and San Remo, on the Rising and Setting Rivieras, and on the edge of Lake Carezza, guarded by some unbelievably fantastic peaks of the Dolomites. Other full length courses are near Rome, Florence and Milan.

Sea bathing, which Italy can hardly claim as a national invention, seems peculiarly appropriate to be enjoyed from the innumerable beaches on this long peninsula bathed by four seas (Ligurian, Tyrrhenian, Ionian, Adriatic). I think there is no other country in either hemisphere where sea bathing is quite so universally popular as it is in Italy. There are hundreds of miles of good, firm sand and it seems that few of these beach miles are neglected. There are public resorts by the score, and *Colonie*, which are private bathing resorts of groups, societies, institutions, literally by the hundred. At many of the resorts good restaurants and bathing cabins are to be found. A single typical example, not too well known to tourism, is *Lido Castel Fusano*, at the terminus of Rome's rail line to (and a little beyond) Ostia, a very pleasant place easy to reach and enjoy. The beaches of Italy, by and large, are one of the country's great and natural assets.

Snow sports may not be associated strongly with Italy in the average tourist mind but actually the facilities and the terrain are quite as good at many of the resorts on the southern reaches of the Alps as they are on the northern, in Switzerland and Austria and France. This is especially true in the Dolomite region, captained by *Cortina d'Ampezzo,* famous in Olympic Games. Piedmont also has many snow-sport resorts, the leaders being *Sestrières* and *Courmayeur*. (This is the *only* part of Italy where French names have crept over the passes.) Even within very easy reach of Rome and Florence there are good Apennine snow resorts such as *Terminillo* (Rome) and *Abetone* (Florence).

In some parts of Italy summer and winter sports unite in a marriage of convenience. Tourists sojourning in Taormina, for instance, may take their choice of descending to such handy beach villages as *Mazzarò* for an ocean dip or ascending to the snow levels of Mount Etna for skiing. Similar, though not quite such striking, contrasts of sport climate are found all along the Riviera di Ponente, especially at *San Remo* and *Bordighera*. During much of the year you may go skiing in the mountains and then top off the exercise the same day with a bathe in the blue Ligurian Sea. That is Italy. There's much of everything in its long leg and foot and in the football of Sicily at its toe.

CHAPTER 7

ITALIAN IN TEN MINUTES WITHOUT A MASTER

THE fact that I know only a little Italian qualifies me, I think, to teach it. If I knew too much I should be telling you all sorts of things that you don't care about and that would be a mere confusion unless you have time to carry on. Marc de Valette of Paris, *Licencié ès lettres,* taught me in ninety lessons, in a book *"L'Italien Par Vous-Même,"* the hopelessness of rushing through an unfamiliar language when time is lacking. In three days I galloped through his 180-page tome, studying furiously morning, noon and night, and at the end all I could say with absolute assurance was *"L'uccello vede il calamaio del professore sulla tavola."* (The bird sees the professor's inkwell on the table.) Not once have I had occasion to use that golden phrase, though I have been primed at all times. Either there was no professor or there was no bird, or if both were present the professor was using a pencil and the bird was looking the other way.

I did find, however, that it was easy to cull from Marc de Valette or any other source a few essential words and phrases which served me with increasing readiness and enabled me to make my way anywhere, even to wrangle a bit when necessary. I found too that Italian makes fairly easy reading for anyone who has had the usual school Latin and who knows some French. It is a very beautiful language, this one formed by Dante, Petrarch and Boccaccio from the degenerate Latin of the Dark Ages. It is liquid and musical beyond all others and, comparatively, it is not hard. Every letter has its value. Every word, almost without exception, ends in a vowel, which has a full syllabic value. Its idioms are much like the French.

One odd quirk it has which should be understood at the outset. The *Vous* of French, the *Sie* of German (as against the familiar *tu* and *du*) becomes in Italian *Lei,* which is literally *she.* It is a survival from obsolete forms of politeness (Your Excellence, Your Worship, etc.) which were feminine. One thus says to a heavily bearded railway porter, "*Ha Lei moneta?*" (Has she change?) meaning, "Have *you* change?" And to the *albergatore* (hotel proprietor), be he ever so masculine, one says, "*Ha Lei una stanza?*" i.e. Has *she* a room? meaning "Have *you* a room?" The plural of *Lei* is *Loro* but this is very unimportant.

Now I am determined in this lesson-by-a-duffer to be rigorously brief, to set down only the prime essentials. Here they are:

Pronunciation

Follow in general the Latin you learned in school unless you are eighty or over, but—

c is soft (like *ch* in cheese) before *e* or *i*.
g is likewise soft before *e* or *i*.
sc is like *sh* before *e* or *i*.
h is silent and hardly ever puts in an appearance except in the present indicative of *avere* (to have).
z is like *tz* or *dz*.
ch is hard like *k* before *e* or *i*.

Stress

You will have little trouble with this, as the stress generally comes "where it ought to," though not in certain common words which might cause question. (*Written* accents, few in Italian, are *grave*, on a final vowel, as città. The *acute* accents marked here are inserted *for purposes of stress only*.)

ferrovía—railway
trattoría—restaurant (of modest type)
lattería—dairy shop
távola—table
amábile—amiable
automóbile—automobile
líbero—free
fiammífero—match
valígia—valise
úscita—exit

Essentials of Speech

One *must* know how to count in cardinals up to twenty (preferably to one hundred); in ordinals up to ten.

CARDINALS

1—*un, uno, una*	12—*dodici*	23—*ventitrè*, etc.
2—*due*	13—*tredici*	(but 28 *ventotto*)
3—*tre*	14—*quattordici*	30—*trenta*
4—*quattro*	15—*quindici*	40—*quaranta*
5—*cinque*	16—*sedici*	50—*cinquanta*
6—*sei*	17—*diciassette*	60—*sessanta*
7—*sette*	18—*diciotto*	70—*settanta*
8—*otto*	19—*diciannove*	80—*ottanta*
9—*nove*	20—*venti*	90—*novanta*
10—*dieci*	21—*ventuno*	100—*cento*
11—*undici*	22—*ventidue*	

ORDINALS

1st—*primo*	6th—*sesto*
2nd—*secondo*	7th—*settimo*
3rd—*terzo*	8th—*ottavo*
4th—*quarto*	9th—*nono*
5th—*quinto*	10th—*decimo*

One *must* know the days of the week. (The first five have a *written* accent, hence also the stress, on the last vowel.)

Monday—*Lunedì*	Thursday—*Giovedì*
Tuesday—*Martedì*	Friday—*Venerdì*
Wednesday—*Mercoledì*	Saturday—*Sábato*
Sunday—*Doménica*	

Also—

today—*oggi* (pronounce *odgi*)	day—*giorno*
tomorrow—*dománi*	yesterday—*iéri*
tomorrow morning—*domattína*	week—*settimána*
tonight—*staséra*	month—*mése*

The days of the month are important if a little less imperative.

January—*Gennáio*
February—*Febbráio*
March—*Márzo*
April—*Apríle*
May—*Mággio*
June—*Giúgno*

July—*Lúglio*
August—*Agósto*
September—*Settémbre*
October—*Ottóbre*
November—*Novémbre*
December—*Dicémbre*

One must be able to discuss the time of day.

What time is it?—*Che ora è?*
Seven o'clock—*le sette ore*
Quarter past seven—*le sette e un quarto*
Half past seven—*le sette e mezzo*
Quarter of eight—*le sette e tre quarti*
Five minutes of nine—*le nove meno cinque* (nine less five)
Noon—*mezzogiorno*
Morning—*mattina*
Afternoon—*pomeríggio*

One should certainly know the Italian names of Italian cities.

Nápoli—Naples
Róma—Rome
Firénze—Florence
Livórno—Leghorn
Génova—Genoa

Miláno—Milan
Toríno—Turin
Pádova—Padua
Mántova—Mantua
Venézia—Venice

The following thirty words (some doubletons) are very busy in the travel vocabulary of every day (along with the elemental *si* and *no*).

grázie (in three syllables)—thank you
prego—"don't mention it"—extremely frequent in use, like the German *Bitte*
permesso—please (let me by or let me through); a prime essential in crowded conveyances
per piacére or *per favore*—if you please
quanto—how much? how many?
basta—enough (That's enough!)

dove—(two syllables) where? *dov'è*—where is, pronounced almost like *dove*
destra—right
sinistra—left
tutto diretto—straight ahead
va bene—all right
súbito (or *presto*)—quickly
qui—here
adesso—now
quando?—when?
troppo—too or too much
grande—large
píccolo—small
questo (a, i)—this, these
chiave—key
in fretta—in a hurry
pronto—ready
il conto—the bill
niente—nothing
che—what?
treno—train
biglietto—ticket
tramvia—tramway
autobus—autobus
a rivederla—au revoir (*a rivederci* to intimates)

The following greetings are tourist essentials:

Buon giorno—Good day—good morning
Buona sera—Good evening
Buona notte—Good night
Entrate—Come in
Ha Lei una stanza (or *camera*)—Have you a room?
Per due persone—For two persons
A che prezzo?—At what price?
(*Qualche cosa*) *meno caro*—(Something) less expensive.
È questa la più económica?—Is this (room) the cheapest?
Cercherò altrove—I will look elsewhere. (This may bring a more generous proposal from the proprietor.)
Ritornerò in pocchi minuti—I will return in a few minutes.

A che ora parte il treno per ——?—At what time does the train leave for ——?
Quale binario?—What track?
Bisogna cambiare?—Is it necessary to change trains?
Quanti minuti di fermata?—How long is the halt?
Due biglietti, seconda classe—Two tickets, second class.
Semplice—One way; *Andata e ritorno*—Return (ticket).
È questo posto libero?—Is this seat free?
Da qui a—From here to—
Quanta distanza c'è da qui a ——?—How far is it from here to ——?
Non ho tempo—I haven't time.
Svegliátemi alle sette—Wake me at seven.
Dov'è il gabinetto (or *toeletta*)—Where is the toilet? (If you have seen the mystic figures oo over a door you won't need to ask. That symbolism is universal in Europe. But WC is also much used.)

When I undertook to motor throughout Italy an entirely new crop of words and phrases began to take root in my personal vocabulary. Here are ten of them.

motore—engine
benzina—gasoline
freno—brake
pneumatico—tire
libretto di circolazione—registration paper
patente (di abilitazione)—driving license
posteggio—parking place
autorimessa—garage
stazione di rifornimento—filling station
Dove posso sostare—Where may I park?

And this is the end of the "lesson." I have been emboldened to offer it because in traveling about one encounters many persons who speak not a word of English and who understand only the magic phrase "O.K." Similarly, in the small *alberghi* of Italy the proprietors often speak no language other than their own, and a few words are certainly better than none. They can be counted on to save their weight in lire.

THE BACKGROUND OF THE PICTURE

CHAPTER 8

THIRTY CENTURIES ON A THUMBNAIL

Races That Made a Race

To the average tourist from overseas it comes as a surprise to discover that the Italian race is decidedly a *composite,* even as the American race is. The melting pot there, however, has been simmering nearly thirty centuries instead of three and a half, so the ingredients have been much more firmly fused.

One of the delights of travel in the peninsula and in Sicily is to come upon the clear marks—we could almost call them branding or tattoo marks on the body of Italy—that have been left, in succeeding ages, by the widely various races that were ultimately cooked into one homogeneous nation. It enhances travel immeasurably if even a few of these marks are easily read and recognized in some of the centers of tourism.

The following comments then, laying no claim to expertness, much less to ethnographical proficiency, are culled from my own pleasures of discovery, made more by chance than plan in Italian travels beginning at the age of ten! The *dramatis genera* shall be presented more or less "in the order of their appearance."

Ancient Rome itself was the first blend of races into a race. Hardheaded history, quite disregarding the pretty story of the Trojan refugees led to Latium by Aeneas, forebear of Romulus and Remus, asserts that rude Latin tribes dwelling on the left bank of the Tiber kidnaped a lot of *Sabine* women from north of the Tiber and thus created the state of Rome. The usual phrase "rape of the Sabine women" may be highly misleading in our current vocabulary. The ladies seem not to have been too upset by the abduction and when their outraged menfolk went to war about it they rushed into the fray, stopped it and said, in effect, "Let's all be one happy family—

and nation." Their suggestion was adopted, and although some fighting occurred later, the new race was never dissolved into its component parts.

The amalgamated Romans built their city, their kingdom, their republic, their empire. Little trace is left of the Sabines as such. *Rieti* is the largest town of today in the old lands of the Sabini, northeast of Rome.

The *Umbrians*, ethnic first cousins to the Sabines, lived north of that tribe, in a region extending from *Spoleto* clear up to *Rimini* on the Adriatic coast. One of the basic parent races of Italy, the Umbrians had their own language, the most important inscriptions in it (sometimes hazily called Etruscan) being the so-called *Eugubine Tablets*, on display in *Gúbbio* where they were found.

The *Etruscans*, an exceedingly important racial stock, lived north of Rome, from *Perúgia*, *Cortona*, *Arezzo* and *Florence* to the Tyrrhenian seacoast. They were, in fact, the Tuscans of their very early day, arriving (unlike the other tribes, which were native) from Asia Minor about 800 B.C. The Etruscan brands on the body of Italy are seen everywhere in the region they occupied, which came, by eastward expansion, to include all of Umbria. Perugia, the capital of the modern compartimento of Umbria, is strikingly marked with Etruscan monuments and relics, the most conspicuous thing, one of the marvels of Italy, being the towering town gate called *Arco di Augusto*. It got its name centuries later when Imperial Rome inscribed this mighty arch with the words Augusta Perusia, still clearly to be read.

The *Greeks*, following the colonizing period of the maritime *Phoenicians*, made Sicily and southern Italy a wonderful New Hellas from the seventh to the third century B.C. Everywhere the traveler goes along the southern and eastern coasts of the island he finds innumerable and majestic remains of Greek culture, as he does also on the peninsula as far north as *Naples*, which name is from the Greek Neapolis (New City). Greek temples and Greek theaters are in almost every town and some of them are in a remarkable state of preservation. The Temple of Concord in *Agrigento* and the Temple of Neptune in *Paestum* (only 60 miles below Naples) rival the Temple of Hephaestus (formerly called the Theseum) in Athens as the best preserved of all Greek monuments of architecture. The superb Greek

Theater of *Syracuse,* which city rivaled Athens even in its great days, is a major spectacle of travel, and the Greek Theater of *Taormina* is one of the lovely sights of that lovely village. And the Greek race? Its blood is, of course, mingled with that of the many other races that have successively occupied Sicily to make the life blood of today's Sicilian.

The *Carthaginians,* who were a later outcropping of the Phoenicians, left few permanent marks on Sicily or Italy, though they were most successful, for a long time, as invaders. Their Punic civilization was of a low and brutal order compared with that of the Greeks or of the developing Romans.

The *Saracens,* alternating in power with the *Byzantines* of the Eastern Roman Empire (Constantinople), conquered and held much of Sicily in the ninth, tenth and eleventh centuries after Christ, holding many of the Christian islanders under Moslem rule for that long period and dominating the entire island for the better part of the tenth century. The Saracens were eager and gifted builders and they left their powerful impress on many communities, especially *Palermo.*

The *Normans* brought the whole island under their sway in the latter half of the eleventh century, this remarkable achievement being the work of *Roger de Hauteville,* who made himself King Roger I, setting up his capital in Palermo. The Norman element is one of the most exotic in the whole composition of modern Italy and by no means the least interesting. Palermo and its marvelous suburb *Monreale* exhibit in the architecture of their great monuments of old an amazing marriage of two types as incompatible, one would say, as any two could be. Palermitan churches think nothing of having several Saracen domes rise from the roof of an otherwise purely Norman edifice, and the mosaics, of Byzantine inspiration, are among the most brilliant anywhere in the world. If you do not know the Phoenician-Punic-Roman-Saracen-Norman-Italian city of Palermo you have a vast treat in store.

Imperial Rome, calling itself the Western Empire after 395 A.D., changed its capital to Ravenna in 402. The nation was sick with decay and in 476 it fizzled out when the last emperor, bearing the appropriately diminutive name Romulus Augustulus, was deposed. Odoacer, a chief of the Herulians, threw out this weakling and ruled as a prefect under the Eastern Empire, but presently Theodoric the Great came along, personally murdered Odoacer and set up the Kingdom of the Ostrogoths, with Ravenna as his capital. Many of the greatest glories of that wonderful city, too little known to tourism, are directly due to Theodoric and his successors. The *Ostrogoths*, or East Goths, stayed in power for only sixty-two years but in Ravenna and all along the Po Valley they bequeathed something of their vigor to the weakened bloodstream of the Romans.

The *Byzantines* of the Eastern Empire succeeded the Ostrogoths and took full control of the Italian peninsula, governing it by means of exarchs, or viceroys, and although their period of complete authority was very short, hardly over a dozen years, their influence on architecture, both before and after their interlude of power, was very significant. St. Mark's of Venice is but one world-known example of the Byzantine stamp left on the churches of northeastern Italy. The domes of the Basilica of Sant'Antonio in Padua give another example, while the Byzantine mosaics brightening the churches of Ravenna and Palermo are perhaps their finest gift of all.

The *Lombards* (Langobards) have been called by John Addington Symonds "a nation in movement," as against a band of invaders (the Herulians) and an army (the Ostrogoths). From 568 they maintained their kingdom for more than a century, with Pavia as capital. The whole of what we know as Lombardy, with Milan as the chief city, has an important physical or ethnological heritage from these rude northerners who emigrated from the region of the Elbe. The early Lombards did not, however, build like the Ostrogoths, and even Pavia shows few traces, except some ancient ramparts, of Lombard construction from the period of the kingdom. (The achievements of the people of Lombardy in the period of the Lombard League and later are quite another story.)

The *Franks*, allying themselves with Papal authority, conquered and took over the Lombard kingdom and on Christmas Day of the year 800, as every schoolboy knows, Charlemagne was crowned Emperor of the West in Rome. For nearly a century (the ninth), Frankish emperors ruled northern Italy, while the Pope was compensated for his support by being given the so-called Papal States of central Italy, an arrangement that held good, excepting for a short interval during the Napoleonic Wars, for nearly eleven centuries, until the unification of Italy (1870) made the popes "prisoners" in the Vatican. That situation, a standing source of friction, was resolved in 1929 by the establishment of Vatican City as a sovereign state.

The confusions of rulership in Italy since the time of the Franks do not belong in this racial review. The *Holy Roman Empire*, really instituted by Charlemagne but specifically set up under that name, or *mis*name, in 962, with Otto I as emperor, was anything but Holy, anything but Roman. It was an affair of *German* emperors, culminating with the Habsburgs, and it was finally abolished only in 1806, by Napoleon. The German rulers were aliens to Italy all that time and certainly need not be considered an element in today's Italy.

The *Tyrolese* of *Alto Ádige*, however, brought to modern Italy a legacy that is encountered and unmistakably recognized by all travelers who make their way to that province. It has been included, since 1948, in an autonomous region called Trentino-Alto Ádige that extends as far south as Riva, on Lake Garda, including that flourishing little city. The entire region, including Riva, spoke German when I first knew it, in 1910, and its people gave allegiance to Austria. By the Treaty of St.-Germain (1919), after World War I, it was assigned to Italy in accordance with demands of the Irredentists, for it had long before been undeniably Italian (i.e. Lombard) soil. The Habsburgs acquired Alto Ádige as far back as the fourteenth century and it was known as South Tyrol until 1919. The rigors developed by the Italian nationalization program after St.-Germain have died down and today tens of thousands of the people of this province still, or again, speak German as their day-to-day language. This goes for such folk as tram conductors and shopkeepers. The blond hair and pigtails of many of the schoolgirls proclaim their background. To the tourist, who need not concern himself with the rights or wrongs of Irredentism in practice, the conspicuous Teuton element of Bolzano (Bozen), Merano (Meran), Bressanone (Brixen) and the western and northern stretches of the Dolomites adds a most interesting racial touch.

Trieste was held by Austria from 1382 to 1919 and of course the German race and language are still in evidence there as they are through all the northern part of Venetia Julia.

Venice was assigned to Austria in 1797 as an incident of one of Napoleon's wars but returned to Italy in 1866. No trace of the Austrian period of power is now to be noticed in the Queen City of the Adriatic, but from the East there is architectural treasure in plenty, for Venice long dominated Dalmatia, the Peloponnesus, the islands of the Aegean and Ionian Seas, Crete, Cyprus and even, for a few decades, the very center of the East, Constantinople. In a special sense Venice brought to the melting pot of Italy the subtle savors, though not much of the physical stock, that made of many races *a* race.

Thirty Dates on Call

I suppose it is an axiom that no other territory on earth the size of Italy has had so much history packed into it, history that has shaped Europe and hence the whole world, including our New World. Rome was born, grew great and ruled her vast empire. She declined and rude peoples who had been subject to her fought endlessly for her rich lands and richer cities, for her ports of commerce, perhaps unconsciously for her encompassing culture, her awe-inspiring name.

Rome became the head and heart of Christendom, till Luther's time. She continues to center *Roman* Christendom in every country.

Italy was born in 1870, reborn in 1946. In the interval she was a European power. Today she is a partner of the West, of us, despite all that guileful Communists can do.

The "splinter history" of Italy's states, her changing combinations of power, her foreign exploiters, her home-grown factions and powerful families, is as complex a structure, and as fascinating, as anything that man has built and rebuilt. You can't dig into Italian history in any competent book without getting buried in it, for every stirring event and personality dissolves into another before your reading eyes.

This book of present-day travel, recognizing the impossibility of sketching Italy's background, along with that of Rome, to even the same meager degree that the Series has sketched the background of other countries covered in earlier volumes, is offering merely a few *roll calls*, first, as above, of the races that made a race; now of thirty dates on call, that can be used as pegs of memory upon which the traveler may hang what history he has or acquires; finally, in Chapter 9, a roll call of selected personalities of the past and another of selected men of art.

Perhaps such drastic curtailment can even be of more practical use to today's traveler than a more pretentious coverage would be. Life in this second half of the twentieth century seems to set too swift a pace to permit most holiday seekers to cope with even so condensed a classic of serried dates as *Ploetz' Epitome,* much less such a classic of good prose as Milman's *Gibbon's Rome,* in six volumes. And now our thirty dates.

B.C. 754 (or 753). The *legendary* founding of Rome by Romulus. He and his twin, Remus, cast into the Tiber as infants but miraculously saved, then suckled by a she-wolf, laid the first stones of the city. They quarreled. Romulus killed Remus and ruled as sole king "happily ever after." The symbol of the twins at the teats of the she-wolf is seen so universally in Rome, and in many other parts of Italy, that one cannot ignore the threadbare myth.

B.C. 264 to 146. The three Punic Wars (Rome versus Carthage) at wide intervals. In the second one Hannibal entered Spain and France, crossed the Alps, won victory after victory, reached almost to the gates of Rome, did *not* enter, leaving on history's pages a major mystery. Scipio Africanus finally defeated the great warrior, fourteen years later. In the third of the Punic Wars, after endless thundering by Cato the Elder *"Delenda est Carthago"* (Carthage must be destroyed), the Punic capital was finally razed, wiped off the map of Africa, its site sowed with salt.

B.C. 102 to 44. The life span of Julius Caesar, who made war on Gaul and Britain, transformed "all Gaul" into a Roman province, wrote his *Commentaries,* so distasteful to generations of first-year Latin students, crossed the Rubicon to defeat his rival Pompey, became Rome's first emperor, and was slain by conspirators during a session of the Senate. His intimate friend Brutus (*"Et tu, Brute"*) was a leading conspirator.

B.C. 31 to A.D. 14. Octavian, given the title Augustus (Sublime) and the name Caesar (which later became a generic name for every reigning "Augustus"), dominated the scene and (from B.C. 27) was recognized as the first emperor to rule over the whole world empire. During his reign a Child named Jesus was born in Bethlehem of

Judea. This event is thought to have occurred actually four years "B.C." The new initials A.D. thus wrongly marked, and still mark, the "Year of Our Lord" (Anno Domini).

A.D. (henceforth) 14 to 68. Rome under the Julian-Claudian dynasty. Four emperors, Tiberius, Caligula, Claudius, Nero, carried the moral tone of Rome from bad to worse. Tiberius was a despot full of suspicions; Caligula a crazy fool; Claudius a weakling, dominated by two successive wives whose names are bywords of evil, Messalina and Agrippina; Nero, the vain tyrant, sadist, arsonist of Rome, persecutor of the Christians.

69 to 96. The Flavian Emperors, Vespasian, Titus, Domitian. In 70, Titus captured and largely destroyed Jerusalem, erecting in memory of this the triumphal arch we admire in Rome. The same year saw the beginning of the construction of the Colosseum, which was finally "opened for business" about a decade later. In Domitian's reign Rome extended her sway over Britain, clear up to Scotland. Agricola was the military hero, but fell out of favor and was poisoned. Persecutions of the Christians in Rome continued.

96 to 180. Rome's Golden Age of Empire. Nerva, Trajan, Hadrian, Antoninus Pius and Marcus Aurelius gave the empire eighty-four years of wise and enlightened rule. Nerva, Trajan and Hadrian were eager builders and did much to beautify Rome. Trajan's column and Hadrian's villa (near Tivoli) are but two of the many relics still admired. Marcus Aurelius, a Stoic philosopher, was one of the noblest sovereigns in all history and his *Meditations* formed a classic of humanitarian thought expressed in prose of deep richness. It is an unfortunate fact that his sense of duty compelled him to continue the rigorous suppression of the Christians (though without sadistic features), on the ground that they gave their first allegiance to Jesus, not to the Roman Empire.

180 to 284. A century of military emperors, among them dissipated Commodus, able Septimius Severus (his triumphal arch in Rome), cruel Caracalla (huge baths in Rome, the ruins now used for summer opera) and wise Alexander Severus.

303 to 325. Triumph of Christianity in the Roman Empire. In 303 Diocletian authorized a general persecution of the Christians, but this was the last one. In 306, Constantine (the Great) became one of

six "Augusti" and from 323 on he was sole emperor. During the interval between these dates, he won a battle (312) against his rival Maxentius at the Milvian Bridge over the Tiber, very close to Rome, and laid the victory to the aid of the Christians' God. He believed he had seen in the sky a flaming cross, with the words IN HOC SIGNO VINCES (In This Sign Conquer). He became a Christian catechumen (*not* a baptized Christian until he lay on his deathbed) and founded the first Church of St. Peter on the grave (probably authentic) of Peter himself.

330. Constantine set up a new capital at Byzantium, renaming it Constantinople, and this was to be a distinctively Christian capital. He still permitted pagan rites in Rome. From this emperor's death the world rule of Rome was split into an Eastern Empire and a Western Empire.

476. The end of the Western Empire came when Odoacer, a Herulian chieftain, deposed the last emperor (see first section of this chapter). Twice, a few decades earlier, Rome had been overrun and pillaged by barbarians, first by the Visigoths under Alaric, then by the Vandals under Genseric, but Rome had not technically been the Western capital since 402, in which year the court transferred to Ravenna. The Ostrogoths, succeeding Odoacer, ruled from Ravenna for six decades (493-555).

590. Gregory the Great, bishop of Rome, became the first pope, in the full sense of the word. He established the ecclesiastical supremacy of Rome and gave order to the liturgy. Every bishop of any see had been called *Papa*, but from Gregory's time the word applied only to the successor of St. Peter in Rome. (The Italian word for pope is still *papa*.)

800. Charlemagne crowned emperor (see first section above) by Pope Leo III, leaving the pope temporal ruler of the Papal States.

January 25-28, 1077. Emperor Henry IV stood for four days in a castle courtyard bareheaded and barefooted as an act of submission to Pope Gregory VII, who was then staying temporarily in the Castle of Canossa. Hence the phrase "to go to Canossa."

1155. Frederick Barbarossa crowned emperor in Rome. This sovereign, unlike others of the long imperial line, wished to restore the old grandeur and authority of Rome, with himself as the chief Roman.

He wished the term Holy Roman Empire to be much more than a polite fiction.

1282. The Sicilian Vespers, one of the most terrible massacres in history. All the French (Angevins) in Sicily were killed in a popular uprising provoked in part by the behavior of the French soldiers. Power over Sicily was transferred to the Aragonese (Spanish) line.

12th to 15th centuries. The Guelphs and Ghibellines, rival political factions originating in Germany under the names Welf and Waiblingen, racked Italy with endless internecine wars. In a general way the great *cities* (e.g. Milan, Genoa, Florence, Bologna) were Guelph and the noble *families* (e.g. Pallavicino, della Scala, Visconti, di Montefeltro, Frangipani) were Ghibelline. Pisa and Verona were anomalies in that they were Ghibelline cities. In Rome, Florence and Milan fierce struggles shook the communities to their foundations. Venice, a separate republic and even an empire in her own right, was not torn by these factional wars. The Guelphs were strongly favorable to the papacy and against the imperial power, while the Ghibellines had aristocratic and imperialistic preferences, so this was the social conflict of that era, interwoven with many other strands, including common or garden jealousies and personal rivalries.

1309 to 1377. The period of the "Babylonian Exile" of the papacy in Avignon. This strange interlude, brought on by the papal detestation of the Ghibellines and the Vatican's consequent reliance on French power, came to an end when Gregory XI returned to Rome.

1294 to 1587. The period of the very powerful noble families, often closely interwoven with the Ghibelline faction. Nearly every city in northern Italy was involved in strife due to the personal intrigues and power politics of these noble families. We associate the della Scala name with Verona; Visconti with Milan; Sforza (later) with Milan; Doria and Pallavicini with Genoa; Este with Ferrara; Gonzaghi with Mantua; Malatesta with Rimini; Frangipani and of course Colonna (for four or five centuries) with Rome; Piccolomini and Chigi with Siena (and Rome); Albizzi, Strozzi and Pitti with Florence and, brightest of all, the long-flowering name of Medici with Florence. From 1434 to 1587, with but two brief breaks, the Medici ruled the city on the Arno. Lorenzo the Magnificent ruled from 1469 to 1492. Both Michelangelo and Raphael were born during his reign and Florentine art quickly developed to its highest pinnacle. This was the period of Borgia ascendancy in Italy, and of worldly pride. Plain piety, of ascetic order, often had tough sledding, as when the Dominican friar Girolamo Savonarola, preaching reform, was burned at the stake as an impostor, in the center of Florence's Piazza della Signoria (May 23, 1498). The profligate Borgia pope "got his man," commanding that the monk was to die "even though he were a second John the Baptist," but now every year, on May 23, Florentines strew with flowers the brass slab in the pavement that marks the scene of the martyrdom. Thus does Florence show its eternal regret for what was, in essence, a brutal lynching instigated by an ecclesiastical monster.

1626. The mighty basilica of St. Peter's in Rome, the church built by Brumante, Michelangelo and many other architects, the church of pontifical splendor and of the masses throughout the world, consecrated by Pope Urban VIII.

1796 to 1815. The Napoleonic "disturbance" in Italy. By the Peace of Campo Formio (1797), the French-dominated Cisalpine and Ligurian Republics were formed, with capitals at Milan and Genoa, while Venice was thrown to the Habsburgs of Austria. Naples had its French-run Parthenopean Republic. After the victory of Marengo (1800), Napoleon reorganized Italy into French puppet states. Tuscany was made first a republic and then the Kingdom of Etruria. Naples presently became a kingdom, first under Joseph Bonaparte as king, then under Marshal Murat. Lombardy, South Tyrol and even Venetia and Istria, these latter taken back from the Austrians (for about a decade, until Elba and Waterloo), formed the so-called Kingdom of Italy, with Napoleon as titular king and Josephine's brother Eugène Beauharnais as viceroy. Piedmont, Parma, Genoa, were ceded outright to France, as was Tuscany, the kingdom episode having run its brief course. The Papal States were boldly incorporated into the French Empire by the all-powerful dictator of Europe, who was himself a Roman Catholic of sorts.

1814. The fall of Napoleon restored the Papal States to the church but left a vastly scrambled political map of the Italian peninsula.

1860. Victories of Magenta and Solferino, won by Napoleon III (France) and Victor Emmanuel II (Sardinia), against Austria. Among the results were the cession of Nice and Savoy (ducal possessions of

Victor Emmanuel) to France and the compensating incorporation of Lombardy in the Kingdom of Sardinia. Garibaldi and his famous "thousand," secretly aided by that masterful patriot Count Cavour and by the noble revolutionary Giuseppe Mazzini (never a royalist but a lifelong republican), made the amazing and successful invasion of Sicily in 1860. The leader could have been named King of Italy, by the people's overwhelming choice, but he bowed out in favor of Victor Emmanuel. Other states flocked to join the rapidly enlarging kingdom. They included Tuscany, Módena, Parma, many of the Papal States and Naples. A curious anomaly of this great development was that the king was of the Royal House of Savoy, and this title was retained by the family despite the distressing cession of Nice and Savoy to France. That explains the shrill screams of the Fascists that broke up certain meetings of the Assembly of the League of Nations, "Nizza! Savoia! Nizza! Savoia!"

March 17, 1861. Victor Emmanuel II empowered by the new parliament to assume the title King of Italy. This was a big moment in history, but some painful gaps remained in this first design of an Italian nation. One of the gaps was filled in, following a successful war with Austria (1866) that resulted in the return of Venice to Italy.

1870 to 1872. Troops of the Kingdom of Italy enter Rome, against the pope's protest and a token show of military resistance. In a plebiscite in the city, 133,681 votes were cast in favor of union with Italy, 1507 against it. After this avalanche vote all thought of papal resistance was at an end. In July, 1872, Victor Emmanuel II entered the Eternal City as its king and made it his capital.

1915 to 1918. World War I. Italy, lured into the conflict by the Allies' siren call, suffered some reverses, won some victories, was rewarded at the end of the war with South Tyrol, the Trentino, Trieste, Istria and some islands off the coast of Dalmatia. The poet-novelist Gabriele d'Annunzio made his fantastic capture of Fiume in 1919, but his sway there lasted only some fifteen months.

1922. Benito Mussolini made his Fascist "March on Rome" and was asked by the intimidated king to form a cabinet. He formed it. No doubt of that. By 1928 he had made himself absolute dictator. Accomplishing wonderful things for Italy, he rode for a sure fall as overweening ambition warped his judgment. His political immorality in the taking of Ethiopia (1935) helped notably to wreck the League of Nations.

1929. The Lateran Treaty signed, whereby the State of Vatican City was set up as a sovereign temporal state—of 109 acres and incalculable world influence. The brilliant celebration of this event in the Church of St. Peter on February 11, 1929, was witnessed by this author and will be briefly described in Chapter 11.

1940 to 1945. World War II, in which Mussolini's ambitions teamed the unfortunate country with Hitler, left Italy a political ruin and in some parts a physical ruin as well. Mussolini, caught in 1945 trying to escape from Italy with his mistress, Clara Petacci, was killed and his body taken to Milan, where it was gruesomely kicked by an infuriated and sadistic mob. His corpse and that of the woman as well were strung up with the maximum of indignity upside down in Milan's Piazza Loreto.

1946 to 1947. King Victor Emmanuel III resigned (1946) and the Republic of Italy was established. A peace treaty was signed in 1947.

Today's Republic

Little need be said here about the new Republic of Italy. It is a going concern and every visitor gets a lift, or should, from watching it go—forward. I have had a better chance than most to watch its course for I have spent some weeks in the country during each of the last four years. In even that short period the gains, immeasurably aided and consolidated by the ERP and its successor the MSA (Mutual Security Agency), have been immense, considering that *every* prospect of gain had been, and still is, fought savagely or subtly by official Communism, made in Russia, whose only hope of power lies in sustaining human misery.

Individual Communism, I may say, is sometimes quite a different, and fantastic, thing in Italy. Little Commies, the shop and tramcar and waiter and home variety, go in thousands to church, to the Roman Catholic church, implacable foe of atheist Russia. They are very often "good guys." They will even express, *sotto voce*, involuntary admiration for America, where many have relatives, though they are always ready, at Communist pep meetings, to join faithfully in the rabid cries against the capitalistic warmongers and imperialists. They like Coca-Cola, an evil and dangerous brew in the official Red vernacular, and if nobody is looking, nobody who matters, they will buy it every time in preference to its pure Communist rival, a beverage called Unità. This latter, by the way, must be moribund or even defunct now. I haven't seen it on this present trip, though the Red newspaper of the same name is omnipresent.

In the above digression I do not mean to minimize the Communist danger to Italy, which is terrible and constant, with something close to a third of the voters voting Red in every election. With its poisonous equivocations and its Big Lies pouring out upon Italy in endless billows of radio, press and poster propaganda, though stoutly and tirelessly answered by strong foes like Catholic Action, official Communism *is* a sword of Damocles, and to me the wonder is that the thread suspending this sword has grown in so few years to a string and now a decent cord of considerable strength. Runaway inflation is also a perpetual threat to Italy, so with prices high and earnings often pitifully low, with the population ever increasing by about 400,000 a year, the Reds have plenty of grist for their mills. It is cheering that Italian common sense and love of freedom have managed to hold the fort against them. Perhaps the secret of it is more clearly seen by those travelers who have read that charming little classic of 1950, Giovanni Guareschi's *The Little World of Don Camillo*.

To turn my unsolicited essay into a fact or two of the modern republic—Italy is governed under a constitution that took effect January 1, 1948. This constitution recognizes Roman Catholicism as the state religion, and incorporates the Lateran Agreement of 1929 between Italy and the Holy See. It also recognizes the complete freedom of the individual to choose what religion he likes, or none at all.

There are two houses in the Parliament, the Senate meeting in Rome's Palazzo Madama and the Chamber of Deputies in the Palazzo di Montecitorio. The Christian Democrats have held the reins of power (up to the present writing) since the inauguration of the republic, with the Communists, calling themselves the Popular Front, always in second place numerically.

The Army of Italy was limited, by the terms of the treaty, to 250,000 men, the Navy to 22,500, and the Air Force to 25,000. These and other limitations on our partner-in-NATO, our partner-in-containment-of-Communism, are now under avid discussion and ways have been found to mitigate the limitations, though the Red airwaves are always filled with bigger and louder screams of warmonger.

Italians love individual freedom quite as much as we do. The press and radio are as free as ours, though with the one stipulation that insulting comment about the pope is taboo. The Poster Wars and Chalk Wars, in evidence on church walls despite laws against this, are as colorful and as libertarian as any of our American Election Wars. I cannot believe that *regimentation*, that recurring curse of Germany, could ever fasten itself permanently upon the Italian spirit. Mussolini probably came as near to doing it as anyone could come, but even in its lustiest heyday Fascism always seemed, to me at least, synthetic and a bit unreal in Italy. The "Roman step," Fascism's edition of the goose-step, seemed always a little comic rather than terrifying, the upthrust hand of salute a perfunctory rather than threatening gesture. Today's Republic of Italy is an eager, friendly fledgling, wallowing in difficulties, determined to surmount them. It is one of our most important associates, one of our most interesting colleagues.

CHAPTER 9

GREAT NAMES ON ITALY'S SCROLLS

In Saintly Life and Influence

No other country in the world can match Italy in the variety and spread of its great names not specifically connected with reigning, with governing or with military enterprises. These three categories, along with the category of the papacy, all more or less covered in the previous chapter, shall be entirely omitted, save for an occasional special case, from the six lists that follow, the purpose of which is to reveal at a glance the basic meaning, in terms of travel, conveyed by the names. Many of these one- and two-sentence "revelations" will be but flashes of the obvious to the average reader. Many others may serve as refreshers of knowledge garnered long ago in school days and half forgotten, while some of them will introduce names that mean little or nothing to most American travelers, though they mean much to Italians. Travel is enhanced if these names too are part of one's cultural equipment in the land one is visiting.

A typical example of the last type is, for instance, Massimo d'Azeglio. If the inquisitive tourist is accommodated in a hotel on Via Massimo d'Azeglio he enjoys his stay more if he knows just who the man with that interesting name actually was. In one of the ensuing lists is the answer. Similarly, if he is told that the Donatello statue he is looking at is of Gattamelata, which seems to mean, and does mean, "Honeycat," it is of far more interest if he knows who the Honeycat was and how he got that nickname.

And now for some saints and their special days, presented by one who is not a Roman Catholic and therefore no expert in hagiology, but who finds the following figures a part of the very fabric of Italy, emphatically including the tourist's Italy.

St. Agnes (January 21), a Christian maiden of pagan Rome, suffered martyrdom at the age of thirteen in defense of her virginity. She is the patron of young country girls, who believe she lends aid in finding a husband. Her remains are supposed to lie beneath Rome's Church of Sant'Agnese fuori le Mura. On her annual festival two lambs are blessed in this church and their wool is later made into *pallia* (Latin for bands), which the archbishops wear on ceremonial occasions.

St. Ambrose (December 7), a scholarly bishop of Milan, was devoted to justice and the public good. To high-placed sinners he was severe, to lowly penitents very gentle. His remains are in the important basilica of Sant'Ambrogio in Milan.

St. Anthony of Padua (June 13), who preached to the fishes when men wouldn't hearken and who rates in hagiology as "the finder of lost articles," is of course among the best loved of saints. He was actually a native of Lisbon but his life is always associated with Padua.

Arnold of Bréscia, never canonized and in fact bitterly condemned by two or three successive popes and by at least one saint, Bernard of Clairvaux, was a monk of impeccable character who fought against abuses in the church. His agitation finally earned martyrdom, for he was executed in Rome, about 1155. His home town, Bréscia, erected a monument to him in the Piazzale Arnaldo.

St. Augustine (August 28) born near Carthage but teaching for a time in Rome and then in Milan, was the very great theologian of the early church, often considered second in influence, over the ages, to St. Paul alone. The marble sarcophagus of St. Augustine, presumed to contain his relics, is in the Church of San Pietro in Ciel d'Oro (St. Peter in the Golden Sky) in Pavia.

St. Catherine of Siena (April 30) was declared in 1939 the patron saint of Italy. Catherine was the last of twenty-five children of a Sienese dyer named Giacomo di Beninenza. She was a twin, but the other twin died at birth. A mystic, always in frail health and often in physical anguish, she wielded enormous influence by her cheerful piety and eloquence. In diplomacy, her talents were great, for it was she who ended the "Babylonish Captivity" by persuading Pope Gregory XI to return from Avignon to Rome in 1377. She was called "the Spouse of Christ" and her mystic marriage was a favorite subject of medieval artists. The House of St. Catherine, in Siena, is almost as popular a goal for tourists as for pilgrims, and the same may be said of the Church of San Domenico, also in Siena, where the saint's head is enshrined within a special chapel.

St. Cecilia (November 22) was a virgin martyr of Rome, whose life is somewhat shadowy though her importance seems to have been great in very early times. Her assumption of the role of patroness of music, and especially organ music, is thought to be purely fortuitous, due to an outright misunderstanding of a medieval document.

Saint Charles Borromeo, or *San Carlo Borromeo* (November 4), was a saint in the broadest sense of the word. Born into a very wealthy family in a castle at Arona on Lake Maggiore and made a cardinal at an early age by his de' Medici uncle, Pope Pius IV, he always lived in utmost simplicity. He devoted his life to reform of the church from within. During a terrible plague in Milan in 1576, he went boldly about everywhere aiding the stricken and burying the dead, with no thought of sparing himself. A colossal copper and bronze statue, seventy-five feet high, of the cardinal-saint stands on a height above Arona. The islet called Isola Bella, darling of the tourist world, was palatially developed by a seventeenth-century member of the Borromeo family.

St. Dominic, or *San Domenico* (August 4), a Spanish monk from Castile, founder of the Dominican Order, died in Bologna, whose Church of San Domenico contains a chapel with the saint's sarcophagus, a magnificent work of art partly by Michelangelo.

St. Francis of Assisi (October 4) is probably the most widely and ardently loved saint in the entire calendar. Wherever the name Francis occurs, in any of its languages and forms, it is traceable to this man of Assisi, for it was almost unknown until his ever-cheerful, humble, charitable and devoted spirit inoculated a world and left its stamp indelibly on succeeding generations. More will be said about this joyously selfless saint, Il Poverello, when this book reaches his famous hill town in Umbria.

St. Januarius, or *San Gennaro* (September 19), is the patron saint of Naples, whose festivals in his honor have been mentioned in Chapter 6. Tradition says that he was persecuted by Diocletian and finally martyred by a sword thrust, after fire had refused to burn him and wild beasts had refused to tear him.

St. Philip Neri (May 26), born Filippo Romolo de' Neri, was of a rich and cultured Florentine family but, although never an ascetic, he gave up his wealth and social advantages to devote his life to the poor and sick in crowded portions of Rome, where his influence reached great heights. Veneration of him is specially associated with Rome's Church of Santa Maria in Valicella and its splendid Oratory.

St. Thomas Aquinas (March 7), born in Aquino south of Naples, became one of the greatest figures of the Roman Catholic calendar because of his dominance of scholasticism, the Christian philosophy of the Middle Ages, a system that is still the church's official philosophy. This brilliant churchman, who lived down the student nickname of "Dumb Ox" earned by his slow speech, was for a time a professor in Rome, but he now lies buried in the Church of St. Sernin in Toulouse.

In Patriotism, Politics, Adventure

Camillo Benso di Cavour (1810-61) was one of the greatest statesmen in the history of Italy and was indeed the father of modern Italy, as Garibaldi was its dramatic spark. Cavour sometimes reached heights of selfless nobility rare in statesmen who are consumed by a single idea, in his case the unification of his country.

Bartolommeo Colleoni (1400-1475) was a hard, brilliant, faithless condottiere, or soldier of fortune, who enjoyed fighting on either side of almost any war. He concluded his career as general-in-chief of the armies of Venice and is commemorated in that city by one of the greatest bronze equestrian statues ever cast. This marvel of art was done by Andrea Verrocchio and stands in front of the big Church of Santi Giovanni e Paolo. The Colleoni Chapel in the upper town of Bérgamo is one of the richest treasures of early Renaissance art. The masterful condottiere rests in it in an over-ornamented but splendid sarcophagus, and his daughter Medea, whom he loved well, is in a simpler and far more gracious tomb beside him.

Christopher Columbus (1451-1506) is claimed as a native of several cities and small towns in several countries, but Genoa's claim is by far the best and is considered authentic by nearly all scholars. In that port city we see the modest little home of his birth at one end of the central town (Piazza Dante), a magnificent marble statue of him at the other (Piazza Acquaverde), and part of his remains in an urn in a central palace (Palazzo Bianco).

Enrico Dandolo (1108-1205) was one of the greatest doges of Venice. He steered the Fourth Crusade into an attack, a successful one at that, on the Byzantine Empire. He led the campaign that resulted in the capture of Constantinople, but death finally caught up with him, and his body rests in a gallery of the church-mosque-museum called St. Sophia in that distant city.

Andrea Doria (1468-1560) was the Genoese admiral, statesman and doge who brought the name of Genoa to its highest peak of fame. Filling the public eye by a spectacular defeat of the Turks in 1519 and capturing Tunis from them some years later, he became, to all intents, dictator of the Mediterranean world. The Palazzo Doria Pamphili in Genoa, now sadly desolated by time and the railway, is the building where this tremendous man of power died at ninety-two.

Giuseppe Garibaldi (1807-82) has been briefly discussed in Chapter 8, but a patriot of such proportions cannot be omitted from the present "scroll." Born in Nice, he became a roving soldier (Brazil, Uruguay, etc.) while still in his twenties. Later he devoted his life to his dream of complete unity for the state of Italy, which he helped so magnificently, if spottily, to make a reality. Often in trouble, even with his king and his warmest friends and associates, his life was a tapestry of adventure. One of its interludes was half a decade spent in New York, first as a chandler and then, during intervals, as skipper of a trading ship. He "made so good" in these five years that he returned to Italy a rich man and bought, for a residence, the islet of Caprera off the north coast of Sardinia, but he devoted most of his fortune to his unceasing patriotic enterprises. Garibaldi is a common noun as well as a proper one. Webster defines it as "a sort of shirt-waist worn by women; from its resemblance to the red shirt of the Italian patriot Garibaldi." My grandmother liked to wear this "common noun," as I remember her telling me.

Gattamelata was the nickname for *Erasmo da Narni* (died 1443), a condottiere is command of the Venetian army. An equestrian statue of this "honeycat," who could tread stealthily and purr gently as he prepared to tear his enemies to pieces, is one of Donatello's finest master works. Until the casting of this statue nothing of the first importance had been done in bronze in Italy since Roman times. Gattamelata in Padua, Colleoni in Venice and Marcus Aurelius, an ancient work, on the Capitoline Hill in Rome, are commonly called the three greatest equestrian statues in bronze ever created.

Nicolò di Bernardo Machiavelli (1469-1527) was, of course, the Florentine statesman, schemer and unscrupulous but brilliant author who gave his name to the word Machiavellian, an adjective suggesting devious political foxiness, quite untroubled by ethics, morality or the need for good faith. His famous book *Il Principe* (The Prince) describes, without pulling any punches, how the Machiavellian head of a state may keep himself in power. The bones of this author, whose cleverness did not enable him to dodge death, lie in a tomb erected by an Englishman (Lord Cooper) in the Church of Santa Croce, the "Pantheon of Florence," as it is often called.

Daniele Manin (1804-57) was a Venetian patriot who spent much of his life attempting in vain to win the freedom of his city from Austria. For a very brief period he did head the so-called Republic of St. Mark. Later, as an exile in Paris, he helped lay the foundations for the establishment of Italy as a constitutional monarchy under the House of Savoy. Manin's body lies in a sarcophagus of marble in the Piazzetta dei Leoni on the north side of St. Mark's Cathedral in his home city.

Giuseppe Mazzini (1805-72) has been already mentioned as a high-spirited revolutionary. He was a powerful supporter of Garibaldi, and his brilliant pen was in considerable part responsible for the founding and unification of Italy. A passionate republican and deeply interested in socialist doctrines, he came, in time, to support the monarchy as the only force capable of binding Italy together as a nation. A statue of this patriot decorates the pleasant Piazza Corvetto in Genoa and he is buried in that city's camposanto.

The Medici of Florence must be the one exception to this list's intention to omit the great ruling families in Italian cities, for they brought their city to its point of highest luster. You may wish to forget Giovanni de' Medici, who first invented the income tax in 1427, but his son Cosimo (known as the Elder) and the latter's grandson, Lorenzo the Magnificent, you will neither wish nor be able to forget. *Cosimo the Elder* (ruled 1428-64) was called *Pater Patriae*.

For twenty years he was practically dictator of Florence and attracted to his court the greatest scholars and artists of the time. *Lorenzo the Magnificent* (ruled 1469-92) was a prince with a genuine gift for poetry. His court fully rivaled in brilliance that of his grandfather, but his morals caused so much scandal that Savonarola was very nearly able to overthrow him. The Medici did not die out of the pages of Tuscan history until 1737. By that time they had thoroughly undone their work and brought Florence to ruin.

Francesco Morosini (1618-94), a famous Venetian soldier and doge, rebuilt the Venetian Empire for its last, brief "Indian summer." A statue of him is shown to tourists in the Sala dello Scrutinio (Voting Hall) of the Doges' Palace.

Marco Polo (1254-1323) left a name that makes every traveler's heart beat faster, for he was the Supreme Traveler of medieval times and luckily he was also a wonderful observer of detail. In one of the most remarkable journeys of history, Marco and his father and uncle made their way, in four years (1271-75), from Venice to Peking, to the court of Kublai Khan. They remained, or were politely "detained" by the great khan, for seventeen years, but eventually were allowed to return and they all got safely back to Venice toward the end of 1295. Four years later, while he was a prisoner of war of the Genoese, Marco Polo dictated to a fellow prisoner an account of his travels and his sojourn in China. It turned out to be one of the keenest and most color-packed travel books ever written.

In Science and Letters

Gabriele d'Annunzio (1863-1938) has been mentioned in Chapter 8 for his impulsive and ill-conceived exploit in the capture and holding of Fiume. It should also be said that this bizarre but brave and brilliant man was a skilled and famous aviator in the service of Italy during the First World War. It is as a novelist, poet and playwright, however, that he has his main claim to fame. One of his best-known novels, *The Flame of Life*, is supposed to deal with his celebrated romance with Eleanora Duse, who is credited with bringing him success as a dramatist. Gabriele d'Annunzio was sharply criticized in his time for the purple voluptuousness of his prose, but he was also exuberantly praised for freeing literature from its shackles of primness. Some forty years ago it was considered a bit "wicked" to sneak a look at a d'Annunzio novel. Lecturers on this author had a ready-made audience, eager to be shocked. On the slopes of Gardone, on Lake Garda, is the villa, called *Il Vittoriale*, long occupied by this versatile man and now containing his tomb, which may be seen by the public. The actual bow of *Il Puglia*, the battle-cruiser which figured in his seizure of Fiume, is built into the hillside and seems to be sailing forth into space. A curious sport is associated with this villa. A group of bold Italian civilians *who parachute from planes into the lake for fun* bears the proud name *Associazione Paracadutisti del Vittoriale* and will be further mentioned when this text reaches Lake Garda in Chapter 25.

Ludovico Ariosto (1474-1533) was a poet of great power and of elegance too, capable of writing a monumental epic in forty-six cantos like *Orlando Furioso*, his one immortal work of genius, and in airier mood comedies and lyrical pieces. He had in Alfonso I, head of the glittering Este family, with seat in Ferrara, a patron who was notably parsimonious but who nevertheless did provide a refuge enabling the poet to get on with his literary tasks. A monument to Ariosto has been erected in Réggio Emília (Via Toschi 7), where he was born, and another (on a column) in Piazza Ariostea of Ferrara. His house, at 67 Via dell'Ariosto, in the same town, is a place of tourist interest.

Giovanni Boccaccio (1313-75) is commonly ranked with Dante and Petrarch as a chief "builder" of the Italian language. Even more than the earlier Dante or than Petrarch, his contemporary, both of whom were devoted Latinists and were influenced by Latin constructions, he was the father of *Italian* prose, reveling in it as a new and wonderful medium, extremely flexible and of infinite capacity to reflect the feeling of the people he knew. Boccaccio's *Decameron*, considered by all scholars as one of the great literary works of all time, has suffered from its reputation as a "dirty" book, featured in the windows of bookstores specializing in pornography. In its hundred stories, "told" to each other by Florentine ladies and gentlemen, it does, most certainly, employ the "rawest" language and depict the most flagrantly sensual scenes, but in its age and in the setting of its Tuscan region it would not have caused elegant eyebrows to rise in horror. Often, in the coarsest tales, its sheer humor and naturalness are enough to relieve it of the indecency which many deplore.

Giosuè Carducci (1835-1907) was one of Italy's greatest poets, winning the Nobel Prize in 1906. He was long a professor of literature at the University of Bologna and his home there is shown on the *viale* that bears his name. A large statue of him stands in a park in front of the Brufani Hotel in Perugia.

Benedetto Croce, born in 1866 in the resort village of Pescassèroli, east of Rome, and still very much alive, is one of Italy's mellow figures of philosophy and of literary criticism. He is a statesman and diplomat and has taken an important part in various Italian governments.

Dante Alighieri (1265-1321), born in Florence, was, of course, one of the world's giants of literature, the father of Italian poetry as Boccaccio was the father of prose. His *Divina Commedia* (*Divine Comedy*), standing on the highest level of expression and of imaginative thought, has perhaps never been equaled in any language in its particular field, which may be called neighbor to epic, though not itself a typical epic. Its general theme, a hero being led through the hereafter by Virgil as cicerone, is too well known to need elaboration in this catalog. Dante's passionate love for Beatrice Portinari, whom he first saw "about the beginning of her ninth year" and who died at about twenty-five, is also too well known to call for comment. The tourist in today's Italy is "always running into Dante," as one expressed it to me, not only in Florence but in Padua, Verona, Ravenna, Perúgia, San Gimignano and so forth. He belonged actively to a political faction (White Guelphs) that was mostly "out" and hence he wandered widely in exile, to the vast benefit of posterity, for when Florence lost a politician the world gained a poet. His remains are in an urn in a chapel called Dante's Tomb (with an adjacent museum of relics) in the city of Ravenna, where the great man died while at the court of Guido da Polenta. An important and authoritative biography of Dante was written by none other than Boccaccio, who did not spend all his time penning "tales."

Galileo Galilei (1564-1642) was a brilliant pioneer in astronomy and physics. He discovered, by experiments with a hanging lamp in the cathedral of his native city, Pisa, the principle that a pendent object will oscillate at the same tempo whether the arc of its swing be great or small, thus pioneering the idea of the pendulum's use. He built the first practical astronomical telescope, though a Hollander had invented the first laboratory telescope. Finally, he accepted and proclaimed courageously the Copernican theory that the earth, with the other planets, revolves around the sun. Forced by the Inquisition in Rome to abjure this "heresy," he rose from his knees and made (perhaps) the muttered remark that has always been associated with his name, "*Eppur si muove!*" (Just the same it *does* move). Imprisoned for a time, he was finally allowed to live in retirement near Florence, pursuing his studies. Some of his experiments in the laws of gravitation took place from the Leaning Tower of Pisa, whose "deformity" lent itself to them. Here he learned that bodies of different weight fall at the same velocity. Memorial monuments to Galileo are seen in the Church of Santa Croce in Florence and on the Monte Pincio in Rome.

Luigi Galvani (1737-98) was a physicist of Bologna whose name crept into the world's languages as indicating a direct electric current. Figuratively, when we are *galvanized* into action we borrow this man's name to express it. Galvani noticed that a charged metal touched to a frog's leg caused a spasmodic contraction. He guessed wrong about the cause, attributing it to "animal electricity," but a fellow-countryman, Volta (see Chap. 27), later established the true cause and really discovered dynamic electricity.

Carlo Goldoni (1707-93), born in Venice and chiefly associated with that city, was a phenomenally prolific writer of comedies, achieving more than 120 of them. Some good ones emerged from this torrent. A statue of the dramatist stands in his native city's Campo San Bartolommeo, near the Rialto. In Perúgia, the handsome yellow *Sala Goldoni*, named in his honor, is a marvelous feature of the University for Foreigners.

Francesco Guicciardini (1483-1540) was an extremely able and illustrious Florentine historian who was an intimate of Machiavelli. He was a diplomat too and at various times held important government posts. The street leading from Florence's Ponte Vecchio to the Pitti Palace is named Via Guicciardini and on this street (at number 17) the historian lived.

Alessandro Manzoni (1785-1873) was a Milanese novelist and poet of international fame, his masterpiece, *I Promessi Sposi* (The Betrothed), being one of literature's supreme romances, translated into countless languages. There is a statue to him in a square in Lecco, the scene of a portion of *I Promessi Sposi*. His funeral in Milan was a state affair of great solemnity and in memory of this man of letters Verdi wrote his beautiful *Requiem*.

Ludovico Antonio Muratori (1672-1750) was a priest, a historian, an antiquarian and, above all, a leading scholar of his age. A statue of him stands on Via Emilia in Módena, where he was archivist and librarian to the local duke.

Petrarch, or *Francesco Petrarca* (1304-74), has been mentioned above as one of the three illustrious men of letters who formed the Italian language. He lived in the time of the "Babylonish Captivity" and spent much of his time at Avignon, though he loathed the papal court, considering it an incubator of falsehoods and intrigue. His most celebrated poems were the exquisite love lyrics in the *Canzoniere*, inspired by his hopeless love for a mysterious lady named Laura who was the passion of his life. She is thought to have been Laura de Noves, the wife of one Hugo de Sade (not to be confused with the much later count who gave his name to sadism).

Torquato Tasso (1544-95), author of the epic masterpiece *Jerusalem Delivered*, a poem that deals with the First Crusade, was born in Sorrento, whose main square has a statue of him, and died in Rome, in the Monastery of Sant'Onofrio, where several rooms and a chapel of the church are devoted to memorials of him. He is, however, most closely associated with Ferrara, where Duke Alfonso II, grandson of Alfonso I, gave him patronage—and incarceration as a madman for seven years in the Hospital of Sant'Anna! This pungent story, too long for inclusion in this list, will be told in Chapter 20, when this book reaches Ferrara.

In Music

The Amati, a celebrated family of violin makers of Cremona, the world's violin town *par excellence*, flourished for nearly two centuries, from about 1550 to 1740. Niccolò Amati (1596-1684) won a double distinction by producing wonderful violins himself and by being the teacher of the craft to a pupil destined to outshine his master. That was, of course, Antonio Stradivari.

Vincenzo Bellini (1801-35), a native of Catania, Sicily, would perhaps be called today a "tunesmith." He wrote operas such as *Norma*, with easy-to-sing melodies. Musical criticism has spent well over a century disparaging his talent, but he is still popular with the musical masses. One of the loveliest civic gardens in all Italy is Catania's Giardino Bellini, named for its celebrated son, who lies in a tomb in that city's cathedral.

Enrico Caruso (1873-1921) is a legend to the American people and to all the world. Born in Naples and attracting attention in that city as an operatic tenor when he was little over twenty, his fame gradually spread to all civilized lands. In New York he was the star attraction of the "Met" for the sixteen years of his connection with it. His romance with, and marriage to, his beloved "Doro," Dorothy Park Benjamin, was popularly recreated in 1951 for the screen and his voice was recreated, in some degree, by Mario Lanza. Probably no other person in the history of music has become the musical idol of so many millions as has Enrico Caruso of *bella Napoli*.

Maria Luigi Carlo Zenobio Salvatore Cherubini (1760-1842) was a Florentine operatic composer who spent much of his life in Paris, where he became director of the Conservatoire. Cherubini was a boy wonder of music, achieving some fame as a composer of religious music when he was but fifteen. His remains are in Santa Croce (Florence).

Arcangelo Corelli (1653-1713) was both composer and violinist. In the field of composition he did much to develop the sonata in various forms and for various instruments.

Gaetano Donizetti (1797-1848) was an operatic composer born in Bérgamo, that lovely double town of Lombardy, which now honors him with a statue in front of the Civic Theater in the Lower Town and with a splendid tomb, surmounted by weeping angels, in the Upper Town. Among his many successes were *Lucia di Lammermoor*, always a popular offering of itinerant companies throughout Italy, and, for the Opéra Comique in Paris, *La Fille du Régiment*.

The Guarneri were another violin family of Cremona, producing superb violins for a century or more (1650-1750). The most celebrated of them was Giuseppe Antonio Guarneri (1687-1745), who was called also Guarneri del Gesù.

Ruggiero Leoncavallo (1858-1919) wrote several operas that failed and just one, *I Pagliacci*, that magnificently succeeded. This tearjerking drama-in-song of Canio and Nedda and Silvio, though so short that it is usually linked with another short opera such as Mascagni's *Cavalleria Rusticana*, is one of the sure-fire favorites of operagoers everywhere.

Pietro Mascagni (1863-1945) was a native of Leghorn. Like Leoncavallo he achieved one short opera, mentioned just above, that won permanent popularity. One or two others, such as L'Amico Fritz, have at least lived on feebly.

Niccolò Paganini (1784-1840), a native of Genoa and still associated, in the world's thought, with that city, was the most fabulous figure ever to hold a violin and draw a bow. He developed a phenomenal technical proficiency that was the wonder of his age and many consider that it is not surpassed, if indeed equaled, by the greatest masters of our time. So incredibly brilliant was his mastery of technique that the public was superstitious about it and became easily convinced that the devil stood beside him to lend him aid, a belief which Paganini himself was not above exploiting for the melodramatic advantage it gave him. His compositions, still considered technical challenges and often played by young violinists to prove their conquest of difficulties, were chiefly of the fireworks type, but with occasional slow passages of tender and genuine feeling. Paganini's favorite violin, a large Guarnerius, is exhibited to tourists in Genoa's Palazzo Municipale. (Lesser but still famous Italian violinists before and after Paganini are too numerous to discuss here. They include Giovanni Vitali, Giuseppe Tartini, Gaetano Pugnani, Pietro Locatelli, Pietro Nardini and Giovanni Batista Viotti, who was an older contemporary of Paganini and who is often called "the father of modern violin playing.")

Giovanni Pierluigi da Palestrina (1514-94) was born in the small town from which he took his surname, Palestrina, a medieval community in the hills some seventeen miles east of Rome. He is called, perhaps with a touch of exaggeration, "the savior of church music" because his beautiful masses are said to have persuaded a commission of cardinals not to ban church music as they had virtually decided to do on account of the flippancy of the compositions then in vogue. Palestrina certainly gave polyphonic music a new lease on life. He was appointed choirmaster of the Vatican's Julian Chapel, then of the Church of St. John Lateran, then of Santa Maria Maggiore and also of St. Peter's itself. In the latter church, in a tomb erected in front of the central altar of the south transept, his remains lie today. On Good Friday, every year, one of his major works, the so-called *Improperia*, is sung in the Sistine Chapel.

Adelina Patti (1843-1919), perhaps not a supremely great singer in a purely artistic sense, was, for a full half century, the darling of concert audiences in America and Europe. Amazingly enough, her debut took place in 1859 when she was sixteen, and her absolutely final "final appearance" in 1908, when she was sixty-five! Many thousands of Americans still remember her charm and her virtuosity in coloratura.

Giacomo Puccini (1858-1924) was born in Lucca and lived during his later years in a lakeside villa at Torre del Lago, on Lake Massaciúccoli, ten miles north of Pisa. This villa, which contains the composer's tomb, is a regular halt of the CIAT tourist busses on their daily runs between Genoa and Florence. The enduring popularity of Puccini with opera lovers is attested by a mere naming of his chief operas: *Manon Lescaut, La Bohême, Tosca, Madame Butterfly, The Girl of the Golden West*.

Ottorino Respighi (1879-1936), a Bolognese composer of our own century, achieved wide and deserved popularity with his symphonic poems built on Roman themes, namely *Pines of Rome, Fountains of Rome* and *Roman Festival*.

Gioacchino Antonio Rossini (1792-1868) was born in the Adriatic town of Pésaro, where his father had the proud post of "town trumpeter," but spent many years of his life in Bologna (26 Via Mazzini). His remains are in Florence, in the Church of Santa Croce.

Domenico Girolamo Scarlatti (1684-1757) was a composer of light works for the harpsichord and piano, chiefly gay, one-movement sonatas. He was a virtuoso on the harpsichord and is considered to have fathered, by his compositions, modern pianoforte playing. The

"Cat Fugue," based on notes picked out by his cat in treading gingerly along the keys, is one of his popular compositions.

Antonio Scotti (1868-1936) was one of the greatest Italian operatic bassos, a contemporary of Caruso, with whom he teamed in many famous duets of opera, and almost comparable to Caruso in popularity with Metropolitan audiences.

Antonio Stradivari (1643-1737), commonly called by his Latinized name Stradivarius, was, of course, the greatest of the Cremonese school of violin-makers and indeed the greatest of his profession "before, during or since." In his youth he was fully under the influence of his teacher Niccolò Amati, but for the last seventy years of his life—he lived to be ninety-three—he put his own individuality and skills into each instrument. His wonderfully long life permitted him to make more than a thousand violins besides eighty celli and numerous other instruments. Wherever violin music is loved, and that is in every civilized land, musicians still debate "the secret of Stradivari." Was it the shape of his instruments that made them superior? Was it the selection of woods? Was it some magic formula for the varnish? Doubtless it was all of these and something more, the priceless ingredient of genius, which cannot be explained by debate.

Arturo Toscanini, born at Parma in 1867 and at this writing still going strong, is surely one of the greatest operatic and concert conductors of all time. His memory is a special phenomenon of the first importance, enabling him to conduct without score a prodigious repertoire of operas, symphonies, choral and orchestral works of vast variety, composed in all ages by men of many nationalities. This capacity to conduct without score allows his remarkably magnetic personality to inspire his players and to lift his audiences to the heights of rapt attention.

Giuseppe Verdi (1813-1901), born the son of a humble innkeeper in a village near Busseto in the Duchy of Parma, would be called "Mister Opera" if political styles were to be transferred to the realm of grand opera. During his life of nearly ninety years he became and remained a legend, as indeed he still is. He championed a new school of singable Italian opera as against the more formal Teutonic style then prevailing. He made his way as a young student to Milan, but actually "flunked" in the courses of the music conservatory there, to the later embarrassment of teachers who had failed to recognize genius in him. A list of Verdi's many successful operas is too long to set down but the most enduring are probably *Rigoletto, Il Trovatore, La Traviata* and the powerful *Aïda*, which far surpasses the others. An odd historical fact of Verdiana is that the five letters of the composer's name came to stand as a secret symbol of nationalistic aspirations during the birth throes of the Italian nation. When young patriots shouted "Viva Verdi" they were really saying "Viva *V*ittorio *E*manuele, *Re d'I*talia!"

Antonio Vivaldi (ca. 1678-1740) was a Venetian priest, feeble in health, who became a violinist of Europe-wide repute and then an astonishingly prolific composer of contrapuntal music. His concerti alone numbered over four hundred and he wrote more than a hundred chamber music works and half as many sacred choral works. His popularity with critics and audiences is gaining both in America and Europe. In Perúgia, a musically erudite city, I recently heard the celebrated "complex of soloists" of Rome's *Collegium Musicum Italicum* perform three Vivaldi works and the response of the listeners was as impressive as the melodious music.

In Contacts with Visiting VIP's

A few non-Italian personages, chiefly literary and chiefly English, coming eagerly from their damp and chilly island to Italy's sunshine, have been so much in love with Italy that they have, in a sense, left their stamp upon it, or at least their names, as devoted visitors, woven into its fabric. Ten or so of these Very Important Persons seem to need inclusion on the Scrolls of Italy, with a few words about the connection of each of them with the land of their affection.

Robert and Elizabeth Browning spent most of their fifteen years of married life, until the untimely death of Elizabeth, in Italy, chiefly in Florence. Their home, called *Casa Guidi*, is pointed out in the Piazza San Felice (Number 9), near the Palazzo Pitti. Elizabeth lies buried in the Protestant Cemetery, as do several other English notables, including Walter Savage Landor. Robert survived his wife for twenty-eight years, death finally overtaking him in the Palazzo

Rezzónico on the Grand Canal of Venice. The Brownings' love for Italy is a legend in itself. Elizabeth worked ardently for Italian liberation from Austria's clutches, and Robert identified himself with Italian patriotic aspirations and was an able interpreter of Italian thought.

Lord Byron, in his much roaming, morally roving life, favored Venice more than most places. The Palazzo Mocenígo, or one of the four adjacent palaces bearing that name, on the Grand Canal, was a principal scene of his more notorious debaucheries. Following that, he lived for a short time in Ravenna, the Countess Teresa Guiccioli being then his acknowledged and honestly devoted mistress. With her relatives, Byron became involved in various intrigues aiming at an Italian revolution. His mansion in Ravenna was the Palazzo Rasponi, an isolated house in the square now called Piazza San Francesco, though it was known until a few years ago as Piazza Byron.

Queen Christina of Sweden, daughter of the great Gustavus Adolphus, conspicuous leader of Protestants in the Thirty Years' War, abdicated her throne in 1654, fled Sweden in the garb of a man, was baptized as a Roman Catholic in Innsbruck and then settled in Rome, where she lived almost as a personal "ward" of the pope. This strange Swedish queen, whose life is still a puzzle to historians, lived for more than twenty years in what is now the Palazzo Corsini at the base of the Janiculum. She was an important "prize" for the Catholic church and there is a monument to her, by Carlo Fontana, in St. Peter's. Her remains lie in a place of special distinction in the Papal Chapel of the crypts under the same church, Pius X and Benedict XV reposing in adjacent coffins. She was the only woman, except saints, ever to be buried in this edifice.

Nicolas Copernicus (1473-1543), the great pioneer of modern astronomy, was of Polish origin, born in Prussia, but he had many contacts with Italy, over a period of ten years. For a year, he was a student in the University of Bologna. Later he lectured on astronomy in Rome. Then, for several years, he pursued various studies in Padua and Ferrara, where he won a doctorate in canon law. In the field of astronomy—it could go without saying—his work had an enormous influence on Galileo.

Johann Wolfgang von Goethe, like many another man of letters, was an "addict" of Italy. Among the many communities associated with his visits are Malcésine, a village on Lake Garda, where he was once arrested (1786) for sketching, on the charge that he was endangering the Venetian Republic; Rome, where he lived for a time at Number 20 on the central Corso; and Castel Gandolfo, hill village of the Papal Summer Palace, where the poet sojourned in a villa on the Albano road.

John Keats lived for the last five months of his life in the very heart of the visitor's Rome in a house at the edge of Piazza di Spagna fronting on the Spanish Steps. He died of consumption in this house in 1821, while still only twenty-five, and lies buried in the older portion of the Protestant Cemetery near the Pyramid of Cestius. The Keats House is a tourist goal of some importance containing items associated with both Keats and Shelley, who also was an Italophile and who also died in Italy.

John Milton visited for a time in the monastery guest house (later called Paradisino) of Vallombrosa, a beautifully wooded hill resort some twenty-five miles from Florence, and paid tribute to the place in Paradise Lost. Vallombrosa is proud of this association with one of the world's supreme poets, as a handsomely carved tablet erected in 1925 indicates.

Florence Nightingale began her eventful and remarkable life of almost ninety years in a villa called La Colombaia, at Bellosguardo, a little way outside the Porta Romana of Florence, for which city she was named. In the cloisters of the Church of Santa Croce is a mural monument to her.

Percy Bysshe Shelley brought his brilliant, restless life to an early and abrupt end by a drowning accident in the overturning of a small schooner off the beach of Viaréggio in 1822, when he was just short of thirty. His fingers, clutching a book of Greek drama, left their imprint on the waterlogged covers. His body and that of a companion named Williams were found about a month later on the beach by his great friend Captain Edward John Trelawny and burned on the spot, in accordance with wishes that Shelley, for his part, had urgently expressed. Souvenirs of Shelley are to be seen, as stated above, in the Keats House in Rome. His ashes are interred in a substantial tomb in the newer portion of the Protestant Cemetery.

Above All, in the Arts

(TWENTY FLORENTINE MASTERS)

No other country—and one does not forget the numerous masters of Holland and Flanders—has ever approached Italy in the number and power of its great artists and sculptors, and no other city of Italy has equaled Florence as a wellspring of mighty talents and achievements. It is not by chance that Florence is the city where the *Medici Art Series* is published, and, of special importance for tourists, that handsomely printed compendium of art, *Wonders of Italy*, compiled by Joseph Fattorusso. This book, enthusiastically mentioned in Chapter 3, has 623 slick-paper pages, as I have said, and therefore cannot be tucked casually into a suitcase, but it seems to me an essential before-and-after book even if carrying it as a companion-book proves impracticable. Its 3265 illustrations, each with brief explanatory text, whet the appetite "before" and nourish pleasant memories "after."

Among the myriads of Italian masters—any comprehensive list names four or five hundred—these scrolls shall limit themselves to twenty who were associated with Florence, fifteen Sienese, Umbrians and Scattered, and ten Venetians, this school developing later than the others and bringing the lingering sunset of Italian Renaissance to its last brilliant coloring. It is not easy to boil the multitude of Florentines down to a selective twenty, but I shall attempt it. The significance of Florence develops like an opening flower as one examines the basic facts and figures of her life of art.

The following artists lived and worked in the thirteen hundreds and are known as Trecentisti (literally *three*hundredists):

Giovanni *Cimabue* (1240-1303). The name means Bull's Head. Hardly was this artist a *trecentisto* but he drew back the curtain for the new century. He was the teacher of Giotto. Some of his work is in the Church of St. Francis in Assisi, and one picture, a Madonna, is in the Uffizi Gallery of Florence.

Giotto di Bondone (1266-1337) was found as a shepherd boy by Cimabue, who noticed the remarkably lifelike sheep he was drawing on flat stones. Cimabue taught him to paint and the pupil far outshone the teacher. In Assisi, in Padua and of course in the Uffizi, we may study Giotto, not forgetting his great campanile, beside the cathedral in Florence.

Taddeo Gaddi (1300-66), a disciple of Giotto. Some of his frescoes are found in Santa Croce of Florence.

* * *

The following Florentines, having done their work in the fourteen hundreds, are called Quattrocentisti:

Tommaso Masaccio (1401-28). The name means "Great Heap" and was given him because of his rather slovenly appearance. His work, however, was anything but slovenly. He is often called the founder of modern painting, and the great ones, even Raphael and Michelangelo, are hardly of greater caliber, in a sense, than this uncouth "Heap." His chief masterpiece, painted when he was but nineteen, is in the Brancacci Chapel of Santa Maria del Carmine in Florence. A small-boy guide who once showed me these frescoes *insisted* that Masolino and not Masaccio did the powerful scene of Adam and Eve being expelled from Paradise, but the boy is contradicted by every art authority. Why, I wonder, should a child be empowered to give tourists officially wrong information?

Paolo Uccello (1397-1475). His, too, was a nickname, meaning "Bird." It was given to him because of his passion for painting birds. He was too mathematical an artist to be really of the first rank and apparently Donatello finally persuaded him to give up painting altogether. Yet Paul "Bird" had great influence on the Florentine school. You will find him not only in the terribly damaged Green Frescoes of Santa Maria Novella but—you guessed it—in the Uffizi.

Fra Angelico (1387-1455) is called The Angelic and also The Blessed (*Il Beato*) because he was officially "beatified." (Joan of Arc, you remember, was beatified before she was at last canonized.) This gentle friar, who joined the Dominican Order in Fiesole, started his art career as a miniaturist but became an important painter of frescoes and church pieces. The terrific political struggles of Florence scarcely touched him at all. Some of his best work is seen in the Museo dell'Angelico in the Convent of San Marco in Florence, where he passed nine years.

Fra Filippo Lippi (1406-69), another monk, was radically different from Fra Angelico. He lived a rather two-faced, disordered life and was always in trouble. He could scarcely paint a Madonna unless his model had really a pretty face. For Saint Margaret he used as model a lively nun named Lucrezia Bute. Giorgio Vasari, famous Florentine art critic of the sixteenth century, says he abducted and ravished her, that she lived with him in Prato and that Filippino Lippi was her son and his. Some apologists now cast doubt on this story and say Filippino was an adopted son. After he was born, the pair got married, having been released from their monastic vows by Pius II in deference to an appeal of Cosimo de' Medici. One of Fra Filippo's pretty Madonnas is in the Uffizi. The artist's body is in a sarcophagus in the cathedral of Spoleto.

Filippino Lippi (1457-1504), a great colorist, was taught by his father and by Botticelli. He completed the celebrated Brancacci frescoes in the Carmine Church. As a human being he was less interesting than his father and less individual. His work too is to be seen in the Uffizi.

Sandro Botticelli (1444-1510). His first name is short for Alessandro. His last was a nickname of his elder brother, who brought him up, and it means "Little Barrel." The painter's real name was Alessandro Filipopi. A passionate lover of beauty for its own sake, he filled his large canvases with beautiful women, very often in the most diaphanous drapery. He did much work for Lorenzo the Magnificent and for the latter's cousin. This "Little Barrel" can be studied to the very best advantage in—the Uffizi.

Domenico Ghirlandaio (1449-94). His real name was Domenico di Tommaso Curradi di Dosso Bigordi, so why should he not change it? Ghirlandaio means Garland-Maker, referring to the wreaths of gold and silver which his father, a goldsmith, made. He is said by Vasari to have regretted not having "all the walls of Florence to cover with frescoes." You and I may be content with the great amount of work he did leave. It is found in the San Marco Museum, in the Hospital of the Foundlings (Spedale degli Innocenti), in the Church of Santa Maria Novella and in the Uffizi. That is not all, but it is enough. His work is far less inspired than some of the other Quattrocentisti, but he costumes his scenes with the very color of medieval Florence.

In other artistic fields Florence points with pride to five great men of the fourteen hundreds towering above many able men of lesser caliber:

Filippo Brunelleschi (1378-1446) founded the architecture of the Renaissance. His dome for the cathedral of Florence was the greatest structural achievement of that era and a thing of sheer beauty. He began his career as a goldsmith, turned sculptor and finally, a boon to Florence, turned architect. Among many other notable "jobs" he designed the rugged Pitti Palace.

Lorenzo Ghiberti (1377-1445) bothered Brunelleschi for a time by "helping" him on the Duomo dome. For a time, also, Brunelleschi competed with Ghiberti as a sculptor. Each eventually found his field. Ghiberti's prize-winning doors on the cathedral's baptistery constitute perhaps the finest bronze relief work in the world. He spent his life on them. It is hard to believe that a man with such gifts was so mean in spirit as Vasari described him.

Donatello di Betto Bardi (1386-1466) was a giant among giants. If Brunelleschi fathered Renaissance architecture, this "Little Donato" certainly fathered sculpture, though one must not ignore Iacopo della Quercia, who is chiefly associated with Siena. About ten years younger than Ghiberti, Donatello once worked on the baptistery doors under his instruction. Soon he mastered this and every other form of sculpture. He could make exquisite little bronzes, powerful equestrian statues, terra-cotta busts, and figures in oak. Whatever he undertook he carried through supremely well. His great contemporaries knew this and graciously proclaimed it, and yet Donatello's fame dimmed and all but disappeared for two centuries. The only parallel to this strange sinking spell is the similar decline and final rise (in the present century) of Bach's fame in the musical world.

Today we know—as Michelangelo knew—that a greater, more comprehensive genius than Donatello's has not existed in the field of sculpture—unless we except Michelangelo himself. Everywhere in Florence, but especially in the Bargello, one finds Donatello.

Luca della Robbia (1400-82) was hardly a giant, but he had a certain genius that was his own and that genius was the making of bright terra-cotta figures. He passed on this talent to his son Andrea, who made the bambini that delight all visitors to the Foundling Hospital.

More bambini and Madonnas and angels by both Luca and Andrea are seen in the Bargello on the floor above Donatello's masterpieces.

Andrea del Verrocchio (1435-88), a pupil of Donatello, achieved a refined delicacy of style that hardly anyone but Donatello himself could match. Also, Verrocchio designed just one tremendous equestrian statue, that of Bartolommeo Colleoni, set up in Venice, as has been mentioned above. So amazing is this great statue in its virility and strength that it is often called unblushingly the finest equestrian statue ever made, and those who dare to say this always mention in the same breath Donatello's own statue of Gattamelata in Padua. How could Verrocchio just once have climbed from graceful little bronzes to such rugged heights?

* * *

Of the *Cinquecentisti* (artists of the fifteen hundreds) who brought glory to Florence three cry out for mention:

Leonardo da Vinci (1452-1519), on the border line between two centuries, is generally thought of as belonging to the later one. He was illegitimately born, of a notary of Florence, by a peasant woman in the Tuscan hill town of Vinci. No one questions Leonardo's place at the very pinnacle of Italian painting, but he was also a sculptor, architect, scientist, engineer, inventor and many other things. You do not have to go to Milan (for his *Last Supper*) or to Paris (for *Mona Lisa*) to find the work of this manifold genius. Two of his greatest paintings are in the Uffizi, namely *Annunciation* and *Epiphany*.

Michelangelo Buonarroti (1475-1564) belongs in some part to Rome, where the dome of St. Peter's and the paintings of the Sistine Chapel are but samples of his mastery in several fields, yet it is fair to call him a Florentine. He was born in Caprese, of Florentine parentage, but while still a suckling went to Florence and was nursed at the breast of a stonemason's wife. Thus, as he liked to claim in later life, he imbibed a fondness for sculpture with his nurse's milk. If I personally were to choose from among the great Florentines the one who means most to me it would certainly be Michelangelo Buonarroti. His *David*, the original being in the Galleria dell'Academia, is the most widely known of all his works in sculpture. In 1949, a splendid and genuinely exciting screen biography of this amazing man was produced by a foreign film company, with Frederic March as "voice." It was appropriately named *The Titan* and one hopes it will be revived from time to time.

Benvenuto Cellini (1500-71) seems something of an anticlimax after the triple mountain peak (sculpture, painting, architecture) of Michelangelo. Cellini was of the first rank only as a jeweler and silversmith, though one must not forget his *Perseus* in the Loggia dei Lanzi of Florence. Cellini's life was one of the most picturesque, hectic and amoral that it is possible to imagine—unless he is grossly lying in his autobiography. For a while he "got religion," but at the age of sixty he plunged gaily into new debaucheries. He had a lot of children, legitimate and illegitimate, and scarcely bothered to keep track of them. One, Costanza, he gave away for a sum of money, and wrote candidly, "I never heard anything about her after that."

The chronicles of Florence are fairly bursting with stories of the city's great sons. They offer the most fascinating field for serious research or for mere random digging. One question, one comparison, constantly arises. Did Athens, in her golden era, shine as brilliantly as Florence? Did Attica produce as much genius, either by bulk or value, as Tuscany?

(FIFTEEN OF SIENA, UMBRIA AND ELSEWHERE)

Siena developed its school of art more or less in the same three centuries that Florence did, while the Umbrian school flourished chiefly in the seventy years between 1450 and 1520. Individual masters of Pisa, Padua, Rome, Milan and Parma brought luster to their respective cities. With the exception of Pisa, which flowered very early, most of these scattered cities developed their native artists at about the same period as the peak of Umbrian achievement. There was, of course, much moving about, as artists of one city were commissioned to do work for others, and it goes without saying that Rome, with its wealth and papal power, commandeered genius wherever and whenever it wished.

Of Siena's great, five demand listing.

Duccio di Buoninsegna (ca. 1255-ca. 1319) founded the Sienese School and left, among other works, one of his greatest masterpieces there, a double painting done for an altar in the cathedral but now shown in the *Cathedral Museum.* Duccio performed a wonderful service for the somewhat faltering Christianity of his day by painting warm, understandable pictures of the life of Christ instead of the stylized and unconvincing Madonnas of the preceding Byzantine period that had left the shrines of worshipers so bleak in emotional stimuli. Much Sienese painting, including that by Duccio, was done in tempera. Semi-precious, and even precious stones, including rubies, were mixed with egg yolk to enhance the glow of the pigments, the whole being then covered with white of egg.

Lorenzo Maitani (1275-1330), a pioneer Sienese architect and sculptor with some gift for painting as well, left as a memorial to his genius one work of surpassing magnificence, the polychrome façade of the Italian Gothic Cathedral of Orvieto. This is generally called, without qualification, the finest major work in polychrome ever achieved anywhere. Maitani did also the bronze angels of the main portal, but he must have "shot his bolt" on this Orvieto work, for the traveler finds few traces of him in Siena or elsewhere and even the omniscient Joseph Fatorusso can seem to find nothing else of Maitani that deserves special comment or picturing.

Ambrogio Lorenzetti (1300(?)-1348) of Siena "was born when he was born," there being no record of the exact year, but he seems to have died of the plague in 1348. He put fresh warmth and power into Sienese art, and the vigor of his frescoes depicting allegories of *Good Government in Siena* and *Bad Government or Tyranny* must have been strong and perennial sermons. They are still admired, in spite of much damage and deterioration, on the walls of the Sala della Pace in his home town's Palazzo Pubblico.

Iacopo della Quercia (1374-1438) got his surname, "of the Oak," from the village of *Grossa Quércia,* just outside Siena, where he was born. This early but greatly gifted sculptor is credited with doing for stonecarving what Masaccio did for painting. He escaped from the spirit of medievalism and established his art on a sculptural rather than a mere pictorial basis. One of his greatest works, and certainly his most popular one, is the Fonte Gaia, or Gay Fountain, a lovely and unusual work seen in faithful replica in the lovely and unusual Campo, a shell-shaped piazza of Siena. This book shall have more to say of della Quercia in Chapter 16.

Il Sodoma (1477-1549), whose actual name was Giovanni Bazzi, earned his unpleasant nickname, according to Vasari, who disliked him and disparaged his talent, because of his unnatural sex habits, but many students think Vasari, whose fitness to undertake his *History of the Painters* Bazzi openly ridiculed, was merely taking his revenge. The artist had an extra family name, Sodona, say these critics, which was quite naturally corrupted to Sodoma. Be that as it may, this Sienese master, though extremely uneven in his work, painted a number of pictures of the first rank. Some good ones are in the churches of Siena, but the most famous work, *The Nuptials of Alexander and Roxana*, is in the Villa Farnesina of Rome, which was, in the artist's time, a Roman residence of the wealthy Sienese banker, Agostino Chigi.

* * *

Of Umbria's great, just five, as in Siena's case, seem to demand mention. They will be listed in the order of their birth.

Piero della Francesca (1420-92), a quattrocentisto who pioneered in the study of perspective and decorative design, achieved a mastery of backgrounds and of light effects that made him a commanding figure in the development of the Umbrian school. His most widely praised masterpiece is the *Legend of the Sacred Cross* in the Church of San Francesco in Arezzo.

Luca Signorelli (1441-1523) was a pupil of Piero della Francesca, but, as happened in so many parallel cases in art and in music, he grew up to exceed by far the achievements of his teacher. It has been Signorelli's fate to remain obscure in popular estimation because he left no work in Florence or Rome or other great cities, but only in small towns such as Cortona (his birthplace) and Orvieto and in the Monastery of Monte Oliveto Maggiore, at some distance from Siena. He was a rich man who could easily have become a shallow sybarite but who worked intensely to perfect himself, especially in the novel field of anatomy. His work in the Capella Nuova of Orvieto's cathedral (see Chapter 16) is almost startling as a forerunner, at least in the anatomical power of its figures, of Michelangelo, who owed a great deal to the Umbrian. Signorelli is very much greater than his fame in the world at large.

Perugino (1446-1523) means simply "Perugian," and the adjective was applied, almost as a surname, to Pietro Vannucci, the name that today graces the main corso of that glorious Umbrian hill city, Perugia. Perugino, like Signorelli, was a pupil of Piero della Francesca, but he developed along utterly different lines. He has always been far more popular and beloved than his fellow-pupil because he found the "formula" for sweet, almost cloying Madonnas and angels (even his warriors and emperors exude sweetness), but students agree that Signorelli was a far greater artist. This book has no desire to belittle an able artist who has been so warmly loved for so many centuries and it shall have more to say of "the Perugian" when it reaches his city (Chapter 16). One of his most satisfying works, however, is not there but in the Sistine Chapel of the Vatican, a fresco of *Christ Giving the Keys to St. Peter*.

Pinturicchio (1454-1513) was destined to carry his affectionately bestowed nickname all his life. It means "Little Painter" and was borne by Bernardino di Betto, an apt pupil of Perugino. His best work is in the cathedral library of Siena, representing scenes from the life of Aeneas Silvius Piccolomini, who became Pope Pius II. These Piccolomini frescoes are of special appeal to visitors because they are wonderfully preserved, as fresh, it seems, as when he painted them in the years 1505 to 1507.

Raphael (1483-1520), whose proper native name was Raffaello Sanzio (or Santi) da Urbino, left the most celebrated name, in painting, of the entire galaxy of Renaissance artists, and had his life not been cut so tragically short—he died of a fever before his thirty-seventh birthday—he would likely have attained a stature fully to match his overpowering fame. Born in Urbino, now a sleepy little hill town of great charm amid a stormy sea of hills, and brought up in the cultured court of the Duke of Montefeltro he never had to struggle, as did his contemporary Michelangelo. At sixteen he became a pupil of Perugino and was drawn into his orbit of sweetness and light, acquiring habits of gentleness in portraiture that stayed with him, in some degree, even in his most vigorous work. He spent a second period in Florence, in association with Leonardo da Vinci and other bold spirits, developing greatly in power. A third period was spent in Rome, where he decorated various *stanze* (rooms) of the Vatican with superb frescoes. Profiting from companionship and rivalry with the great artists of his time, including Michelangelo, he became very great himself. He did, in fact, become a legend, one of the most courted and admired men in all Europe. His output of master works, supported by many assistants, was astonishing for so short a life and one finds him represented in many a city all over Italy and all over the world, Rome and Florence exceeding others in this wealth of marvelous compositions. Raphael lies buried in the Pantheon at Rome.

* * *

Among the Scattered Great, five cities and five men must be listed.

Pisa: Nicolò (or Nicola) *Pisano* (ca. 1210-ca. 1278) was the greatest of a great family of Pisans—hence the name—who were pioneer sculptors and especially pulpit builders. They are called *Dugentisti* because the two outstanding ones, Nicolò and his son Giovanni, lived and worked in the twelve hundreds. Nicolò's finest pulpit is doubtless the elaborate hexagonal one of marble in the baptistery at Pisa. More will be said of the Pisani in Chapter 19.

Padua: Andrea Mantegna (1431-1506) was a "revivalist" of classic styles of Greece and Rome, a sort of one-man art school which was destined to die with him. He was a supremely gifted line engraver as well as a painter, and left his work not only in Mantua, from which city he got his name, and in Padua, whose art he influenced, but in Milan, Florence, Venice and several other cities.

Rome: Donato Bramante (1444-1514) was the real founder and moving spirit of the Roman school of Renaissance architecture and for that reason, although he was born in Umbria, near Urbino, and did much early work in Milan, he seems to fit in this "Scattered" group of individual leaders as a Roman of the Romans. He had a major hand in the design of St. Peter's, which, however, Michelangelo and Bernini altered very substantially after his death. This very great architect and able-enough painter allowed his life to be warped and his work to be somewhat hampered by a gnawing jealousy of his younger and more versatile rival, Michelangelo.

Parma: Antonio Allegri da Corregio (1494-1534) was born in the town, not far from Parma, which is his surname. He headed the Parmesan school and brought it great fame, but so eminent a critic as

John Addington Symonds has blamed his "affectation, . . . his all-pervading sweetness, his infantine prettiness" for wreaking havoc with Italian art for centuries. Others, agreeing that Corregio's influence was enormous, have found his work tender, beautiful, joyous and of special interest for its mastery of chiaroscuro. All agree that he had sensuous power. A traditional *Leda* of his once shocked a visitor in a German gallery to such extent that the outraged man cut off, or cut out, the head of the lady from the canvas in punishment for her "vice" but the head was later restored to Leda. Corregio's best work is right where it belongs, in the cathedral and picture gallery of Parma and in the same city's Church of San Giovanni Evangelista.

Rome: Giovanni Lorenzo Bernini (1598-1680), like Michelangelo a sculptor, architect and painter, was born in Naples but is chiefly associated with Rome. He had such outstanding talents that he was able to dominate the artistic projects of the papacy for half a century. The huge colonnade encircling St. Peter's Square is his best-known work and several of the most famous fountains in Rome were designed by him.

(TEN OF VENICE IN A SWAN SONG)

The Venetian masters, forming a school of art second only to Florence in its wealth of great and near-great artists, do not fall into any neat classification, as the Florentines do. In general, they were of a much later vintage, flourishing chiefly in the fifteen hundreds and then managing a creditable revival, the swan song of the Renaissance, as late as the seventeen hundreds. The Selected Ten shall be presented here in the chronological order of their birth, regardless of how long they lived and worked.

Giovanni Bellini (1430-1516) was the fountainhead of Venetian art, teacher of such masters as Giorgione, Palma Vecchio and even the mighty Titian. Influenced at first by the classical and almost ascetic techniques of Mantegna, who was his brother-in-law, he developed gradually a much more mellow, not to say sensuous, style. Venice itself is the one satisfying place to see Bellini's works and they are at their best in two of the city's churches, Santa Maria Gloriosa dei Frari and San Zaccaria. As so often in Italian art, Bellini was but one, the leading one, of an able family of artists. Iacopo, his father, and

Gentile, his brother, were both gifted men and would loom larger had not Giovanni so far outshone them.

Vittore Carpaccio (ca. 1450-ca. 1522) is best known as a colorful painter of historical scenes and of Venetian pageantry, with its reflections of the venturesome spirit of Marco Polo. His most famous works are in his home city in the Accademia di Belle Arti and the Church of San Giorgio Maggiore.

Giorgione (1477-1510) has been called by Frank Schoonmaker, who wrote well on art before he turned to the study of fine wines, "the first painter of symphonies—of pictures wherein a dozen different but interdependent themes were combined to produce a single end and a single effect." The critic credits Giotto with being the first to bring life and action into painting; Masaccio with being the "first and perhaps the greatest realist," and Giorgione, whom he dubs "the third prophet of Italian art," with introducing "symphonic splendor." Giorgione's name is as mysterious as himself. He was long thought to have been the natural son of a member of the noble Barbarelli family by a peasant girl of the Venetian mainland, but modern research seems to show that this story was a bit of "bragging" invented by the Barbarellis after he became famous. He was probably of extremely humble, but legitimate, peasant parentage and may have borne the surname Zorzon. The date of his birth is sheer guesswork.

Palma Vecchio (ca. 1480-ca. 1528) was a short-living contemporary of very-long-living Titian and studied for a time under Titian, though the latter was about eight years his junior. Palma Vecchio, as a name, means simply Old Palma to distinguish him from Young Palma (Palma Giovane), who was his grandnephew, a painter of mediocre attainments. Old Palma was a master of unquestioned ability, just a shade or two below the first rank of greatness. He is notable for his rich coloring, as seen, for instance, in the six paintings of Venice's Church of Santa Maria Formosa. A favorite face in his portraits is of a beautiful girl named Violante who is said, by tradition, to have been his daughter and is said also to have been at one period Titian's light o' love.

Titian (1477-1576) lived an almost incredible ninety-nine years, *if* he himself was "telling it straight" about the date of his birth. He was called by his contemporaries Tiziano Vecelli da Cadore, the last name being from the region of his birth, Cadore, in the Upper Piave Valley amid fantastic Dolomite peaks. Titian was a giant of painting, one of the supremely great of all time and of all lands, yet he was Venetian of the Venetians, bringing the rich coloring and portraiture of that school to its loftiest levels. He started painting when he was a youth, yet when in his nineties (again *if* he was truthful about his age) he was still wielding a skillful and untrembling brush. Venice, it goes without saying, is the natural place to study Titian. He is seen everywhere, in the Old Library (near St. Mark's), in the Doges' Palace, in the Accademia, in the Church of Santa Maria Gloriosa dei Frari (where he is entombed in a fine sarcophagus) and in many another church of the city. He is also seen, in the full power of his genius, in the great galleries of Florence, in Milan's Brera, in Rome's Borghese Gallery and in Naples' National Museum. Other Titians are hung in galleries all over Europe, all over the world, for this artist had a lot of time to work. In sacred and secular paintings he had equal success, but in the latter category his Venuses do not *bulge* like those of Rubens and the other Flemish masters. That must be, we are sure, from observation, because Italian women do not, in general, bulge like those of Flanders. Titian's brilliancy in red is, of course, the origin of the popular adjective Titian-haired.

Tintoretto (1518-94) was christened Iacopo Robusti and the diminutive by which he is universally known is a nickname meaning Little Dyer given to him because his father was a full-sized dyer (*tintore*) by profession. The Little Dyer was called also *Il Furioso* because of his furious speed and tirelessness in work. He did oil paintings by the hundreds, some of them huge, and he covered walls with frescoes by the acre, it seems. An oil painting of *Paradise*, in the Hall of the Great Council in the Doges' Palace, is claimed to be the largest picture in the world (24 feet by 74, with several large "jogs") by any recognized master, but one wonders if the claimants have forgotten the Mexican muralists. It is, at any rate, probably the largest *oil* painting, with about five hundred figures in it. His forty canvases on Old Testament themes and on the story of Christ, seen in the School of San Rocco in Venice, are considered his finest achievement, as they are also his most titanic undertaking. (*Life*, in its issue of December 2, 1951, devoted twenty pages to the reproduction of these works in color.) All Italy and indeed all Europe is fairly plastered by Tintorettos and much of the painting is very good. It is said that this artist aimed to combine in his own work the color mastery of Titian with the power of draughtsmanship of Michelangelo. He was indeed a mighty man of art and if only he could have managed, by disciplining his wild spirit, to become *Il Moderato* instead of Il Furioso it almost appears that he would have achieved his vast ambition. His works are everywhere in Venice. It would be hard for the hastiest tourist to miss the Little Dyer.

Paolo Veronese (1528-88) acquired his surname, according to the frequent custom of the time, from his home city, which was Verona, but at an early age he transferred to Venice and that became his permanent home. The artist's real name was Paolo Caliari. Like Carpaccio, he loved the glitter of pageantry and whether the subject matter of a composition was religious or worldly he could rarely resist painting pomp and splendid clothing and accouterments. Venice is appropriately rich in his works, and the Church of San Sebastiano is almost a personal monument to him. It is filled with his paintings, on walls and on ceiling. The organ was built to his designs and he painted its panels. Finally, the church for which he did so much serves as his resting place, for he was buried here a few days after his death.

Giovanni Battista Tiepolo (1696-1770) is called by Fattorusso "the last of the old painters and the first of the moderns." He was a first-rate colorist, with a master's knowledge of perspective. His art is seen in several churches and, as one would expect, in the halls of the Doges' Palace, but one of his most appealing works is the decoration of the Colleoni Chapel in Upper Bergamo.

Canaletto (1697-1768) was a nickname actually given to two Venetian painters, a teacher and his pupil, who was also his nephew. The teacher, whose dates are given above, was Antonio Canale and the nickname is therefore a mere diminutive. The pupil, who did not, in this case, measure up in talent to his teacher, was named Bernardo Bellotto. The older and more important Canaletto, a native of Venice who spent a few years in Rome and a few also in England, where he painted landscapes in the vicinity of Eton, devoted most of his artistic career to depicting color-rich scenes of his own city, especially the Grand Canal and the unique ensemble of the

Doges' Palace, the Piazzetta and St. Mark's. The older Canaletto was almost an exact contemporary of Tiepolo and shared with him in rendering the swan song of the Venetian school.

Antonio Canova (1757-1822), a relatively modern Venetian sculptor who attained great fame, can certainly not be considered as of the Renaissance, even in its Venetian swan song, but he is too important to be excluded from the list. He was the leader of a brief Classic Revival in Italy and left some notable works which are admired as much in our day as they were in his. Among the finest of these are two statues of Venus for which the sculptor used as a model Pauline Borghese, sister of Napoleon I. Pauline, however flippant and sexy and selfish, was certainly a very pretty young lady and the *Venus Victrix*, in the Villa Borghese of Rome, is one of the most popular statues with tourists, in all Italy. Canova made several imposing tombs for popes and royalty (the exiled Stuarts), and in the Frari Church of Venice is his own tomb, designed by him and executed by his pupils. With the passing of Canova, who seems almost like a *reflection* of Italy's past, the Scrolls of the Great in Art come to an end, until some miracle causes a rebirth of the talents that must surely lie dormant in the Eternal Peninsula.

YOURSELF IN THE PICTURE OF ROME

CHAPTER 10

THE ROME YOU ENTER NOW

Approaching and Settling

However you enter Rome, whether by plane, train, motor coach or private car, you are likely to "dismount" in its very heart, its tourist heart that is, by which I mean Piazza Esedra, with its main artery Via Nazionale, and the adjacent lungs, stretching east to that large park and larger square (Piazza dei Cinquecento) upon which the incredibly large railway station fronts.

To abandon metaphors and bring on facts, the coaches that carry arriving travelers into the city from Ciampino Airport deposit them in the Hotel Quirinale on Via Nazionale if the service is BOAC or BEA, in the new air terminal within the railway station if the service is Air France, Pan American, TWA, KLM or any other. All trains except those of the Ostia Line and the old Viterbo Line deposit travelers in the same far-spreading structure, the Stazione Termini. The motor coaches that traverse the trunk highways, meaning chiefly those of CIAT, weaving their intricate patterns up and down the peninsula, come to rest *in* Piazza Esedra, in front of the head offices of CIT and CIAT.

If you come by your own car, things may be a bit different. Coming from Florence or anywhere in the north you will probably find yourself bowling along the Via Flaminia to the Porta del Popolo. From here it is easy to reach the tourist center through the Borghese Gardens to Via Véneto, or by way of Via Babuino to the Piazza di Spagna and straight on (passing through the tunnel) to Via Nazionale, etc. Coming from Naples and the south, you could use the so-called New Appian Way, to enter by the Porta San Giovanni, near St. John Lateran; or, much more pleasurably, by the brand-new road through the Exposition Grounds called EUR (see end of Chapter 11), continuing by the splendid avenue named for Columbus and in a later stretch for the Baths (Terme) of Caracalla, and so to the Colosseum. I am beating the gun to mention this new approach, for it is not quite yet open, though I hope it will be when you read these words. It is soon to be a wonder road, the whole way, starting from Naples by way of Posíllipo, cutting through a tunnel and then hugging the seacoast clear to Fórmia, finally traversing the reclaimed Pontine area (Latina, etc.) to reach Rome.

Few tourists realize that Rome is still a walled city and that there are no less than fourteen named *Porte*, or Gates. In two stretches the Tiber serves as wall and there are a few small gaps where the ramparts have yielded to modern pressures, but in general the wall we see, and penetrate by one means or another, including the railway tracks, is the same one that Emperor Aurelian undertook to build in 271 A.D. to keep out the barbarians. They do not keep out the tourists, the invaders of today, even though a few of them (us) do act like barbarians.

Rome has spilled far outside its Aurelian Walls. Four centuries ago, in the period of the city's worst decline, the population had sunk to 32,000. By the census of 1951 it had exactly 1,600,011 inhabitants and, by press estimates, was growing at about the same rate as Los Angeles. Tourist population grows with it and the scores of large hotels are often bursting at their seams, even in spring and fall, not to mention the high travel season of summer. Forehandedness in making reservations in Rome (as in Florence, Venice, Naples) is highly advisable, and for those who can come only at the time of the greatest influx, it is almost essential.

Problems of Orientation

Street maps of Rome were slow in catching up with events and for years after Mussolini cut through some new streets, maps that were offered to tourists often showed the former labyrinths instead of the newer, simpler design. A notable case in point is the broad, up-to-the-minute street of air offices (and of Rome's finest cinema, "Fiamma"),Via Bissolati. Shortly before the new air terminal was established in the railway station, I once came by plane and arrived in a coach at Via Bissolati very early in the morning. The map in a newly published guidebook ushered me into the Department of Utter Confusion. There was no Via Bissolati on the old map in my new book and it took me a good quarter of an hour of footwork and map correction to determine just where I was.

At last this annoying situation has been largely cleared up and good maps in a variety of forms are easy to pick up. Let me enumerate a few.

The *sectional* maps in the Nagel guide are excellent, as clear as a May morning. A general one of the city, four sectional maps, a special one of the forum area, another of the Vatican and St. Peter's, give the tourist all he usually wants. The only difficulty is that *book* maps are hard to use in tourist practice in the big cities of Europe.

Ente Provinciale per il Turismo, glowingly mentioned in Chapter 3, with its Rome office at 47 Via Barberini, publishes really wonderful maps. The one called simply *Rome* is a little booklet, no bigger than a fat letter, with twelve sectional maps, an assemblage of them all as key, a clear plan of St. Peter's, with its monuments, and one of Vatican City, a motorist's chart for entering and leaving the capital, a directory of all the city's streets and squares, and finally, to enhance all this, twelve pages of condensed guidebook facts, in English. The Ente office also publishes a small *Pianta di Roma* (Plan of Rome), about eight inches by ten, with the chief bus lines (*Autobus* and *Auto-pullman*), tram lines (*Linee Tranviarie*) and trolleybus lines (*Linee Filoviarie*) listed on the back with their respective numbers and the routes they traverse. To give background to all this, it publishes an English-language *Guide of Rome,* in 80 packed pages, with a clear general map pasted in it. This guide, detailed and well done, deserves much more than the parenthetical mention here being given.

The best one-page map of Rome I have seen at all seems to be nameless, a thing apparently designed for the advertising uses of travel organizations. On its title space (on the back) the following words appear: *Pianta di Roma; Offerta da,* but no firm or airline name is stamped on mine to indicate by whom it was "offerta" to me! Perhaps I lifted it from the table of some tourist or airline office. I really wouldn't know. But I hope that by good luck one will be offerta to you, or that you likewise can gather one in somehow. Its sides and its reverse are packed to the gunwales with all the trade and entertainment listings and transportation routes and *Indirizzi Utili* (Useful addresses) you could possibly want.

Failing the luck to pick up the remarkable map-without-an-author, you'll find that any Rome bookshop (*libreria*) will have a variety of offerings for sale. A wonderfully complete one, now not too easy to come by after the lapse of years, *was* the *Jubilee Year Plan of Rome*, specially published in 1950 by SEAG (Società Editoriale Anno Giubilare), with a separate transportation map thrown in. One wishes this could be kept alive. Another large and fairly clear one, but without any listings of any kind for tourists, is published by Lozzi Editore, 57 Via della Frezza.

A half hour's concentrated study of any good map *before* starting out on Roman rambles can save ten times half an hour in wasted steps in wrong directions, though, in another sense, it is hard to waste time in *any* direction in this incredibly scene-rich city. Those who like to systematize their thrills may find it convenient to divide Sightseers' Rome into six sectors, somewhat as follows:

Hotel Rome, from the Termini Station to the upper end of Via Véneto, though the newest and largest hotel of all, Hilton-managed, is to be on Monte Mário, on the far northwestern fringe of the city, on the Tiber's right bank. The old-established hotel sector, for orientation purposes, should certainly include the magnificent Pincian Gardens and the park called Villa Borghese, with the Borghese Gallery, the whole glamorous section being reached from Piazza Trinità dei Monti (Hotel Hassler Villa Medici) or from Via Véneto (Hotel Excelsior, etc., etc.).

Shoppers' Rome is the section west of the hotel belt, extending to the central Corso. Among the chief shopping streets are Via Nazionale, Via Venti Settembre, Via del Tritone and the whole crowded gridiron of little streets that fill the wedge of Rome between the Corso and Via Babuino, with its extension through Piazza di Spagna to Largo Tritone. The Corso itself, continuing for three-quarters of a mile from Piazza Venezia to Piazza del Popolo, is a shopping stem of venerable standing, with a galleria near its central point, though this does not compare with the larger gallerie of Milan and Naples. *Santa Maria Maggiore* and *St. John Lateran*, two of the supreme Christian basilicas

Italian State Tourist Office

The immensely rambling Vatican, with Michelangelo's great dome of St. Peter's in the background.

St. Peter's Square on "any day," with priests, fountain and the Bernini colonnade.

Italian State Tourist Office

Italian State Tourist Office

(Upper) A tower's-eye view of Milan's Cathedral Square.

(Lower) The Neptune Fountain in Rome's Piazza Navona.

Italian State Tourist Office

(Upper) One of the two bronze Moors that ring the bell on the clock tower of Piazza San Marco in Venice.

(Lower) Sicily's coast line and Mt. Etna seen from Taormina.

Ediz. A. A. Mag. Standa, Perúgia

An archway of Perúgia, hill city of the ages.

The village of Vinci, in Tuscany, where Leonardo, "genius of all trades," was born in a peasant home.

Ditta Stefano Venturini, Siena

The shell-shaped Campo in Siena, second in glamor only to Piazza San Marco in Venice. Here the celebrated horse race of *Il Palio* takes place.

Italian State Tourist Office

The towers of San Gimignano, near Siena, were familiar to Dante.

Brunner & Co., Como

A glimpse of Florence from Fiesole. The cathedral, with its celebrated dome, is flanked by Giotto's Tower.

The six pills, symbol of the Medici, seen everywhere in Florence and throughout Tuscany.

Italian State Tourist Office

Michelangelo's drunken Bacchus in the Bargello of Florence. Note that a sly faun behind the wine god is trying to give him more grapes.

Italian State Tourist Office

(Upper) The motor bridge over the Ádige into and through Can Grande's Castle in Verona.

(Lower) The Bargello's courtyard in Florence, formerly a place of execution, now the center of a great museum of art.

Ediz. Pratesi, Florence

Italy's most famous bridge, the Ponte Vecchio of Florence. Its interesting shops, offering many a good buy, jut out over the Arno.

Italian State Tourist Office

The grape harvest provides gaiety in many parts of Italy.

Casa Rag. Cav. Alfredo Reffi, San Marino

One of the three hilltop towers of the tiny Republic of San Marino, embedded in Italy. San Marino is a marvel of travel, too little known.

Italian State Tourist Office

The magic of Venice, as the plane sees it. The quay in the foreground is Riva degli Schiavoni.

A gondola cortege on the Grand Canal during a local festival.

of Rome, rising at opposite ends of the broad Via Merulana, may be roughly included in this sector.

Forum Rome, including the Capitoline, the Colosseum and even the Baths of Caracalla.

The Tiber Pocket, containing infinite treasures of Ancient Rome, an area that tourism too often neglects, with the one exception of the Pantheon.

St. Peter's and the Vatican, with the *Castel Sant'Angelo* as corollary.

Trastevere, meaning The Other-Side-of-the-Tiber, an appealing area almost totally overlooked by tourists except for the Janiculum Hill, which looms above it.

A few of the great sights of Rome do not fall within any of the six chief areas, for instance, the Church of St. Paul-without-the-Walls, the Pyramid of Caius Cestius and Mussolini's showy Foro Italico, lavish in statues, lavish in tribute to the Caesar-who-fell; also, and nowadays importantly, the EUR Exposition Grounds, of which I shall say more at the end of this chapter.

The original Seven Hills of Rome, hardly more than hillocks, with an average above-Tiber height of but one hundred feet, are the Palatine, the Capitoline, the Quirinal, the Aventine, the Esquiline, the Viminal and the Caelian. Such popular heights as the Pincian and the Janiculum are upstarts in the picture and Monte Mário is a hill-come-lately that is destined for much more importance when its new palace of tourism is completed.

Simplicities of the Fixed Tours

All Rome's travel offices arrange guided tours of the city and its environs and all the hall porters of the chief hotels are eager middlemen in the business. In my opinion, the concern that is the most Roman of them all—of course I mean CIT—is especially well equipped to take you where you should go and to explain in clear, authoritative terms the meaning of what you see. I have found its guides educated rather than glib, honest in their patter rather than flippant or (as guides in all lands too often imagine) "entertaining," by use of unabashed distortions thought to be exciting, or jokes thought to be funny.

In two morning trips and two afternoon trips, CIT covers the essentials of Rome. (Trips to the environs will be discussed in Chapter 13.) The coach calls for you at your hotel and at the conclusion of the tour delivers you at your hotel. Canned tours have their frank devotees ("It's *so* much easier") and their firm detractors ("You don't catch *me* going in a herd"). If you are in the latter category, give some thought to breaking your rule in Rome. Of all the tourist cities I know, including London and Paris, none, I think, matches Rome in its complexity of lures, and if you want a touch of everything without burdening your budget by the hire of a private car and guide, consider these well-run, dignified tours. The "best people," I assure you, will be your companions, including plenty of tourists who could well afford the Cadillac-and-courier method of viewing the city.

American Express (38 Piazza di Spagna) is, of course, an eager and recommendable purveyor of city tours, providing some circuits that are not duplicated by others. *Cook* (offices at 11 Via Véneto and 83 Piazza San Silvestro) is another old hand at the game, backed by decades of experience. *Carrani Travel Service* (95 Via delle Terme) is, I believe, still another dependable office, though I have never happened to try it. *Via Travel Service* (105 Via Due Macelli) seems to specialize on palpitating Rome-by-Night tours. You should not expect another Paris, so far as night clubs and naughtiness go. However, you may certainly expect to see some grand and moving sights in the floodlighting of ancient, medieval and modern Rome, and the nightspot specialties *are* special to this city as will be explained later in this chapter.

But Finding Is Keeping

Having paid my respects to the fixed tours I must offer a tribute of personal affection to the Rome that is *found*—by personal trial and error. There is no other city that rewards so lavishly the aimless stroller, and to give Mussolini his due, the rewards are much greater than before his energies uncovered Ancient Rome to its present extent, revealing and cherishing hundreds of charming bits from classical times.

Just for instance, I was strolling aimlessly one day in the "Tiber

Pocket" when I came upon Piazza Zanardelli, as I had known it many years before. I found that sign on a building, but mysteriously beside it I found another and a newer sign designating the square as *Piazza di Tor Sanguigna*. This puzzled me until I saw that *inside* a moderately new and large apartment house just off the square there was a big chunk of what I took to be the lower portion of the tor for which the square had been re-named. Mussolini, I assumed, had forbidden the builder to remove a single classic stone. The structure must accordingly enfold it.

But what was the Tor Sanguigna? In vain I ransacked all my guidebooks—I had a lot of them—and two or three encyclopedias. Finally, an Italian friend with a rare nose for following historical scents dug up for me the fact that a noble family named Sanguigni did indeed live here—until 1300 when this clan died out—and did indeed have a tor (torre) here, in the bellicose spirit of their era.

Finding is keeping, and since I found the Tor Sanguigna I *kept* it, far more than anything that was presented to me in a prepared talk by a fluent professional guide.

And for a different sort of instance, I was meandering one sunny April afternoon down the lower portion of Via Nazionale when I saw crowds of people in what seemed to be a garden up aloft on top of ramparts. How to get there without a scaling ladder? I asked two or three passers-by and they didn't have the faintest idea. Finally, by considerable footwork, I found the entrance, on a side street, Via Mazzarino, and climbed the steps to one of the loveliest and most lavish displays of azaleas I have ever seen. It was Azalea Week, I learned, and this was the *Giardino Aldobrandini*. Its southwestern side loomed very high above Piazza Magnanapoli, and beyond this was that prodigious "Wedding Cake," the Monument of Victor Emmanuel II.

These are but two samples of my own chance discoveries, which it would be easy to multiply. You too will find things from the Classic World, the Church World, the Art World, even from today's new and newer world. Discoveries won't be exhausted, for no book and no series of guided tours can do more than brush the scintillating surface of the Eternal City.

In personal exploring, intelligent use of public transportation, in place of taxis and horse-drawn cabs, may add to one's pleasure rather than detract from it. It is necessary, of course, to procure an up-to-date list of the various city lines, bus, trolleybus and tram. Their numbers occasionally change. For instance the trolleybus from the Termini Station to Piazza di Spagna and Piazza del Popolo, known to tourists for years under the sign EF, became 78 a while ago and starts now from the station square instead of from just beside the Hotel Continentale. An even more conspicuous trolleybus route, however, running from Piazza Esedra by way of Piazza Venezia to St. Peter's Square, seems content with its established letters: MB. The three chief *starting points* for transportation lines, so far as tourism is concerned, are the above-mentioned Termini Station Square; Piazza San Silvestro, in front of the main post office; and Largo Chigi, just off the central point of the Corso, beside the big Galleria.

The Restaurants of Rome

In Rome, as in Paris, the visitor who arranges his stay on an American Plan basis, all meals to be taken in the hotel where he lodges, robs himself of one of the most exciting adventures in gastronomy, for there are scores, perhaps hundreds, of good restaurants, serving Italian, not French or international, meals and there are certainly a dozen or more of superior quality. There are others, in plenty, of special character in food or setting, and still others, as briefly mentioned earlier, where one may eat, and *well,* under the moon and the stars, or under gay lanterns.

Among the established city restaurants, perhaps the most celebrated is the *Hostaria dell'Orso,* at 93 Via Monte Brianzo, close to the Tiber bridge called Ponte Umberto I. It is a place of assured elegance, of very special atmosphere and of wonderful and special food, though I've never had bear meat there, as its name, Inn of the Bear, would seem to suggest. It is a massive sort of place, and with its *trecento* style (of the 1300's), its stone work and its fireplaces, it seems like a retreat for the Frangipani and their Ghibelline cronies. The claim is seriously made, especially by the proprietor and the head waiter, that a more celebrated personage, Dante, who was not a Ghibelline but a White Guelph, actually lived here for a time. His very room is pointed out, and in it one may eat. It is asserted also that Leonardo da Vinci, two centuries later, often partook of food and wine here, and there is no question that many literary men have frequented it, including the two named in an earlier chapter, Montaigne and Rabelais. Today it is a retreat for those who relish epicurean fare in an unforgettable restaurant—and are willing to "pay accordingly." It is one of three Roman restaurants with an official de luxe rating, the other two being *Casina Valadier* and *Casina delle Rose*, already mentioned with enthusiasm as places for "eating under the sky."

Another restaurant of wide fame is that of *Alfredo*, located on Piazza Augusto Imperio, just off the Corso. This is now the only restaurant in Rome actually presided over by *the* Alfredo himself. Two others, on Via della Scrofa and in Trastevere, bear his name and lure some tourists from the "original and only." Alfredo is not particularly bashful. He calls himself, on his menus, his chinaware, his glassware, his napery, IL VERO RE DELLE FETTUCCINE (The Genuine Noodle King) and the specialty of the house, set forth in vast capitals on the bill of fare and urgently advised by all the waiters, is: *Maestosissime Fettuccine all'Alfredo*. The first word means, of course, "most majestic," like the climactic movement of a mighty symphony. Alfredo himself, looking maestosissimo with his distinguished bearing and his wide white mustache, holds the baton, a double baton in the form of a large spoon and fork, often the solid gold implements given him by Douglas Fairbanks and Mary Pickford, and mixes the platter of fettuccine, doing the task with incredible gusto and flourish in a ceremony that rivals, for pomp and circumstance, the preparation of the numbered duck in *La Tour d'Argent* of Paris. Upon conclusion of the ceremony, he places the noodles before the patron, bowing ceremoniously and intoning "È l'originale." It is a good show and a wonderful dish. Don't miss either.

The restaurant called *Alfredo alla Scrofa*, at 104 Via della Scrofa, is most cheerful and excellent, even if the maître cannot declaim its *original* status. It is gay and bright, with strolling musicians wandering in and out during the dinner hours, in the casual manner so common in Rome.

Fagiano, on Piazza Colonna, is a first-class place in the very heart of the city, with an appealing terrace from which one may watch the beating of the Roman heart as one lunches or dines in leisure. The name Fagiano means Pheasant and perhaps the management sometimes suits the menu to the word, but in any case you may eat well and glamorously here.

San Carlo, on Piazza San Carlo al Corso, halfway between Piazza Colonna and Piazza del Popolo, has and deserves a good rating on any list. The management freely admits this, widely advertising itself as *il ristorante più rinomato di Roma*.

Ranieri, at 26 Via Mario dei Fiori, near Piazza di Spagna, is a place of elegance and first-rate cuisine, specializing in game.

Bel Sito and *Faro*, in the Monte Mário sector, have many devoted clients.

Roma, *Rupe Tarpea*, *Nino*, *Passetto*, all first-class, are but four more of the many pleasant places to eat in Rome. The abundance of good-to-excellent restaurants and the surprising quality of "the funny little place around the corner" begin to put Rome in the league with Paris and New York, though of course in a smaller way, since this is a smaller metropolis. Rome's Ente Provinciale per il Turismo puts out an exceedingly informative and sprightly pamphlet called *Gastronomy in Rome* that is packed with expert comment on the capital's restaurants and their specialties.

Ristoranti Caratteristici, meaning, in Rome, chiefly cellars of song, where bottles fill ample wall recesses from floor to ceiling and where guitars strum and singers sing, are numerous. They are wonderful fun and a couple of them need special mention.

Taverna Ulpia, on the east side of Piazza Foro Traiano, near Piazza Venezia, is definitely "characteristic." Its food is of top quality, its drinks, captained by a so-called nectar, an alcoholic concoction of cognac and Strega served in a Greek amphora, are—*heady*. Its atmosphere is awash with the sort of life that would be called *Stimmung* in Bavarian cities. A statue of a Roman emperor is on the landing of the stairway leading down to the cellar. The emperor is Nero! What he's doing there I can't figure out, except that he liked good liquor.

La Biblioteca del Valle, fronting on the Largo Teatro Valle in the Tiber bulge, is more Bohemian than the rather elegant Ulpia. The food, featuring *Cannelloni Valle*, is about as good, and the drinks, featuring a smooth wine oddly called *Acqua di Trevi*, quite as potent. This "Library," its "shelves" filled to repletion with bottles, suggests to me the atmosphere of Montparnasse.

Two other (among many) restaurants that are often in character classification are *La Cisterna*, at 13 Via della Cisterna, in Trastevere, and *Da Canepa* on Via Terme di Diocleziano, opposite the Grand Hotel. The former is perennially popular.

* * *

Open-air summer restaurants abound during Rome's long summer. Two conspicuous and luxurious ones have been mentioned above. Several other Roman gardens of gastronomy are found on the highways outside Rome's gates, for example *Belvedere delle Rose*, on Via Cassia, beyond the Milvian Bridge, and *San Callisto*, on the Appian Way; and a pleasant garden, gayed by lanterns in the evening, is to be found in the very center of tourism, on the corner of Via Véneto and Via Boncompagni.

* * *

Student-type eating places may be found in Rome (more easily if you have a student friend) and one of them that I know favorably from several trials is a double-decker place called *Alla Taverna e All'Orto degli Artisti* (The Artists' Tavern and Kitchen-Garden) at 54 Via Margutta, a place very near the Piazza di Spagna but deceptively hard to find. From the square you walk a few steps down Via Babuino, turn right on Via Aliberti and then left on Via Margutta, a lost little street in the lee of Monte Pincio, entering finally an art-school-looking courtyard and bearing left till you find the entrance to the Taverna—and if you don't find it at all *be bold and ask*. Just the word *ristorante*, in a rising inflection, will do the trick. For a dollar, and perhaps well under (it costs less in the Taverna than in the Orto) you can buy a thoroughly good meal with a small carafe of wine. Members of the Artists' Association pay still less than their "amici" and a notice on the menu even asserts that *non-soci* may not enter without a "little ticket" furnished by a member. "This doesn't mean anything," said the head waiter to me. "It enables us to keep out persons we don't want, but any who come quietly and appreciatively will be welcomed." I like that, and since your serenity and appreciation measure up to the requirements, you will like it too, as you will like the food, a minestra item, a meat or fish dish (I had a luscious *polpo,* or octopus, delicacy here) and something tasty from the contorni sector. The Taverna is a large, cheerful upstairs room, filled with good student talk, and the Orto is up aloft. BUT, on my most recent visit I found the entire establishment closed for a Mostra (Exhibition). I was assured it would reopen "in a few months" and sincerely do I hope the assurance will have become a fact when and if you seek the place.

On side streets are scores of tiny restaurants where a dollar, or at least a dollar and a half, will still buy an adequate meal, sometimes very well cooked. Typical perhaps, though mentioned quite at random, is the little hole-in-the-wall called Trattoria Colline Emiliane, at 22 Via degli Avignonesi, a narrow canyon of a street near Piazza Barberini. Another, a trifle more expensive and much brighter to the eye, is a basement place called *Ristorante Véneto,* on Via Viminale at the corner of Via Principe Amedeo. I could go on with many more but you will *see* such places and will need no list. A restaurant that is full of patrons at meal time always attracts me. It is likely to be good, else it wouldn't be sought. One that is nearly empty, and there are lots of these, probably lives on the fringes of trade.

Bright Nights and Dim Ones

The reader is referred to the roundups in Chapter 6 "About Music, for All Brows" and "About Evenings in the Cities" for the essential facts about Roman entertainment, early, late and later, but some facts on theaters, movies and night clubs may here supplement the earlier comment.

Theaters offering plays in Italian necessarily have a limited appeal to visitors whose Italian is limited—as is my own—but a *Rivista* (Revue) is always good fun and if you go to one in Rome you will very likely find that compatriots of yours will be among the stars in song-and-dance offerings. Three theaters of the capital purvey revues, the *Barberini,* in Piazza Barberini, the *Bernini,* at 36 Via Borgognona, near Piazza di Spagna, and the *Quirino,* on Via dell'Umiltà, off the Corso. A back-number issue of *This Week in Rome,* now before me, lists as the star attraction of the Barberini, *Benny Goodman, il clarinista magico,* and as the star of the Quirino, *Josephine Baker col suo eccezionale spettacolo.*

Movie houses, known throughout Italy and all Europe as cinemas, are very numerous in Rome. The weekly guide lists ninety-two of the chief ones. Italy's own film industry, centering just outside the capital, has taken a leading role in the postwar world, as we all know, and virtually all the foreign films now shown in Italy are dubbed in with spoken Italian, so that, again, the plots are difficult to follow if one's knowledge of Italian is slight, though it *is* wonderful practice, as a langue lesson, to look and listen. When you behold Van Johnson, James Cagney, Loretta Young or Mitzi Gaynor spouting torrents of colloquial Italian you perhaps have a fair idea of what they *would* be saying, and this may add interest to the lesson.

Two cinemas, however, *Arcobaleno,* on Via Pastrengo near Piazza Esedra, and *Fiametta* (Little Flame) in the same building (around a corner) as the sumptuous *Fiamma* (Flame), on Rome's air-office street, Via Bissolati, almost always present films in the original language, usually English, sometimes French. Both of these small houses are of luxurious quality and comfort.

Top-ranking cinemas with reserved seats, but showing films that speak Italian, are the *Fiamma,* the *Rivoli,* on Via Lombardia, and the *Capranichetta,* on Piazza Monte Citorio.

Locali notturni, or night clubs, more often known as "Dancings" in Rome, are not numerous, especially when compared with cabaret towns like Paris and New York, but there are some first-rate places, especially in certain leading hotels (*Excelsior, Palazzo e Ambasciatori,* etc.). Among night clubs not in hotels two *summer places* of outstanding charm and quality are *La Lucciola,* in Villa Borghese Park, and the *Pincio,* a part of the much-mentioned Casina Valadier, on the Pincian Hill. Other places are *Florida* (18 Via Francesco Crispi); *Kit-Kat* (28 Via Liguria); *Whip Club* (73 Via Sistina); *Jicky Club* (13 Via Véneto); *Open Gate Club* (2 Via San Nicolò da Tolentino). Such boîtes as *Broadway* (87 Via Boncompagni) and *Nirvanetta* (on Via Maroniti, not far from the Largo Tritone) are anything but exclusive.

Night clubs in any large city shift about in quality, in name, in location, like the sand bars in a rip-tide sea, so a *book* is no place for discussion of them. *This Week in Rome* is the place to look, though there is nothing in the least discriminatory about its flat, all-alike listings. If you are in an exclusive, best-people mood you may stick to the top-rated cabarets in hotels and luxury gardens. If you are exploratory and don't blench or blanch or blush when a pretty signorina addresses you in "hostess English," try any of the places listed. It will be no surprise that these hostesses enjoy sipping thousand-lire drinks as they entertain(?) you with their pretty prattle. They make no secret of their expensive tastes. Their sisters are like that in every city in the world.

CHAPTER 11

FIVE ROMES IN A CITY'S FABRIC

Preliminary Thoughts

What shall we do about Rome? This city is a world in itself, *several* worlds in itself. No other city, not even Paris, presents such a problem to the traveler whose time is limited. The visitor to Paris generally has at least a vague idea of what he wishes to do and see, but one's approach to Rome is roiled with so many countercurrents that one is in danger of sinking in the whirlpool.

I believe it is possible, with copious use of philosophy, to enjoy Rome in a week, or even in half a week, if the traveler definitely accepts the limitations of time. The chief difficulty is that most of us do not accept these limitations. We rush around feverishly trying to see everything, and thus, to all intents, see nothing. It is necessary to think well before entering the Eternal City. Which of the three obvious Romes really interests you most, the Rome of the Romans, the Rome of the Christian Church and the popes, or the Rome of today? Or do you wish to see the very highest spots of each? Each is interwoven, as a matter of fact, with the others and you could not quite miss any of the Romes if you would. Modern Rome is especially pervasive and surprising to those who knew the capital a long time ago, even before Mussolini's energies took hold of it.

I think sound strategy suggests that, in any case, the first-time visitor give himself at least a couple of the fixed tours of CIT or some other dealer in city trips. This provides a sort of moving map of the terrain to be attacked, so that the nature of the attack can then be determined by each individual. But you will show sound generalship and not attempt to conquer Rome by a frontal attack on all its strongholds at once.

If the rolling wheels of a tourist chariot are good, for first impressions and basic facts, an inquiring mind, a rugged constitution and two sound feet are the best possible supplements. A great number of the noblest and most fascinating things Rome offers are well bunched in the half mile southeast of the Piazza Venezia and many others are within easy walking distance of the Corso. Walking is the thing, and furthermore, wheels simply will not climb the lofty Campidoglio Steps, nor even the Spanish Steps.

Roman Rome, with a Word About Il Duce

The devotion of the Departed Duce to the grandeurs of classic Rome is too well known to need retelling, and yet no one who knew the city three or four decades ago and has not seen it since can credit the immense changes that took place in revealing the Rome of the Romans. No such wholesale remaking of an old city has been achieved since Baron Haussmann remade Paris.

Just what were these mighty changes, since generalities are unsatisfying? First, there is the Mussolini-built *Via Impero*, a city boulevard with no parallel in the world, just as there is no parallel to the Colosseum. This imposing avenue, where motor cars speed like racers, was cut through the incrustations of centuries from the Victor Emmanuel Monument past the *Foro Traiano* (Trajan's Forum) and the *Foro Romano* straight as a great arrow to the Colosseum, opening to view this unique monument of the past.

Second, the *Campidoglio* was isolated and brought gloriously into the sun by tearing down the masses of decrepit structures that used to conceal it. The ensemble of this historic hill (the Capitoline), with the strange, bare church of Santa Maria in Aracoeli and the glittering, if garish, monument of Victor Emmanuel II in Brescian marble, seems to throw all three Romes into one, no matter from what angle you gaze. The approach to the Campidoglio consists of broad steps bordered by a lovely strip of verdure.

Third, the *Tarpeian Rock*, which was once a thing you hunted for and found if you were lucky, is now as conspicuous as it is lovely, a two-tier park so beautiful that it would be a pleasure to be thrown over and killed there, as foes of the state were in olden times. At the base is a large cage, inside which a she-wolf paces restlessly back and forth, a descendant, no doubt, of her who suckled Romulus and Remus.

Fourth, the *Theater of Marcellus,* whose two top tiers the Orsini Family converted into a palazzo in the Middle Ages, was opened to view by a wide, curving avenue called Via del Mare, leading from the base of the Capitoline to the Temple of Fortune and the lovely round Temple of Vesta beside the Tiber.

Fifth, the impressive semicircle of *Trajan's Market* was brought to the light of day by sloughing off numerous medieval hovels. (This market is not mentioned in old Baedekers for the good reason that it was *buried* in slums.)

Sixth, the *Circus Maximus,* a stadium between the Palatine and Aventine Hills, so large that the greatest bowls in America are mere beginners (there were seats for about a quarter of a million persons) existed until Mussolini's day only as an indefinable green hill. Then, for the first time, it was brought to light by excavations.

Seventh, the important *Mausoleum of Augustus,* formerly missed altogether by most tourists although it lies within a stone's throw of the Corso, was cleared of the residential and business debris around it to reveal it to the world.

It would be easy to go on and on like a publicity release, but I have no wish to sound like a propagandist for the Sawdust Caesar, whose mighty sins against the world should not blind us to certain fine things he did.

* * *

A good way to develop some faint sense of personal acquaintance with classic Rome is to select some one famous building or ruin and "make it your own" by reading its life story, preferably on the spot. Suppose, for instance, you select the most conspicuous of all, the Colosseum (sometimes spelled Coliseum), secure from some bookshop an authoritative volume (there are many) and settle down for a couple of hours *in* the Colosseum to let this symbol of Roman power—and brutality—reveal itself to your consciousness. There are few dramas in all history so vivid.

Act I portrays the henchmen of Vespasian lashing twelve thousand Jews to forced labor constructing this gigantic stadium on the site of Nero's private lake, in front of his Golden House. Vespasian dies but Titus and Domitian carry on and at last the Colosseum is completed. It was at first a marine stadium for mock naval battles and accounts state that sailors used to rig a vast awning over the entire structure for the comfort of spectators. Soon the "lake" was filled in and the floor raised, to provide a great stage for combats and spectacles.

Act II shows ninety thousand citizens of Rome watching within the arena a gladiatorial contest. The emperor is present too and all the glittering dignitaries of state. With the emperor, in places of honor, are the Vestal Virgins, dainty creatures so pure that a single misstep from the path of virtue would result in their being buried alive. They are frantic with excitement, literally screaming, as they signal with the others for the death of some gladiator whose exhibition has failed to satisfy them.

Act III, Scene I. A gala show in which seven hundred wild beasts and six hundred gladiators participate. All—*all*—meet death to entertain the lust-fed spectators. The Virgins, still unsullied, are watching, as usual, from their places of honor.

> All pity dieth in that glaring look.
> They clap to see the blood run like a brook;
> They stare with hungry eyes, which tears should fill,
> And cheer the beasts on with their souls' goodwill;
> And wish more victims to their maw, and urge
> And lash their fury, as they shared the surge,
> Gnashing their teeth, like beasts, on flesh of men.

The lines are from Elizabeth Barrett Browning's translation of a contemporary Latin description.

Scene II. Another gala show. Gladiators' blood has become a common sight. Lions and tigers rolling in agony are likewise too common to be interesting. Jaded appetites must be titillated, so hundreds of exotic creatures are slaughtered to please the multitude. There are elephants and stags and wild boars, even giraffes and ostriches. As a *pièce de résistance* two naked women, Christians who are said to worship an ass, are hoisted in a net in full view of ninety thousand pairs of eyes. Then bulls are let loose to gore the women.

Tumultuous applause rocks the Colosseum. A decidedly amusing act this. But there should have been four or five women, or a dozen.

Act IV, Scene I. The Colosseum is a medieval fort, the cages of the animals turned into barracks for soldiers installed there by the powerful Frangipani Family.

Scene II. The Colosseum has become a quarry. Thousands of workmen are busily engaged in removing its blocks of fine travertine. Many medieval palaces, including the Palazzo Barberini and the Palazzo Farnese in Rome and including one or two in distant Venice, are built from this quarry, two-thirds of its total bulk being removed.

Scene III. A cloth factory is in operation in the arena. Far above, one man, a professor sort of man, is wandering along the looted tiers of seats, peering intently here and there. He is a botanist trying to classify the more than four hundred varieties of flowers that have sprung up on these stone benches.

Act V. Benedict XIV consecrates the blood-soaked structure as a sacred relic because of its role as a place of martyrdom. A cross now rises from the center of the arena.

If you do not care for my gory selection, there are plenty of a nobler nature to choose from. Even in Imperial Rome, brutality and debauchery very often yielded to loftier strains of character, and many a ruin has an inspiring story to tell. The unstarred bit is often the most fascinating of all. One discovers, as stated in the previous chapter, amazing outcroppings where least expected, and it is an interesting game to run these discoveries to earth. Each time-worn stone and brick is zealously guarded by Italy's Republican regime, and it was by the former Fascist regime, for the treasure that it is. One such outcropping, a curious and very conspicuous one, is a long stretch of the city wall of Servius Tullius, King of Rome in the sixth century before Christ, jutting out into the square at an awkward tangent from the enormous gleaming façade of the modernistic Termini Station. Despite heinous sins and sadisms, Old Rome has always been, and still is, an inexhaustible well of fresh power to subsequent generations.

Church Rome

Of Rome's three hundred churches and more, some eighty of which are consecrated to Mary, how many do you wish to know personally? I should say that the irreducible minimum for travelers who have little time but who do not wish to ignore this all-important phase of the city is four, namely, St. Peter's; St. John Lateran; St. Paul-without-the-Walls; Santa Maria Maggiore; and, for its view, Santa Maria in Aracoeli (St. Mary-on-Heaven's-Altar). *Many* others, like San Pietro in Vincoli for its great masterpiece of Michelangelo, the world-famous statue of Moses in an angry mood at finding his people worshiping a golden calf, and the Pantheon, technically named Santa Maria dei Martiri and popularly called, from its shape, La Rotonda, as burial place of Raphael, have some special and equally strong appeal; but the latter, at least, is hardly to be considered a church at all. It is more a national monument, being the best preserved of all the buildings left by the Roman Empire.

St. Peter's, officially *San Pietro in Vaticana*, is the largest, greatest, most important church of Catholic Christendom, though it is *not* the cathedral of Rome. No one, it is safe to say, ever entered St. Peter's for the first time, or the twentieth, without being profoundly impressed. You cannot, for one thing, get away from its *size*. Four acres of ground it covers and eighty thousand persons it can hold. Companies of soldiers could deploy in the transepts without being seen in the nave and scores of eagles, it seems, could soar about within the dome that Michelangelo built and never cross each other's path. This dome is supported by four colossal piers, each 234 feet in circumference. There are about 150 columns in the church and some 30 altars. The statuary is on the same proportional scale as the structure itself. The tiniest cherubs are the size of a man, and those at some height from the floor are eighteen feet tall, though they seem of normally modest dimensions. In the ball on top of the dome eight people could stand erect.

Some claim that it is *only* the size of St. Peter's that impresses, but it is certainly far more than that. There are warehouses in New York and Chicago considerably larger. It is the sublimity, the smooth harmony, of St. Peter's, that lifts you out of the ruts of life and makes you feel like hurling your guidebook into some dim corner. The bells, captained by *Il campanone*, an eleven-ton monster, peal overhead and penetrate the church only as the rumble of some heavenly diapason millions of miles distant. A child is lifted by its mother to kiss the smooth burnished toe of that vapid thirteenth-century figure (St.

Peter) that sits near the beginning of the right transept. And under Bernini's baldaquin, with its fat writhing columns, lies—according to a tradition which has very strong historical support since recent discoveries were made in the crypt—the actual body of him who denied his Lord thrice before the cock crew—and then "went out and wept bitterly."

St. *John Lateran* is another colossal church, and in the ecclesiastical sense it takes precedence over St. Peter's itself, for it is the "mother and head of all churches," the cathedral of Rome and of the world, claiming as spiritual, though certainly not architectural, children even such mighty cathedrals as those of Chartres, Reims, Seville and Cologne. Constantine founded it and gave it (though not this actual structure) to the popes. Here, then, was established the first chapel of the Bishop of Rome. It is now second in world importance only to St. Peter's, and here, in the adjacent Lateran Palace, the treaty was signed, in 1929, which made the pope a temporal sovereign. The brilliance of the marbles and frescoes and mosaics is very cheerful in its whole effect and worth long study in detail.

An adjunct of this church, the *Scala Santa*, is quite as celebrated as the church itself. This Holy Stairway, brought from Jerusalem by the crusaders, is "believed to be the stairway that led to Pilate's hall," and consequently trod by the feet of Jesus; so says the English version of the placard posted on a pillar at its base. The French, German and Italian versions, as I carefully noted, say it *is* the stairway, etc. The placard also states that Saint Helena, the mother of Constantine, had it brought to Rome, but other authorities set the date many centuries later. At any rate, it was set up here in the sixteenth century. To all who ascend its twenty-eight steps upon their knees in prayerful mood, Pius VII announced the granting of nine years' indulgence "applicable to souls in purgatory." Pius X, in 1908, deeply impressed with the stairway's sanctity, granted plenary indulgence *in perpetuo*.

A dark stain under a glass covering on the top step is venerated as the actual blood of Christ.

I have watched with enormous interest, on several occasions, the attitude, and especially the faces, of those who were engaged in kneeling out of purgatory some relative or friend. On one occasion I counted nineteen women, four men and one small boy. The expressions on certain faces were extremely moving. Some of those women certainly were praying for dead sons. What mother would not kneel her way up twenty-eight hard steps to pull her son nine *days* nearer to heaven, let alone nine years or the whole long journey? The little boy on the steps, however, was plainly doing his stint, as he would have sawed twenty-eight logs. The levity of one group was amazing, to say the least. Two young women and a man, all Italians, approached the Sacred Stairs. One of the women knelt down on the lowest step and started to say a prayer. The other woman and the man openly laughed, rather loudly laughed, and mocked their companion, who thereupon hastily rose and rejoined them, blushing furiously. With much laughter and banter they strolled out of the edifice. Perhaps the mockers were Communists.

St. Paul-without-the-Walls. The veriest upstart among Rome's churches, being less than a century old, this structure houses the body of St. Paul. So, at least, a raggedy little girl lurking about in the church told me, and so many of the faithful believe. The authentic body *was* very probably in a metal coffin five feet square (the Apostle was short and the head is in the crypt of St. John Lateran), but that was in the old church on this spot and whether or not the Saracens, when they rifled this tomb, stole the sacred bones, no one can say. The church, second in size (among those of Rome) only to St. Peter's, is magnificent, a vast glory of granite, marble and bright mosaics, with some of the daylight seeping in through alabaster windows. A frieze high in the nave contains portraits of all the popes, from St. Peter to the present pontiff. Despite its glories, or because of them, St. Paul's gives the impression of a show piece, and for that reason it leaves me a trifle cold, though the adjacent cloisters are very beautiful and restful to the eye. I do warm to the mosaic chancel-arch of Galla Placidia, salvaged from the original church and re-erected in the present structure. The princess who built this arch (in the fifth century) lies in Ravenna in a chapel of surpassing loveliness. When you reach Ravenna, and Galla Placidia, do not fail to think back to this arch.

Santa Maria Maggiore. This is one of the most luminous and truly beautiful of the huge churches of Rome, and Americans may feel a special proprietary interest in its beauty since the wonderful gilded ceiling which Sangallo designed is covered with the first gold brought by Columbus from the New World.

I like this greatest of Mary's Roman churches, this basilica built on the spot selected by the Virgin herself and delineated by her with an August snowfall! I think you will like it too.

The use of the word basilica above may warrant a word of explanation, for non-Catholic visitors often think the word implies something specially sacred. It is, in fact, merely an architectural term indicating an oblong church built in the general shape of a Roman court of justice. The word cathedral, on the other hand, is, of course, an ecclesiastical term, indicating that the church is the seat of a bishop.

If you would crown your brief survey of Church Rome with the full realization of how utterly hopeless it is, in anything shorter than a full lifetime, to familiarize yourself with the subject, climb to some high spot, perhaps the porch of Santa Maria in Aracoeli, beside the Campidoglio, and survey the sea of baroque domes spreading out in widening circles toward the Janiculum and St. Peter's. One feels, in the presence of this city, one's incurable littleness, but the air up here on heaven's altar is so fresh, the scene so lovely, that what there is of us feels also incurably alive.

Città Vaticana: *A Small State Within a Large City*

On February 11, 1929, being in Rome, I took it into my head to see the city, as was then a clumsy custom for tourists, from a rubberneck *tram*. It was a long and tedious business by such a conveyance and I was the one and only passenger. The guide—for this was an official civic *Servizio Turistico*—kept up a perfunctory patter, mostly dates, about what we were passing, and it was a question whether he or I was the more bored. But suddenly his monotonous drone ceased.

"Ecco! Ecco! Signore!"

He pointed excitedly to a yellow and white banner being hung from a window.

"Ecco! It is the pope's flag! The treaty has been signed!" and sure enough, that proved to be a historic moment. Soon we saw dozens, hundreds, of yellow and white flags being raised. Significantly, they were often crossed with Italian flags. The Italian press had been severely silent on the subject of this treaty—by compulsion—and though I had heard rumors and whispers, I had no idea that the thing was so imminent.

Excitement filled the streets and now that the treaty was a *fait accompli*, the newspapers rushed the full story to the populace, including one American who was on a tram seeing Rome. How wonderfully dramatic the ceremony of signing the concordat must have been. A motor car swept up to the Lateran Palace bearing a man in scarlet cape and hat, even scarlet gloves and hose. It was Cardinal Gasparri. Another motor car brought Il Duce himself, extremely modish in morning coat and silk hat. There were, in all, four emissaries from each side. These and two photographers made up the total gathering. The eight seated themselves on ebony chairs sent to the pope from China. The documents lay before them on a table sent from the Philippines. The cardinal toyed with a specially made pen of solid gold, dipped it in a gold inkwell. The dotted lines were indicated, the concordat was signed by the high contracting parties, and for the first time in sixty years State and Church could exchange civilities without losing political ground. No longer was the pope a "prisoner." The cardinal could and did chat with the dictator as informally as Mrs. Smith would chat with Mrs. Brown.

The accord was to be celebrated next day in St. Peter's, and I, though a non-Catholic, succeeded in wangling a ticket from an English-speaking monsignor living in Rome. It was presumptuous, certainly. My argument was that of the small boy to his parents. I *wanted* a ticket. I wanted it very much. "No," said the monsignor, "absolutely no. It cannot be done." But I asked once more and looked very unhappy, so he gave me a ticket.

I have never seen excitement to compare with what I witnessed in St. Peter's, and I say this with full recollection of certain athletic victories of my alma mater when I thought my voice (and my hat) would never survive. My pink *ingresso* ticket to the church landed me in a knot of South Boston priests in the right transept, who were in turn lost in a veritable mob of other priests from many lands. I heard French and German and Spanish, and I saw Orientals and even Negroes who were of the cloth.

The Leviathan among churches was presently filled to the last possible inch with at least eighty thousand persons whom hundreds of brilliantly garbed papal guards attempted to control. It was like a lavish scene from an opera. The famous Swiss Guards, carrying swords or halberds according to rank, wore slashed purple and yellow uniforms designed by Michelangelo, these being partly covered by the shiny steel cuirass worn on state occasions, and topped by a ruff and a plumed helmet. Various other functionaries, were equally resplendent, some wearing rose-colored breeches and hose with chain mail shirts and shiny steel breastplates. There were "Elizabethan" ruffs in plenty and white-plumed visored helmets and many noble black busbies.

The pope was late and South Boston grew restive. I was charmed by the slangy humanness of these holy Irishmen. "Shove up, Jack," said one of them to his pal. "What's the use of being polite?" And another, apostrophizing the pontiff, exclaimed, "Let's go, Holy Father. Let's go. It's getting late."

After two or three false alarms, a wave of electric excitement announced that the pope was really coming. Two or three thousand nuns across the way in the left transept ran out their necks like turtles, straining for a glimpse of their spiritual chief. There was a distant blare from the famous silver trumpets, then a momentary hush, followed immediately by a roar "as of a rushing, mighty wind." The roar waxed greater. Every throat, it seemed, of the eighty thousand strained to greet the Sovereign Pontiff. Yells of "*Viva Papa! Viva Papa!*" rang over the general roar, the second word being pronounced exactly as it would be in rural sections of New England.

Finally, from my position, I could make out the head of the papal procession slowly advancing toward the Bernini baldaquin. It included papal gendarmes in mountainous black busbies and gleaming white breeches, chamberlains in their lace ruffs, wearing gold chains, Knights of Malta in white cloaks adorned with scarlet crosses, bishops and archbishops in brilliant purple robes, and then a double row of cardinals in scarlet robes, with ermine capes. They were only partly visible through the chinks in the dense mass of heads. Then came the Holy Father himself, carried high on the *sedia gestatoria*, or ceremonial chair. He wore a white silk cloak embroidered in gold, and the triregnum, or triple crown of gold and precious stones, supposed to symbolize the triple authority of Christ's vicar over Heaven, Earth and Hell. Behind his chair, as a background, the two *flabelli* were carried on poles. These are immense ostrich-feather fans used to add splendor to such scenes. Surrounding the chair of His Holiness walked Swiss Guards, carrying their great serpentine swords, and some high lay dignitaries in medieval costumes, with slender rapiers at their sides. The pope continually raised his right hand, on which glistened the green fisherman's ring, and waved his dignified blessings over the throng.

When the procession came to its goal before the high altar the pontiff took his seat on a specially prepared white damask throne and the beautiful music of the high mass began to ring through the church and hush the excited crowds.

From where I stood I could look up into Michelangelo's dome and see in huge mosaic letters—they are six feet high, blue on a gold background—running around it these words:

TU ES PETRUS ET SUPER HANC PETRAM AEDIFICABO ECCLESIAM MEAM
ET TIBI DABO CLAVES REGNI COELORUM

(The Latin words, from Matthew 16: 18-19, mean, Thou Art Peter and upon This Rock I Will Build My Church and I Will Give unto Thee the Keys of the Kingdom of Heaven.)

I could not but picture Peter's utter amazement had he been able to look through the telescope of time to this glittering event in a church named for him and built over his grave.

Since that event, Vatican City has surged forward, temporally speaking, as impressively as Rome itself. The changes since 1929 have been almost incredible. Consider, for instance, that great pile of buildings that houses the papal art collections, being by far the largest assemblage of valuable antiquities in the world. In 1929 one circumnavigated St. Peter's and by following Baedeker's directions very closely succeeded in finding, at the end of a sort of alley, an unimpressive little doorway, which was the museum entrance. Today, one goes by bus or otherwise to Piazza del Risorgimento, walks around a corner of the Vatican wall and there beholds an immense gateway surmounted by figures of Michelangelo and Raphael, with the papal emblem, a miter over crossed keys, between them. These two Titans of art, so utterly opposite in temperament, were the mainstay, artistically, of Julius II, who, with his successor Leo X, brought the papal court to so brilliant a level.

Entering the building, one is fairly dazzled by its splendor. An enormous new ramp, beautifully designed and built of marble and bronze in a double spiral for mounting and descending, leads to the *Vatican Picture Gallery*. Along the side of this ramp, in large bronze letters, appear the names of the popes, from the earliest holders of that office to Pius XII. His predecessor, Pius XI, is honored as the Pontifex in the Years 1932-33, when this reconstruction was completed. Incidentally, two elevators of great size supplement the ramp.

On the upper level is a papal post office where scores of tourists are always busily engaged in sending off post cards bearing the papal stamp and cancellation.

One pays a fee for admission and enters the series of museums. Inside the barrier, one finds oneself in a shiny sea of masterpieces. In the *Pinacoteca Nuova*, for example, are the ten famous Raphael tapestries (designed by him and woven in Brussels), now housed in most sumptuous brass-rimmed, plate-glass cabinets. You step out on the balcony of the Pinacoteca and see many evidences of the papal zeal that has developed the new hundred-acre state. Armies of gardeners planted, sodded and edged its gardens for months, following the signing of the concordat. All was done with taste, and certainly with money, for the new state received from Italy in 1929 a huge sum in settlement for the lands taken from the Holy See in 1870. The money had long been refused by the popes on the ground that they, as "prisoners," had no voice in making the agreement. Each year since 1870, the Italian parliament had voted the payment and each year it had been steadfastly refused. In 1929, however, an independent state could accept it without an act of subservience. So fresh cash came within the walls of Vatican City and there was no unemployment crisis. New buildings were erected to meet new needs, a sacred broadcasting studio, for example, a marble railway station and a government building. An older institution, the Mosaic Factory, was extended and re-equipped.

One hundred acres constitute one-sixth of a square mile and that is the area of this state. You can walk completely around it in half an hour, and yet it contains untold wealth. If the pope were disposed to sell to some wealthy manufacturer (ghastly thought) the *Apollo Belvedere*, to another the *Laocoön group*, to an ambitious gallery the *tapestries of Raphael*, and so on, he could raise, I suppose, enough to make every one of his few hundred subjects a millionaire. Such a course would also give a good many experts employment in removing the shiny and rather ridiculous new fig leaves which were superimposed upon the old statuary in fairly recent times. One may possibly condone the painting of drapery on the figures of Michelangelo's *Last Judgment* on the altar-wall of the *Sistine Chapel*—this was done by the Cinquecentisto Daniele Volterra, at a papal command, and won for him the nickname of "The Tailor"—but the placing of fig leaves, in carload lots, on glorious Greek statuary in a museum is carrying modesty rather far. It certainly emphasizes what it is supposed to conceal.

I would urge three things in connection with a visit, however hasty, to the Vatican. First, do not fail to take a few moments to gaze from the balcony of the Pinacoteca Nuova toward the dome of St. Peter's. You will see it as Michelangelo wanted you to see it and surely you will never forget that view. It would have made the master boil with rage could he have known that fifty years after his death his dome would be absolutely hidden, by Maderna's façade, from those who approach St. Peter's through the square.

Second and third, acquaint yourself here in the Vatican with the personalities of Raphael Sanzio and Michelangelo Buonarroti. Pope Julius II got on wonderfully with the gentle artist from Urbino and not at all well with the obstinate, irascible Florentine. And yet many of us would reserve our greater admiration for the latter. Hardly ever has so much artistic genius been heaped upon one human being. In sculpture, in architecture and finally in painting he reached the very utmost pinnacles. It is said that his bitter rival Bramante persuaded the pope to commission Michelangelo to do the ceiling paintings of the Sistine Chapel, thinking secretly that the Florentine would make a fool of himself. Michelangelo demurred, begged to have Raphael do the work, said plainly that he knew little of painting and could not handle the task. He was overruled, however, and thereupon *learned* to paint, and achieved what some critics consider the greatest frescoes of all time, the gigantic picturing of *The Creation of the World* and *The Fall of Man*. The virile, sculptured nature of his figures is always evident and even the layman can invariably detect the stamp of his genius. (*Life* printed twenty-two pages of color reproducing this magnificent masterpiece in a special issue of December 26, 1949, and this is richly worth looking up in some library.)

"I have finished the chapel which I painted," wrote Michelangelo to a friend. "The pope is very well satisfied." And Bramante, green with jealousy, plotted other ways to entangle his rival.

Today's Rome, New and Newer

The way to see what new and newer Rome is like, meaning the city itself, is to make a private tour with a hired guide, or to take one of the bus tours (consult your hotel porter) that more or less concentrates on the fine modern buildings such as the huge *Air Ministry*, on up-to-date developments in housing such as the extensive *Città Universitaria*, on the ramifying new athletic stadia and on current residential districts of the greatest elegance. Certain not-new specialties of interest are always included, such as *Villa Torlonia*, which Mussolini appropriated for his private home, and *Villa Savoia*, a royal residence of Victor Emmanuel III for forty years but now the Egyptian Embassy. These are only relishes, however, on the main dish of What's-New.

The newest and most sumptuous part of residential Rome, with some marble apartment houses of really astonishing magnificence (these, however, built, or commenced, just before the war, when such luxury was not inappropriate to the times), is the *Parioli section*, between the Borghese Gardens and the National Stadium, just east of Via Flaminia. A street of very special *luxe* is the curving Via dei Monti Parioli. Others, still newer, are Via Panama, Via Polonia, Via Bruxelles and the whole network in the neighborhood of Piazza Cuba, each named for a country or a city.

The *National Stadium* is near this section and might be impressive were it not thrown completely in the shade by the *Foro Italico*, called also the *Campo della Farnesina*, across the Tiber. The Farnesina complex of stadia and of buildings and fields for sport and physical development remains as one of Mussolini's self-glorifying modern wonders, guarded by an obelisk nearly sixty feet high, with the word MUSSOLINI so deeply carved in it that the authorities of republican Italy, who have expunged Il Duce's name wherever they could possibly do so, were faced with the alternative of leaving it here in the imperishable stone or destroying the fine monolith altogether. So far they have retained the obelisk.

When fully brought to completion the Foro Italico will certainly be one of the most impressive, if also over-showy, centers for athletic competitions in Europe. Its *Stadio dei Marmi* (Stadium of the Marbles) is adorned—if that is the right word for such an explosion of sculpture—with sixty large marble statues of athletes, each given to Rome by a different Italian city. Each athlete represents a different type of sport—one would hardly have supposed sixty varieties to exist—and each well-muscled youth wears, if I may mention it, an athletic supporter as his sole garment. Perhaps Il Duce had a gentleman's agreement with Il Papa to keep Fascist statuary modest, but like the Vatican's fig leaves these garments seem to draw attention rather than divert it.

The Stadium of the Marbles is said to seat 40,000, but the unfinished *Stadio Olimpico* in the same wide-spreading complex will ultimately seat 120,000, if the predictions of Roman enthusiasts is to be credited. A small stadium, also having marble seats, is used for tennis matches only. Near it is a handsome pool for swimming matches and in adjacent parts of the vast ensemble are facilities for almost every conceivable sport, perhaps even sixty, as the marbles suggest.

The usual tour of New Rome includes a visit to the summit of *Monte Mário* (on which the big new hotel is to take form), providing the best obtainable view anywhere of the whole ensemble of Rome. The sharp gazer, aided by the guide, will see many new housing developments, high-cost and low-cost, designed to combat the often tragic overcrowding of the city. Among the low-cost ones are up-to-date multiple dwellings at moderate rentals erected by the so-called *Fanfani* organization.

One of Rome's finest modern office-building developments, and one of the easiest to reach, is seldom if ever shown on the fixed tours and it is hard to understand Roman reticence on this. I refer to the mass of buildings between the Corso and the Tiber, near the Mausoleum of Augustus. In strolling to this worth-while goal from the Corso, one first enters the newly built *Largo dei Lombardi*, lined by five-story buildings of travertine and tawny brick, then passes through an archway to a nobly pillared court surrounding the vast *Piazza Augusto Imperatore*, with the emperor's now-unhidden mausoleum looming very close at hand. The office buildings, with arcades of shops, restaurants and open-air cafés, are so tasteful, so cheerful and so typical of New Rome that they constitute a sight of the city, however seldom viewed. As I have earlier reported, Alfredo all'Augusteo has his restaurant in one of these arcades, so those who hunt up this King of Noodles will, even if inadvertently, see a significant business center of Rome, and with it the untrumpeted but magnificent imperial mausoleum.

The Subway to Tomorrow—EUR

Rome's first subway was tentatively opened in 1952. It has been extended and is supposed to be in full operation "any day," as soon as all the lagging equipment, chiefly the rolling stock, has been secured. The line runs—when it runs—from the Termini Station to the Colosseum to the St. Paul Gate and so, three miles southwest of the city, to EUR, which is the Rome of Tomorrow.

The mysterious initials stand for Esposizione Universale Roma and the buildings and grounds of this Universal Exposition are the Rome of Tomorrow.

Tomorrow was to have commenced in 1942. Mussolini planned to make EUR the most extensive, expensive, exhilarating, explosive affair of its kind ever seen on earth, but before those exuberant ex's could be transmuted into facts he made his—exit, by choosing war instead. Several of the buildings were nearly completed and the landscaping was well under way. The whole thing was to cost, even with the very low scale of wages for Italian labor, some two billion lire, then meaning one hundred million dollars.

The postwar republic found itself stuck with this vast "white mammoth." What to do? A committee was organized to study and report. Oddly enough, money was needed, *is* needed. A Niagara of money could do the trick but the lire come only in a thin, frustrating trickle. Even so, EUR is something to behold. Consider just one of its buildings, the *Hall of Congresses*. In this we see one of the most imaginative of Tomorrow's buildings. The huge reception hall is an exact 132 feet by 132 by 132. It is enhanced by great frescoes and much marble, hundreds of large slabs of the stone having been ingeniously split to create clever symmetrical designs. The roof is sustained by elegant pillars of interestingly varied marble. The building contains two more-than-modern theaters, one inside, with superb acoustics, the other, of Greek inspiration, on the open roof, with a marvelous view of Monte Cavo and the mountain town of Rocca di Papa. This lofty theater, all of marble, has a stage that might have been trodden, it seems, by Athenian actors in the Age of Pericles, though they would have been a bit surprised by the curtain, which is a compact row of jets of water illuminated to cut off vision from the auditorium. The remainder of the roof is a series of little gardens that are to serve collectively as a summer café and restaurant terrace. This terrace, say the optimists, will be ready for business—"practically now," and I ardently hope their predictions are coming true.

Other structures of EUR, nearly done, half done, quarter done, are the Reception Building; the Palace of Italian Civilization, destined to house the National Library; the Museum of Science; the Museum of Roman Civilization. These are but conspicuous "samples." The area of the grounds is just about the same as that of the city of Florence. There will be hundreds of neat villas for private residence. A forest was planted in one corner—for 1942—and besides this, 28,000 separate trees. A very fancy artificial lake was planned and may yet be realized, the subway station being on its northeast bank. The new highway from Naples, now a-borning, will pass through the exposition grounds.

Under the cornice of the very wide façade of the Reception Building a long motto is carved that has in it elements of pathos, but elements too of justified hope. It reads: LA TERZA ROMA SI DILATERA SOPRA ALTRI COLLI LUNGO LE RIVE DEL FIUME SACRO SINO ALLE SPIAGGE DEL TIRRENO. It means: The Third Rome Will Spread over Other Hills Along the Sacred River as Far as the Beaches of the Tyrrhenian Sea. The "Third Rome," be it understood, was Mussolini's Rome. This went into a sudden decline and collapsed. The Fourth Rome is the free republican one of today. The Fifth Rome, it seems to me, is aptly symbolized by EUR, so perhaps the motto's second word should read Quinta. You'll be amply rewarded, and more so as construction and improvements continue, by taking some conveyance, perhaps the subway, emerging at its outer terminus into the very middle of Tomorrow.

CHAPTER 12

PERSONAL ZIGZAGS IN ROME

A Fountain Tour, Self-Conducted

THE fountains of Rome, more numerous and of more artistic interest than those of any other city anywhere, have been an unfailing source not only of water, for many centuries, but of expressions in poetry, in prose and even in music, notably that of Resphighi. They make their own music, babbling, splashing, often melodiously roaring, and generations of visitors have loved them with a special devotion.

On the fixed tours of the city these fountains—a very few of them —are shown in passing, with a hasty word of comment, but the only way one can really be *with* them is to organize one's own fountain tour. A guidebook and a map are necessary but not a guide. Of the myriads, six or eight or ten, according to one's strength and time, may be selected and visited on foot, or with the aid of a taxi or carriage, hired by the hour. Little retracing of steps will be necessary if one's tour is carefully planned with a map. My own plan, perhaps quite different in arrangement from yours, might have these nine fountain halts.

The *Fountain of the Naiads*, centering the great circle of Piazza Esedra, is of modern construction, having been designed at the turn of the century by an artist named Rutelli. It is perhaps not great, as Roman fountains go, but it makes a lovely effect with its single lofty jet surrounded by lesser jets, the whole thing marvelously illuminated every evening and visible for half a mile down Via Nazionale. Piazza Esedra—it is worth while to note—takes its name *and* its shape from the *exedra,* meaning the apse, semicircular in form, of the west court of the colossal Baths of Diocletian, larger in their day than even the Baths of Caracalla.

The *Fontanone dell'Acqua Felice,* in Piazza San Bernardo, only a long block northwest of Piazza Esedra, is a composite fountain whose central figure of Moses was done by an aspiring young artist with the optimistic name of Próspero Bresciano. He proved to be anything but prosperous, and his statue, in the manner of Michelangelo but utterly lacking the master's touch of genius, aroused such storms of contemptuous comment and ridicule that the unhappy designer drowned himself in the Tiber. Several able sculptors, including Domenico Fontana and Giovanni Battista della Porta, completed the affair we see today, still not too successfully, and it was named for Sixtus V, whose name prior to his elevation as pope was *Felice* Peretti. The water, of exceptional purity, comes from a point some fourteen miles distant in the Alban Hills.

The conspicuous *Quattro Fontane* (Four Fountains), one of Rome's familiar tourist sights, are at the crossing of Via Venti Settembre (two blocks down from Piazza San Bernardo) and Via Quattro Fontane. The innocuous little fountains, not of much importance but very pleasing there amid the traffic, are supposed to represent the four seasons.

Fontana del Tritone (Fountain of the Triton), in the center of the very busy Piazza Barberini, a few steps from the Four Fountains, is one of the well-loved masterpieces of Giovanni Lorenzo Bernini. In the middle, cynosure of all passers-by, a Triton, sitting on a giant shell supported by four dolphins, blows a generous jet of water high aloft from a tipped-up conch.

La Barcaccia, in Piazza di Spagna, is a fountain in the form of a leaking war vessel designed by one Pietro Bernini, by no means to be confused with the great Giovanni Lorenzo Bernini. This is not an important work of art but travelers love it, chiefly, I think, because they love the square in which it stands and the wondrous Spanish Steps that mount from in front of its meager waters to the Church of Trinità dei Monti.

Fontana di Trevi (The Trevi Fountain), reached from Via del Tritone by Via Poli or Via della Stamperia, is certainly the greatest, as it is the largest, of Rome's fountains. Bernini (probably) designed it and the work was ordered by that tireless pope-of-construction, Sixtus V. It has the broad, high wall of Palazzo Poli as a back and its central figure is an imposing Neptune being drawn in a winged chariot by Tritons and rearing horses. The ensemble of the fountain is a huge thing, full of statues in niches. Somehow, with all its elaborations, it escapes being *fussy*. Everybody loves the Trevi, whose satisfying sound fills the whole neighborhood, and it makes even the sharpest critic of Bernini forgive him for his occasional artistic atrocities, such as the heavily conceived baldaquin he did for St. Peter's. It is a tradition of very long standing that on the last evening of a stay in Rome the visitor shall toss a coin into the fountain to insure his return to the city. And here is a question for the gods of tourism. *Why*, since the world of travel venerates the Trevi, is there no appealing open-air café on the square before it and no attractive hotel—it could be reasonably modest and in appropriate taste—beside it? I, for one, would certainly pay double for the privilege of going to sleep some night to the Trevi's rich roar.

Fontana delle Tartarughe (The Fountain of the Tortoises), in the tiny Piazza Mattei near the broad Via Arenula and (in the opposite direction) near the Theater of Marcellus, takes a lot of finding and may prove wearying, but it warrants real effort, for this is a masterpiece of sheer charm and of lively action. Four young boys, each wrestling with a dolphin, manage also to keep a hand free to lift a tortoise to the edge of the fountain's upper basin to give the eager reptile a drink of water. Giacomo della Porta designed this, with the co-operation of a Florentine artist named Landini.

The *Piazza Navona Fountains*, three in number, are an institution in themselves. Two of them, the central and southerly ones, are Bernini masterpieces and the central one, called the Fountain of the Rivers, is almost as grandiose and turbulent a work as the Trevi itself. Four human figures of heroic size represent the Danube, Ganges, Plata and Nile, the latter shielding his eyes from the "horrible" Church of Saint Agnes close by on the square's east side. This fancy was attested by Bernini himself, though this was obviously a sour joke, since the church was not finished until some years after the fountain. He did, at any rate, seize every opportunity to belittle his rival, Francesco Borromini, designer of Saint Agnes. Borromini couldn't take it, and though he did some fine work, certainly including this church, he was so utterly chagrined at his rival's greater success that he finally committed suicide.

The two *Fountains by Carlo Maderna*, on the north and south sides of St. Peter's Square, are impressive for the simplicity of their towering columns of water that send their spray far and wide on windy days, even to the ramp that ascends to the basilica. Bernini fountains, always very exuberant, would hardly do for this dignified and all-important square, surrounded though it is by that artist's mighty colonnade. This famous structure measures 1115 feet (north-south) by 768 feet (east-west) and can "hold within its arms," by a conservative estimate, a quarter of a million people, when the pope blesses the multitude on great days. For such a square, plain and lofty fountains are admirably suited.

These nine above are but whetters of the fountain appetite. If you become addicted to this fare you may satisfy the hunger, or thirst, by almost endless browsing in search of new architectural tidbits from among the hundreds of fountains in the city. For a personal example, I found in the Borghese Gardens (near the Gallery) the *Fountain of the Sea Horses* and became mightily attached to it because the sea horse is the symbol, and name, of my home on Cape Cod. With such a vast variety of designs, it will be remarkable if you do not find some little-known fountain that likewise has a special significance for you.

Beloved Corners in the Sun

Rome, with seven hills celebrated throughout the centuries and two more that are quite as appealing in their different ways, possesses a great many well-loved corners that invite a sort of blissful lethargy. Some travelers have the folly or the courage, I don't know which, to accept the invitations even at the expense of their travel education. Rome is, after all, so incomparably rich in works of art (some thirty museums and galleries), in churches (over three hundred), in ruins of real significance, that perhaps it is defensible, in the interests of a balanced diet, for us to steal a portion of each day for sheer lazying. Where then shall we go for our siesta? I suggest the following loafing grounds for your consideration:

The ever beautiful *Pincian*, as lovely as it is familiar. It is not by any preconcerted agreement that all the world pays homage to this hill. Outside the Seven Elect, it preens itself in the copious sunshine and reveals to all who come here the grandeur of Rome, seen *near* the vantage point.

The *Janiculum* (Gianicolo in the Italian spelling), another outcast from the Seven, but very commanding. This hill is *"trastevere"* (across Tiber) and seems especially designed to honor the Garibaldi family. Giuseppe has sat his horse here for sixty years but only in relatively recent times has Anita, his Uruguayan wife, also been given a place of honor. A very remarkable woman was Anita, a devoted companion to her husband and, like him, an intrepid warrior. Against the western sky she fiercely reins in her steed, making a brilliant picture for Romans to see from their windows. Near by is a beacon which flashes green, white, red, the colors of Italy.

The *Borghese Gardens*, as a setting for Titian, Correggio and Raphael in the Borghese Gallery, one of the thirty, by the way, *not to be missed*. You may easily walk to and through these gardens from the Pincian. They have a hundred sunny corners to invite your soul, in case your body grows walking-weary, in the gallery or otherwise.

The *Tiber bridges*, any one of the twenty, saturated with history for ages. The most distant one, Ponte Milvio across the river's northern bend, marks the spot, to repeat from a background chapter, where Christianity captured the Western World. Here, in the crucial Battle of the Milvian Bridge, Constantine sharply defeated the forces of the pagan emperor, Maxentius. From then on the destiny of the new religion was assured.

The *park on top of the Tarpeian Rock*. And if, while here, you wish to add some modern touches to your art education, step into the *New Museum*, which was called the Benito Mussolini Museum in Fascist days, and have a look. Canvases are replaced from time to time and a puzzling, blue-eyed, flaxen-haired nude seems to have vanished from its walls. When she was on exhibition, at the time when I earlier visited this gallery, she was being attended by a man of sorts and I remember asking myself if she was an honest wife having her back scrubbed by her husband or a pensive harlot who found her client unattractive. As antedote to this peculiar work, I admired a lovely little painting of Augusta Perusia at sunset. It was a foretaste of what I was to see when I headed north from Rome to the lovely Umbrian center (Perúgia).

The lone bench at the *top of the steps leading from Via del Campidoglio to the Forum*. This is a superb spot from which to see the *whole* Forum and, while seeing, dream.

A wisp of a girl approached me here and asked me to read her some lines from my guidebook. I did so—it was in English—and she nodded her head, pretending solemnly that she understood it all. Then she asked, "Francese?"

A Kit of Facts, with Some Surprises

Rome is a fact mine. You can dig up facts, always interesting, occasionally startling, in every street and square, in every church, in every ancient ruin, and make them your own. I shall reach into my kit and take out a few, as samples, of those that I have been tumbling into it, trip by trip. Some of them are of Baedeker character, though perhaps no less interesting on that account, and some may contain elements of surprise for you as they did for me. I shall extract them at random, for neatly ticketed information would become a lecture and this is not a lecture but a bag of chances.

The *Quirinal*, originally a hill of the Sabines, was named by them for the god Quirinus, later identified (arbitrarily) by the Romans as Romulus. This last was a neat trick and the emperors made it stick.

The world-known *Quirinal Palace,* which rose on this hill, was first a summer residence of the popes, then (from 1870) the palace of Italy's kings, and finally, today, the home of the president of the republic.

The *Chigi Palace,* in the Piazza Colonna, became the Foreign Ministry during Mussolini's day and has remained so under the republic.

The *Palazzo Montecitorio,* adjacent to it, is the home of Italy's Chamber of Deputies.

The *Palazzo Madama,* near the well-fountained old Piazza Navona, is the present meeting-place of the Senate.

The *Palazzo Venezia,* in Piazza Venezia, is the historic building where Mussolini embarrassed his callers by making them walk across the marble floor of an enormous room to arrive within range of his desk in a far corner. The building's balcony is the one from which, jutting his chin and popping his eyes, he made his clangorous speeches to the multitudes. The Palazzo Venezia now houses an art gallery and a library of archeology and art.

The *Palazzo Barberini*, on Via Quattro Fontane, originally built for Pope Urban VIII, who was a Barberini, is one of Rome's grandest palazzi. A standing joke in the Middle Ages was: "What the barbarians didn't appropriate in Rome the Barberini did." In certain wings of the vast structure special art exhibitions are set up from time to time. One that I have seen, with due horror, was a so-called "Exhibition of Demoniac Art," the ghastly works being mostly of the Flemish school, with several canvases by that master of mad fantasy, Hieronymus Bosch.

The above six palaces, be advised, are about 10 per cent of those usually recorded on an "abridged list."

The ancient Romans liked *round* temples, the Pantheon being their supreme achievement in this type of structure. Note also the lovely little *Temple of Vesta*, perfectly circular, near the Tiber's Ponte Palatino; the *Temple of Divus Romulus*, a sort of entrance, or narthex, to the *Church of Santi Cosma e Damiano*, on the edge of the Roman Forum; the remains of the round temple in the *House of the Vestal Virgins*; the huge round *Mausoleum of Augustus*; the equally huge round *Mausoleum of Hadrian* in the celebrated Castel Sant'Angelo; and for that matter, by heritage, the innumerable round domes of Rome's churches, including the supreme one surmounting St. Peter's, directly inspired, in this case, by the Pantheon.

Consider some widely assorted facts, perhaps insignificant and certainly disjointed but all corollary to the above paragraph. The bronze of the Pantheon's ceiling went to ornament St. Sophia in Constantinople (Istanbul), and other bronze from it was used for Bernini's baldaquin in St. Peter's. The Tiber used to flood the Pantheon frequently until the building's floor was raised and the river's walls built higher, in the late nineteenth century. Even after that, in 1900, a terrible flood inundated that entire part of Rome. The terrace of the Castel Sant'Angelo is the setting for the last act of *La Tosca*. In St. Peter's, on one of the main bronze doors to the nave, is a fifteenth-century representation of Nero sentencing Peter to be hanged upside down. There are said to be 2800 shades of color in the mosaics of St. Peter's—there are *no* paintings or frescoes in the church. On the floor of the nave are markers indicating the length of other great churches of the world. Even such edifices as St. Sophia and Westminster Abbey are comparatively Lilliputian, their marks being about half way from the wall of the apse to the church's entrance.

Oddities of Rome, ancient and modern, are headed by that colossal and bizarre Monument of Victor Emmanuel II, symbolizing Italian unity. The *Tomb of the Unknown Soldier,* which is a part of it, has real artistic merit, but most of the soaring mountain of marble and bronze is merely big. I was told that twenty-five journalists once ensconced themselves in the belly of the horse which the king rides and drank a toast to Italy; that the whiskers of the horse are three feet long; that the king's sword is eleven feet long; that the wings of victorious Rome, centering the vast ensemble, are thirty-eight feet in length.

Another thing noted for its size rather than its quality is a prodigious marble head, with fragments of the limbs, of Constantine the Great, in the *Palazzo dei Conservatori,* on the Capitoline.

The *clustering museums* on the Capitoline are, like our kit, full of facts, with some surprises. Among the great art works in the *Capitoline Museum* (left as you enter the square) are such celebrities as the *Dying Gaul,* an ancient and excellent marble replica of the original bronze; the *Resting Satyr,* being Hawthorne's *Marble Faun,* and the universally known *Capitoline Venus,* an ancient marble copy, more or less, of Praxiteles' Venus of Cnidos. The goddess is divine in body but if your eyes chance to rise to her face you will note that it is extremely earthy, dull, commonplace. In the museum's upper gallery a mosaic of doves on the edge of a bowl, from Hadrian's Villa, is often called the finest small mosaic ever made.

Among the masterpieces in the Palazzo dei Conservatori on the right (south) of the square, are such items as the *Boy Removing a Thorn from His Foot* and the bronze *She-Wolf,* familiar symbol of Rome, made by an Etruscan artist twenty-five hundred years ago. That statue long stood in a grotto on the Capitoline Hill but was struck by lightning centuries ago, leaving a scar which you and I may plainly see on the wolf's left rear leg.

One more oddity of the Capitoline may claim our attention, an oddity in headgear, always enjoyed by visitors. This is the "millinery" worn by Castor and Pollux in the statuary flanking the entrance to the small square. Each hat is a perfect half of an egg shell, no more and no less. The twins were, of course, children of Leda and the swan, who was Jupiter. Had *Leda* been the swan we would suppose one of her eggs was being thus halved and used for hats, but as it is, the whole affair is so confusing!

CHAPTER 13

THE RING OF WONDERS

The Appian Way to the Catacombs

LATE in 1951, Hollywood presented the Appian Way to breathless millions of moviegoers in the most pretentious and expensive color film ever made, *Quo Vadis*. Some twenty months prior to that I had encountered the stars, Robert Taylor and Deborah Kerr, at work on certain scenes of the supercolossal spectacle in Italy. Taylor's hair was convincingly long, for the part of Marcus Vinicius, and wherever he went gaping throngs looked on and whispered to each other in awe, "Guardi! Quello è Roberto Taylor!"

It was on the Appian Way, half a mile outside Rome's St. Sebastian Gate, that one of the most moving dramas of all time took place, according to a legend that does not fade. Here rises now the little church called *Domine Quo Vadis*, supposed to mark the exact spot where Peter, having no taste for martyrdom, was fleeing from Rome only to meet his Lord coming *toward* Rome.

"Lord, where goest thou?" he asked in consternation.

"I go to be crucified again," replied the Master, and impetuous but rock-fast Peter turned in shame and went back to Rome to accept his own fate.

The ancient Appian Way, not to be confused with the much-traveled New Appian Way, is as well known to the world as is the crisis that overtook "the first pope" while on it. The highway, chief of all Roman roads of old, and lined with ancient relics, took its name from Appius Claudius, who built it in 312 B.C. It leads to the most famous of the Christian catacombs, named for St. Calixtus, and continues thence to Capua and clear to distant Bríndisi.

We are told that the early Christians built more than forty separate catacombs around Rome, serving primarily as burial places but also as secret refuges from persecution. How they ever achieved it in secret, and where they deposited all the tufa that they excavated from those endless miles of subterranean passages, would seem to be problems for engineers to ponder. Sometimes these labyrinthine ways are four or five layers deep, like mines, and it is said that all the corridors, if stretched out in a single line, would run from the border of Switzerland all the way to Sicily!

Tourists in thousands visit the catacombs, and while I personally do not enjoy such dank Stygian explorations, guided by a friar with a lantern or torch, the historic and spiritual appeal of these winding passages is undeniable. The Christians who patiently dug them must have believed *totally* in their Redeemer, to endure what they did. Here, as in all early Christian memorials, one finds the crude sign of the fish, and sometimes, as in the grasswork outside the St. Calixtus Catacombs, the word for fish, in Greek characters ΙΧΘΥΣ. This was a universally understood cryptogram standing, as near as one can reproduce it in Latin letters, for *Iesu Christos Theou Huios Soter,* meaning Jesus Christ, Son of God, Savior.

A Papal Palace and the Mother of Rome

Castel Gandolfo, town of the summer palace of the popes, seventeen miles from Rome by the Appian Way, is thought to be on the very site of Alba Longa ("White Long"), which was the Mother Town of Rome. Tradition says that a son of Aeneas founded Alba Longa about 1050 B.C., that it was later the birthplace of Romulus and Remus and that infant Rome was its favorite daughter, though this daughter, when grown, destroyed the mother, fearing her power as capital of the Latin League.

The *Pontifical Palace,* built by the same Carlo Maderna who designed the façade of St. Peter's, is magnificently located on the lofty volcanic rim of Lake Albano, a splendid blue oval over six miles in circumference. About four hundred years before Christ, the Romans tunneled an outlet for the lake, to obtain a supply of water, and this was renewed in imperial days. Called by the Latin word *Emissarium,* this outlet can be visited today by tourists, but few bother to do so when merely *looking* at the glorious bowl of blue from up aloft is so infinitely appealing. From the town's main square, beside the palace gate, and all along the line of a famous avenue named *Galleria di Sopra* (Upper Gallery), glimpses are had that saturate the senses with the beauty of these Alban Hills.

To come down to earth with a slight bump, Castel Gandolfo may be reached by train from the Termini Station in Rome or by an electric tramway whose Roman terminus is very close to the station, on Via Amendola. The halt for Castel Gandolfo, on the Rome-Albano line, is *Ercolano*, whence a path is ascended in ten minutes to the goal. This tramway system, with conveyances that are like the offspring of railway coaches mated with streetcars, is very well worth knowing, for its various lines reach every place of importance in the Alban Hills. Personal study of the timetables, in Pozzo's tome or in the system's waiting room on Via Amendola, can be very rewarding. However, the vast majority of tourists (myself included when time is brief) visit this region, as they always have and always will, the easy way, by means of prepared tours. This sort of group travel tantalizes by its haste, but it does save a lot of wear and tear, to avoid which, otherwise, one must go to the far greater expense of hiring a private car and guide.

Castelli Romani, *Hill Towns of Wine*

The *Castelli Romani* have been mentioned in Chapter 5 as the source of the most popular Roman wines, corresponding, in a very partial way, to the "château wines" of France. Travelers who visit the Alban Hills will thereby visit these "Roman Castles," which are not castles at all, be it understood, but lovely towns and villages at various heights in the hills. The name Castelli Romani is a term used to designate all the communities in this limited volcanic area, which was, alas, a war area also, in World War II, many scars still remaining. Nearly every place of importance has its "name wine," originating from the vineyards that surround it.

For convenience, since most visitors go in group tours, I shall mention the leading towns—after Castel Gandolfo—in the order customarily followed by the big busses. (CIT, at the moment, does not operate this full tour. Your hotel porter may be consulted.)

Albano, still on the Appian Way, a mile or two beyond the path and road up to Castel Gandolfo, is a well-liked summer resort with an exceptionally beautiful public garden and with a most curious pair of conical towers of an Etruscan-style tomb.

Aríccia, a mile or more farther on, is reached by crossing a remarkable viaduct a thousand feet long and two hundred feet high, consisting of three rows of arches, one superimposed upon the other, constructed about a century ago.

Genzano, a wine town and also, in season, a strawberry town of note, lying two miles beyond Aríccia, is one of the glories of the Alban Hills. This "Roman Castle" looms almost perpendicularly, high above Lake Nemi, which is a jewel of smaller dimensions but no less beautiful than Lake Albano. The lake took its name from the *nemus*, or grove, of Diana, to whom a temple was erected on the bank. It was the play-lake of Tiberius and then of Caligula, and one of these emperors, or both in turn—chronicles seem to disagree—constructed two huge pleasure barges with marble floors and "every modern convenience," including the best imperial plumbing. The existence of these fabulous barges has long been known and three attempts were made in the last sixty years to raise them. The third, in 1931, was successful, after much of the water had been drained into Lake Albano. The barges were placed in shelters on the shore but these constructions could not shelter them from bombs! In 1944 German bombs shattered the two craft and their shed to splinters, but patient reconstruction has been undertaken and it is hoped that the floating palaces—for that is what they once were—will some day be again on display.

Velletri, which suffered from the war beyond the average of its neighbors, is farther from Rome and is not generally included on the fixed tours, but its name wine is popular.

Marino, just north of Lake Albano (and Castel Gandolfo), is notable as being a medieval home of the Colonna family, its town hall, heavily damaged in 1944, having been the actual Palazzo Colonna. One of the most famous members of this famous family, Vittoria Colonna, was born in this palace. She came to be recognized as a poetess of genuine ability, but her life was tragic. A woman of very great beauty and unquestioned purity of life, she maintained an unflagging devotion to a husband who did not value the treasure he had. To her we owe an enormous debt, for she was the chief inspiration of Michelangelo for years. He wrote sonnets to her and admired her immoderately, though no breath of scandal ever blurred the friendship. It is said that the Virgin in the scene of the *Last Judgment* on the altar wall of the Sistine Chapel is a faithful portrait of Vittoria Colonna.

Grottaferrata, a little to the northeast of Marino, is known for its ancient abbey, with art works and a library of important old manuscripts, but most visitors, intoxicated by the beauty of the Alban Hills, and perhaps slightly mellow too from sampling the good wines here and there, are content to accept this place merely as another castle of wine.

Rocca di Papa, reached by the electric train-tram but not ordinarily by the tourist busses, is the highest and most spectacularly located of all the Castelli Romani. It was originally a papal fortress, hence its name, but later passed to the engulfing Orsini family and then the Colonna family.

Frascati, most famous Roman Castle of them all in vinous terms and the most sumptuous and important of them as a holiday town for Romans, is celebrated for its palatial villas, notably the *Villa Aldobrandini*, with a park that is remarkable even in park-rich Italy for its landscaped magnificence, including a so-called Theater of the Waters.

Tivoli for Temples and Scenery

Tivoli, the most popular tourist goal in the vicinity of Rome, is not in the Alban Hills, is not one of the Castelli Romani, but it is often added to the Castelli as a climactic halt because of its marvelous scenery, keyed to gushing cascades and larger waterfalls. Oftener still it is a half-day trip in itself, enhanced by visits to *Hadrian's Villa*, a ruin of stupendous extent, for this was once the Roman World's largest and most luxurious country palace—guides tell their flocks the Hadrian estate was once ten miles in circumference—and of course the fountained splendors of the medieval *Villa d'Este*.

Tivoli is a symphony of water sounds, an achievement in polychromy of water, forest and vineyard sights. The water is from the considerable Ánio River, which used to flood the town frequently until a double tunnel was completed (in 1835) to harness the stream's madness and lead the water through a portion of Monte Catillo. The *Great Falls*, called also the *New Falls* because it *was* new in 1835, plunges from the tunnel's mouth, dropping over 350 feet. One may enter the Villa Gregoriana to see this attraction at close range, but better views of the whole ensemble are obtained from the winding *Via delle Cascatelle*, along which the tourist busses roll, stopping at appropriate belvederes. The spectacle is still an interesting one, though industry has eaten *sadly* into its grandeur by the construction of a hydroelectric power station. (On Sundays the flow is usually ampler.)

Lunching at Tivoli can be as grand as viewing it. A very favorite place to lunch is the *Sibilla*, an open-terrace place on the mountainside close to two ancient temples that were dedicated to Vesta and to the Sibyl, and close also to the waterfalls. The location is so exciting that it robs you of your appetite. The food is so good that it woos you from the view. You end up by achieving a satisfactory compromise, and that's life. Another place of great popularity and of equally fine view is the *Sirena*.

Villa d'Este and Its Fifteen Hundred Fountains

Villa d'Este and its fabulous garden of fountains is a part of Tivoli, and its waters are from the Ánio. The palace and garden were built in 1550 for Cardinal Ippolito d'Este but this magnificent prince of the church, a member of that long-flowering family whose central stronghold was Ferrara, could not, with all his wealth, stave off death. With a brother he lies in a tomb in the palace chapel, the tomb bearing the Latin inscription *Hippolyto et Aloysius Principibus Atesti*. The surname Atesti is a form of d'Este and one may note in passing that northern Italy's River Ádige is said to be still another form of Atesti or d'Este.

In this Roman Garden of the d'Este clan there are many things to marvel at, some to admire. A feature that never fails to catch the eye upon first arrival—I trust it will never be discontinued—is a "growing calendar." In the shrubbery directly below the palace appears *today's date* in fresh green box. The gardeners have all the needed numerals ready for quick transplanting each morning, and the month names are similarly ready for use when needed. I recall, as a treasured snapshot in one of my memory cells, the date when I first saw this calendar of verdure pictured in box: 20 Aprile 1950.

The garden descends from the palace in a series of terraces, and the first one is famous as the *viale delle Cento Fontane*, with a hundred jets (I didn't count them to see if the name tells the truth) spouting forth like the "waterwind" section of the symphony. There is a central circle in the garden, surrounded by imposingly tall and beautiful cypresses, said to be the tallest in Italy. They seem like giant guards and remind us inevitably of the seven-foot palace guards corralled in a former age for a Prussian monarch. In one of the arboreal lanes a remarkable trick of perspective has been achieved, making the short lane seem very long and the palace very distant, and if we are in the mood to be reminded of things, this lane will recall to those who have visited Vicenza the amazing optical illusions in the scenery of the sixteenth-century *Teatro Olimpico* in that city.

There is an odd and perhaps over-cute *Rometta* in the Villa d'Este garden, being a "Little Rome," with miniature reproductions of various well-known temples of classic Rome. This may quickly pall, but the symphony of the fifteen hundred fountains will live in the mind. Imposing ones such as the big baroque Fountain of the Sibyl are seen here and there, and very queer ones are numerous, as, for instance, the grim figure whose nostrils spout water. Others are the Peacock Tail Fountain, the Deluge Fountain and the Organ Fountain, which once operated an organ by means of water pressure. Cardinal Hippolito d'Este must have had quite a time for himself with all these aqueous playthings, and conceivably he may even have found occasional hours to attend to his ecclesiastical duties.

Latina, a Wonder of Reclamation

At its lowest estate, in the Middle Ages, the city on the Tiber had but a few thousand war-torn, disease-racked inhabitants. It was utterly despoiled and forgotten, given literally to the dogs. Today it is the great metropolis we see, clean, vigorous, afire with ambition. Its main shopping streets are brilliant, its newer living quarters as up to date as any in Europe.

As concrete (and stone and plaster) proof of Rome's energetic and creative spirit I offer first a child of the capital, born in 1932, by name *Latina*. You may reach Latina in an hour by train from the Termini Station, to see something quite out of the well-trodden tourist pattern. This fledgling town, which was earlier named Littória, is the new center of the reclaimed Pontine Marshes, a district uninhabited and uninhabitable, because of malaria, for centuries past. In 1930 or thereabouts, Rome, meaning Mussolini at that time, decided that this unhealthy region could be reclaimed, and with extraordinary zeal set about to do it. Armies of laborers, droves of long-horned white oxen and fleets of tractors were sent thither. Scores of square miles of sodden, useless, disease-giving marsh were slowly tranformed into good arable land. Hundreds of small *poderi*, plaster houses painted blue, with red tile roofs, were erected to give shelter to those who were assigned to various plots of this new land. Then came Littória (Latina), the gleaming new-born city. You could almost watch it take form before your eyes.

In the spring of 1933 I sat me down in what was then the incipient city's only café and watched what was going on. Plasterers and masons were all about me and the café had no window glass, but who cared? Things were moving. A giant bell across the way was in position to be hoisted to the tower of the unfinished city hall. The church, the schoolhouse and the post office seemed to be having a race to see which should first reach completion. The name Littória, outlined in white stones, was worked into a patch of sward. Public buildings were fairly springing into the air and a theater was half built. In the main square were knots of subcontractors holding committee meetings. Truck loads of building materials kept rolling in.

What was the source of all this stimulating activity? Of course the answer was obvious. It was written, as a matter of fact, in stone, in the unfinished city park. On the tastefully designed wellhead here one read the words ROMA A LITTORIA, and below these words was carved a she-wolf suckling two infants.

The development of the reclaimed area, now significantly called Agro Pontino (Pontine Fields), was slowed almost to a halt by the war, but has gone steadily forward under the direction of the postwar republic. Three hundred and fifty thousand acres have been drained and healthfully irrigated, thousands of houses built, and there are now at least four more pleasantly named Pontine towns: Sabáudia, Pontinia, Aprília, Pomézia. Latina itself has some 25,000 inhabitants. Agro Pontino is one answer, at least in a strong whisper, to Italy's fearful problem of overpopulation.

Ánzio and Nettuno for Memorials of '44

Two of the grimmest place names of World War II were Ánzio and Nettuno. At these two beach resorts, less than forty miles below Rome, the British and American assault troops respectively disembarked with great and successful secrecy as the night of January 21, 1944, turned into the morning of January 22. These beaches are to the Italy campaign what the beaches of the Cotentin were to the Normandy campaign in May of the same year. The troops, achieving outright surprise in this case, succeeded in forming a bridgehead that held out for exactly three terrible months, until, on May 21, relief finally came from the Allied forces that had landed at Salerno, south of Naples, and had worked their perilous way northward, by way of Cassino, to effect a junction.

At Nettuno there is an American cemetery, with the bodies of nearly 7500 officers and soldiers, and at a point two or three miles north, on the road that leads to Aprília, is a similar British cemetery.

Ánzio (Antium of old) was a tribal capital in earliest times of the Volsci, whose most famous leader was Coriolanus, and in Roman republican and imperial times it was the leading resort of the rich families of Rome. Cicero was an enthusiastic property owner, as were Caligula, Claudius and Nero, the first and last of this trio of Julian emperors having been born here. Nettuno is of less historical interest but more scenic beauty. It is supposed to have been first settled by Saracens.

To everyone except "confirmed historians" the two beach names now recall only the ghastly quarter-year in which greatly outnumbered soldiers of the Allies, aided by superior air support, fought to a standstill five crack Nazi divisions rushed up under Kesselring at

Hitler's personal command to "lance the abscess" that he feared as a threat to Rome. Those who wish to see these Tyrrhenian Sea resorts of heroic memory, one only a mile from the other, may do so, without the cost of car hire, by taking a train (via Campo Leone) from Rome's Termini Station. The fast trains, very few in number, make the run in an hour. This visit may be combined with a visit to Latina, which lies but eighteen miles south of Campo Leone on the main line to Naples.

Óstia for Relaxation

Óstia is a name taken from the Latin word for the mouth (ostium) of the Tiber, and Old Óstia (Óstia Ántica) was Rome's mighty port until, due to increasingly bad malarial conditions, it declined rapidly in the fourth century A.D., as the empire itself began to do. One character who died here (387 A.D.) and who should perhaps have been listed in our scroll of saints, was Santa Monica, the mother of St. Augustine.

Nowadays, despite the really remarkable excavations to be seen in the old part of the double community, few visitors to Italy think of Óstia save as the Lido of Rome, a place for holiday fun and swimming, and in that department I may offer some advice so that you will not make the error I did, the first time. One takes a clean little electric train from Rome's *Porta San Paolo Station*, not to Lido Centro but to *Lido Castel Fusano*, at the very end of the line. My initial error was to undertake a sea bath from one of the huge central bathing establishments—they run in an almost solid line for two miles—but later I learned how infinitely more pleasurable is a bathe taken from the Lido Castel Fusano. The sand is whiter, the water cleaner, and the people—without wishing to sound snobbish—more "desirable." There is also an exceedingly attractive sea-terrace restaurant at Castel Fusano where a first-rate meal may be had—in one's bathing suit if desired. There are private cabins for rent, with bathing gear and towels also available. In the enormous *Stabilimento Balneare Roma* of the Centro, one may take a dip of sorts, Coney Island fashion, from almost black, volcanic-looking sand, whereas in Castel Fusano one may dip and dine in genuine relaxation.

YOURSELF IN THE PICTURE OF ITALY

CHAPTER 14

TO NAPLES AND ITS FABULOUS BAY

Fórmia or Cassino on the Way

THE *Nastro Rosa,* or Pink Ribbon, of CIAT divides itself into two routes between Rome and Naples, one the direct, bee-line route via *Fórmia,* in five hours, the other a somewhat longer arc with a lunch halt at *Cassino* and a sightseeing halt at *Caserta,* an eighteenth-century "Versailles"—with imposing palace and sumptuous park—of the old Bourbon kings of Naples.

It is hard to say which route deserves the more stars, in a book like this. Fórmia, on the curving shore of the wide Gulf of Gaeta, with a dramatic view of Gaeta's old castle on a point jutting into the sea, is extremely beautiful and its *Grand Hotel Miramare,* once a royal residence, is one of Italy's most insistently appealing resort hotels. Located on a bluff directly above the bay, it is cooled by gentle Tyrrhenian breezes and its quiet aristocracy is supported, in a practical way, by the artistry of a notable chef. Any meal, every meal, including a "one-course snack" served to hurrying motor tourists, is very good, but if special delicacies are wanted they are to be had at the drop of a hint. (CIAT travelers should know that the coast-road coaches stop at the Miramare for lunch on the *north*bound run, Naples to Rome, but not on the southbound run.)

The longer route is richly worth the little extra time involved if history, including recent tragic history, is your chief interest. *Cassino,* a considerable town that served as a key point of the "Gustav Line" so obstinately held by the Nazis, was rubbed out by the bombardments of the war as effectively as any enemy was ever rubbed out by rival gangsters, so it has started from scratch to rebuild itself and it is now a new town, by no means a thing of beauty, yet worth seeing for the moving memorial it is.

The ruins of the lofty *Abbey of Monte Cassino,* glimpsed from several points along the highway, recall the awful days from February to May, 1944, when this most celebrated abbey of Italy, founded in 529 by St. Benedict as the home of the Benedictine Order, took an air-and-artillery pounding such as perhaps no other great monument has ever suffered in all history. Cloisters, church and convent went up in smoking rubble and splinters but the archives and the valuable books were mercifully saved. This prolonged Allied assault, undertaken because the Germans were using the abbey as an observation post, proved unsuccessful until the enemy finally was forced to withdraw because of the cutting of supply lines. It was an experiment that taught us the futility of trying to bomb out an enemy solidly protected by masonry and rocks. The abbey will be rebuilt in time, and even now it is worth the climb to it, requiring a stopover by those who use the CIAT busses, for the superlative view it offers. Polish shock troops showed wonderful bravery in the assaults on Monte Cassino and there is a monument to them near the summit. The Polish Cemetery, with several thousand graves, is a little lower down. A huge new monument to the troops of *all* nations involved in this tragic offensive operation is at present under construction a few miles to the south of the city and the mountain.

Caserta is one of that numerous company of "Versailles" of which there are examples in virtually all the countries that were ruled by kings contemporary with, or subsequent to, Louis XIV. The big, glittering royal palace in Caserta, with some curious decorations in Vesuvian lava, has special interest, above the general run of palaces, because it served as Mediterranean Allied Headquarters during the war and it was to this building that the humbled Nazis had to come, on April 29, 1945, to surrender Italy.

The vast *park* of the palace is exciting for its fountains and water fantasies, or would be so if one had not seen the greater (though far less extensive) wonders of Villa d'Este's garden. The park is two miles in length (one *rides* in the bus), from the palace to the main cascade, an extremely showy affair. In a pool there, Diana and her maidens disport themselves in marble nudity and a mythical ogler—I believe he was named Ateone—who couldn't resist looking, found himself turned into a horse-headed creature with a bevy of curs yapping at him. You see the whole drama in the statuary.

Settling at Santa Lucia

Looming directly above Naples' small-boat harbor of Santa Lucia, one of the most undebatably romantic spots in all Europe, are the city's leading hotels, a whole row of them lining the inner side of Via Parténope, the seafront boulevard bearing the ancient name of this mellow metropolis. The best of them, each with a luxury or first-class rating, are, to name them from east to west, *Excelsior*, *Santa Lucia*, *Vesuvio* and *Continental*. The newest of them, and the only one whose bedroom balconies virtually overhang the gaieties of Santa Lucia, is the Vesuvio, with the new office of American Express in a street-floor corner.

Hotel Vesuvio is to me one of the half-dozen most glamorous hotels of all Italy's thousands, and its really marvelous cuisine matches its physical glamors. I like the hotel for many things, but first of all for its unsurpassable location facing Santa Lucia, backed by the frowning Castel dell'Ovo and the fishermen's quarter called the Borgo Marinaro, where, as guides assert, Nelson met Lady Hamilton. (Other guides say that this occurred at the luxurious Villa Roseberry in Posíllipo.) The whole great bay, with its famous islands, lies beyond this ensemble and of course the volcano for which the hotel is named. I like the Vesuvio because I can have my breakfasts, and anything else I order, on my own personal balcony overlooking these wonders. I like it also, as an admittedly comfort-loving American, for its modernities. It is, in fact, of such modern vintage (1950), though there was an earlier like-named hotel on the same site, that it is not yet as widely known to travelers as older luxury hotels, but its newness provides creature comforts and features of decoration that the older places cannot match without total rebuilding. In décor these items include lovely flower tiles in some of the rooms and baths, products of the craftsmen of Vietri, and in the department of creature comforts, last-word plumbing and built-in wardrobes of ultra-modern design.

To conclude this paean with a fact or two, the hotel has 180 bedrooms, each with bathtub and shower except for one smaller room on each floor with a shower only. There are no rooms with windows looking solely on the court. The stone used so lavishly throughout the Vesuvio's interior is called *trani*, being like marble in appearance but with a soft buff color. The seventh and eighth floors are largely devoted to luxurious suites, and the ninth floor is chiefly a summer roof garden and restaurant, so high above the water that one may look over the lofty battlements of Castel dell'Ovo to Capri and all the contours of the lovely bay. And as a special Vesuvio feature, it has a regular 36-hour laundry service, the work being done in its own laundry, at standard charges.

Other hotel areas of Naples are the central Piazza Municipio—I have stayed with satisfaction in the *Grand Hotel Londra*—and the lofty, winding Corso Vittorio Emanuele, where *Parker's Hotel* provides first-class accommodations along with its grand outlook. The official *Annuario* lists 132 hotels and *pensioni* of all categories in Naples, including several in the Santa Lucia sector of more modest status than those mentioned above. In a general way, any place with an official second-category listing should prove entirely acceptable. Among the pensioni, few in Italy have a listing higher than the second category, and those with a first-class rating are to be considered, says the *Annuario* succinctly, "equivalent to hotels of Cat II." The only two in Naples rated "Cat I" are the *Pensione Maurice*, at 3 Via Partenope and the *Pensione Panorama* on Via San Pasquale a Chiaia.

Sights and Scenes of Napoli

Naples is one great city, I think, that should certainly be seen rather than "sightseen." There are a thousand typical things to experience, generally alluring, sometimes irritating, always colorful, frequently unkempt, but of tourist sights that mustn't be missed I admit only three, the *National Museum*, the *Aquarium* and *San Martino*, a hillside treasure that very frequently *is* missed even by experienced travelers.

Naples is *different* and if you condition yourself and get in the mood for it you will love it, from its volcanic setting to its volcanic temperament, from its elegant beauties to its perennial rackets. Even at the moment of arrival you will be made violently aware of this city's difference from others in Italy and this will be tenfold emphasized if you have not reserved lodgings in advance, for all Naples, it seems, is personally concerned with your problem.

You secure a *facchino* to tote your bags, for stowage in a checking place while you look for a room that calls you. Then you stride right into the maelstrom.

First you walk through a bedlam of hotel porters, some in uniform, others mere touts, and then a bedlam of hoarsely shouting taxi men and/or whip-cracking cabbies, and then you find yourself escorted by a bodyguard of perhaps a score of Neapolitans, young and old, crack troops made up of the very finest scum of one of the most crowded port cities in Europe.

"You want a hotel, mister?"

"You want some post cards, mister?"

"Want some beads, mister?"

"Carry your bag, mister?" (It is actually a typewriter that you have elected to keep hold of personally.)

You decide to brazen things out in dignified silence, but one gamin, bolder than the rest, actually tugs at your typewriter. You have to struggle, physically, to keep possession of it. This is the proper time to lose your temper, and you lose it.

"Get away, you! And you too! All of you!"

The troops fall back a pace or two and you march proudly on, but in a trice they are all with you again.

"Carry your macchina, mister?"

"You want a hotel?"

It suddenly strikes you funny and you laugh right out—which is an enormous tactical blunder, as it proves to your bodyguard that you are weakening.

"Hey, mister! Hey, mister! You want a hotel? Post cards? You want to see a good show? Want to buy a Parker 51 very cheap?"

Perhaps you look at the pen, and if you unscrew it and look at the barrel very closely you will find that the inscription reads *P. Arker. Type 51.* The vendor hopes you didn't notice the period after the P. He tells you earnestly that a sailor friend smuggled it ashore and you can have it for next to nothing, say five dollars. You beat him down to one dollar, even fifty cents, which may still be too high for the junk he offers you. Then you tell him off, pointing out the fraud. Dejectedly he turns away to hunt for another victim.

The curtain is lowered and raised to denote the passing of half an hour. You have proved your mettle, found accommodations and are setting out to see Naples, to become a tourist "super" on the stage itself. The procedure just pictured may actually be enjoyed by college students and sound-nerved men who like a lively battle. To all others I strongly recommend definite advance selection of your hotel *in Naples*. (In any city north of Naples, perhaps excepting ever-crowded Rome, it is much less necessary.)

We are eager to be out treading the streets of Naples, lineal descendants of the paths of Parthenope. We all know that Naples, since time immemorial, has been called the City of Parthenope, but a few of us do not know exactly *why* until we have looked it up. It seems, then, that the siren of Capri was madly, hopelessly, in love with Ulysses and when, cold to her charms, he escaped her and fled, she flung herself despairingly into the sea. Her body was washed up where Naples now lies and the local colonists, from the island of Rhodes, gave their settlement her name. It has clung through twenty-seven centuries and it still clings to Naples' superb shore boulevard.

Neapolis means, of course, New City and modern Italy has succeeded by vast efforts, in making this name partly true, in spite of, or perhaps because of, the war ravages that laid waste big areas, especially along the harbor, necessitating drastic rebuilding operations. If you do not see much difference at the dock or the station, and if the incorrigible night-life racket still goes on, it is nevertheless true that Naples has had her face a little bit lifted and partially scrubbed. Efforts have even been made to improve the ethics of those humble folk who batten upon tourists in the streets and restaurants, but with dubious results. Old Naples is still going her easy way and perhaps you would hardly want to change her. Steep little streets, festooned with drying linen and ripe with alley smells, still exist in plenty; the tarantella is still danced and "Santa Lucia" is still sung to the accompaniment of twanging guitars.

The throbbing center of this very populous metropolis is the **Galleria Umberto Primo**. Search it out and settle for half an hour in one of its cafés and you will see half the city pass before your eyes under the Galleria's great glass roof. What a mob! What an endless, seething, eddying whirlpool of humanity! And how unceasingly interesting!

If you can tear yourself away from this human panorama and from the assorted street scenes of one of the world's most vibrant cities to view some of Naples' unique treasures, you will be very richly repaid. A celebrated sight of the city, the *Museo Nazionale*, contains many of the most important antique sculptures in the world, dug up for the most part from the volcanic material that buried Herculaneum and Pompeii. (Volcanic mud covered Herculaneum, imparting a dark hue to everything that has been found there, while lava and ashes buried Pompeii, leaving a greener hue on statuary and other things exhumed from that city.) The museum contains, for a few examples, the marble *Farnese Bull*, the *Dancing Faun*, the *Narcissus*, the reposing *Mercury*, the *Drunken Silenus* and half a dozen "Veni," of whom the most famous is the *Venus Callipyge*, though this is an ancient copy of the original. The fame of this statue is frankly due less to the quality of the execution than to the unusual emphasis on anatomy. The compound Greek word tells the unblushing truth, that this is the Venus-of-the-Beautiful-Behind. The museum's bronzes and marbles are equally well known; and its Pompeiian frescoes, done largely in a red that subsequent artists have never been able to reproduce, are perhaps the most famous of all, though they seem greatly unsuited to the sixteenth-century barracks in which the museum is housed.

The *Gabinetto Pornographico* at the end of the mezzanine corridor is not exhibited except to those with a special permit, but a museum attendant manages to make a good thing out of tourist curiosity. He winks suggestively to men, indicating that after their women have withdrawn he will show them some frescoes that *are* frescoes. What he actually exhibits are perhaps merely a few nudes and a nearly obliterated hermaphrodite, less sensual by far than what is shown to every woman tourist in the Ara Pacis hall of the Uffizi, in the Borghese Gallery of Rome and in many another gallery, less sensual, in fact, than the conspicuous phallic lamps and ornaments on open display in this very museum.

The *Aquarium of Naples*, though perhaps not up to the level it maintained before the war, is still a wonderful attraction, offering a weird and in some features an almost unique display of life in "the sea around us." The collections of the aquarium were world famous long before Vicente Blasco Ibañez saw them, but the Spanish novelist, in *Mare Nostrum*, added fresh luster. He quite frankly forgot all about his novel and left his adventuress standing about in the corridor while he discussed for fifty or seventy-five brilliant pages the finny and tentacled monsters here and even in the great deep. It is a fascinating exercise in research to get hold of *Mare Nostrum* and read or reread his encyclopedic discussion. After doing so you'll be ready to see the Aquarium.

The park in which this building lies is one of the loveliest shorefront parks in any European city, for the peerless bay is directly before it, the waves slap the sea wall, and across the bay lies Vesuvius. No mountain in the world, not even the Matterhorn or the Jungfrau, has quite the universal appeal of Vesuvius. If there is any appreciable activity in its soaring hulk (sometimes it seems almost dormant) it will seize and hold your gaze. By day its plume of shifting smoke, by night its pillar of fire, proclaim that it is one of the main doors of that terrible fiery furnace where even Shadrach, Meshach and Abednego could scarcely abide in comfort.

A little over two thousand years ago the gladiator Spartacus, defying Rome, took refuge with his followers in the very crater of Vesuvius. It was cold then, stone cold and choked with vines and brambles. The gladiators, in fact, made ropes of the vines and so escaped the Roman legions which had apparently trapped them. For a hundred and fifty years Vesuvius bided its time, as cold as the corpse men thought it, then burst forth (79 A.D.) in pent-up rage so terrible, so unutterably violent, that it has become a symbol of destruction throughout the ages. Some seventy times since then it has scorched with hot ashes or drowned in boiling lava the villages that dare to climb its flanks, and it gives no sign of improving in temper.

In April 1906, to reveal my rare early vintage, I was with my parents on the good ship *Thetis* of the (then) Austrian Lloyd Line nosing into the Adriatic harbor of Cáttaro, a good three hundred miles from Naples. We all noticed that a peculiar white powder was falling thickly on the sea, on the *Thetis*, and more particularly on us. Continuous brushing of our clothes did little good. It was uncanny, inexplicable, and no one, from the captain down, could hazard a guess as to what caused it. Only next day did we learn that Vesuvius had again blazed forth in wrath, the worst outburst possibly since 79 A.D. It was then that the roof of the Neapolitan market hall, weighted with ashes, crashed down on screaming victims, and frightened tourists scampered from Naples as though the last trump had sounded.

The very uncertainty of Old Vesuv' is part of his fascination. You love him, you admire him, you deplore him. Sometimes still you have cause to fear him, but he is a fixture in the Neapolitan scene. You can no more think of Naples without this mountain than of Rome without its Colosseum. The Colosseum is unlikely to destroy even the most delicate flower that blooms within its crater, but the mountain is different. Tomorrow, maybe, or century after next, it will once more breathe out threatenings and slaughter.

* * *

A third sight of Naples, quite lacking in fame and very often ignored even by eager repeater-tourists, is to me the most exciting of all. I refer to the *National Museum of San Martino*, in a Carthusian monastery of the fourteenth century perched high on the side of the Vómero Hill beside the Castel Sant'Elmo above central Naples. The museum itself, housing countless souvenirs of the city and of the old Kingdom of Naples, plays somewhat the same role here that the Musée Carnavalet plays in Paris, but I do not urge its collections upon you, interesting though they are. Rather, I urge the vast rambling building that contains them. From several rooms and corridors, and more especially from the little room called the Belvedere, you find yourself hanging in mid-air, unbelievably *straight over* Naples, as if in a helicopter. The magnificence of this prospect of city and bay and volcano makes mere words of encomium ashamed to be uttered or written. See it yourself and judge whether adjectives can do anything for San Martino.

The CIT city tours and those of other companies take their passengers to the very doors of this monastery-turned-museum, on a lofty street called Via Tito Angelini. They let you get out and exclaim about the wonderful but limited view. The guide points out some terrace restaurants a few steps from the street (Renzo and Lucia; Paradiso; Belvedere), all with engrossing views, but then, perhaps after you've bought some souvenirs or post cards from the crowding vendors, it is time to board the bus and move on. You have not even entered San Martino and the views you have seen are merely A* views instead of A***. To give yourself all the best, flag a taxi or, more natively, board a city bus on Via Partenope (Number 244, plainly marked San Martino), and go straight to your goal. The terminus of the line is squarely in front of the museum entrance. This wonder of travel is yours for the taking and you may devote to it an hour or two instead of a minute or two.

Tourist Geography of the Bay

Too often, travelers with limited time for Naples' bay master its tourist geography and learn its excursion possibilities only as they are leaving it altogether. Half an hour's advance study would easily forestall that phrase of frustration, "If I'd only known!" Here then are some facts-in-advance.

The city's information office of the EPT is at 15 Via Vittorio Emanuele (formerly Via San Carlo), very near the central Galleria. The organization publishes numerous alluring and useful folders, maps and even a pamphlet guide in English, *Naples and Surroundings*.

CIT has several offices, the large main one being at 72 Piazza Municipio, a few steps down the slope from the Ente office. Its list of guided tours, set forth in various leaflets and booklets, seems to me even more comprehensive than that offered in the Rome office, and here, as in all large cities of Italy, CIT picks you up at your hotel and, upon concluding the tour, delivers you at your hotel. Ten different trips in Naples and its environs are now offered, ranging in length from half a day to two full days, and these include, of course, the boat trips to the islands of Capri and Ischia, with motor trips on those islands. Smart selection is a real problem for those who have only a week or less.

Tourist geography of the bay comprises a horseshoe of wonders. The inner part of the curve is the stretch from the city itself past Herculaneum and Pompeii to the thermal resort of Castellammare di Stábia. The north prong of the horseshoe is Pozzuoli, backed by the volcanic Campi Flegrei, with the "extension islands" of Prócida and Íschia. The south prong is Sorrento, with the Isle of Capri in its front yard. Beyond this prong, but definitely a part of Naples' tourist geography, is the Gulf of Salerno, with the unsurpassably lovely coastal towns of Positano, Amalfi, Ravello and so forth. The traditional "grand tour," two days in length, covers Pompeii, the Amalfi Coast, back by a different highway to Sorrento (overnight) and by steamer to Capri for the second day. On the afternoon of this second day another steamer carries the trippers to Naples' Beverello Quay, where busses pick them up for transportation to their respective hotels.

If only one major trip can be taken the above is undoubtedly the most important and diversified, but I happen to be a devotee of forgotten Íschia and shall trumpet the charms of that neglected island later in this chapter.

The Fields of Vulcan and the Lake of Hell

The *Phlegraean Fields* (*Campi Flegrei*), back of the port of Pozzuoli, are hotbeds of disturbance, not made by Communists in this case but by Vulcan himself. The traditional tourist trip features a substantial halt at the *Solfatara*, where one may make the closest acquaintance with a miniature volcano and with various other volcanic phenomena. Guides announce that if you wear any nylon garments you shouldn't come too close, for Vulcan has a warm affinity for this product. I *did* approach, nylons and all, and nothing happened. I didn't even explode or go up in smoke.

The tour usually includes a halt at the impressive *Vespasian Amphitheater* in Pozzuoli—the ancient Puteoli, a flourishing city of commerce when Paul landed here after his adventures in Crete and Malta—but to see the region of the Phlegraean Fields in its entirety calls for a private car and a guide, or else for a laboriously managed all-day trip by railway and carriage, too complicated to set forth here.

The whole region abounds in interesting sights, many of them saturated with history, and I shall list here half a dozen of the chief ones, though the order in which the visitor sees them may vary greatly.

Báia was the very smartest and most magnificent beach resort of imperial Rome and many sumptuous villas were erected here, some of them rising directly from the sea. Corruption and sybaritic profligacies brought the place, in time, to utter decay and then to utter ruin.

Bácoli, farther out on a small peninsula, is the place where the playful Nero murdered his mother Agrippina in 59 A.D. A tomb called that of Agrippina is shown near the village.

The *Piscina Mirabile* is an ancient reservoir of classical times adjacent to the ancient peninsula port of *Misenum*, built by Agrippa for one of his fleets. Misenum (now Miseno) is supposed to have taken its name from that of the trumpeter of an early "tourist," Aeneas!

The little lakes name *Fusaro* and *Lucrino* were oyster-bed lakes of the old Romans and are of similar luscious use again for the moderns, including such traveling moderns as ourselves.

Cumae (now Cuma) was the abode of the very celebrated *Cumaean Sibyl*, rival in fame of the Delphic Oracle as a mysterious and ambiguous prophetess. The Sibylline Books originated here.

Lake Avernus (now Averno) was the very entrance to the hell of the Greek world, as every schoolboy knows who has taken a course in ancient history, though very few boys, or their parents, probably realize that the mouth of Hades is in a suburb of Naples. It was into this lake that the Sibyl led the intrepid Aeneas. Emperors Augustus and Agrippa made the lake into a naval harbor by building a canal from it to the sea and thus robbed it of its age-old terrors. Agrippa also built a tunnel from Lake Avernus to Cumae and until the Second World War of our own tortured times it was entirely practical to walk through it—three-quarters of a mile from one end to the other— but bombardments heavily damaged it. Avernus became a modern Lake of Hell and the tunnel a Roman wreck.

Herculaneum, Pompeii and Their Mountain of Murder

Herculaneum, the only community ever to be named for Hercules— this hero was locally worshiped as a god—was a wealthy resort, while Pompeii was a commercial city of prestige and importance, but Vesuvius, in a spirit of impartiality, buried them both. The layer of volcanic mud and lava over the former attained, through all the eruptions, a depth of from forty to a hundred feet, while the latter was submerged in ashes and pumice to a depth of only seven or eight feet above the roof tops. It follows naturally that only a few valuable finds have been exhumed with difficulty from Herculaneum, whereas much of Pompeii has long since been excavated and laid bare before our eyes, exactly as Vesuvius left it nearly nineteen hundred years ago.

Very few tourists who visit Naples briefly use any of their precious time on the *Scavi di Ercolano* (Excavations of Herculaneum), but virtually everyone allots some time to Pompeii. The bus tours similarly skip by Ercolano with a few words of comment from the guide and concentrate on Pompeii. Most tourists make their visit in a guided tour, but if you feel in a more rugged mood, be advised of certain rugged facts. 1. There is a light railway system called the *Circumvesuviana*, its Naples station on Corso Garibaldi (at Number 387), a few blocks south of Piazza Garibaldi. From this station trains roll out at intervals of about an hour and creep around the base of Vesuvius. 2. If Herculaneum is your goal, you descend at the station of *Pugliano*, which is part of the village of *Resina* built upon the engulfed resort. 3. About a quarter of a mile from Pugliano Station is the starting point for the *Vesuvian Electric Railway*, which toils five miles up toward the crater (more later on this). 4. The Circumvesuviana meanders along for about an hour, covering a grand total of sixteen miles, to the station called *Pompei Scavi* (our spelling of Pompeii is an odd invention, the name having but one *i* in Italian) and here you enter the exhumed city, most famous of its sort. You are ready to visit the world of 79 A.D., when Titus was emperor of Rome and when many persons still lived who had talked with Jesus Christ.

* * *

Since most tourists go as the bus goes, this swift text shall do likewise.

Torre del Greco (literally Tower of the Greek), a considerable town just beyond Herculaneum, is the center of the craft of carving coral, shells and minerals, a big business, second in importance locally to the manufacture of macaroni. Much coral is drawn from the harbor all along here. Much more is imported for carving. Always the tourist busses stop at one or two of the large factories for a visit to the salesrooms. Always the women glow, burble and buy. Always the men look on—and pay. But the stuff is fascinating. The guides, who presumably are rewarded by the factories, are ever ready with torrents of information, as are the salesgirls. They point out, in addition to fine corals, various shells susceptible of fine carving, and dark minerals, some almost chocolate colored which they call sardonyx from Cuba, others of delicate reddish hues which they call carnelian from Madagascar. Wonderful effects are achieved by the carvers and some of the cameo and intaglio work reaches the level of artistry.

Torre Annunziata, five miles beyond the "Tower of the Greek," is famous in the Naples area as the spot where the dreadful lava flow of the 1906 eruption stopped, at the upper end of the town. Of course the faithful saw a miracle in this, but one hopes they took time out to mourn the fate of neighboring communities where the hoped-for miracle did *not* occur. Vesuvius' flanks, by the way, all along this bay shore hereabouts, form the center of the culture of vines that produce the delectable wine called *Lacrima Cristi* (Tear of Christ).

The wonders of Pompeii are far too numerous and extensive even to list here and it is quite unnecessary anyway, since local guidebooks and guidebooklets abound for the use of those with time for more than the usual cursory viewing. An English-language pamphlet of sixty pages by Dr. M. Della Corte, Director of the Excavations and member of the Archeological Institute of America, is to be had at the entrance. Its down-to-earth text and its numerous illustrations, together with a plan of the excavated streets, make it something of a treasure in small compass.

The hastiest visitor to Pompeii senses the awful suddenness of the tragedy that overwhelmed this city. The volcanic material formed perfect molds of many persons—two thousand were killed; twenty thousand or more escaped—and even of many animals. The stuff became rock-hard and gradually the body within the mold decomposed. All the excavators had to do was to pour plaster carefully within these molds and they had plaster casts of the persons and animals. In the museum at the excavations we see a woman thus recreated in plaster. She had lain on her stomach, trying desperately to shield her head from the rush of poisonous gases. We see the whole thing and we see *her*, a well-formed woman with pretty legs and callipygian curves. We even see her interesting hair-do, still in plaster. Similarly we see a plaster dog in his last agonies, striving in panic to bury his head beneath his paws.

The local guide (required) allows little time for such grim contemplations. Summoning his finest phrases ("Let's go, folks. Okeydokey. You haven't seen nuthin' yet."), he herds his sheep outside the museum and into the ancient city, where, under his leadership and lectureship, we see the Pompeian temples, forums, markets, theaters, hotels, baths, brothels and, above all, the superb mansions of the rich. We see a score or more of city streets, often revealing ruts in the stones worn by the constant pressure of cart and chariot wheels. We see, too, many a hint of the way of life of first-century Pompeii. In the Temple of Diana we see a statue of that goddess, with a hole in the back of her head through which the voice of a priestess, who lurked below, could be cleverly piped when it was desired that the goddess should utter a prophecy or some advice—for a consideration.

In such splendid mansions as the Vettii House, the House of the Golden Cupids, the House of Menander and the Villa Juliana, each surrounding its own handsome patio, we see the wealth and ease of life of the Roman rich, also their frequently amoral habits. Elaborate frescoes, depicting, for instance, the initiation of a maiden into the mysteries of Dionysos, including her ecstasy at the revelation of the phallus, were considered entirely suitable for the walls of a sumptuous home. In the building numbered 40 on the Della Corte plan, a building thought to have been Pompeii's most important hotel, a *cella meretricia* is shown under the staircase, this being the chamber of the prostitute of that hotel, as an appropriate symbol over her door made plain to male guests. An interesting item on the other side of the ledger is evidence, scratched on the walls, that in this very hotel Christianity was first proclaimed to the Pompeians by a missionary from Puteoli. His name is not given but he was probably one of Paul's converts.

Pornographic pictures, sculptured figures and decorations are numerous, fancy lamps, for instance, being favored, whose ingenious designs present a trio or quartet of powerful phalli supporting the chains that hold up the oil containers. In the *Lupanar*, a pretentious two-story brothel, many obscene sketches are scratched on the walls, and the clients who came here did not hesitate to scratch their names as well, along with those of "hostesses" who had pleased them. In a small house near one of the exits of the city is a special Pornography Room, shown to male tourists and frequently to women as well, "if you can take it, ladies," as the guide warns. Of the bus load on one recent visit of mine, every lady, without exception, "took it," and then came out of the room endeavoring to look bored.

Pompeii is unquestionably one of the most remarkable travel sights in the world and its special "oddities"—shall we say—should never obscure its solid wonders as an open book of life in the world of commerce and society at the beginning of our era.

* * *

I have mentioned the Vesuvian Railway in connection with the station of Pugliano, on the Circumvesuviana. This mountain-climbing affair ascends by two stretches of adhesion railway and one of rack-and-pinion a distance of five miles to the lower station (2500 feet altitude) of what *used to be* the funicular to the crater's rim. This funicular was destroyed by the eruption of 1906, was painfully rebuilt, was again destroyed by the eruption of 1944. Again—they say—it is being, or to be, rebuilt. If the job is ever completed it will make this the world's most undiscourageable rail line. Meanwhile one climbs up to the rim, in a guided tour if desired, by a rough-on-shoes path in fifty minutes, to win an exciting view of the crater itself and a stupendous one of the glorious region over which the mountain broods. The altitude of the rim is about four thousand feet.

Beauty in Crescendo: Amalfi, Sorrento, Capri

The classic of Neapolitan tourism, to repeat here the itinerary, is the two-day tour that starts with a visit to Pompeii; continues by road to the Gulf of Salerno; winds back along Amalfi shores to Sorrento (dinner and over night); proceeds next morning by steamer to Capri, for a day on that island; returns by steamer to Naples in the late afternoon. The beauties of the first day are so overpowering that anything like a crescendo seems quite impossible, until the second day proves that it *is* possible. The outgoing road crosses the Peninsula of Sorrento by way of Scafati, Nocera, Cava (one groans to hear the guide call this lovely area "the Neapolitan Switzerland"), to descend to the sea at Vietri, the "tile town," only a couple of miles short of Salerno. Travelers who plot their own course may easily diverge for a visit to that port city, whose ruins still proclaim the bitter Allied landing in September 1943, and to *Paestum*, on the far side of the wide gulf, for a view of some of the best-preserved temples of the ancient Greek world. Those who follow the course of the busses, however, will double back at Vietri to skirt the sea for many miles on the highway that leads to and beyond Amalfi.

The Amalfi Drive, the darling of travel ever since it was completed in 1852, is still and always a blue ribbon highway, or shoreway. As I think of it I feel almost inclined to recant my words about the Capri Climax. The road is carved out of the solid cliffs for nearly thirty miles and where the cliffs give way to gulleys, hewn by the rain-made *torrenti*, it leaps across them by means of airy viaducts, often five hundred feet above the sea. Below the road one views in narrow coves the most improbable fishing villages, reachable, it seems, only by helicopter. Above the road one sees eagle-nest villages clinging to any cleft they can find.

Consider some of the double-star communities along this road, from east to west.

Marina, Cetara, Maiori, Minori, Atrani (whence the climbing road to *Ravello*), and then AMALFI.

This key town of the drive was an independent republic, and an important one, for several centuries, vying for a time even with Venice. It had seventy thousand inhabitants and boasted a very extensive Mediterranean trade. Its maritime code, called *Tavole Amalfitane*, was the recognized code for the whole Inland Sea, but the Normans of Sicily, and then the Pisans, attacked the republic and reduced its importance. A frightful storm in 1343 delivered the *coup de grâce*, drowning and wrecking much of the town. Its destiny, from then on, was merely to bring delight to visitors as one of the most romantic communities of Italy both in appearance and in setting. The cathedral, of Lombard-Norman style, with a black and white zebra-striped portal, is interesting to look at, interesting also to reach, if your heart and wind and limbs are up to it. The broad stairway consists of sixty-two steps.

Ravello, a thousand feet above Amalfi, was once an important part of the Amalfi Republic, is now a sleepy village of rare loveliness in a setting which many favor as the best of this whole drive. Its Romanesque cathedral and, of special appeal, its Norman-Moorish *Palazzo Rufolo*, in which Boccaccio used to be a frequent visitor, give it distinction. Wagner is said to have composed *Parsifal* in Ravello.

Beyond Amalfi, still to the west, the scenery of the shoreway maintains its incredible average of beauty. *Conca dei Marini* is one of the first villages encountered and it lies 916 steps above its tiny harbor, where its menfolk fish at night with the aid of lanterns. An Italian friend who took his bride to this village for his honeymoon told me that "half the inhabitants now live in Brooklyn." He met one woman who asserted solemnly that she had *twenty* nephews in Brooklyn!

The road passes high above the cove village of *Furore*, with twenty-four inhabitants, and *Praiano*, with forty-eight, finally to reach *Positano*, the paradise of painters. The Norman-Moorish influence, stemming from Palermo, is extremely evident here. Many of the homes have Moorish domes or cupolas and the little church needs only a minaret to look like a genuine Moslem mosque. All around Positano, and indeed all along the whole drive, olive groves, vineyards, fruit orchards and above all lemon groves, in endless miles, add their touches of opulence to the landscape. The lemons must number high into the millions, all told, and many of them grow under trellises that are partly netted, or even thatched, to protect the fruit from this coast's occasional frosts.

A few miles beyond Positano the road becomes literally a high way, zigzagging up more than a thousand feet to cross the backbone of the peninsula and descend to Sorrento on the bay side.

Sorrento is the very shrine of tourism, with animated streets and a handsome "view park," with many good hotels, many lively cafés and countless shops and sidewalk vendors specializing mostly in lace and woodwork. Of the hotels, by far the largest and most conspicuous is the *Excelsior Grand Hotel Vittoria*, under the same ownership as the big Vesuvio across the bay. It is on the cliff directly above the town's steamer landing, having its own private elevator from wharf to hotel, and is specially relished for one of the most inviting café-terraces anywhere on the bay. Here, if accommodations can be had, tourists usually put up for the intervening night of the two-day classic, but two or three other first-class hotels are available, if this one proves to be full. The *Europa Palace*, also squarely on the front, was completely rebuilt in 1952 and is first-class in every way. Others on the edge of the cliff are the *Imperial Tramontano*, *La Terrazza* and *Loreley* of first, second and third category, respectively. The first-class *Cocumella* is farther from the center.

Essentials of Capri, from Tiberius to Axel Munthe

Those who take the two-day special tour have the essentials of Capri—*some* of them, I should say—neatly prepared and wrapped up, and perhaps this is the best way to see the island for the first time, but Capri has such wonderful riches, often quite hidden from the eye of the bus, that a *personal* visit, of as long duration as possible, cries to be had. It is even defensible, I think, if one has but two or three days for the Bay of Naples, to spend the *whole* time on Capri.

On a visit to Naples between the World Wars I set out to "do" the southern half of the bay, "on my own." After a short stay at Sorrento and a night on Capri I was going to continue on to Amalfi, Ravello and Salerno. Amalfi especially called me. I remembered having been convoyed thither, from Sorrento, years before by a cabby named "Honest John," so disreputable in his extortions that the trip had been half spoiled. I wanted to repair the damage by this new trip. Then too, like everyone married during the first quarter of the century, I had as an ornament of my home the *Monk of Amalfi*—a wedding present. But despite even that call I remained for three whole days and nights on Capri. I went further and gave this island a niche in my personal hall of fame.

My claim is that those who associate the place primarily with group travel, with clicking camera shutters, with untidy orange peels and with tempests of exclamatory ohs and ahs, have missed the real Capri. This hullabaloo centers around the village square, the Grande Marina, the Villa San Michele and the Blue Grotto, but those are not the total of Capri's attractions, by a very long shot.

What is the essential Capri? I must explain myself. Rise early some morning and climb from the Grande Marina the steep zigzag path that leads past Axel Munthe's villa (that is important but it will keep); then stroll on to oriental-looking Anacapri and locate the path to *La Migliara.*

You will arrive at that lost point, after a considerable hike, most unexpectedly. Apparently you are strolling through pied meadows as quiet as a Devon pasture, when, to your utter astonishment, you find yourself looking straight down—nine hundred and sixty feet— to the bluest crinkled sea imaginable. Flowers, almost as blue, are all about you, amused at your astonishment. They know all about these tremendous cliffs of the Punta Carena. They know the Faraglioni and are not afraid to climb up and down, clinging where no human hands or feet could cling. Below, like tiny figurines fashioned by a clever carver, two fishermen are seated in two painted hollow chips waiting for their big cork-buoyed net to fill. One of them bethinks himself of an anecdote, a grievance, a joke, and speaks out to his pal in the the other boat, who interrupts with a counter-anecdote, a counter-grievance or a counter-joke. For two or three minutes their voices, very faint but clear as distant cowbells on a Swiss alm, float up to you. Their minuscule hands fly about. Then suddenly the excitement is over. The fishermen have yielded the air to a couple of screaming gulls. All this is Capri.

Or again, visit the grim, half-terrifying *Villa of Timberio,* to use the local Caprian name for old Emperor Tiberius. There may be some native claptrap here, perhaps a dubious character trying to dragoon you into hiring him as a guide. Shake him off and press upward towards the ruined villa. A determined tout, male or female, may try to sell you some wine, offering incidentally to show you the precise point from which the blood-gorged emperor threw his victims into the sea. Shake off this pest too, and continue on your way. At length you are beyond such importunities on the very crest of that superb hill where Tiberius made his home—if one can call a tyrant's den a home. It is a hundred and fifty feet loftier than La Mígliara and just as precipitous.

Finally, if you would discover "unguided" Capri, stroll, as dusk settles, to some deserted spot on the Anacapri road and watch faint lights across the bay prick out the contours of Naples. This is one of the grandest sights I know, and the perfume of invisible orange and lemon groves plays its seductive role in shaping one's mood to sensuous appreciation.

* * *

Neither the *Blue Grotto* nor *Villa San Michele* should by any means be missed merely because they are double-starred items of any prepared trip. For the Blue Grotto one takes a launch or rowboat from Grande Marina to the Grotto's mouth and a smaller rowboat to and within it. The effects within are so wonderful, all of a luminous, pervasive, indescribable blue, that they demolish the spirit of iconoclasm with the first splashing of an oar. The whole grotto is like a jeweled water-sky and each time the boatman dips his oars into the blue they come up dripping with sapphires. Capri has a Green Grotto and a White Grotto on the opposite side of the island, but the Blue one receives and deserves most of the attention.

The *Villa of San Michele*, home of Axel Munthe made famous by his book, *The Story of San Michele*, was built by the Swedish doctor-author lovingly and carefully over a period of twenty years, being in large part the reconstruction of a Roman villa that stood here. The lady guide who now shows the place to visitors, hundreds of them every day, says that she is a daughter of Rosina, who still lives, and a granddaughter of Pasquale, now dead, both of whom readers of the book will remember. Munthe himself died in Stockholm in 1949 at the age of ninety-two. He had been the lifelong crony of King Gustaf V and lived for many years with him in the royal palace. His passion as a collector is very evident, for the villa is packed with finds he made. These include a Medusa head he found in the sea off Capri and a skull with gold coins in its mouth that he dug up in his own garden. They include also a marvelous Roman mosaic table he acquired from a washerwoman. Discovering the laundress slapping out her wet clothes on this wonderful old treasure, he offered to get her a nice new wooden table, so much more convenient and easy on her hands, and exchange it for her old one. Eagerly she took him up on this swap!

Some practicalities may conclude my Capri paean, commencing

with the suggestion that Italians are naturally pleased when tourists pronounce the island's name correctly, Cápri. Few do so nowadays, apparently because a perennially favorite popular song, first brought out years ago, demands for its own rhythm that the ictus be on the last syllable of the "isle of Caprí."

Direct steamers connect Naples' "tourist quay" with Capri's Grande Marina, while more luxurious steamers make the longer trip to the island by way of Sorrento. Motor boats supplement the steamers, so there is certainly no lack of service.

A funicular ascends from the wharf to the center of the village-capital, which is seated on a strikingly handsome saddle, its two feet in the stirrups of its two harbors. From here workadays busses may be taken to Anacapri and to Píccola Marina.

Hotels of all classes are numerous on the island. The only one of de luxe rating is the *Grand Hotel Quisisana*, but the *Morgano e Tiberio Palazzo* is a large place of first-class rating. On the three-day stay mentioned above, I ensconced myself very pleasantly in the *Hotel Grotta Azzurra* (Blue Grotto), humbly third-class but wonderfully located just above the Grande Marina. At Anacapri there are two hotels, the *Caesar Augustus* and the *Eden Paradiso*, of the first category. Farouk, before and after abdication, thought both of them worthy of his royal patronage. The Caesar Augustus, hanging dizzily in mid-sky on the cliff's edge, has a view you'll never forget.

* * *

To sum up the hiking challenges of the island, I shall list here five superb walks that radiate from the Capri saddle, placing them in the order of my personal preference.

Anacapri and La Mígliara. (Allow 3 hours out and back; or, if bus is used to Anacapri, the time allowance may be halved.)
Monte Tibério. (Allow 2 hours.)
Punta Tragára, with its magnificent *Belvedere.* (Allow 1 hour.)
Arco Naturale, a grand Natural Arch. (Allow an extra half hour to include this with 2 or 3 above.)
The road to Píccola Marina. (Allow 1 hour.) This touristical but very lovely road was built by Friederich Krupp of Essen and it

was formerly named for him, but the name now has decidedly unpleasant connotations to Italians, so it has long since been rechristened Strada Cesare Augusto.

* * *

An old Capri booklet dating from between the World Wars lists a galaxy of emperors, from Caesar Augustus to Wilhelm II, and a still more luminous group of literary celebrities: Meredith, Conrad, Norman Douglas (have you read *South Wind?*), Francis Brett Young, Compton Mackenzie, Booth Tarkington, D. H. Lawrence and Axel Munthe, whose names are associated with Capri; but then, in sudden panic, it disavows any blue-stocking tendencies and reminds you of the jazz band of *Caffè Hiddigeigei.* That "in-town" place is now utterly eclipsed by Gracie Fields' luxurious establishment, a restaurant, swimming pool and night club in the Piccola Marina sector, called *La Canzone del Mare* (The Song of the Sea). The charm of Capri cannot be lightly ticketed. It is as old as Parthenope herself, who would not, however, like my adjective. She lived here and lured bold mariners to their doom. It is as new as tomorrow morning's dewdrops. Ulysses managed to escape. I wonder if you and I can summon fortitude enough to do likewise.

Forgotten Íschia

Íschia, largest of Naples' islands (21 miles in circumference), is curiously neglected by tourists and for that reason those who do make their way here often consider it a treasure island beyond price. In a bay less rich in wonders than this one, it would be *the* place to visit and might thereby lose some of its simple charm.

The steamer trip between Naples and the chief port of Íschia, with a stop en route at the smaller island of Prócida, consumes two hours each way, but this may be shortened by taking the *Metropolitana,* an underground of sorts, from Piazza Amedeo to Pozzuoli and there boarding a smaller steamer for the islands.

The Port of Íschia is a sight in itself for it circles the shore of a perfectly round lake that once filled an ancient volcanic crater but was cut through to the sea about a hundred years ago to form this ship haven. The whole island is called by guidebooks, "the debris of a submarine volcano," to which one adds in admiration, "and *what* debris!" Just off the Porto d'Ischia rises the striking islet called simply *Castello,* now a complete ruin, where once lived the chaste beauty Vittoria Colonna, serious friend and inspirer of Michelangelo.

The standard trip includes lunching at a hotel, perhaps with a chance for a sea bath, though the brand-new first-class *Hotel dei Pini* is a little way from the beach in a pine grove, and then a two-hour circuit of the island. Stops are made at *Serrara Fontana* for its lovely view, with the Punta Sant'Angelo in the foreground, and at *Forio* for its fumeroles, reminding us "that there's fire in old Ischia yet. There is actually fire in the *sea* also, off this southern coast. It heats the water for a considerable area. A potato will be nicely cooked here in fifty minutes. The water is hot but not scalding. It is possible to swim in it, "but keep moving," says the guide, "or you'll cook too!"

Other stops of the circuit are at *Lacco Ameno,* with the church of Santa Restituto, patroness of the island (big celebration on her day, May 17), and at *Casamícciola,* because it is the most important resort. The return to Naples may be made from here, since the steamers make it a port of call.

Those who can afford time for a sojourn in forgotten Casamícciola of forgotten Ischia will find a second-class hotel, the *Miramare e Monte* and a modest but good Swiss-run place, the *Bellavista.* Another inn, bearing the name *Pithaecusa,* which the island itself bore in ancient times, is also of modest rating, but it seems all right and it has a terrific situation, hanging practically *over* the resort.

Henrik Ibsen, to whom there is a monument near the wharf, died in Casamícciola, where he is said to have written a part of *Per Gynt,* but such a fate will hardly overtake us, for this is as soft and salubrious a resort as one could find. It has a considerable appeal for the traveler who likes "untrodden ways" and towns.

Tangents to Heel and Toe

The heel and toe of Italy, with the arching instep between them, form no specific part of this book, since these regions are seldom visited by tourists, and transportation there is comparatively little developed, but it should be known by avoiders of beaten paths that there are lovely, unsung things to be seen and that prices are much lower in the south, for the obvious reason that they are 100 per cent *Italian* prices. The flow of foreign tourist trade has never had its chance to raise them appreciably.

It should be known too that Naples is the natural take-off place for all the south and that railways and highways, though sometimes they are bumbling private lines and sometimes dirt roads, circle *the entire perimeter*. Of all the cities in the far south two stand out, *Bari* and *Táranto*.

Bari, the capital and metropolis of Apulia, with some 300,000 inhabitants, is easily the largest city of the whole region and it has the distinction of being the only one imbued with a touch or two of tourist consciousness, though its propaganda is beamed chiefly at vacationing Italians. The *Maggio di Bari* is a spring festival—art, music, drama, ballet, folklore dances, sports—of some drawing power even in the crowded calendar of Italy.

The city's anatomy is rather curious in that a large and lively New Town seems to clutch in its arms an ancient little mother Old Town that almost slips away into the Adriatic. In the New Town the visitor finds broad avenues, impressive buildings and a university complex of enormous bulk. In the Old Town, much of it dating from the twelfth century, there is a labyrinth of little streets that are almost as hard to follow on a map as the tortuous salizzade and rughe of Venice. The three chief things to see there are the *Castle of Frederick II of Swabia*, the *Duomo* and the *Basilica of San Nicola*, which last is Bari's great and special pride. It is an imposing structure designed in the Apulian version of Romanesque and begun as early as the eleventh century. On its model scores of imitative basilicas were built in other Apulian towns.

The region of Bari, especially to the south and southeast of the city, abounds in interesting villages and hamlets, and one feature that makes them interesting is the existence, in thousands, of strange round huts of stone with roofs that are perfect stone cones. They are called *trulli*, and if you would like to see what they are like in photography rather than in words you may find some striking pictures in an old number of the *National Geographic Magazine*, that for February 1930.

The article which they accompany is "Stone Beehive Houses of the Italian Heel," by Paul Wilstach. If you would like to see what they look like "in the very stone," without a smidgen of mortar, you'll simply have to visit Apulia, and in special particular the village of *Alberobello*, some forty miles southeast of Bari by a private rail line whose trains make the trip in two toiling hours. Alberobello is the undisputed champion of trulli villages, with more than a thousand of these never-never homes.

Táranto, with about 200,000 inhabitants, is a strikingly placed city, partly on an island, and it has its fair quota of star-worthy sights, but Italians know it chiefly for the two distinctions of its double harbor, divided by a promontory called *Punta della Penna* (Feather Point). One part is a military harbor of the first importance, the other part *raises oysters* by the million, enough to supply all Italy, with some left over for export. They are de luxe bivalves, not common or mudgarden ones.

Like Bari, this city is a doubleton, Old and New, and in this case the modern developments perhaps outrank in interest the medieval portion of the city. A splendid seafront promenade, beautified by oleanders and symmetrical palms, and a public garden called *Peripato*, on the "Periphery" to the north, give touches of elegance to the whole.

In the orbit of Táranto one goal stands out from the rest, namely *Metaponto*, for this was, of course, the Hellenic city of lustrous name called by the Romans *Metapontum*. It was a powerful and highly cultured metropolis of *Magna Graecia*, as all this southern part of the peninsula was called. Pythagoras taught in this city and here laid the foundations of the philosophical school called Pythagorean. From the Hellenic era several ruined temples remain.

Magna Graecia is today only a name in textbooks, but the ankle and smartly shaped foot of Italy remain. They are neglected parts of the country, so far as tourism goes, and to a few venturesome souls they are especially alluring for that very reason.

CHAPTER 15

THE SPECIAL WORLD OF SICILY

How to Go and Where to Stay

SICILY, known as Trinacria to the Greeks who settled here in such numbers, is an island with a past of tremendous proportions and incredibly many racial colors. Without trying to sort these colors in any detail, it may be stressed that those travelers who are primarily interested in *Greek* Sicily will find its well-preserved Hellenic beauties in almost every city, town and even village all along the extensive east and south coasts. Those whose chief interest is *Byzantine-Saracen-Norman* Sicily will find it, in amazing splendor, in Palermo and vicinity. And finally, those who wish to see something of everything will do well to start their Sicily travels at Palermo, reaching that port by LAI plane from Naples (with Rome connections) or by *Tirrenia* steamer (over night) from Naples. There are definite practical reasons for this, as will be explained later in this chapter. Travelers to Greek Sicily only may take an excellent night train from Naples, with sleeping cars that are ferried across the Straits of Messina, to reach Taormina early in the morning and even Syracuse before 10 o'clock. Planes of the LAI system fly to Catánia, midway between the two goals just mentioned.

Weather is a thing to keep well in mind when planning a visit to Sicily, for most of the island is uncomfortably hot during six months of the year and tourist transportation is then sharply reduced. On the other hand, if a bit of heat fails to deter you and if you revel in the thought of having Sicily to yourself, with all the room in the world at every place of call and with the keepers of such hotels as remain open eager to welcome you at bargain rates, Sicily can be a delight even in high summer. Trains, however, must be chiefly depended upon rather than the big, comfortable motored chariots of tourism.

Hotels of all categories are numerous in the Sicilian towns. The official *Annuario* lists about 170 of them, so there is almost an embarrassment of offerings. Only two of the lot are given de luxe rating by the government, namely the *Villa Igea* at Palermo and the *San Domenico Palace* at Taormina. Perhaps these two warrant a brief description.

The *Villa Igea* is of Victorian appearance and presumably of Victorian construction. The plumbing in many of its private bathrooms has the pioneer quality of olden times—but don't let such considerations bar you from enjoying a luxury hotel with one of the most delightful seaside gardens in many-seasided Italy.

The *San Domenico Palace,* at Taormina, is a palace indeed, as is evidenced by the fact that no less a palace denizen than Farouk of Egypt, when he was king, considered it worthy of his patronage while on his honeymoon with Queen Narriman. Press reports stated that he "made do" with a mere sixty rooms here, for himself, his bride and the royal entourage.

The structure of the hotel is an old Dominican monastery, hence the name. Its comfortable "cells," of modern furnishing and decoration, all bear *names*, that of mine, which made me feel unnaturally holy, being *Amor Sanctus*. Those on either side bore the names *Agnus Dei* and *Stella Matutina*. The public rooms of the San Domenico Palace are a treat to the senses, being veritable museums of fine furniture and objets d'art, and many of the corridors are real galleries of painting. The view from the hotel's garden, one of the loveliest carefully casual gardens of flowers and flowering shrubs I have ever seen, covers the whole majestic sweep of Etna and the curving Ionian Sea. It is one of the very great views of all the world, in the class of Rio's views from the summit of Sugar Loaf or Corcovado.

Among the less famous hotels of Sicily, a very few, in five towns, may be mentioned here.

In *Palermo: Grand Hotel delle Palme*, in the heart of the city, is of first-class rating.

In *Agrigento: Hotel dei Templi* is the newest and leading place, officially rated second category but surely "on the edge of first," with a fragrant orchard-garden from which, as from many of the bedrooms, one has a perfect panoramic view of the fine old Greek temples on the slope-to-the-sea below. The *Grande Bretagna e Gellia* is another good second-class place, while the *Belvedere* is a bit more modest but recommendable. I once stayed there pleasurably years ago.

In *Syracuse: Grand Hotel Villa Politi*, in a suburban garden setting, complete with antique statuary, is a thoroughly delightful first-class place, convenient to the city by bus services; *Hotel degli Stranieri* (Hôtel des Etrangers), formerly also bearing the name Politi, is on the seafront of the island part of the city, directly overlooking the famous Fountain of Arethusa.

In *Catánia: Hotel Centrale-Corona* is a long-known first-class hostelry of this metropolis of eastern Sicily, located on the central Via Etnea, within a block of the superlative Giardino Bellini, named for a native son, the composer Vicenzo Bellini.

In *Taormina:* four first-class hotels (one of them, the *Villa Riis*, a pension) supplement the luxurious San Domenico Palace. Of these, the vine-bowered *Timeo*, adjacent to the Greek Theater, especially caught my eye. The others are the *Excelsior* and the *Miramare*. Among second-class places, the *Villa Flora*, near the Greek Theater, and *Hotel Metropol*, squarely on the same view-front as the San Domenico itself, seem to me highly recommendable.

Palermo, Where Saracens and Normans Met

Palermo is a large city, the sixth in size in Italy, with about half a million inhabitants. In the number of racial strands that have formed it and left their rich legacy of culture to the citizens—and tourists—of today it probably ranks first, and this despite the fact that it almost wholly lacks the legacy of Greek culture, so important on the southern and eastern coasts of Sicily.

The Phoenicians founded Palermo, the Carthaginians conquered it, and then the Romans, the Goths and the Byzantines in turn did likewise. Continuing the kaleidoscopic process, the Saracens seized it in the ninth century and the Normans in the eleventh. It was, in fact, just five years before William conquered England that his fellow-countryman, Roger de Hauteville, conquered this Sicilian city. It was held by the Normans until 1282, when the historic massacre known as the Sicilian Vespers "liquidated" them. It passed to the House of Savoy, then to the Kingdom of Naples and finally, through the campaigns of Garibaldi, became a part of modern Italy. It was from the union of the Saracen and Norman elements, as different in culture as one can possibly imagine, that most of the great works of Palermitan art and architecture were born. We find mosaics that have never been surpassed, except, perhaps, in Ravenna, and we find queer domed churches, some of which were Moslem mosques until the Normans came. Few cities of the Mediterranean have so checkered and thrilling a past as has Palermo. For those with time to read its story, the remarkable buildings and mosaics take on vivid meaning.

To be specific about the attractions of the Sicilian capital, the following things, all shown, if hastily, by the city tours of CIT, call for much more than a casual glance.

The *Cappella Palatina* in the old royal palace (small fee to the monk who shows it). Does it seem extravagant to call this "the most beautiful chapel in the world"? It is often called just that. Its mosaics, scintillating rather than subdued, are on a color base of lustrous gold; the floor is of varied marbles; the ceiling is *artesonado,* meaning that some portions are sunk and others raised, which was a Moorish idea. Painted arabesques and strange figures of all sorts run riot on this extraordinary ceiling, which the monk illumines by flashing on concealed lights. The Palatine Chapel is indescribable. Do not by any means allow yourself to miss it. If you are there in April you will more than likely find a wedding going on. The priests will not perform marriage ceremonies in May, a month dedicated to the Virgin, so hundreds of young couples wishing a spring wedding rush to the altar before the deadline. All of Palermo's churches are busy every day in April.

The *Cathedral,* a very imposing structure, though not to be compared with many others in Italy. The interior is as bare as a barn, most of its splendid porphyry, jasper, lapis lazuli and so forth having been stripped off and sold more than a century and a half ago. But do not overlook the imposing sepulchers of the Norman kings and queens, found in two of the chapels. These give an idea of what the cathedral must once have been. The sarcophagi of King Roger II and his daughter Constance are of special importance. Note also that in a solid silver tomb in a chapel of the right transept lie the remains of Santa Rosalia, patron saint of Palermo.

Churches. Three stand out, *San Cataldo,* a Norman church with three Saracen domes, the *Martorana,* another Norman church, with a most interesting campanile of four stories, and *San Giovanni degli Eremiti* (Saint John of the Hermits) graced by an exceptionally lovely flowered cloister. One of the plants in this cloister, I must record, is called in Italian "mother-in-law's tongue" because its large, tongue-like leaves flap constantly even in the lightest zephyr! This Church of the Eremiti, like so many other old structures of Palermo, shows clearly the union of Saracen and Norman ideas. King Roger II, a Norman of the Normans, built it in 1132 but he obviously liked the bulging domes of Moslem mosques and probably employed a Moslem architect. The structure's pink-red domes seen against a blue Sicilian sky, make a picture that is never forgotten.

Monte Pellegrino, towering in majesty two thousand feet above the city. Its views are striking and its *Sanctuary of Santa Rosalia* is a curious feature. This saint is greatly beloved by Palermitans and especially by those who go down to the sea in ships. A huge anchor was lugged up here by mariners who credited her with saving them from a tempest. On the night of September 3-4 thousands of pilgrims climb to the shrine, many of them barefooted, for a pre-dawn mass, followed by a day of festival doings.

Assorted attractions of Palermo shown to tourists include: (a) the Bourbon-built *Favorita Park,* with an oddly misplaced *Chinese Casino,* this being a fancy of Ferdinand of Bourbon; (b) the adjacent *Ethnographical Museum,* one of the most interesting of its kind in Europe; and (c) a visit to the gay beach called *Lido Mondello,* beside whose very fishy harbor you will see shellfish being cooked to order, though it is to be doubted that you will order any.

Above everything, the visitor to Palermo should not miss its celebrated suburb *Monreale.* The cathedral of this once-royal retreat is incomparable for the combined richness of its mosaics and its setting. The mosaics are even more lustrous than those in Galla Placidia's chapel in Ravenna and nearly as perfect, and in amount they are twenty times as extensive. The setting is quite as glorious as anything in Sicily—and that includes Taormina.

Enter the adjacent Benedictine cloister, a sight in itself, and presently a monk (rewarded by a tip) will unlock a door and let you through to the cloister garden, which commands a view so unpredicted and so literally *shocking* in its beauty that it would sober Bacchus. You are not in his league, but you will, at any rate, be shocked into a feeling of awe. I suppose there are other views as fine —in fact I know there are and have mentioned some hereinbefore—but hardly ever does one smite you so suddenly and unexpectedly. The village and the cathedral itself have shut away every bit of it *except from this garden*. Below, and a very long way below, lies the verdant valley of the Orcto, oranged and lemoned to its limits. In the distance lies Palermo in its famous *Conca d'Oro* (Shell of Gold). All about are loftly brown hills and above is a sky as blue as any twelfth-century mosaicist could have colored it. It must have been this view that induced the Norman kings to erect here their Royal House of God.

Rolling Out the Golden Ribbon

The travel revolution that has occurred in Italy since World War II has been even more complete and widely acclaimed in Sicily than on the mainland. By this I mean that whereas train travel was the accepted thing before the war the CIAT motor-coach circuit, called here the Ribbon of Gold (*Il Nastro d'Oro*), is the accepted thing now, and it is infinitely more convenient. I have "done" Sicily both ways and have full knowledge of the contrast. But, as stated earlier, there is one possible hitch in planning to use the motor-coach tour. The company operates it only from November 1 to April 30. Before and after that period demand is so light, due to Sicily's warm weather, that it has not proved profitable.

The complete excursion, moving counterclockwise, west-south-east-north-west, starts and concludes at Palermo, taking six days, Monday morning to Saturday evening, and at present it is made only once a week. The sightseeing in Palermo itself is not included, but must be done in city tours, as mentioned above, quite apart from the round-island journey. Subject to space being available, any part of the Ribbon Tour may be made separately. Many travelers devote but three days to it, starting at Palermo Monday morning and terminating the trip at Taormina Wednesday evening. The tour halts in that wonderful Etna-side resort for two days and three nights, one day being given over to an Etna trip up to the snow line, and continues on Saturday in a long twelve-hour run along the island's north coast, back to Palermo. The first three days thus provide most of the varied colors of the circuit. Monday brings the coach to templed *Agrigento*, by way of *Segesta* and *Selinunte* (this name deriving from the word for wild parsley), both also towns of ruined Greek temples. Tuesday morning offers Agrigento itself and then continues to *Syracuse* (Siracusa) for the night. Wednesday morning offers Syracuse, a double city, old and new, on a small islet and the main island, while the afternoon run carries northward to *Catánia*, a large city of limited interest, and then to peerless *Taormina*.

Three Towns of Trinacria

(AGRIGENTO; SYRACUSE; TAORMINA)

The first Greek settlement in Sicily, in 735 B.C., was on a promontory below Taormina, the second, founded one year later, was, and still is, Syracuse, whereas Agrigento, called Akragas by the Hellenes, was founded as "recently" as 581 B.C. Sicily rapidly became a sort of New Hellas, some cities, notably Syracuse, rivaling even Athens in glory and culture. The Romans, efficient and warlike, finally conquered it and cast their blight upon it about five centuries after the beginning of Greek colonization, but the blight was far from complete, for two-thirds of the entire coastal belt, from Segesta around the south to Taormina, is saturated with Greek remains.

Agrigento is *the* Temple Town above all others on the island. There are temples to Heracles (Hercules), Concord, Jupiter Olympus, Castor and Pollux, Demeter and Persephone, and Vulcan. The town of today sits on a steep hill with arbored promenades, whence the stroller may look down upon the array of many-columned ruins, some of which are so well preserved that they hardly deserve that word at all. The *Temple of Concord* ranks, indeed, with the Temple of Neptune at Paestum as one of the two best-preserved temples in all Italy. Marble statues and items of ancient pottery, vases, lamps, little earthen gods, are so abundant that almost any property owner may dig them up at will.

A Temple Tour is provided as one of the features of the Golden Ribbon, and even ruin-shy American businessmen confess to finding it interesting. I will mention just two features, among many, that make it so. In the Temple of Concord the columns and the roof are so designed that one of the aisles, as we look through it, outlines a perfect *amphora,* or two-handled Greek vase, that is, a vase of pure Sicilian *sky.* It is an amphora of cobalt blue, so perfectly formed that you feel you could pick it up, if you had the strength to hold so large a thing. The other feature that I have in mind is sheer luxuriance of flowers, shrubs, almond orchards, like carpets of snow in winter's spring, and citrus groves. In one of the hotels I was shown a phenomenal lemon, locally grown, that weighed exactly *one kilo,* which is two pounds and two-tenths. It was about the size of a child's football.

Syracuse is like a double star that astronomy reveals. The new city is on the small island called by the Greeks Ortygia. The ancient city, with some modern residential sections, is on Sicily itself—one can hardly call it "mainland"—and stretches far and wide, for this was a Hellenic metropolis of great proportions.

On Ortygia Island the so-called *Fountain of Arethusa* is the chief attraction, being a large basin of fresh water at the sea's edge filled with reeds and marine plants. It seems that the river-god Alpheus was annoying the nymph Arethusa way off in the Peloponnesus. He chased her so persistently that Diana came to the aid of the fleeing girl, turning her into a spring and causing her to flow under the sea and come up for air in distant Ortygia.

In old Syracuse the sightseer's sights include the *Roman amphitheater,* the *Greek amphitheater,* where classic plays are given in May, and the caves of the *Latomie,* ancient quarries that gave up the stone for so many large structures.

The most famous of the caves is called the *Ear of Dionysius,* an enormous twisting grotto carved out of the solid rock, narrowing in its upper section to a hole that emerges, or formerly emerged, to the surface of the earth. The acoustics of this cavern are amazing. The guide strikes a match and it sounds like a rocket going off. He tears a sheet of paper sharply and it sounds like a cannon shot. The tradition is that at the orifice of the great ear Dionysius, a tyrant of Syracuse, liked to listen to the talk of his political enemies imprisoned in the cavern below.

Taormina is the darling of tourism and will be so as long as tourists like "atmosphere" that is genuine, scenery that is enchanting, shops that are full of good things to buy and a climate so balmy that sea bathing (from the beaches of Giardini and Mazzarò far below) is possible, and even probable, in January and February. The *Greek Theater*, wonderfully placed on a lofty ledge on the town's shoulder, is the only sight of importance, but the entire town, a mountain village really, is its own best sight.

In saying that Taormina deserves all the gushing encomiums that have been heaped upon it one says the bare, minimum truth. It would hardly be possible for words to exaggerate its beauty, its quaint, "unrehearsed" graces and its outlook, as broad as the world, one would say.

And Taormina shops, those tempters of the unwary and conquerors of the wary, are enough in themselves to draw visitors to this flank of Etna. Blouses and lingerie, daintily embroidered, handkerchiefs, scarves, napery, textile novelties, angora wool sweaters—but I won't go on. You know what I mean better than I do. It takes the average woman about twenty-five minutes a block merely to walk along the town's main street, allowing nothing for the time spent *in* the shops.

If you sometimes find exclamatory tourism a bit too dominant in this glamor village, you may escape it by a number of rough but surpassingly lovely mountain paths. One of these (and there is a winding road as well) leads up to *Mola*, a small, unkempt village high above its de luxe and haughty cousin. In the tiny church square of this backward village I witnessed an "outdoor play" so winning, so joyously comic, that I can never forget it. I was alone in the square save for two black kids, *goat* kids, hardly bigger than kittens. Each had a smoke-gray nose and smoke-gray ears and tail and each wore around its neck a huge white ribbon with red polka dots. They were tearing around the deserted square like mad, tumbling awkwardly over each other, jumping in the air in absurd little leaps, all four baby legs taut, then darting suddenly up a side street as though the devil were after them and back again as though they had seen the evil one farther up.

It was one of the most riotous comedies I have ever watched on any stage, but I dared not laugh aloud for fear the actors would misunderstand and call off the performance. The back drop for this comedy had obviously been designed by one who knew color values —if not theater values. At times this curtain threatened to steal the show. It depicted a limitless stretch of blue crinkling sea bordered by a broad irregular band of verdure from which rose a majestic, snow-crowned Smoking Mountain.

High above Taormina and its Mola satellite, soaring from a base that is nearly a hundred miles in circumference to an altitude of 10,784 feet, this mountain, Etna, the highest volcano in Europe and one of the two or three largest in the world, keeps its threatening watch over the scores of communities that cling to its sides and cluster around its foundations. The tours take passengers to a snow-line inn for lunch (skiing is practical for two or three months every winter), and on the day when I made the trip a brand-new smoke hole appeared near the inn, on the side of the mountain! Its sudden appearance gave ample evidence that this smithy of Vulcan, whose eruptions, about 140 of them, have been recorded by man for at least twenty-five centuries, is still by no means too old to smoke or too old to have fits of fiery temper that frighten villagers out of their wits but can never quite drive them away from their ancestral homes.

CHAPTER 16

CITIES THAT "CANNOT BE HID"

Two Hill Routes to Florence

THE towns and villages of Italy that have "risen to the top" in Latium, Tuscany, Umbria, the Marches and other regions of the Apennines are a company so numerous and so full of special character that the very multiplicity of their charms and glamors tends to blend them into a pleasant composite in the tourist mind. Combating this, I have found it profitable to carry some one great character, an artist, a saint, a brigand or a poet, away with me as a souvenir from each hill community. Mere names have thus become, through vivid association, breathing human beings. Instead of languishing on an upper shelf of some library, they have traveled with me, revealing lots of intimate things from their experience.

Two traditional hill routes, a western and a central, between Rome and Florence, are traversed, in both directions, by the daily busses of CIAT, and substantially the same routes are followed by other companies and by the chartered busses of various American travel purveyors.

I have followed both routes several times with undiminishing pleasure, the most personalized and unhurried of the guided tours being one that I made on the central highway under the aegis of a home-town organization, Boston's Metropolitan Travel Service, mentioned in an earlier chapter. Ernest Ruegg, the company's Swiss-born director, who was in Europe on a scouting mission, joined us-of-the-bus and whenever necessary to smooth our way he dispensed one of his Swiss languages, Italian, with the fluency of a Florentine. His wife dispensed tact—a busload of Americans can use plenty of that commodity—while Signor Silvio Giacalucci, our erudite lecturer, gave out with facts, spiced to our taste, and Renzo, our driver, despite some pretty girls of the group whose faces he could see in his mirror, kept his eyes mostly on the road. It was all good fun and good camaraderie, occasionally enlivened by Stateside songs, and there was just enough instruction in art and history to satisfy those bent on sheer holiday and to incite to serious study those who wanted a cultural dividend from their trip. It gave me a new picture of what a predigested tour can be.

On several CIAT tours on both highways I have enjoyed the really surprising bonhomie that bus travel of this distinctive type seems always to develop. The passengers are a United Nations of the Road, the English, French and Italian languages being usually of about equal prominence. All of these languages, and German as well, chiefly for Swiss patrons, are spoken as a matter of course by the hostess-guides and it is fascinating to hear their speech leap nimbly about from language to language like glottic chamois.

The personality exuding from these modern bus-hostesses is often remarkable. I have looked at and listened to a dozen of them for many hours on end, and only two or three were on the humdrum side, reciting their prepared lines with mechanical care. The others were as various in style as so many well-educated girls in any walk of life. I remember vivacious Hebe, unruffleable by any crisis, earnest Vittoria, who wanted so much to come to the States, irrepressible Gioia, chock full of jokes and repartee, quiet Mariella, devoted to Tuscany and its rich background, and pretty Giuliana, who was looking forward with excitement to marriage "after three more trips." I rode for a thousand miles or more in the lee of Giuliana's scintillating personality and when I finally parted from her bus and herself in Siena I took her hand and said, "It breaks my heart to leave you, Giuliana. You're a traveler's dream." An American newspaper man in the bus overheard this tender tribute, took down the exact words and printed the anecdote in his paper. That is bus life in Italy. You never know what will happen next.

* * *

In using the CIAT busses, *stopovers* for one or more days may be made at various points, but those who elect to continue by the same bus will discover that at only two towns, italicized immediately below, on each route from Rome to Florence are the halts long enough so that even a racing visit may be made. The *Western Route* goes by Viterbo, Lake of Bolsena, Orvieto, *Acquapendente, Siena;* the *Eastern Route* by Terni, Spoleto, *Assisi* (with Santa Maria degli Angeli down in the valley), *Perúgia,* Lake Trasimeno, Arezzo.

In striving to be as helpful as possible to travelers who journey by bus, this chapter shall offer brief notes about places on these two routes or very close to them, which can be visited *by stopping over*, with separate and somewhat further descriptions of the towns where, by usual custom, a *sosta per la visita* (halt for visiting) is provided in the itinerary. A later section of the chapter will discuss certain hill towns and villages of outstanding charm that are visited easily by means of a private car but only with some difficulty by public conveyances. I have mentioned the CIT *Guide to Italy*, but it should be stated here that CIAT also puts out a small paper-covered booklet in English, named *Pink Ribbon* that covers virtually *all* the routes traversed by its busses north of Rome.

The Western Route shall be here outlined first.

Viterbo, where a halt is made for a few moments only, not in the old portion, is a picture town of the Middle Ages, properly walled and turreted. It was once a residence of the popes and for three centuries was a serious rival to Rome. Its *Medieval Quarter,* at its evocative best only in a small area of the city, carries you back in an instant to the thirteenth century. The *Palace of the Popes* was so damaged in the war that it is not supremely worth hunting up, though it is still of interest, but the congested old area around Piazza San Pellegrino and another square with a jawbreaker name, Piazza Scacciaricci, is wonderful. You have to pinch yourself to see whether you're awake in the twentieth century or dreaming of the thirteenth.

North of Viterbo, the bus passes, without any real stops, two points of special interest. The first is *Montefiascone,* where the Swabian canon, as described in Chapter 5, drank himself to a happy death on Est! Est!! Est!!!, the excellent local wine that still goes under that name. Virtually every restaurant, café and bar in town and in the whole surrounding region now carries the sign Est! Est!! Est!!! on its advertising. Making a special visit to Montefiascone, I tried a couple of such places, but thought two Ests, with two exclamation points, would be quite sufficient.

The town has a main stem steeply ascending to the cathedral, its dome by Carlo Fontana, and above this the towering bulk of *San Flaviano*, where one big church seems to carry another on its shoulders, "as did Aeneas the old Anchises bear."

The second place of interest is *Bolsena*, where the Miracle of Bolsena, wonderfully pictured by Raphael in one of the stanze of the Vatican, occurred. (During a Mass, blood spurted from the host, bringing belief in transubstantiation to a doubting priest.) Far below the village of Bolsena is the large and striking *Lake of Bolsena*, filling an extinct volcano.

Orvieto, the second official halting point, where about two hours is usually allowed, is of great importance and will be discussed presently.

Acquapendente ("Hanging Water") is the halfway halting place on this route to Florence, but warrants no special attention.

North of this, entering from Latium into Tuscany, three interesting places are passed at intervals: *Radicófani*, whose loftly fortress is associated with one of the campaigns of Frederick Barbarossa; soaring *San Quérico d'Órcia*, whose chief church has three doors of three queerly different styles, all excellent; and *Buonconvento*, an extremely photogenic town with medieval ramparts.

Siena, where an hour's stop is made, will be described separately. *San Gimignano*, twenty-three miles from Siena at a northwesterly tangent, is so much a satellite of that city that it calls for coverage while on this western highway and it too shall be described separately, for it is unique and far too important to "tuck in" with a few swift sentences.

Florence, the overnight, or many-night, halt of all the busses, from whatever direction, is forty-four miles due north of Siena.

Orvieto on an Upthrust Fist

Weird and lonely is *Orvieto* on a tufa rock that rises like a great clenched fist pushed up from the surrounding plain to a height of six hundred and fifty feet. The bus, toiling up by many a zigzag, leaves you in the Piazza Vittorio Emanuele, heart of the city, and one of the precious two hours of the halt is devoted by most tourists to lunch (with a good bottle of Orvieto wine), presumably at Hotel Palazzo, on Via Garibaldi. With so much, of such special quality, to see, the use of half the time for eating seems a sin of travel, but a stopover of twenty-four hours will obviate this sin. Such a stay, needed, I admit, by virtually every hill town of the first rank, seems here an undebatable must.

Perhaps you will have come to Orvieto by train, and in that case, unless you are a veritable mountaineer, you must take the funicular from the station. It plunges up and through the rock, under the old *Fortezza*, and emerges in a broad open area, whence a bus proceeds a half mile or so to the center of the town. It is richly worth the effort, after settling at the historic *Hotel Palazzo*, which actually was a nobleman's palace, or at the more pretentious *Grand Hotel Reale*, to return to the Fortezza for the handsome public garden laid out upon it and for its brilliant outlook over the valley and the tumbled Umbrian hills. The *Well of San Patrizio* is here too, a most curious affair designed by Antonio Sangallo in 1527. The ingenuity of it is remarkable for its day. Boring the rock to a depth of two hundred feet, to pure water, it provided *two* spiral ramps, each completely independent of the other. Men with donkeys *de*scended by one ramp, *a*scended by the other, bringing water.

Do not, I urge you, go from the central piazza or from the funicular terminus *direct* to the cathedral by the usual route. I did just that the first time, and later regretted it, for I thereby forfeited a first-class thrill. The flanks of Orvieto's *duomo* are merely zebra stripes of black and dusty yellow, but the west front is a riot of color, a riot kept under intelligent control by its masterly thirteenth-century designer. In order to come face to face with this west front, one should approach the cathedral by the street that bears the artist's name, Via Lorenzo Maitani. Thus the whole glory of its astonishing façade bursts upon one's vision. It is the quintessence of Italian Gothic, with the upward spring of Chartres or even Beauvais made brilliant and colorful by rich gold-tinted mosaics that the French cathedrals would spurn with horror.

I could wish for every visitor the stroke of luck that befell me on another occasion, namely a sharp and sudden shower followed by an equally sudden burst of sunshine—afternoon sunshine straight from the west. The effect produced by this "New England weather" was weird and wondrous. The wet polychrome surface of Maitani's masterpiece gleamed like a jeweled châsse in the powerful rays of the declining sun, which poured straight through the artist's street as though steered by the hand of a celestial picture director.

Inside the duomo is another supreme achievement of art, less evident to the layman than the gay façade but no less stirring if one takes a bit of time to grasp its splendor. I refer to the frescoes of Luca Signorelli in the *Cappella Nuova*. Signorelli is the man I "took away" with me from Orvieto. I confess he had been only a name, and rather a dim one at that, until I saw his art at its stimulating best.

Luca Signorelli was peculiarly gentle, affectionate and courteous, according to Vasari, who was in a position to know, since the critic clearly recalled Luca's visits to his uncle. The master was fond of rich clothing and high, though not gluttonous, living. One cannot imagine a temperament more at variance with that of Michelangelo, yet the two are invariably linked together. Michelangelo greatly admired Signorelli, who first taught the world that the human figure could be made to look human, and the mighty Florentine borrowed very freely from the older master's work. Some of his angels and demons in the Sistine Chapel, for instance, are the next things to copies of Luca's angels and devils here in Orvieto.

One moving story Vasari relates, though it may be mere gossip. He says that Luca had a son of rare beauty to whom he was devoted and that this son suddenly died in Cortona. Luca thereupon had the boy stripped nude and "uttering no complaint and shedding no tear . . . painted the portrait of his dead child, to the end that he might still have the power of contemplating by means of the work of his own hand, that which nature had given him, but which an adverse fortune had taken away." (Translation of Mrs. Foster.)

No other man then living could have thus solaced himself, for Luca Signorelli alone had mastered the fundamental principles of portraying the nude form naturally.

In the fullness of years Luca died at eighty-one. Though palsied and infirm, he was still "in harness." He died almost in the act of painting a fresco on the palace chapel of the Cardinal of Cortona.

In Orvieto's Corso Cavour I was once treated to a very different form of Italian art, the music of Verdi. An opera, apparently from Rome, was being broadcast by the lusty radio of a sewing-machine shop, and the narrow street, although it is Orvieto's broadest, became crowded as a goodly percentage of the town's inhabitants gathered for the concert. The rain came and fell gently, persistently, on the throng, which, however, did not in the least diminish. For some hours Verdi filled the Corso and indeed the whole town, for Orvieto is almost tomblike in its normal stillness. As the invisible tenor soared to ever new heights and the rain-drenched crowd hummed its approval, I sneaked back to the Cappella Nuova to have one more look at Signorelli's bold Michelangelesque conceptions of what is to happen when the sun and the moon shall be darkened.

Siena's Sleepy Splendors and Its Seething Palio

Siena, sprawling about upon three hills and the valleys that separate them, is perhaps the most medieval-looking *city* of all Italy, hardly matched in this respect even by Perúgia. It is, accordingly, a wonderful town for leisure, except twice a year, on July 2 and August 16, when it goes exuberantly mad with excitement over its festival called *Il Palio*, the greatest, brightest, most fanatical festa in the whole Italian calendar of them. I love the town in both moods, but perhaps more in its slow, reflective mood.

There is an excellent hotel in Siena, the first-class *Excelsior*, that invites the soul for as long as the body can stay in this lovely city. I like this hostelry immensely because it is one of Italy's *personalized* inns of travel, which means fine food along with informal comfort and quality. The personality is injected by a widely known hotel couple named Stoppini, who direct the place. I like it too for an odd and geographical reason. Located on a corner of the Piazza Gramsci, many of its balconied rooms look out at bulky San Domenico and at the hill that is crowned by the duomo, and immediately *down*, steeply down, upon the hotel's terraced flower garden and the Civic Stadium. The windows of the cheerful dining room also look straight down into the stadium and it will be rarely bad luck if you do not, during your stay, have the chance to watch a track meet or an inter-city soccer game.

While on the subject of creature comforts I should mention that there are some character restaurants in Siena, one of them, the *Trattoria Tullio*, on the little Vicolo di Provenzano, having an artymedieval look that is perhaps too self-conscious, though the place and its food are genuinely good and no mere trap for tourists. In the peerless Campo, of which I shall have much more to say, are two good places, each with extra tables in the open air, *Ristorante al Mangia* and *La Speranza*.

The Siena of Sleepy Splendors suggests one special personage of art. Do you know Iacopo della Quercia? He is on our scroll—any scroll—of Italy's great-in-art and of course his name and his position as a pioneer in Renaissance sculpture are known to all who love what Italy has wrought, but he becomes real and vivid here, for he was Siena's own, a sculptor happily not without honor in the place he called home. Clearly he is the artist to make *your* own in this city. His best-loved work is the *Fonte Gaia* in the Campo and it *is* gay, as its name says, though the theme of its sculpture is religious. The original, now preserved on the upper floor of the Palazzo Pubblico, is so sadly damaged by the centuries (it was taken from the square to this place of retreat only in 1904) that it hardly reveals the sculptor's infinite zeal for detail. For once, the reproduction in the Campo is more satisfying than the original. If you can dream by the edge of this fountain in a square outshone in grandeur *only* by St. Mark's of Venice and keep from falling in love with Siena, you are a strong individual and can be depended upon to resist all attacks of sentiment.

The Campo is unique in its shape, which is that of a shell, unique in that indefinable something so lamely called atmosphere. Among the important buildings surrounding it are the above-mentioned *Palazzo Pubblico*, a structure of medieval elegance, and the sky-piercing *Torre del Mangia*, to whose summit you climb for a view that is quite as unique as the square below. The stairs are winding and narrow and in large part dark and there are 395 steps, as I know from painful count, but what a reward awaits the climber. This is one of those sights that we cross oceans for!

As for the Campo, at the tower's base, one must congratulate Siena on its strength of mind, or perhaps its fortunate neglect, in resisting the invasions of tourist trade that could ruin the harmony and native grace of this wonderful "Shell." It is still *of the people*. The humblest dwellings and native shops surround it. When I open my cobbler's shop it will certainly be here and probably in the once elegant Palazzo Sansuedoni.

There are many superb things to see in Siena, but the greatest, not even excepting the Campo, is the *cathedral*, a magnificent structure with the usual Tuscan (Pisan) stripes of black and white marble but with twenty other colors of marble also in its composition, the glorious building being further enhanced by its unique Piccolomini Library. Located on the roof of Siena, so to speak, the cathedral is a marvel of beauty and the Sienese have made the most of it. Each evening it is illuminated by a battery of pale greenish floodlights which make its three-gabled façade and its striped wall and campanile stand out with weird clarity, visible for twenty miles. A portion of the structure is flooded with pale lavender light from concealed bulbs and if this color scheme sounds cheap and carnivalesque, I beg you to withhold judgment until you have seen it. To me the effect seems marvelously beautiful.

The cathedral square is surrounded by imposing buildings and "around the corner" is another square called Piazza Iacopo della Quercia which is—you would never guess it unless you look *up* to see soaring, unfinished walls—none other than the nave of the so-called "New Cathedral," which was started in the fourteenth century on an incredibly large scale—a bitter rivalry with Florence being the spur—but was abandoned after sixteen years of folly. The old (present) cathedral was to have served as the "crossing" and the two transepts. The "right aisle" of the non-existent New Cathedral is closed in to contain the *Opera del Duomo*, or *Cathedral Museum*.

One of the most surprising features of the whole cathedral complex is the *Baptistery*, reached by descending a very long flight of steps from the New Cathedral (square). The little structure directly beneath the cathedral's apse yet opening onto its own little piazza, is oddly cold, and I mean *cold*, on the hottest summer day, but a little shivering is repaid by viewing its works of art, the finest, as you have came to expect, being a font by della Quercia.

The things to see inside the cathedral are almost beyond numbering. Most immediately we see the famous floor paving of many vast marble blocks, enlivened by some sixty scenes in *graffitto intarsia* (the design inlaid with lead lines) of Bible stories. There are numerous other special masterpieces of art, such as a Pisano pulpit, called by Sienese enthusiasts the greatest pulpit ever built (but Pisa would challenge this), a St. John statue by Donatello, and some excellent stained glass windows. A feature of perennial interest is the *Chapel of St. John the Baptist*, enshrining, guides assert, the right arm of the forerunner of Jesus, but the climactic sight of all is the *cathedral library*, built by Cardinal Francesco Piccolomini in Columbus' time.

So irresistibly bright and cheerful is this library that one's spirit positively soars. The famous Pinturicchio frescoes are embossed very cleverly with raised gold work and jewels to make the adornment of the figures stand out more sharply. I enjoyed these frescoes far more than most others in Italy for two definite reasons. First, they are as fresh as though just completed instead of having been done more than four hundred years ago. I cannot work up a frenzy of enthusiasm over wall paintings so damaged by time that they are half obliterated, like those of Uccello, for example, in the *Chiostro Verde* of Florence's Santa Maria Novella. One is supposed to be enraptured by these and many others almost equally damaged, but I cannot achieve it. I like my pictures to look like pictures and these of Pinturicchio certainly do.

Second, I like the subject of these frescoes, dealing as they do with the life of Aeneas Silvius Piccolomini, uncle of the cardinal who built the library. Aeneas was a pleasure-loving gentleman who became a pope. He traveled widely and I first felt a sense of intimacy with him in distant Bruges, a city which fairly bowled him over, as it did me, though for different reasons. Bruges, in Aeneas' day, was the brilliant metropolis of northern Europe, with the extravagance and wickedness of a medieval Babylon. He wrote of his visit with a certain shocked wistfulness that is charming and understandable.

Before drifting away from the cathedral and its accessory buildings I should say a further word—two words—about the *Cathedral Museum*.

It is full of famous art works of the Sienese school, and its upper terrace commands a very striking view of the city. The most important art work is the so-called *Maestà*, a large painting by Duccio de Buoninsegna, housed in a special Duccio Room. This and his method of painting have been mentioned in the Scroll of Arts (Chapter 9).

Of the almost "discouraging" number of fine old churches in Siena, two or three must be given some attention.

San Domenico is an enormous Gothic structure on its separate hill. It boasts famous frescoes by Sodoma and the still more famous reliquary containing the head of Saint Catherine, who was associated with the Dominican Order.

San Francesco is another great, bare-looking church on the tip of a conspicuous promontory, its zebra-striped walls showing up for miles around.

Santa Maria dei Servi, on still another prow-like promontory, appealed to me strongly because of several individualistic features. I liked the quite unsung but noble king-sized cedar of Lebanon in the square in front of it, a tree to match the famous one beside the cathedral in Tours; I liked the church's cozy red-brick floor; and finally, I liked the view of the Torre del Mangia from its front steps. This is a good place to work up admiration for yourself if you are among those hardy and perhaps foolish persons who have climbed to the tower's top. From Santa Maria dei Servi it appears to split the heavens and then keep on going up!

The medieval palaces of Siena match its churches in number and splendor. The *Palazzo Piccolomini* houses the State Archives. The *Palazzo Buonsignori* is filled with great paintings of the Sienese school. The *Palazzo del Magnifico* was once the mansion of a "magnificent" dictator named Pandolfo Petrucci. The *Palazzo Salimbeni* and the *Palazzo Spannochi*, both in the Piazza Salimbeni, are put to commercial and banking uses. From a high cornice of the latter oddly staring stone faces, in a long row, peer out and down.

Finally and most importantly, the *Palazzo Chigi-Saraceni* serves as one of the most important centers of music study in the whole of musical Italy. Count Chigi, the present owner of this palace and a native of Siena, is a very great and earnest patron of music. Every summer, advanced students come here from all over the world to study, and they are taught by Italy's finest musicians. The palace may be visited when the school is not in session. It contains many treasures, including a black walnut grand piano on which Liszt gave concerts, a rare Stradivarius cello and a library of music manuscripts hardly matched elsewhere. There is also a most attractive concert hall, where concerts are given during the winter. As if incidentally, the whole palace is an important private gallery of paintings.

To many Roman Catholics the importance of these luxurious palazzi pales into insignificance before the humble *House of St. Catherine*, which has been a house of prayer, with many small oratories, for the past five centuries. This patron saint of Italy (since 1939), whose life has been briefly outlined in our Scrolls of Italy's Great (Chapter 9), has an enormous hold on popular affections. On the only occasion when I have entered her house I had literally to push my way in, so crowded was it with awed visitors. In a chapel here is shown the painted crucifix before which Catherine was kneeling when she noticed the stigmata in her hands.

* * *

Siena's festival, called *Il Palio*, to shift the scene a bit suddenly, is a veritable bomb-burst of excitement, the like of which I have rarely witnessed anywhere. After two or three near misses I managed finally to see it and I was swept into the vortex as if by a tidal wave of popular emotion, the vortex centering in the Campo, which was ringed by thousands of grandstand and bleacher seats. (For a full account of the pageantry, with wonderful illustrations in color photography, see the article by Major General Edgar Erskine Hume in the *National Geographic Magazine* for August 1951.) The affair started with a long procession of men in brilliant medieval dress, ten great groups representing ten divisions (*contrade*) of the city. (Siena is composed of seventeen contrade but ten are chosen by lot.) The procession around the square lasted an hour or more and was featured by a competition in skillful banner-throwing.

Finally the festa worked up to its climax, the famous horse race, each horse, be it understood, having been previously blessed and sprinkled with holy water in a church of its own contrada. In this event, each year, the ten chosen jockeys ride their mounts into the square amid a continuous din of yells and whistles. At a signal they gallop on their bareback steeds furiously three times around the Campo, the winner receiving as prize a *palio*, or banner, of the Virgin drawn to the square on a chariot by four white oxen.

The excitement of the race I saw was beyond my previous imagining. It was terrific, even downright dangerous. Frequently riders were thrown and sometimes seemingly trampled. The *horse* that comes in first, *even* without his jockey, wins the race. So it was on this occasion. The horse of the Contrada of Valdimontone came in first, though his rider was thrown (and somewhat hurt) at the second-from-the-last turn. Men of the Istrice Contrada, losing by a narrow margin, wept openly in anguish—I saw this happen—and men of Valdimontone hugged and ecstatically kissed each other in their exaltation.

An evening and a night of noisy revelry followed and then Siena seemed to wrap her shawl about her shoulders and shrink back to quiet spinsterhood.

Sortie to San Gimignano—Which Can't Be True

In the Baedeker Era, of pleasant memory, I used to experience real difficulty in forgiving the Sage of Tourism for devoting, in his abridged *Italy*, one hundred and forty-six pages to Rome and but seventeen words to San Gimignano. I still have the tome, of 1928, and here are the words:

"Then, on the hill to the right appears the little town of San Gimignano, with its towers."

By careful pruning he could have sheared this down to five words— "Hill right, San Gimignano, towers." One might have thought the cicerone to be sending a cable to New Zealand or China, with each word costing a worrisome number of lire. Certainly he gave his faithful reader no hint that this village was, and is, absolutely unique in Italy, in the world, for that matter. (Nagel, I'm glad to mention, finds it possible to devote an entire fine-print page to this marvel.)

The trouble-dodging tourist will visit this lofty community by hiring a car in Siena for the 24-mile ride, but the untiring type can make it without too much of a struggle by taking an accelerato (train) from Siena to Poggibonsi and a bus from that station up to this hill goal. There is also, be it carefully noted, an inexpensive CIT tour from *Florence* to San Gimignano daily in summer, priced now at hardly over $5.00, lunch included.

San Gimignano's skyline is quite as remarkable as that of New York City, even more so in a way, since it tops an 800-foot hill. As your bus struggles upward in sharp zigzags this skyline unfolds before your unbelieving eyes, and you are finally forced to acknowledge that the thing is not a queer dream but an actual place of human habitation. Thirteen towers, from 50 to 175 feet in height, some of them tipsy, pierce the Tuscan sky in a weird and glorious ensemble. It simply can't be true, and yet you find you can walk the streets of this town and even climb its towers. No wonder Italy proclaimed (in 1928) the whole town a national monument. I know of no other town in Italy (though there may be others) where every inhabitant—and San Gimignano has four thousand—is proclaimed a museum piece. I wonder if the green umbrellas of thick cotton which are considered smart in this town were also modish when Dante trod its streets. But, no, it can't be. Umbrellas were only "invented" about 130 years ago when an eccentric traveler first demonstrated the utility of this new-fangled device.

The first open space reached in the huddling town is *Piazzo della Cisterna*, named for the thirteenth-century cistern in its center. Here are the two inns, *La Cisterna* and *Leone Bianco*. If you cannot stay overnight try at least to have lunch on the terrace of the first-named inn, which has a grand view.

Over the medieval houses of this square rise the two dominating towers of the *Famiglia Ardinghelli*, a leading clan of the Guelph faction of old. In periods of tension, and there were many, it must have been nerveracking to live here, for only fifty yards away, in Via San Matteo, are the equally grim towers of the *Famiglia Salvucci*, fierce partisans of the Ghibellines. At the drop of an insult either family was ready to loose deadly arrows on any member of the rival one.

The *Piazza del Duomo* (Cathedral Square), only a step from the other, serves as a stage for open-air opera on certain summer evenings, and *what* a stage! It offers to one's astonished gaze six of San Gimignano's thirteen towers. They make a striking group. Think what this town must have been when not six or thirteen but fifty-six, and some say seventy-six, towers were grouped about this spot. San Gimignano was a patrician town, with many proud families of Guelphs hating and fearing equally proud families of Ghibellines. Every important family, on either side of the political fence, built a tower, as a matter of course, above his house, so that it might, in case of need, resist a long personal siege. But towers did not suffice to save this town from itself. Torn by perpetual strife, it finally fell under the domination of Florence and from that date (1353) it became virtually the dead but very beautiful museum it is today.

Ghirlandaio and Lippo Memmi and Benozzo Gozzoli left good frescoes in the cathedral and the Palazzo del Popolo, but it is likely to be the poet Dante whose company we wish to cultivate or *begin* to cultivate. He is so vast in name and meaning that we cannot associate him solely with this hill town, nor with his native Florence, nor with Verona, where he took refuge, nor with Ravenna where he died and lies buried. We must be content to catch occasional glimpses of the man as we work our way through Italy.

To San Gimignano Dante came in the year 1300, but not as a poet. Beatrice Portinari, the passion of his youth, had died ten years before, the wife of another man and scarcely conscious of her admirer's existence. Recovering slowly from his deep gloom, he finally plunged into politics and this brought him to San Gimignano, where he attempted to heal the breach that existed between Guelphs and Ghibellines by making the town side firmly with the Guelphs. He made a speech from the balcony of the Palazzo del Popolo, a balcony to which you and I may mount, but he failed, and in selfish mood we may rejoice in his failure, since it was strife that built this town and strife that left it for us. Had it turned to peaceful and harmonious ways those towers would surely have been razed.

Halts on the Central Route

The *Central Route* from Rome to Florence, by way of Assisi and Perúgia, is quite as full of important halts and unimportant but very lovely hill villages as is the Western Route, and the succession of these places shall be dealt with here as the other succession was before, merely by mentioning the best *little* places, while saving Assisi and Perúgia for a following description.

On the way from Rome to the first CIAT halt (Terni) travelers pass two especially eye-catching towns, *Civitacastellana*, a pottery-making town that perches on the edge of a great gorge, and *Narni*, once the home of that soldier of fortune Erasmo da Narni, better remembered as Gattamelata, the "Honeycat" whose magnificent equestrian statue Donatello fashioned to decorate Padua. From the rear balcony of Narni's little *Caffè d'Italia*, in the main square, a superlative view is had of the River Nera far below, but regular bus passengers are unlikely to be allowed time to see it.

Terni, an established halt though only a quarter of an hour or so is given to it, is an industrial city (steel) of nearly a hundred thousand inhabitants and lacks the glamor of the towns of art, but it is a good center for tripping, enjoyed by those who stop over.

Spoleto, the next halt, is a compact and very striking town of medieval look dramatized by two special features, a hilltop ducal castle called the *Rocca Papale*, once a papal fortress, and a mighty bridge over the Tessino, tying the town to the *Monteluco Hill*. This bridge, the *Ponte delle Torri*, is one of the most utterly spectacular ones in Europe, yet it was built six centuries ago. To give a statistic or two, it is 262 feet high and 754 feet in length and it strides across the valley in ten great arches. Monteluco, regardless of the bridge, is a goal worth reaching—this can be done by bus in summer—for it lies at an altitude of more than half a mile, and its crest, crowned by the sprawling Monastery of St. Francis, offers a view unusual even on this route of views.

North of Spoleto, high on a hillside, lies dramatic little *Trevi*, whose name graces Rome's best-loved fountain. (Speaking of fountains, the springs called *Fonte del Clitunno*, forming a charming lakelet fringed by willows and surrounded by a poplar grove and lush meadows, are on the main road two miles short of Trevi as the bus rolls north. The beauty of this spot has been sung for ages in poetry and prose, but I found that it was forbiddingly difficult to enter its fenced-in loveliness. One must get permission from some hard-to-find office in Spoleto! I didn't try, but contented myself with gazing from the road.)

Foligno lies in a valley north of Trevi and from Foligno (but CIAT makes no halt here) the traveler may make a side trip by bus, in seven miles, to the hill village of *Montefalco*, universally called "the balcony of Umbria." I made the effort and was indeed rewarded by a magnificent panorama, to be well viewed, however, *only* by climbing the Town Hall tower. Montefalco is more of a *cupola* than balcony. At any rate it is not my idea of an *open* balcony, for houses insistently shut off the splendid outlook. Happily there are other and opener balconies in Umbria, every bit as good, including Assisi and also that master balcony, Perúgia itself.

The graceful little town of *Spello*, with Roman walls as "railing," juts out from Monte Subásio on the Central Route, just north of Foligno. This is seen only "in passing" by bus travelers, yet it has at least one major sight, the little old *Church of Santa Maria Maggiore*, rich in art works, especially in frescoes by Pinturicchio. One of the smilingest priests in the world showed me these marvels of art. On leaving the town I passed him and tried to wave a greeting, but by this time he was absorbed in his prayer book.

Assisi, to be discussed separately below, is a major CIAT halt of more than two hours (including luncheon), with another half hour devoted to the Church of Santa Maria degli Angeli, on the valley floor.

At *Ponte Giovanni* the highway crosses the very young Tiber, no "Father Tiber" here but a youth making his way in Italy.

Perúgia, chief city of Umbria and one of the very special communities "that cannot be hid," will be separately treated.

Lake Trasimeno, a handsome sheet of water that has no affluent or effluent of any importance, is made a halt of the CIAT itinerary because of the beauty of the peaceful scene (with lakeside cafés for which the bus allows very little time) and the grim history of the plain on the lake's north shore. It was here, in 217 B.C., that Hannibal's Carthaginians defeated the legions of Rome, under Flaminius, in perhaps the worst disaster that Rome ever suffered. The defeat was total, the slaughter terrible, and Flaminius, in failure, committed suicide. On a small bridge crossed by the highway is a stone bearing the inscription: "Remember, passer-by, that these are the hills and lake of Trasimeno where more than twenty-five thousand Romans perished by the ferocity of the Carthaginians and Hannibal in the defense of the integrity of Roman civilization." One of the hill villages above the lake bears the commemorative and sanguinary name of Sanguinetti!

Cortona, sheltered by its lofty medieval fortress, is the first town on this highway lying inside the borders of Tuscany. In ancient times it was one of the "Twelve Etruscan Cities" and in medieval times it won fame as the native town of Luca Signorelli and of St. Margaret (of Cortona).

Arezzo serves as an official bus halting point, though for a quarter of an hour only. Those who can give it a day may fortify themselves by a first-rate lunch in a character restaurant, the *Buca di San Francesco*, in the Piazza San Francesco. Arezzo really warrants a stopover, though few accord it one, and this is not a great problem, since it is but two hours distant by rail from Florence. This considerable city, of such early origin, was within the framework of the Florentine Republic in the great days of Florence. Vasari was a native of Arezzo, and Petrarch, who is honored by a spacious park and large memorial in the upper part of town, made it his lifelong home. Bombs, no respecters of persons, demolished Petrarch's house during World War II but it has been restored and is the headquarters of the Petrarch *Accademia*.

Three other items of special interest in this city are the curious twelfth-century church called *Pieve di Santa Maria*, with its equally curious storied campanile; the widely celebrated frescoes (Legend of the Holy Cross) by Piero della Francesca in the *Church of San Francesco*; and the *memorials to Guido Monaco*, including a statue in the square bearing his name. The name Monaco means monk, and this Guido was one. He was also a musician, and is universally credited with having invented the form of musical notation that we still use. This interesting friar was called also Guido d'Arezzo and, meaning the same thing, Guido Aretino.

And so to Florence, the highway closely following the River Arno for the last fifty miles of the journey.

Assisi and Its Famous Poverello

Assisi is probably the most powerful magnet to travelers of all Italy's hill towns, large or small, and offhand this seems a strange thing, for it is a one-man town, a one-*saint* town at that, and its popularity is certainly not restricted to Roman Catholics or to those travelers with a pilgrim complex. It extends undiminished to those who travel for the sake of culture, art, the humanities or the sheer beauties of nature. Assisi means many things to many people, so I shall state my own liking for it in highly personal terms.

I think, then, for one thing, that it is as beautiful in location as any hill town in Italy. It thrills me through and through just to think of the majestic panorama from outside the Porta San Giacomo, from the little park in front of the Santa Chiara Church and from a dozen other vantage points. All of Umbria, it seems, is spread out below, hazy purple and green, with a fretwork of rivers the color of platinum. Patches of shadow drift continually across the picture or, if the day is stormy, little gusts of rain like flocks of draggled sheep. At night the horizon fairly glows. The hills of Umbria are lit with bright villages as if with a score of beacon lights, and Perúgia, the capital, though fifteen miles distant, is the brightest beacon of all.

The second part of this Assisian apology, and certainly the most personal part, is slightly absurd. I like the town because of the grand old frescoes of Giotto and Cimabue in St. Francis' church, and I like those artists not only for themselves but for the childish sentiment which their names recall. When I was in the three *r*'s period of boyhood my parents took me to Assisi. They took my brother too, and as a pair of young art students we earned marks close to zero. So my mother, thinking to stimulate our zeal, told us that if we would really try to understand these Assisi frescoes and listen to what was said, we should each have a goldfish when we got to Florence. We did listen, or tried to, and when we reached Florence we got the goldfishes. Of course you will have guessed that my mother promptly named them Giotto and Cimabue. I chose the former and mentally spelled the unfortunate fish Jotto.

My third score for Assisi, and my greatest, a true bull's eye, is the town's celebrated saint, Francis. Now there is a saint for you! If you do not positively *like* him, which sometimes means much more than "love" or "venerate," it must be because you have not had the good fortune to know him. This mighty *Poverello* was strong, sweet-natured, gay, humorous, tender. Few human beings in history have matched him. He was a poet of rare originality, with a gracious and nimble wit that took all sorts of unexpected turns. Scholarship kneels at his feet and then goes out to ransack the world for information about him. The Public Library of Boston devotes a considerable room entirely to hundreds of books and incunabula about this man. Yet his greatest wish and prayer was not for learning but for "the treasure of poverty."

Chroniclers say that Francis, a millionaire's son in the money of that time, was a frivolous and pleasure-loving youth, tarrying rather long at the winecups and filling Assisi's quiet streets with the sounds of revelry. Can you imagine it? Can you picture him "throwing a party" for the *giovanezza dorata* (gilded youth) of the region? It is not so difficult, at that, to conjure up such pictures. Francis' incurable gaiety survived his conversion to saintly poverty, and his love of song lasted till he lay on his deathbed.

During his last long illness he sang incessantly, not with forced bravado but from sheer, unquenchable happiness. The doctors cauterized his hand one day and he stopped singing for a bit. "See here, Brother Fire," he said, in effect. "I have always loved you and treated you fairly. Have the kindness to requite me. Do not hurt me more than you can help." He died at forty-four, worn out by hard work for others and by self-denial, and two short years later—an interval so brief as to be almost unparalleled in Roman Catholic annals—he was canonized.

Almost in his last hour, Francis earnestly begged the pardon of Brother Body (his own) for having so ill-treated it. Always gentle to others, always severe to himself, he seems a perfect man in this imperfect world and yet one *likes* him.

Do not devote quite all your time in Assisi to this saint and his double church, but spare a little merely to walk the silent streets. If you are there on a personal sojourn quite out of the tourist season you can hardly believe that the town still lives. The beat of its pulse is scarcely perceptible. But presently you are sure to wander into its central square and here you discover that modern Italy has not been too busy to give a thought even to Assisi. Beside the charming old *Temple of Minerva*, some two thousand years old, is a modern post office, designed with such skill that it actually does not clash with the pagan temple. One can almost picture the goddess herself dropping in here to dispatch a letter. This square seems to tie the centuries together, knotting them about the Poverello as the town's chief treasure.

* * *

To present an overdue fact or two of practical use to stayers-over, there are several good hotels in Assisi, though none is officially rated above the second category. The *Subásio* is the largest, in number of rooms, the *Windsor* and the *Giotto* next. The appropriate *name* of this last place may have a certain appeal to travelers, but for me the Windsor's superlative situation, at the Porta San Francesco only a stone's throw from the great double church, easily outweighs this consideration. It is a most attractive hostelry of some fifty rooms, half of them with bath. Only on my second visit did I discover that its director is Giulio Stoppini, a brother of the well-known hôtelier of Siena, earlier mentioned.

* * *

The *Church of Santa Maria degli Angeli* lies on low ground, near Assisi's railway station, two or three miles by a road that descends by many zigzags below St. Francis' Town. It is *the* pilgrim church of St. Francis, for it was here, in the *Cappella del Transito*, that the saint died, and it was here, in the so-called *Oratory of the Porziuncola*, under the great dome, that the Franciscan Order was cradled.

High atop the façade of the church, which is of really imposing dimensions, is a large gilded statue of the Virgin. Millions of the faithful stoutly assert that the statue occasionally *bows*, in a grand gesture of graciousness, to pilgrims gathered below. I was assured that the Virgin had been seen to bow a total of sixty-five times. Renzo, our driver on the Metropolitan tour, told me that he himself had seen the phenomenon five times. On a transatlantic steamer an American lady, a fellow-passenger, told me that she had certainly witnessed this miracle.

"And what was it like?" I asked.

"It was a deep, graceful gesture with her right arm and hand," said the lady, "something like this, but of course with wonderful majesty, a beautiful thing to watch. And there's a strange twist about it all.

I must tell you that the friend who was with me saw the very same gesture, but *she* saw the Blessed Virgin do it with her *left* arm and hand!"

Perúgia, the Grand Balcony of Umbria

The customary halting time of the tourist busses in Perúgia is but half an hour northbound and two hours (including time for lunch) southbound, this being obviously no better than tantalizing. *By all possible means* stop over in Perúgia for one or several nights if you can possibly achieve this, for the city is *marvelous* by any holiday or cultural measuring.

The city has one first-class hotel, the *Brufani e Palace*, excellent in its physical properties, quite unusual in character and a sort of "glorious contradiction" in location, being in the very heart of the city yet jutting almost *over* the valley, a sort of balcony on a balcony. Some seventy-five of its south-facing bedrooms, each with bath, seem to the occupying guests like take-off points for members of a glider club.

One portion of this hotel, for it is a *double* building like its double name, rises from the relics of a vanished temple to Minerva. The story of its proprietors and their forebears is a story of energy, foresight and a bit of luck paralleling many a success story of American industry. Suffice it to say here that the father of one of the co-proprietors in its management went to London with but twenty lire in his pocket to learn the hotel business. He learned it all right, partly there, partly also in North America, where he worked successively at Boston's Hotel Vendôme, Washington's Mayflower and Quebec's Château Frontenac. My enthusiasm for the Brufani eagle's nest, including its cheerful dining room, backed by a superior cuisine, is practically boundless. Even if I didn't like Perúgia—but I love the town—I would go there as often as I could just to enjoy that clifftop albergo.

The main street of Perúgia is *Corso Vannucci* and this proves a pleasant little shock to the tourist, for he has discovered that practically every town in Italy, clinging to old habits, names its main *corso* for Garibaldi, for Cavour, for Umberto Primo or for one of the Victor Emmanuels. Who, then, is this Vannucci that he displaces patriots and kings? If course he is *Il Perugino*, the town's great pride, the gifted if somewhat saccharin painter of angels and Madonnas. Some of his work is seen in Rome, in the Sistine Chapel, more of it in Florence, but here in his native town are the best things he ever did, especially in the ancient *Collegio del Cambio*, the headquarters of the medieval "brokers" and exchange men. He was a great artist, no use denying that, but you always want to shock his angels, and even his emperors and warriors—Pericles, Trajan, Scipio, Leonidas—to see if they can develop a bit of resentment, or even wrath. All are so beautiful, so oval-faced, with such grave, haunting eyes. His famous Solomon, for example, in the Cambio, looks like a bearded choirboy. Obviously he has just been up to mischief and so he gazes from those limpid orbs with a look that is twice as virtuous as virtue itself. But to give the painter his due, Perugino's portrait of himself, on the central pillar of the Exchange, is not saccharin. The features are heavy, the chins billowy and the eyes not tender and grave but severe, almost suspicious of us who gaze at him.

Adjacent to the Exchange is the medieval *Palazzo dei Priori*, called also the *Palazzo Comunale*, with the National Gallery of Umbria on its top floor. Perúgia is a very musical and music-loving city and in that upper gallery I once heard the brilliant "complex of soloists" of Rome's *Collegium Musicum Italicum* give a memorable concert of old music, chiefly Vivaldi.

The north side of this palazzo, facing the Piazza IV Novembre and its wonderful Pisani-decorated *Fonte Maggiore* (Great Fountain), has an unusual outside stairway and porch and above this a curious ornament on its façade, namely an old chain, attached to Perúgia's symbols in bronze, a lion and a griffin. The chain was taken from the gate of Siena after a victory over that rival town quite a while ago—in 1358 to be exact. The rivalry between these hill cities still goes on, but in friendly, not bloody, fashion. On a visit to Perúgia in 1952 I happened to see a historic ceremony (May 11) by which the students of the two universities "signed the peace," concluding it with a most hilarious "tourney" in medieval costumes in Perúgia's lofty stadium.

Perúgia has a score of interesting things to see, the *Church of San Pietro*, almost a Perúgian Pantheon, the *Oratory of San Bernardino*, whose gay façade is the one outstanding masterpiece of Agostino di Duccio, the house where Pinturicchio was born (on Via Pinturicchio), the seventh-century *Chapel of San Prospero*, a primitive jewel of a church inside a farmyard, never shown on tours and rarely by privately hired guides, and, to many visitors the most impressive thing of all, the awesome, loftily looming *Etruscan Gate*.

Don't fail to find this gate, often called on maps *Arco di Augusto* because the upper portion of it is Roman, bearing the inscription AUGUSTA PERUSIA. It is a tremendous thing, overwhelming to the senses, and makes you vividly aware of the rude strength of the Etruscans. The gate is reached by ducking down the steep Via Rocchi or the curving Via Cesare Battisti at the northern edge of the city.

One day, as I was gazing up at its massive masonry, I came face to face with the very model that Perugino must have used many times when painting a Madonna and Holy Child. A young mother was carrying her babe through the gate into Piazza Fortebraccio and a more beautiful mother and child I know I have never seen. Their faces were oval and sweet, but extremely lovely too. An almost startled exclamation escaped me. "That woman is beautiful!" They do, it seems, still grow in Perúgia the sort of beauties Perugino liked to paint.

In one respect this little provincial capital seems quite different from all the other hill towns both of Umbria and Tuscany. It is amazingly full of life, the life of today. Its Corso Vanucci is crowded with those bent on business and with pleasure strollers too. There are good restaurants here, like the *Trasimeno*, good cafés, like the *Falci* and the *Vitalesto*. Most interesting of all, there exists in Perúgia a university for foreigners, giving special attention to those who wish to study Etruscology. Thousands of foreign students of some forty nationalities have enrolled, and I am quite certain that when I undertake to perfect my Etruscology, to say nothing of my Italian, it will be in this Etruscan city of "Perusia," which was old when Emperor Augustus added his name to it two thousand years ago. The *Università per Stranieri* is located, by the way, in the *Palazzo Gallenga Stuart*, adjacent to the Etruscan Gate. Its golden *Sala Goldoni* has already been alluded to in the Scrolls of the Great (Chapter 9).

There are still other things to see in Perúgia but I think it is defensible to spend most of one's time, if time is limited, in merely enjoying its physical beauties—surely including its feminine beauties—and its aboundingly vigorous street life. And of course its views are inescapable. One that matches the outlook even from the Brufani's south windows is that from the tiled piazzetta reached through the flower market. Built in 1932 above the city market overhanging the old Etruscan town wall, it lends itself to reveries, inviting a parade of the centuries, but perhaps the most challenging century of them all—to us at least—is this one.

CHAPTER 17

THE HILL COUNTRY BY FIAT

THE joy of seeing Italy by car, your own brought from home or one rented in Italy, can be more or less imagined, but the reality makes the imagining pretty tame stuff. In my case the reality was, and is— for I write these chapters in intervals of touring—the "Fia*tina*" referred to in Chapter 1, a little Belvedere station wagon made by Fiat of Turin. Tina has opened up an Italy I had always dreamed of, an Italy without timetables, an Italy where any town or village seen in the distance or on the crest of a hill may be captured by a liter or two of gasoline and where any city may be *explored* at one's motored leisure. This chapter is a catalog, rigorously weeded down to ten hill towns of Umbria and Tuscany, with an extra opening word on L'Áquila, capital of Abruzzi, that were brought within my ken "by Fiat." Without motor power of my own it is most improbable that I would ever have seen any of them, and it goes without saying that many of the towns even on the main Ribbon Routes were *seen*, by means of this personal transportation, instead of merely passed through.

L'Áquila is *The* Eagle, its name requiring the definite article, represented by the Italian *L*. If you look it up in guidebook and hotel indices under *A* you won't find it there. The Eagle is the capital and chief city of Abruzzi Province, that wonderful region, rarely visited by overseas tourists, that stretches from Italy's highest Apennines, called the Abruzzi, to the Adriatic Sea. It is about sixty miles by road, and likewise by a branch railway of sorts from Terni, on the main highway from Rome to Perúgia. So striking is this unspoiled capital, both in itself and in its setting amid snow-capped mountains towering to heights of nearly ten thousand feet, that it is worth visiting, even by toilsome train if necessary. You may find accommodations for the night in an establishment of the first category imaginatively named *Grand Hotel*.

L'Áquila has its full quota of starrable churches, especially *Santa Maria di Collemaggio* (Saint Mary of May Hill), an ancient pink-and-white structure, and *San Bernardino*, reached by a lot of steps that are restfully broad and easy. It has its full quota of specialties too, a fifteenth-century *Fountain of Ninety-Nine Pipes* (but try to count that many!) and a notable castle built by the Spaniards four centuries ago, now housing art works. But man-made sights are dwarfed for most visitors by the mountains that nature planted near by. One of them, *Corno Grande* (Big Horn), a peak of the group called *Gran Sasso d'Italia*, is the highest one in the Apennines (9558 feet). From Assergi, fourteen miles northeast of L'Áquila, a *funivia*, or cableway, ascends to *Campo Imperatore* (6860 feet), where there is a modest albergo. I didn't ascend to this height and have kicked myself for the omission. I may mention, as a footnote of history, that Benito Mussolini *did* ascend the Gran Sasso, as a refugee from the wrath of his collapsing Italy, and it was from here that a daring Nazi airman rescued, or kidnaped, him late in 1943.

Three hill towns in the ensuing list seem logically in the Perúgia orbit and four in the Siena orbit, while three more are satellites of Florence. I shall mention first the towns I reached from Perúgia.

Todi, about twenty-eight miles due south of the Umbrian hub on the lightly traveled road to Orvieto, is like a strikingly designed helmet on the head of its hill. It builds the hill higher instead of attaching itself just below the crest, with a lofty *Rocca* (fortress) serving as its acropolis, as is the case with so many of its rival towns. You see Todi from a distance, but when you are near it the whole town is hidden, from some angles, by the hill's broad shoulder.

The main square, *Piazza del Popolo*, is a wonderful, eye-filling thing, surrounded on three sides by medieval *palazzi* and on the fourth by the thirteenth-century duomo. The *Palazzo del Popolo*, with queer arcades jumbled under it and a queerer flight of steps leading up to it along the façade of a neighbor palace, is easily the finest structure in the square. At a tangent to this square is another and smaller one named for Garibaldi and centered by a statue of that patriot, who asks the town to excuse his back while he gazes out over the parapet down to the broad valley and across to other hills.

There is no good hotel in Todi, and you will hardly need one, but you will need to eat and fortunately there is a modest restaurant, the *Umbria,* so dizzily placed that it seems almost to be hanging by invisible chains from the dome of the sky.

Gúbbio lies twenty-five miles northeast of Perúgia by a dirt road of a thousand twists and turns, revealing endless views of such ravishing beauty that if you take this route you won't regret it, though there is a longer and considerably better route by way of Umbértide.

Ancient Gúbbio, retaining its medieval look to a remarkable degree, is a hill*side* town, struggling up and up and inviting the visitor likewise to struggle, but how delightedly, through rude passageways and on steps in the virgin rock. The finest thing of all, however, can be reached by your car, *was* reached by mine. This is the *Piazza della Signoria,* with its fascinating *Palazzo dei Consoli* brooding over the lower lifts of the town.

This Palace of the Councilors contains an art gallery and a museum, the latter featuring one of the priceless treasures of Italy, the famous bronze *Eugubine Tablets,* mentioned in the historical review in Chapter 8. These tablets have long inscriptions in two languages, the primitive *Umbrian,* related to Etruscan but not the same, and *Latin,* thus forming a workable key to one of the earliest languages to take written form on the Italian peninsula. The Umbrian characters read from right to left, like Hebrew, and the inscriptions are said to deal with matters of religion. You and I, glancing at the forest of odd hen tracks, would be the last to deny this.

The palace has many other strange sights quite its own, the most curious being its toilet arrangements, which were amazingly adequate for the early period, about 1400, when this building was erected. We've all heard of our early-American two-holers and even three-holers, but the Palazzo dei Consoli had a twenty-six-holer, though the facilities are not arranged in any neat row. "It was a great novelty, sir, in those days," said the palace custodian to me solemnly. Another peculiarity of the building is a contrivance whereby the councilors, enjoying the seclusion (and the magnificent view) of a lofty covered gallery, could talk to the populace in the great hall below through a sort of speaking tube cut through the masonry. By such aloofness they were able to enhance their prestige.

From the Piazza della Signoria a most unlikely looking archway leads to a ramp, up which one may toil to see the cathedral and the fifteenth-century *Ducal Palace*. Both are well worth finding but they don't hold a candle to the Palace of the Councilors.

The popular festival culminating in the *Corsa dei Ceri* (Race of the Candles) on May 15 is an affair of absorbing interest to the populace, but if you attend it don't look for candles that can be *lighted*. Once upon a time they were real candles of wax but nowadays they are merely wooden replicas, of monumental size, that are carried on poles by competing groups of citizens who *race* uphill with them. I saw these huge shafts of wood and wondered *why* men should half kill themselves annually to race uphill with such vast and heavy contraptions. The answer seems to be, "It takes all kinds of people, etc."

Urbino, birthplace of Raphael and once the seat of the Montefeltro dukes, with the most dazzling court in Italy, is commonly and conveniently thought of as an Umbrian hill town, though strictly speaking it lies just across the provincial border in the Marches, that province that claims its share of the Adriatic littoral between Abruzzi on the south and the Romagna on the north. It lies some forty miles north of Gúbbio and can be included with that town in a one-day motor circuit from Perúgia, returning by a different pass, to make a *round* trip. I know this can be done in one day because I did it, but I should never do so again. There is too much to see, too much to savor slowly, with undiminishing pleasure. Particularly needless is it to make a rush of this tour because there is a really pleasant, though unpretentious, hotel in small Urbino, by name the *Italia*.

One reason for my own miscalculation in pushing along at such a pace was that I hadn't reckoned on such *scenery*. The road to Urbino is in part the famous *Via Flaminia*, that same Roman road by which ancient chariots and modern motors made and make their exit from Rome itself. North of Schéggia, only eight miles from Gúbbio, the Via Flaminia takes you in charge, and the next thirty miles are a series of scenic glories, culminating, just beyond Acqualagna, in the *Furlo Gorge*, as breathstopping a defile as you will find in all Italy, not forgetting the Dolomites and the Valley of Aosta. The mountains aren't especially high here, but the cliffs are as sheer as the man-made cliffs of New York City. There is *just* room for your road, a good one, and for the pellucid green River Metáuro flowing beside it.

More scenery awaits you all around Urbino, and on the way back from the Marches to Sansepolcro, on the main Tiberside highway down to Perúgia, your car must wriggle up and over two passes, the *Passo di Spugna* (2500 feet) and *Bocca Trabária* (3500 feet). Such wriggling keeps the motorist constantly on the alert and to enjoy the big scenery in a big way one must make frequent halts to gaze up and out and over and down, in awe at what nature can do when she really puts her mind to it.

Urbino is a hill town of special character (as if *all* of them were not special) so far as the tourist is concerned, the character stemming from two individuals, Raphael Sanzio, or Santi, and Duke Federigo di Montefeltro.

Raphael is certainly not without honor in his home town. That part of the town where he lived is the Contrada Raffaella and the street of his home is Via Raffaello. It ascends like an Alpine climber—your car almost needs a pickax and rope—to a lovely view-park on the crest of one of Urbino's two hills and in the center of this charming belvedere is a showy marble statue of the artist, holding his brush and palette. *Raphael's home*, at Number 57, is a very simple house, and perhaps the more evocative for that reason. In the room where he was born the attendant shows a fresco of a *"madre e bambino,"* mother and child, done by Giovanni Santi, Raphael's father, who was himself an able painter and doubtless hoped that his boy would grow up to be a good artist too!

The *Palace of the Dukes of Montefeltro*, on Urbino's other hill, became, under the ambitious Federigo, the greatest palace in the Italy of the Quattrocentisti. Built chiefly in the years from 1460 to 1480, when the Umbrian school of painters was attaining its zenith, it attracted to the ducal court the leading personages of Italy, not only in the arts but in literature, science and philosophy. Urbino shone from its remote and lofty crests like a beacon of culture, and the duke, no shrinking violet, basked in all this glow. He capitalized his exalted position by filling his palace with the finest art works his power could command or his money could buy. A Montefeltro duchess of a later generation married a Medici of Florence and the art works of this ducal palace then became the nucleus of the collections in the Uffizi Gallery. What a dowry *that* duchess brought to her Florentine lord!

Throughout the magnificent apartments of the palace and in the stonework of the exterior we read in large letters FE DUX, but despite Duke Federigo's well-known vanity he ruled well, as did his son Guidobaldo after him, and as had his forebears. For more than two centuries Urbino enjoyed peace, wealth and the leisure to pursue its bent for the arts. It was too good to last and in 1626 Pope Urban VIII "acquired" this whole dukedom for the Papal States.

* * *

From Siena one hill *idea*, one hill hamlet and two hill towns, not counting San Gimignano, already discussed as a Sienese satellite, are a bit more insistent than the rest for the motorist's attention.

Pienza is my hill idea, though not mine, after all, but that of Aeneas Silvius Piccolomini, who was born there. At the time of his birth it was not an idea at all but a mere hill village of little interest, by name Corsignano. When he became Pope Pius II he renamed it for himself *Pienza* and commissioned the great architect Rossellino to rebuild it *totally*, from the ground up, as a planned town of the Renaissance. The ambitious pope died prematurely and the work stopped, but a part of it had taken shape and that is what we see today. The *Piazza Pio II* is a model of unity unique in the hills of Italy. Bounded by a duomo and three palaces, the masterpiece being the *Palazzo Piccolomini*, it bears the strong stamp of the strong man who planned it. A look at this Unfinished Symphony will spur one's interest to view again the Pinturicchio frescoes in the Piccolomini Library of Siena's cathedral.

Monteriggioni is my hill hamlet. It is so tiny that its name appears on none but the largest-scale motor maps, yet there is no more striking vignette in Italy. Dante contrived to see it, without even a bicycle, referring to it in the thirty-first canto of the *Inferno* "as with circling round of turrets Monterigion crowns his walls." It lies about eight miles north of Siena, on the Florence road, and can be climbed into by your car. It was by mine. Monteriggioni is a hamlet that has slept on its crest since the 1200's. It has a perfect ring of walls from that period, topped by fourteen towers. There's *nothing* to see when you climb to this community, nothing except itself, an ancient hermit on a hill.

Certaldo, high above the road that leads from Siena to Émpoli, is claimed by Florentine tourism as a town of its orbit, but it is somewhat nearer Siena and only eight miles, by a rough branch road I admit, from San Gimignano, so it seems to me a proper outpost of the lesser city. Aside from its striking appearance and its fine old buildings, notably the Palazzo Pretorio, its clearest claim to attention is as the home of Boccaccio. This very gifted spinner of yarns was born in Paris but lived in little Certaldo probably during his early youth and certainly during the two or three years just prior to his death. The town is rightly proud of him, for he, even more than Dante, was the godfather of the modern Italian language. His home, high up in the ascending town, is a major show piece, though it suffered from World War II and has had to be partly rebuilt, and of course the street is named Via Boccaccio. A tribute that some might consider of doubtful appropriateness, in view of his well-known tendency to "uninhibited" prose, is a monument to the fourteenth-century author in the *Church of Santi Michele e Jacopo*. Feeling quite incompetent to research the Boccaccian soul, I am content to enjoy all these tributes and the medieval town to which he brought such fame.

Volterra, thirty miles or so west of Siena, is a hill town to see almost at random, not one to "do," guidebook in hand. It is a city of five lives, Etruscan, Roman, Free Communal, Florentine, Italian, but it is its first life that commands our chief attention, for the place is unique in that it *looks* Etruscan in almost every part. Perúgia looks Etruscan in some parts, and so does Gúbbio, but Volterra positively exudes Etruscanism.

Find your way, if you can bear to leave the stupendous view from the parapet outside the walls, to the Piazza dei Priori. *Austere* is the word that's always used of this square and this town, and no word could be fairer. You won't feel like singing any roundelays, but you will be impressed, even overwhelmed.

The *Etruscan Museum*, which takes a bit of finding (at 11 Via Vittorio Emanuele), won't do a thing to lighten your mood, for its chief display is of cinerary urns, literally thousands of them of all sizes, but this more-than-austere collection again impresses you with the hoary age of Volterra, grand patriarch of all old hill towns.

My selection of towns to emphasize in the Siena area will be sharply criticized, and why not? I shall be sternly asked, "What about lovely *Montepulciano*, as much a 'ward' of Siena as is Pienza? What about *Monte Oliveto Maggiore*, with the well-known frescoes of Sodoma and Signorelli in the cloister of the Benedictine Monastery? What about *San Quírico d'Órcia?*" Well, that shows the advantage of *writing* a book instead of reading it. You can emphasize anything you like, *because* you like it!

* * *

The orbit of Florence is so broad, so encompassing, that any sort of selection seems arbitrary. One thinks of *Prato*, with its wealth of art and architecture, but this is a valley town, not a hill town. One thinks of the pottery village called *Impruneta*, of the upland resorts called *Montepiano* and *Consuma*, but none of these is important in the shining galaxy of Tuscany. Let's be arbitrary anyway and choose personal favorites.

Vinci is a gem that began to sparkle only in the year 1952, the five-hundredth anniversary of Leonardo's birth, which event, a milestone in the world's development, took place in a rude peasant home some two miles distant on the road that winds up the slope of Monte Albano. This half-millennial year marked the opening, in Vinci, of an exceedingly interesting *Vinci Museum* in a castle donated by Count Giovanni Rasini di Castelcampo. The castle in its setting is a sight to see, warranting a considerable effort to reach it even in castle-rich Italy. The view from its upper terrace warrants climbing the many steps to it. But the contents of the castle prove more enthralling than its construction or setting.

One of the most significant things about the Vinci Muesum is the series of show cases, running around all four sides of one room, each case holding an exhibit to attest a *different* facet of Leonardo's universal genius. Here is the list of fields in which he was at least well versed, and in most cases expert and far ahead of his time: MACCHINE; MECCANICA; IDRAULICA; GEOLOGIA E GEOGRAFIA; BOTANICA; OTTICA; ANATOMIA;

INGEGNERIA MILITARE ARMI; INGEGNERIA CIVILE; ARCHITETTURA; MUSICA; FILOLOGIA; FISICA; ASTRONOMIA; MATEMATICA.

Leonardo's home, called *Anchiano* (don't miss the sign at a Road Y), is the rudest of the rude. This farmhouse too was bought and preserved for the public by Count Rasini di Castelcampo. In a room at the right, visitors see where "Lionardo," as he was christened, uttered his first inquisitive cries. It is the essence of rural simplicity, proving again the validity of a venerable cliché. Genius, like lightning, strikes where it will.

Vallombrosa, mentioned in Chapter 9 in connection with John Milton, *was* the birthplace and home of the Vallombrosian Order, a branch of the Benedictines. (The convent was suppressed in 1866.) It *is* a mountain-forest retreat of great peacefulness and charm at an altitude of about 3400 feet, some twenty miles east of Florence. Its best hotels, in the adjacent resort of Saltino, have all sorts of tourist amenities, including even tennis courts, which may seem incongruous, but actually Saltino doesn't impress you as too sophisticated. The all-encompassing forest serves as guardian of the repose for which this region has always been famous. There are many lovely walks and bridle paths.

Montecatini Terme and *Montecatini Alto*, less than thirty miles west of Florence by the excellent *autostrada* (no cross roads), form a remarkable team—one can by no means call them twins—and they invite a well-rounded holiday sojourn that can be pleasurably prolonged from a day to a week or longer.

Montecatini Terme itself is one of the most important thermal resorts of Europe, with magnificent *stabilimenti* (bath establishments) and equally magnificent hotels. There are an unbelievable *hundred and sixty-nine* hotels and pensions in the official listing of the *Annuario Alberghi*, but the *Grand Hotel Plaza* is the unrivaled center of Montecatini life. When its huge patio café, surrounded by shops, opens in May, the season, to all intents, commences. When this closes, about November 1, the season ends. The Plaza, pronounced "Platsa" in Italian, is a big hotel, with a big and beautifully manicured garden. Half the marble of Carrara, you will say, must have been devoted to its shiny hallways and public rooms. Yet there is no stuffed-shirtism about the place. While heading up the social and musical doings that are always a part of so popular a spa, it manages also to maintain a relaxed air of holiday.

Montecatini Alto, officially known as *Montecatini Valdenievole*, is a fitting epilogue to this catalog of a few—a *very* few—of the Tuscan-Umbrian hill towns, as seen by the motorist. It is quite feasible to drive up to it, though it is nine hundred abrupt feet above its fashionable cousin. A funicular, with frequent service, provides easier access and is perhaps more fun, though it is wonderful fun too to watch the glorious Tuscan panorama unfold, curve by curve, as your motor climbs.

The goal, when reached, reveals itself as a charm-laden little old town quite unspoiled by its proximity to the modern thermal world at its base. There are things to see, like the weathered *Church of Santa Barbara*, but High Montecatini is its own best sight. After strolling its lovely promenades and climbing its steep streets, you'll want to take a table in some open-air café and do your "home work" with picture post cards, as others about you are doing.

CHAPTER 18

FLORENCE, STRONG LOADSTONE OF TRAVEL

Your Shelter in a Much-Sought City

THE MAGNETIC pull of Florence on travelers, and especially, but by no means exclusively, on women travelers, is an axiom of tourism. I suppose the city's power is hardly surpassed by Rome itself, one reason for its special drawing power being obviously *shops*. The shops of Via Tornabuoni, Via de' Cerretani, Via de' Fossi, are almost as alluring as are the shops of rue de la Paix, rue de Rivoli and rue St.-Honoré. The outstanding specialties of Florentine shops are majolica, woodwork, silverware, art reproductions and fine photographs, tooled leather goods, items in tortoise shell, gloves, and of course exquisite silks, lingeries and embroideries.

What's more, prices of things-to-buy in Florence are reputed to be cheaper than in other Italian cities, and in general they certainly are cheaper. This city has been regarded, for a century or more, as the most inexpensive large city in Italy and chiefly for that special reason— I have this tidbit on good authority—Florence was first selected as capital of modern Italy, serving in that capacity from 1865 to 1870, when the preponderance and historical significance of Rome drew the honor to that city.

Don't look for miracles of cheapness in lodging or food. Good hotel accommodations and meals in the best hotels cost *plenty* here, as they do throughout Italy, but that is to be expected in a city of such vast popularity. It is the expatriates, especially retired people, electing to *live* here, year after year, who chiefly benefit by the lower costs; but to a certain extent tourist shoppers benefit too.

There are three de luxe hotels in Florence, the *Excelsior-Italie* and the *Grand*, both on Piazza Ognissanti directly beside the Arno, and the *Savoy*, on the Piazza della Repubblica in the center of the city.

On one of my stays in Florence I "rose to the top" by taking a balcony room overhanging the Arno in the Excelsior-Italie and loved it, as you will if you stay there. The Arno panorama, including the Ponte Vecchio a little way upriver, is unceasingly interesting, despite the terrible destruction wrought at various points by the 1944 fighting, now offset in part by a vigorous rebuilding program. On a second brief stay at the same hotel I was unable to secure an Arno room and "made do" with a fourth-floor room in the back, on the Via Borgo Ognissanti. To my astonishment I liked it even better, for it brought the skyline of the city right to my balcony. Santa Maria Novella and San Lorenzo, with the Medici Chapel, were near neighbors and Brunelleschi's dome of the duomo, flanked by Giotto's tower, loomed up only a little farther away.

The public rooms of this widely popular hotel are as light and cheerful as any I know in Italy, their marble splendors being held sternly in check by good taste. As a personal point, of remarkable insignificance, I would report that I like the outsize metal "tags" of the keys to bedroom doors. Each is stamped with the figure of Michelangelo's David.

Having mentioned the fighting of the Second World War, I should re-emphasize what was stated in Chapter 2, that central Florence, including its most important buildings, now shows few signs of this violence. Most of the fighting took place on the banks of the Arno, for the Nazis chose to make this river a line of stubborn resistance. It took eighteen ghastly days and nights for the Allies to dislodge them, and before retreating, the Germans destroyed all the city's bridges except the Ponte Vecchio, which was barricaded at both ends with veritable hills of rubble. The destruction would have been infinitely more extensive and tragic had not General Mark Clark started the dislodgment by taking a full, laborious month to surround the German troops in Florence so that their retreat could be more quickly forced. This saving strategy, and the energetic efforts of the Florentine authorities to rebuild the wasted mess have combined to restore the well-loved city and present it intact to this generation of travelers. The wounds of war are still amply visible but they are no longer depressing.

The tourist amenities of Florence, to return to more cheerful topics of this incurably cheerful city, are impressive. Official listings report well over a hundred hotels and pensions, plus several more at lofty Fiésole, the city's famous hill suburb. They are, of course, of every category. Two humble but neat-looking pensions whose location I have noted with interest, though I have never stopped there, are the *Novella* (third category), directly on the Arno, near the Excelsior-Italie, and the *Pendini* (second category) on the upper floors of a building directly on that bright, exciting, but undeniably *noisy* central square, Piazza della Repubblica. If you are of the type that likes to look down on seething crowds, cafés with orchestras going full blast, tornados of traffic, with its snarls and taxi men's quarrels, the Pendini may well call you. I *am* of that type. I even like to go to sleep to the music of a city's bedlam sounds, but I realize that in liking such melodies I am of a very small minority.

At Fiésole there is one hotel of the third class, the *Aurora*, that catches every eye. It is in the lofty main square, just at the point where trolleybus F, having commenced its run from Florence at Piazza San Marco, and toiled up (in twenty minutes), comes to a halt, yet the hotel's verandas and many of its bedrooms hang over the widespreading metropolis as if they were on top of a mammoth campanile. This place is worth a thought, since transportation to the city is so frequent and inexpensive.

Florentine Facts and Tourist Pleasures

The EPT of Florence, with office at 15 Via Tornabuoni, is very active and publishes various treasurable brochures, including a two-pamphlet city guide of eminent practicality. One part, the *Tourist Guide to Florence*, gives concise coverage of the historical and cultural attractions, and the gardens and belvederes, with an excellent city map, the other gives *Tourist Information* on every conceivable topic, and the two together take up no more room in your pocket or pocketbook than a fat business letter.

CIT is prominent in Florence, as one would expect. It operates several different guided tours every day devoted to the chief sights of Florence and Fiésole, also a Florence-by-Night tour. This last may surprise you, but Florence *is* rather lively at night and the floodlighting of the churches and public buildings makes it beautiful to the eye. Longer CIT trips are made through neighboring parts of Tuscany, even to San Gimignano and Siena and to Pisa. *American Express* is at 8 Lungarno Corsini, *Cook* at 7 Via Tornabuoni, and there are many more good travel offices.

Tourist pleasures in Florence are a frequent cause of astonishment to visitors, especially to those doubting males who consider that they have been dragged to this city by their womenfolk for no other purposes than to pay for purchases and to sop up culture.

Fine food, cooked in the superior olive oil of the region, is native to Tuscany and it finds its natural home in Florence, whose cuisine is, on the whole, the most notable in all Italy. There is a local saying to the effect that "in the beginning God created the world in the form of a leg of veal, with tripe and beans on the side," and if you look at a map of Tuscany you will see what is meant. The shape of this province *is* remarkably like a leg of veal, trimmed, if your fancy goes so far, with the delicious *trippa* that is supposed to go with it and with a few *fagioli*. The latter garnishment includes, I suppose, the dozen or more islands, one of them Elba, of the so-called Tuscan Archipelago.

I am no expert on Florentine restaurants, though I should like to spend six months becoming one, but I can record some notes of at least half a dozen places I have enjoyed.

Doney, a name familiar as a super-café in Rome, is that of a restaurant and tearoom in Florence, at 57 Via Tornabuoni. Any place bearing this name would have to be good and this Doney certainly is.

Sabatini, on Via Panzani near Santa Maria Novella, is a place of wonderful cuisine but narrow "geography," the main room being almost a corridor. It is enormously popular, attesting its quality, and if, at mealtime, you can get a table there right off you're doing better than I did.

Buca di San Ruffilo, at 7 Piazza del Olio, very close to the Duomo Square, has a church-and-cloister background but is now a frescoed cellar restaurant of the very first quality, famous for its luscious meats and their sauces. Music goes with your meal here.

Buca Lapi, at 1 Via del Trebbio, adjacent to the Palazzo Antinori, is another cellar place of quality gayed for tourists by many striking wall posters of travel and of steamship lines. It is a *ristorante caratteristico*.

Giovacchino, at 2 Via Tosinghi, a little to the Arno side of Duomo Square, is a place of literary-theatrical appearance and standing, where many "greats" have eaten, as the caricatures, sketches, even manuscripts framed and hung on the walls proclaim. The personages here represented include Chesterton, André Gide, Stefan Zweig, Hermann Keyserling, Richard Strauss, and may well include you one day, if you are, or become, that famous.

Paoli, at 12 Via dei Tavolini, between the duomo and the Palazzo Vecchio, is a character place calling itself the oldest restaurant in Florence. It calls itself also the Grand Dukes' Restuarant because medieval grand dukes, we are assured, used to come here, sit at the counter and eat good meals for a payment of *seven centessimi*. You will pay just about thirty thousand times that much—in lire and centessimi—which is to say about three dollars, for a good dinner with chianti. Paoli's walls are frescoed with scenes from Boccaccio (but don't expect Pompeian frankness!) and adorned with the coats of arms of all the towns of Tuscany.

La Loggia, on the famous Piazzale Michelangelo (with the David statue), on the far side of the Arno, is a restaurant-café-tearoom of the front rank, very suitable for relaxation after a full stint of sightseeing.

Da Zi' Rosa, finally, is near the Arno-side hotels. It is a little hole-in-the-wall at 12 Via de' Fossi, near Piazza Goldoni, and relies on no special tricks of eye-appeal but merely on good food in a cheerful setting. It is open well into the small hours of morning and can serve a hot pizza pie that one remembers. At least I remembered mine, a rich small-hours pizza lubricated with Orvieto Secco.

Among the good *tearooms* that abound in central Florence, notably on Via Tornabuoni, *Doney*, already named above, is perhaps the most sumptuous. *Giacosa* and *Leland* are two other tearooms on the same elegant shopping street.

Among *outdoor cafés*, four or five of them centering in a huge way in the Piazza della Repubblica and its arcades, one that I have several times enjoyed for its good music is the *Birreria Wührer Extrabar*, known to prewar tourists as Paszkowski. Scores of its little tables fill a considerable part of the square, and most of the patrons who sit at them seem actually to be *listening* to the music, a pleasant phenomenon that I used to witness in a few special music cafés in Paris, though it is now almost a thing of the past there. I have been genuinely impressed with the *restraint* of artists I have heard here. The girl violinist doing the slow movement of Mendelssohn's Concerto did not turn on extra power to drown out a group of boisterous students walking through the square. The operatic tenor did not attempt to bellow des Grieux's tender song from *Manon* above the clatter of a motorcycle that roared into the piazza. Perhaps the artistic spirit of Florence held them on its leash, whatever the provocation.

I have just stated that Florence is a night town. The EPT's *Tourist Information* lists half a dozen cabarets, or dance restaurants, open in winter, and a similar number of garden places for summer patronage, along with two, *Club Parterre* and the *Baglioni Roof-Garden* that operate throughout the year. The latter, on top of Hotel Baglioni, near the Central Station is considered the dean of Florentine nightspots. Its gay lights add a distinct touch of cheer to the city's late-evening silhouette. *Tourist Information,* by the way, lumps *all* the nightspots, rather roughly, as "Dance Halls," which most of them certainly are *not*, in America's derogatory sense of that word. The Baglioni Roof, the only place I personally know, offers due dignity along with its infectious gaieties. I believe this is true also of the *Pozzo di Beatrice*, a night club in Palazzo Feroni (Piazza Santa Trinità) that flourishes during the winter season.

Letting Florence Seep into Your System

To *enjoy* Florence, within the limits of a short stay, is a fine art which many travelers fail to master. The hurried step and the worried look are familiar features of the Florentine picture and of course the reason is obvious. There is so much to see, so infinitely much, and 80 per cent of it is of the very first importance. It has been said that half the great paintings of the world are in this middle-sized city by the Arno; and its sculpture is hardly less dominant. Its churches, too, and medieval palaces are numbered by the score and almost any one of them would "make" an ordinary tourist town.

I am convinced that there is only one way to enjoy, in a few short days, this City of the Medici, this inspirer of the Renaissance, and that is to kill one's conscience even if it involves hurling your Nagel into the river. I do not mean to imply that viewing art works is in itself a burden to anybody. The person who really *cannot* enjoy a lovely painting or sculpture—if such a person exists—may even skip Florence altogether. Of course it is surfeit that kills, and to surfeit one is driven by the "tourist faith," whose high priest is the Complete Guide.

Florence should seep into our spirits and we can enjoy this phenomenon in the space of two or three days or even in a one-day stay if that is positively all the time we can afford.

I propose, first of all, a leisurely two-hour stroll, as if a full month lay ahead for the enjoyment of the city. The *Duomo* beckons, and who on earth could turn away? Brunelleschi's superb dome, a pioneer that settled in Florence five hundred years ago, broods maternally or grand-maternally over the widespread community, dwarfing all the lesser domes. *Giotto's Tower*, which is the duomo's campanile, is no less marvelous. A gay, square, Gothic belfry adorned with the richest marbles, it is a sort of miracle, having been achieved a hundred years earlier than Brunelleschi's dome by a contemporary of Dante. Giotto, furthermore, was primarily a painter of frescoes rather than an architect, which makes the miracle even more astounding. (You may climb the tower if the thought of its 440 steps does not deter you.)

Across the way is the cathedral's *Baptistery*, completing one of the greatest church ensembles in Italy. The bronze doors of Ghiberti, especially the so-called *Portal of Paradise* directly opposite the cathedral, excited Michelangelo to rapture, and well they might, for Ghiberti had overcome, in open competition, even such rivals as della Quercia and Brunelleschi. He also achieved genuine *perspective*, a thing that had not before been mastered in the medium of bronze.

From the Duomo Square—and if you have not entered the cathedral the heavens will not crash—it is but a short stroll to that other most appealing Florentine square, the *Piazza della Signoria*. What a noble scene this offers! If imitation is flattery, then the world has flattered

Burano, an ancient island town in Venice's lagoon.

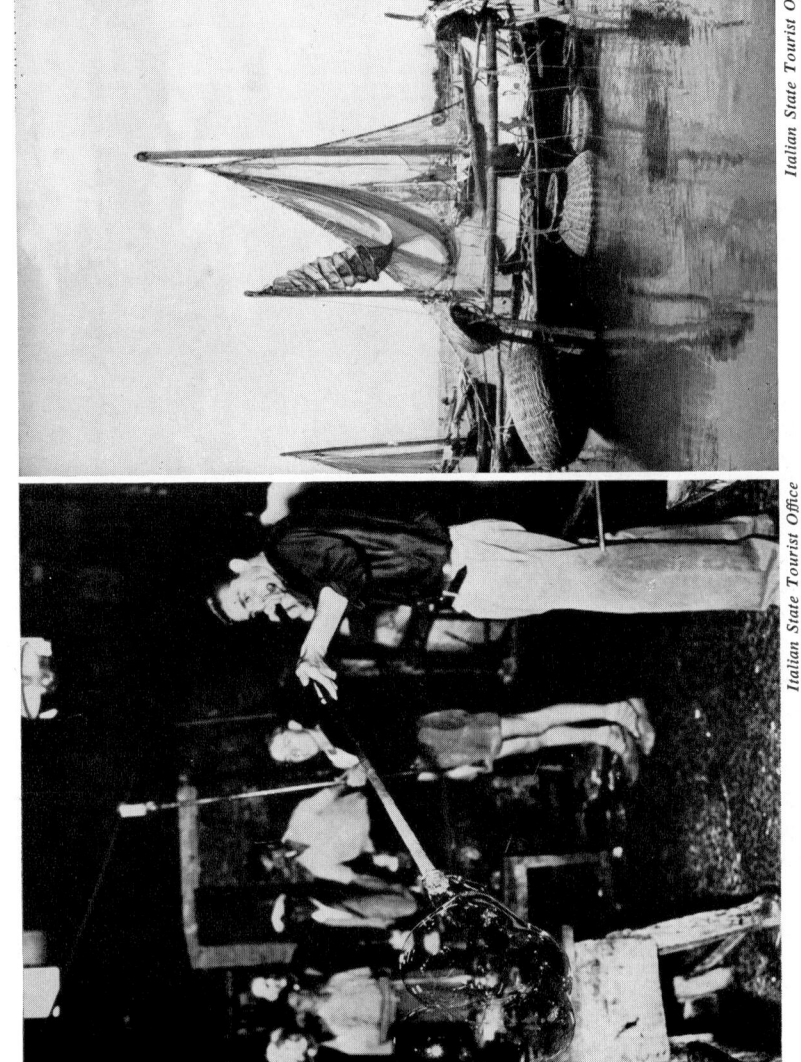

Glass blowers of Murano, in Venice's lagoon.

Fishing boats at Chioggia, an Adriatic suburb of Venice.

Italian State Tourist Office

(Upper) A milk barge goes the rounds in Venice.

(Lower) Hotel guests at the Lido try a rubber of bridge, while others loaf.

Padua's strange Basilica of St. Anthony, with many domes and towers like minarets.

Italian State Tourist Office

Italian State Tourist Office

(Upper) *"Il grandioso garage"* in Venice, perhaps the largest and finest in Europe. The picture was taken soon after its completion by Mussolini's architects. The fascist symbolism has long since been removed.

(Lower) The Anatomy Theater of Padua's university, first of its kind in the world.

Foto Lario, Como

Campione d'Italia, an Italian enclave on Lake Lugano. Its casino is a gamblers' goal.

Provincial Tourist Office, Naples

Gracie Fields' lively bar-restaurant-pool on Capri. Its name is *La Canzone del Mar* (The Song of the Sea).

Brunner & Co., Como

The Western Gardesana, a spectacular road from Riva to Gardone, on Lake Garda. It plunges into tunnels seventy-three times.

A thirteenth-century chapel on the mountaintop at Avelengo.

J. F. Amonn S.A., Bolzano

A basket swings its passengers to Avelengo, a village high above Merano. Several chapters of this book were written in that lofty retreat.

Ediz. Ghedina, Cortina

Ediz. Cartovendita, Bologna

Rock towers in the Dolomites.   Two leaning towers in the heart of Bologna.

Peaks right side up or upside down. Lago di Carezza, in the Dolomites.

The garden of one of Italy's most famous hostelries, Hotel Villa d'Este, at Cernobbio on Lake Como.

Italian State Tourist Office

Italian State Tourist Office

Lake Como, the favorite of tourism. View taken from above Bellagio.

Brunner & Co., Como

A belfry of a village church at Ospedaletti, located on Lake Como.

Air France

The campanile of Santa Francesca Romana, in Rome, seems to fill an arch of the Basilica of Maxentius.

Italian State Tourist Office

(Upper) The fabulous Alfredo, Rome's King of Noodles, mixes a dish with a gold spoon and fork given him by Douglas Fairbanks and Mary Pickford.

(Lower) The fruit market in Bolzano, Upper Ádige.

The photogenic harbor of Portofino, on the Riviera di Levante, near Genoa.

Italian State Tourist Office

this square. The superb *Loggia dei Lanzi*, where Cosimo de' Medici posted his lancers—hence the name—has a very poor replica in the Feldherrnhalle of Munich. And of the admirable Palazzo Vecchio tower there exist numerous copies, including the tower of a fire station in Boston, Massachusetts!

There is much to study in this tremendously significant square, from the *Perseus* of Cellini, the only first-rate statue that the roistering silversmith ever achieved, to the bronze disk before the *Neptune Fountain* marking the exact spot where Savonarola was burned, but if, on this joy stroll, you miss the details and enjoy the whole, what does it matter? You pass the *Uffizi Gallery*—yes, *pass* it—to the Arno, walk a few steps along the quay of this lovable river to the Old Bridge, the famous *Ponte Vecchio*, and across that five-hundred-year-old structure encrusted with goldsmiths' and jewelers' shops and little cubicles where souvenirs of every type are sold, along with attractive blouses and lingerie.

There is no Latin Quarter on this Left Bank nor any bright café, but there is much to compensate. For an infinitesimal charge you may enter the celebrated *Boboli Gardens* and enjoy their formal loveliness. But do not get lost. The Gardens are large and the exits painfully few. The main entrance, by the way, leads directly under the lee of the *Pitti Palace*. Priceless canvases are over your head, but for the present you do nothing at all about them.

Half a mile upstream, along the Arno's left bank, lies the approach—by a long bosky path—to the *Piazzale Michelangelo.* Ascend to this grand square and you will find all Florence at your feet. There is no Florentine view to compare with it unless, perhaps, the more distant view from Fiésole. Michelangelo's *David* is here, not the original but a bronze copy, and the chances are you will like it so much that you will want to find the marble original in the *Accademia di Belle Arti.* The sculptor was a youth when he wrought this marvel from a block of stone abandoned as useless. It is extremely interesting to compare the three great *Davids* of Florence, the bold, gigantic youth of Michelangelo, the tender boy of Donatello in a curious Sister Susie hat, and the delicate yet strong conception of Verrocchio, who was Donatello's pupil. The two latter *Davids* are in the Bargello (discussed later in this chapter).

Have placid wanderings and thoughts of the boy David, who was very dear to medieval Florence, so lulled your conscience that you have lost all sense of worry lest you miss something you wish to see? If so "slip up" to *San Miniato,* just a few steps distant, and revel in the exuberant marbles of that very ancient Tuscan basilica. It is given fewer stars than many a church in Florence but you will like it.

Seven hundred feet above Florence on the opposite side of the Arno lies that delectable hill suburb mentioned above, *Fiésole,* the home of Fra Angelico. From there you see Florence as the birds see it and I believe the trip is worth the two hours' time it needs for proper "seeping," no matter how short your stay. If I may risk insulting your travel awareness, Fiésole is pronounced in four syllables, with the accent on the antepenult, Fi-é-so-le.

From the lofty terminus of this line the little Street of St. Francis (Via San Francesco) leads up to the Franciscan convent. I often think of a tiny terra-cotta shrine on a lowly native house in this street that caught my eye on my first ascent. It was an *annunziata* on a gaudy blue background with fresh white narcissi placed on either side. The shrine was in imitation of the della Robbia technique. One sees such bits frequently in Florence but this particular one, so gay and so immoderately blue, seemed to put me in an expansive mood. From the viewpoint just above it I watched the distant duomo, and then Florence itself, burst through a local blanket of mist to present one of the loveliest city pictures I have ever seen. There is nothing stupendous or dazzling about this view and yet it has a popular and deserved appeal which hardly any similar view can equal. Of course it is Florence itself, with all its wealth of significance, that gives the view such flavor.

Selection versus Surfeit

How shall one plan intelligent selections from the whole world of art which lies in the City of the Medici? With some amazement at my own boldness in offering any answer at all, I would suggest that your time, if very limited, be spent on two or three of those shrines of art which can be seen in a relatively brief period, AND on the *Uffizi-Pitti Galleries*. (Hours of admission—which change from time to time—will be found in EPT's *Tourist Information*.) In the former group, but with due apologies, I would place, for personal selection, the following Big Eight:

1. *Cathedral Museum*, with the celebrated *Cantorie*, or *Singing Children*, some by Luca della Robbia, others by Donatello. The latter's "boys" were pals of mine when I too was a boy, for a carved oak reproduction of them adorned the space above the library fireplace in our home. It is an odd fact of art that Donatello, who never married, was able to sculpture children better than any other of the Great Florentines.

2. *Church of San Lorenzo*. Cosimo the Elder is buried here, under the dome. The spot should be sacred to all who love this city. Without Cosimo we would scarcely have had Florence. The church is replete with works by Donatello, Brunelleschi, Verrocchio and others.

3. The *Medici Chapels*, adjoining the "Medici Church" of San Lorenzo. The *Chapel of the Princes* is an enormous octagon of marble with several huge sarcophagi adorning its walls. The Medici crest is very conspicuous: *five pills*, significant of the name, with a sixth pill for Catherine de' Medici, this one bearing a fleur-de-lis. The *New Sacristy* was designed by Michelangelo but he lost his temper when the Florentine Republic was overthrown and abandoned the work, leaving his pupils to carry on. Despite this sudden halt, the little room contains some of the master's finest work in marble.

4. The *Foundling Hospital (Spedale degli Innocenti)* in the Piazza dell'Annunziata. Just walk through this square and you will see the world-famous white-on-blue *bambini* of Andrea della Robbia between the arches of the hospital's colonnade. Even if you are not a parent or grandparent and even if you have been wont to consider that all babies look alike, survey these charming terra-cotta infants and be convinced that babies are as various and as interesting as adults.

5. *Church of Santa Croce*, often called (and first by Byron) the Westminster Abbey of Italy. This is the largest of all Franciscan churches (interior length 384 feet) and a simple and majestic edifice, though its bright polychrome ceiling may strike you as a bit "fancy"

for a church of Assisian inspiration. You will find in Santa Croce, even without the aid of pestilential guides, an amazing array of tombs and monuments.

Tombs	Monuments
Michelangelo (his body smuggled from Rome as "merchandise" by the Medici)	Verdi
	Cavour
Machiavelli	Raphael
Vittorio Alfieri	Da Vinci
Charlotte Napoléon Bonaparte ("digne de son nom")	Galileo
Rossini	
Cherubini	

—"and others too numerous to mention."

In connection with the Musical May of Florence, concerts are given in this basilica by as many as five hundred musicians, supported by rich organ harmonies from two thousand pipes!

6. The *Church of Orsanmichele*. This tall box of a structure, a church built on the site of an old corn warehouse, is notable chiefly for a wonderful *tabernacle*, the masterpiece of Andrea Orcagna. Its marble and mosaic splendors are so bulky that the thing almost blocks you from entering at all.

7. *Santa Maria Novella*. Both inside and out, this lavishly decorated Dominican church is one of the most "rewarding" in Florence. Ghirlandaio's masterwork is in the choir. But if you can derive much artistic nutriment from the decomposed frescoes of Uccello, in the *Chiostro Verde*, you have my admiration. Yes, I know they are famous.

8. The *Bargello*, with its *Museo Nazionale*. It is wicked, I admit, and I hang my head, to include the Bargello among those things which can be "briefly" seen, but if you climb the Bargello Stairs, famous in their own right, and devote your time *only* to that one upstairs room where you find the *Young Bacchus* of Michelangelo and the two *Davids*, by Donatello and Verrocchio, you can enjoy that much in half an hour.

Michelangelo's wine god is not a fat old fellow, Rubens style, but a young drunk at the happy-foolish stage. You can't help liking him, though he is deplorably over the bay, and you'll be fascinated by the young imp of a faun at his derrière, who is slyly offering him a bunch of grapes, though how these are to be transformed into an intoxicant we are not told.

Donatello's bronze David is a marvelous, flawless work. The young hero has his foot on the decapitated head of Goliath and the wings on the helmet of the dead giant twine themselves ingeniously about the bare legs of the victorious youth. Donatello's mastery of anatomy seems here to be every whit as perfect as Michelangelo's own.

Now I, in my turn, must frankly beg advice. I want to know how to see the *Uffizi* and the *Pitti* in one day, or one week. Although lying on opposite sides of the Arno they are always linked together in our minds, as they are physically linked by a gallery running over the Ponte Vecchio. Taken together, they constitute certainly the greatest art collection in the world. Neither one is large, as galleries go, yet almost any one of the Uffizi's thirty rooms or the Pitti's fifteen, deserves *all* the time one has to give, be it little or much. I remember once encountering an elderly tourist couple in the six-hundred-yard passage that connects the two galleries. (The war wrecked it but it was rebuilt.) They were puffing along nicely at a mile and a half an hour and as I passed them the woman exclaimed to her husband, "Oh, Charles, I call this a *dear* passage." Now *there*, perhaps, is one way out of the dilemma. That woman was placid, as placid as an Alderney cow whom much grazing in lush meadows has satisfied. I am sure she had missed practically everything in the Pitti and was going over to miss it also in the Uffizi, but at least she was enjoying both galleries. If, however, such divine—not to say *bo*vine—placidity proves impossible, one must search for other means of enjoying these galleries in limited time.

Perhaps a little thought at the outset, on the general evolution of Florentine art, may help. It was *Cimabue*, we remember, who really started things, conceiving ways to bring out the third dimension in painting, and *Giotto*, his pupil, advanced that technique. *Masaccio* "founded" painting as a modern art. *Uccello* learned how to foreshorten scenes. *Fra Filippo Lippi* first painted *real* faces. His pupil *Botticelli* learned how to create marvelous effects with drapery, usually diaphanous. He also introduced black-and-white effects for the first time, as seen in *Calumny* in the Uffizi. *Perugino* was the earliest master of proportion. *Leonardo da Vinci, Raphael* and *Michelangelo* brought the art of painting to the highest pinnacles it has ever reached, and all of these masters, with many, many more, are to be seen to advantage in the Uffizi, though not quite all of them were Florentines. Even Michelangelo, who did only one *easel* painting in all his life, is represented in the Uffizi by that one. It is called *The Holy Family*.

The obvious problem posed by the Uffizi is how to be selective. Almost any of Italy's great artists can be advantageously studied here. If we weed out the Venetians, who are superb in this gallery but equally good in their native city, we still have a dozen or fifteen or twenty important Tuscans and Umbrians to cope with.

Suppose we select Raphael himself, the man whom many have decided to call the greatest of all, though this is like "deciding" that Mont Blanc is a greater mountain than the Matterhorn. In the so-called Raphael and Michelangelo room (XIII) of the Uffizi are two of the Umbrian's great achievements, the *Madonna del Cardellino* (meaning goldfinch) and the *Portrait of Pope Julius II*, Raphael's patron. In the former picture there is something remarkably gay, natural and animated in the way the Holy Child is stroking the head of the little *cardellino* that Cousin John is holding. And the portrait of Pope Julius, keen, brainy-looking, with noble snowy beard flowing over the crimson cape, is something you cannot forget. The Raphael *red* has perhaps never been matched by other painters. Old Pope Julius knew what he was about when he engaged this man to paint the papal *stanze*, a job that Perugino, and even Signorelli, could not do to his satisfaction.

Across the river in the *Pitti* there are at least six Raphaels, three of which are among the master's finest works. You know already his celebrated *Madonna del Granduca* (Grand Duke) and *Madonna della Sedia* (Chair), and if the portraits of *Angelo and Maddalena Doni* are not familiar, you now have the great opportunity of knowing them from Raphael's own hand. Some critics do not give the Umbrian quite first place even among Italian painters. What do "you yourself personally" think? They are all here ready for comparison.

What did the war do to these galleries? I rejoice to report that it did not do very serious damage. Some frescoed ceilings of the Uffizi crashed into pieces when the Germans blew up the Ponte alle Grazie, but the pieces were painstakingly collected and ultimately put back. The patching is very evident, of course, but the effect is not ruined. The Pitti Gallery largely escaped war damage. This structure was a solid stone palace erected by the Pitti Family, discomfited in politics, to outrank the Medici, if possible, in magnificence. During the days of the Italian monarchy, a part of this palazzo served as a royal residence for the House of Savoy. Its *White Hall*, built for chamber music concerts, has perfect acoustics and is used frequently for its avowed purpose during the city's festival season.

Maggio Musicale Fiorentino

The three words of this title blossom each spring all over Italy, all over Europe in fact, and in the travel windows and literature of America. Florentine Musical May has become, in recent years, a cultural event of the first magnitude, ranking with the Salzburg Festival and with Holland's Music Festival. It will be recalled that in 1951 even Communist Russia broke down, as has been mentioned in an earlier chapter, and allowed her topflight artists, including her leading ballerina and her leading violinist, to be seen and heard here, though taking due care to guard them against capitalist contamination.

The events always extend far into June, but alliteration seems to be demanded for advertising purposes, so May gets the play. The festival comprises six or seven weeks of musical treats. Opera, ballet, symphonic and choral music, church music, chamber music, light classics in garden settings, musical dramas and melodramas, recitals by leading soloists in song and instrumental music, these follow one another in swift succession, afternoons and evenings. The heavier events are usually held in the *Teatro Comunale*, in the western part of the city, near the Arno. Occasional operas, as well as concerts, are presented in the *Boboli Gardens Amphitheater;* chamber music, as mentioned above, is given in the *White Hall* of the adjacent Pitti Palace; religious music, sometimes with large choruses, is presented in *Santa Croce;* light operettas are often staged in the *Teatro della Pergola* near the duomo. Internationally famous soloists also hold forth in this more intimate and beautiful theater.

The Teatro Comunale is an enormous thing and the orchestra seats are unusually roomy and comfortable but do not look for the glitter of nineteenth-century magnificence here, in the manner of the opera houses of Milan, Rome and Naples. You come to this vast theater to look at the stage, not the ceiling, the boxes or the crystal chandeliers. On its stage I once saw the New York City Ballet give an eminent performance that brought prolonged applause from the sophisticated audience.

In the Teatro della Pergola I saw Rossini's *The Touchstone* (*La Pietra del Paragone*) and hugely enjoyed it. Nothing could be lighter, in theme or in music, than this tangle of plotting and lovemaking, but it was gaily and exuberantly done, and with my less-than-meager knowledge of Italian I could follow the plot, helped by a little synopsis printed in English on the program.

The Musical May of Florence is a wonderfully attractive potpourri of all that is easiest for multi-nation audiences to look at and listen to. Without sacrificing one whit of its dignity or its musical virtuosity, it manages to maintain the buoyant mood of spring, the "May" that lingers even to the first day of the solar summer.

CHAPTER 19

PISA AND ITS NEIGHBORS

Lucca as Foretaste

Lucca is lost in the welter of artistic wealth that Tuscany enjoys, but it should not be lost, for it has a personality quite its own and it offers much to the traveler. It has the misfortune to be a few miles off the highway, between Florence and Pisa, traversed by the CIAT motor tours. (Says the CIAT booklet *Pink Ribbon*, "Far to the right we see the town of Lucca with its towers, belfries and churches.") It has also the misfortune to be a few miles off the main rail lines, but perhaps there is solace in all this. Those who do find the town, make it their own and reserve for it a special place in their affections.

One of its special characteristics is its ramparts of the sixteenth and seventeenth centuries, which have been transformed by Luccan labor into tree-shaded promenades. You may walk or drive clear around the city, your gaze shifting as if on a swivel, first inside, at the medley of wonders, then outside at the Tuscan verdure, backed by hills. It challenges your eyes to try to take in a quarter part of what they see.

In some ways this city, with its churches in black and white stripes, is a foretaste of Pisa itself, with reflections too of Siena. Iacopo della Quercia is seen at his best in the cathedral; and there are some good reliefs by the elder Pisano, pride of that city whose name he bears.

You will note that there are many things wrong with Lucca. The cathedral, as a matter of fact, is almost as "disordered" as the famously jumbled one at Toulouse, but this one is beautiful, while that of the Languedoc capital is ugly. The city's smaller churches often display the same queer mixture of styles. Critics seldom praise them lavishly. Baedeker used to allow no stars at all to creep into his coverage of Lucca, a judgment that sorely puzzled me, but I am relieved to note that today's Nagel is not so hard to please. He allows himself four. Quite regardless of critical stars or the lack of them, every visitor likes Lucca and revels in its churches. You will surely do likewise when you see, for instance, *San Michele*, a structure that was born as early as 1143 and "just growed," like Topsy. And while in wide-eyed mood don't fail to look at a group of dwelling houses on Via Guinigi that date from the 1300's. They are called the *Case dei Guinigi* and if you find that canyon of a lane you won't be able to miss these big rambling mansions that were old when Columbus was young.

Pisa's Marbled Meadow

In the 1200's, before Florence rose to pre-eminence, Pisa held the stage in a commanding way. It was not only the foremost city of Tuscany but actually the leading power in the whole of the western Mediterranean. Of course it was a mighty seaport then, but the Mediterranean deserted Pisa and a powerful maritime metropolis was brought to ruin and then to peaceful, beautiful stagnation, preserving, however, some wonderful evidences of its Golden Age. The population is now but a tithe of what it was, though the city has staged a genuine revival in this century, to reach a new position of importance.

Pisa's greatest glories are grouped in a green meadow to which the tourist busses roll directly, though it is not in the town but on its northwestern edge, rather far from the railway station on the southern edge. All travelers, by whatever means they come to Pisa, hasten straight to what leaflets like to call the Meadow of Miracles. It *is* indeed a Meadow of Miracles—three miracles in one, and it was four until the grim coming of the Second World War.

The three unspoiled wonders are the Cathedral, its Baptistery and its Campanile, that Leaning Tower which could sensibly claim to be the most widely known structure in the world. By the fourth feature, the one that *was*, I mean the Camposanto, a cemetery enclosure that was rich with marble statuary by Renaissance sculptors until the shelling of the Second World War. It was rich also with frescoes, especially by Benozzo Gozzoli, and fortunately some of these had been removed and are now being painstakingly restored. One devastating missile struck the roof on July 27, 1944, and set it afire. Tons of melted lead rained down in a metal cloudburst, raising havoc with all that lay beneath. One can see plenty of marble art works that are still gray with lead spatterings, but the place looks far less dreary nowadays, since a solid new roof has finally replaced the old one.

The *Cathedral,* to return to the more cheerful buildings, was built in a style that is called Romanesque-Pisan from its mixture of these two so-different styles (the stripes of black in the white marble give the Pisan touch) and it is surely one of the richest churches in all Italy, its exterior full of interest, its interior crammed with marvelous art works. It was first erected in the eleventh and twelfth centuries, to commemorate a victory over the Saracens, but was damaged by fire five centuries later and then faithfully restored. Among its art works are the huge mosaic of *Christ between Mary and John,* a masterpiece begun by Cimabue; the familiar *St. Agnes,* by Andrea del Sarto, modeled, it is said, from his wife; and of course the very celebrated *pulpit* by Giovanni Pisano, of which I shall say more below. Among the duomo's special features is the "lamp of Galileo," a lovely bronze one hanging from a great height. Its swing, the great physicist noted, took always the same length of time, regardless of whether it covered a small or greater arc. This established what scientists call the principle of the isochronism of the pendulum, though it was much later that Galileo applied this principle in the making of an astronomical clock.

Pisa's *Baptistery,* round as a dollar, is famous as a favorite haunt of the nymph Echo. The uniformed guard who takes your fee at the entrance stands beneath the dome and sings lustily, and rather well, four ascending or descending notes, and they return to you as a rich, resonant chord, lasting so long that you half suspect a trick. This remarkable effect was not planned by the architects. It is caused by the contour of the dome and by the fact that it is a *double* one, with air between its two layers. There is a superb Nicolò Pisano pulpit here in the baptistery too, but like the other one, it needs special mention below.

The *Leaning Tower* leans almost fourteen feet out of the perpendicular and when you climb to its summit, by 294 steps, you feel that you must be in the Crazy House of some amusement park. As you go round and round, you are *climbing* hard one minute, *coasting* the next, and so on and on. There are five halting places, on the five upper stories of the cylinder, and in most places there is *no railing*, so watch out! A fall from the sloping side would be very easy to achieve and probably very fatal, and certainly you don't need to fall to establish the law of gravity. Galileo helped to do that by dropping things from the tower's sloping summit long before Newton's apples started falling. You and I will concern ourselves with simpler matters such as the *view*, which is, indeed, amply worth the climb. The whole city is spread out before us, the whole marbled meadow is beneath us, and the Arno is a rope of shimmering silver as it lazily winds to the sea.

The story of this campanile is more or less familiar to all the world. It was begun in 1173 and was well along when the foundations on the south side sank alarmingly. It did not appear to settle any further, and after some decades, work on it was resumed, the architects striving to correct the difficulty by "tipping back" the upper stories a little to offset some of the inclination. Scientific Cassandras say the Leaning Tower will continue to lean just a little more and a little more—six inches per century, for instance, is mentioned as the current pace of increased leaning—until it sometime overplays the balancing act. They even have a date for its collapse, namely 2160, quite disregarding the fact that engineers constantly study the problem with a view to strengthening the foundations. One suspects that dire predictions may be more in the nature of publicity than anything else. The press likes to receive these warnings from time to time. They give point to such cartoons as that memorable one in *The New Yorker* showing a group of timid tourists looking up at the tower from the *safe side!*

Two great Pisans seem to overshadow all others in this Meadow, namely, the Pisani, father and son. Both were born even before Giotto, so they are pioneers in point of art. They were pulpit-builders extraordinary and have left admirable examples of their work in various cities. We have already found a Pisano pulpit in Orvieto, for instance, and another in the cathedral of Siena. Here in Pisa, Nicolò, the father, built the baptistery pulpit, while Giovanni, the son, built the one in the cathedral. Nicolò was possibly the greater artist, if only because he had so little precedent to help him, but Giovanni had more boldness in execution.

Giovanni's pulpit, in the cathedral, was broken up after the edifice was damaged by fire centuries ago, and its parts were distributed to various other churches, but as recently as 1926 it was reconstituted, with amazing skill, from the original fragments. You will admire the marvelous artistry of it—Giovanni worked almost day and night for nine years on this alone—and you will be amused at two oddities. One of these is a tall woman representing the Roman Catholic Church and she is suckling two babies, who are the Old Testament and the New Testament. She has little milk for the Old Testament and that unfortunate infant, a poor and skinny thing, sucks futilely at her empty right breast. The New Testament, a fat and lusty infant, is nursing happily at her full left breast. The pulpit's other oddity, a modern one, is the absurd towel of bronze affixed for modesty's sake *in 1926* to the nude marble loins of a worthy lady representing Prudence. The bronze *cache-sexe* is painted white, but the guide taps it and it has the ring of metal.

* * *

Those who can spare a little time in Pisa from the well-grouped miracles will find much else that is worth seeing. The Piazza dei Cavalieri, for instance, is really a notable old square. In one corner stands a palace built by Giorgio Vasari, with a tower that is called *Torre della Fame,* or *Tower of Hunger,* in recollection of a former tower on the same site, in which, as a very strong tradition has it, Count Ugolino della Gherardesca was imprisoned, along with his son and his grandsons, *all* of them condemned to die of starvation because Ugolino, as admiral of the Pisan fleet, had lost a battle to the Genoese. An item of far happier background in the same square is the *Church of Santo Stefano dei Cavalieri,* also by Vasari, with amazing trophies in it captured by Pisans from the Turks in the Battle of Lepanto and the Battle of Bizerta. We see on the walls the bowsprits, sterns and lanterns of Turkish galleys and of course many captured flags. This church was half wrecked by the Second World War, its bell tower being struck by a bomb and collapsing upon it, but the damage has been largely repaired and we see on its gold ceiling the proud crimson cross that was the emblem of the Knights of St. Stephen. It is appropriate that the city's newest and best hotel, *Albergo dei Cavalieri,* is named for these knights.

In addition to the clustered buildings of the Knights' Square, the visitor will find in Pisa many a small church of black and white marble hardly less deserving of his admiration. The most amazing of these is also the most obvious, *Santa Maria della Spina*, which means Saint-Mary-of-the-Thorn. Like the jeweled reliquary of some great cathedral, it is guarded jealously by the city which is fortunate enough to own it. It is not, however, hidden away. Its location actually on the sidewalk of the Lungarno Gambacorti overlooking the river—in the Middle Ages it rose *from* the river—makes it so conspicuous an object in the Pisan scene that it seems under the personal protection of every citizen. It is often illuminated evenings by concealed lights and the effect of it then, doubled by reflection in the Arno, a fuller stream here than in Florence, is indescribably beautiful.

Pisa was a Ghibelline city, like Verona. Florence was a Guelph city, like Milan and Genoa. In Pisa's long struggle with her Tuscan rivals she was finally forced to yield, and thereupon the sea, as if only a fair-weather friend, deserted her miserably. There is pathos in that, but pathos is only an enhancement of beauty, and the beauty of Pisa has survived in undiminished measure.

The Game of the Bridge and the Night of Lights

Pisa has two special festival events of which it is justly proud, the *Game of the Bridge (Il Gioco del Ponte)*, on the first Sunday in June, and the *Illumination of the Arno's Banks*, on the evening of St. Ranieri's Day, June 16.

The Game of the Bridge splits Pisa into two rival parties as the river splits it into two geographical halves. The party on the northern bank is called *Tramontana*, that on the southern bank *Mezzogiorno* (literally Noon), and all the participants wear medieval costumes, no matter how torrid the sun may be. Five teams are chosen to play, and for that word Pisans substitute "fight." After a colorful parade by both parties on both Arno banks, the big fracas gets under way on the wide Ponte di Mezzo, which is anything but medieval, having been built in 1948 to replace an old one destroyed by Nazi mines in 1944. There is a fifteen-minute period during which Tramontana and Mezzogiorno try to take "prisoners" from each other on the bridge, and this is no pussyfoot play or stage battle. When I saw it both sides got fighting mad and the terrible-tempered fellows in coats of mail and helmets were a sight to behold. Standing on a balcony near by, I was tense with excitement.

Feeling on the bridge cooled gradually and then, at the signal of a canon shot that seemed to shake the very river, the contest was on. A 24-man team from each party advanced under its own squadron banner to clash in a "push-of-war" in the center of the bridge, each trying to push the traditional sledge (a massive affair on wheels on a temporary track) over onto the other side's territory. There were five such contests of strength, and on the occasion when I witnessed the Gioco, Tramontana won three, and hence the *Palio of Victory* (a silken banner). I was on the Mezzogiorno side of the river and "my" side was glum almost to tears, but from Tramontana, across the way, came heaven-splitting whistles, shouts and roars of elation. Celebrations "raged" far into the night.

The *Luminaria di San Ranieri*, on the night of June 16, is a pageant of quite another color, the color coming from tens of thousands of little "tumbler lamps" made by placing wicks in small glass jars of oil. They illuminate every window of every building on both banks of the river and the whole spectacle shines in duplicate, the Arno's waters reflecting the lights above. I have seen this only in photographs, but if the actuality lives up to what the camera's lens proclaims, it must be a thing of magic.

Tuscan Neighbors, South and North

Those who have time enough to make Pisa their excursion center for several days of tripping in northwestern Tuscany will find this ancient, now-reviving city a delightful headquarters, and as convenient as it is delightful. Its new *Albergo dei Cavalieri* (mentioned above), in the station square, is up to the minute, and its cooking is so excellent that it is proud to let you *watch* it being done as you sit at your table in the dining room. Through a glass wall you can look into the spotless kitchen and see the cylinder-hatted chefs at work. Two other good hotels, the *Nettuno* and the *Victoria*, are directly on the right bank of the Arno, not far from the Ponte di Mezzo.

* * *

Leghorn, whose anglicized name is a curious corruption of the Italian *Livorno*, is known to us chiefly as a word for white hens and straw hats, neither of which is to be found there now in any significant way. To military folk, including the American forces in Europe, Leghorn is known as one of the very important seaports of Italy. Being that, it took a terrible beating in the Second World War and some of the most fantastic ruins in Italy are still to be seen in the heart of the city.

In the richness of tourist Italy, this lacerated port has very little pulling power for tourists, but the coastal road to it (and beyond it) from Pisa *is* delightful. The road beside the Arno from Pisa to Marina di Pisa is eight miles of sheer charm. You roll between rows of splendid plane trees, and suspended over the river you see the hugest imaginable fishing nets, stretching almost from bank to bank, ready to be lowered when the fish are there. On reaching the sea, your road runs through various beach resorts, Tirrénia north of Livorno, Ardenza and Antignano south of it. A charming place to lunch, on the very edge of the Tyrrhenian Sea, is the *Bagno Acquaviva*, on the southern outskirts of the city.

The coastal highway running northwest beside the Ligurian Sea from Pisa to Genoa is the one followed by CIAT and it passes several points of exceptional interest before crossing the line from Tuscany into Liguria. Three, at least, need mention.

1. *Torre del Lago—Puccini*, its hyphenated name being a twentieth-century device, was long the home of Giacomo Puccini, as mentioned in the Scrolls chapter. His many operas are, of course, quite as dear to the music world as those of Verdi. The villa in which he lived and worked is at the roadside, within a few yards of the pleasant *Lake Massaciúccoli*. The CIAT busses are supposed to make a brief halt here to let passengers enter the Puccini villa, but sometimes the hostess may need a reminder from those of her "flock" who are sincere music lovers.

The villa is packed with memorials of the composer, his piano, his writing materials and some manuscripts, his pipe, his spectacles and even his pills. Among his souvenirs is an elaborate wooden screen, inlaid with ivory and mother-of-pearl, given him by the Japanese imperial government when *Madame Butterfly* was first produced. In a rear room of the villa is Puccini's marble tomb, a large and lachrymose affair in the manner of Italy's cemetery statuary, and on a lawn near the lake is a bronze statue of him, wearing overcoat and felt hat and looking rather remarkably like Toscanini in middle age.

If you visit Torre del Lago "on your own," with some spare time, you may find refreshment at the lakeside café called *Chalet Emilio*, across the street from the villa.

2. *Viaréggio* is reached by a handsome lime-tree avenue, bordering a part of the extensive pine forest for which this littoral is famous. There is an equally extensive forest of bathing cabins lining the beach almost continuously for twenty miles, for Viaréggio is certainly one of the most popular beach resorts in Italy. Its sands are smooth and clean, its surf of generous but not frightening proportions. It was not the surf but a sudden squall of wind, capsizing his sailing craft (see Chapter 9), that brought death by drowning to Shelley.

3. *Carrara*, lying at the extreme northern tip of Tuscany, means *marble* to all of us, and even those who hustle by this town—it lies three miles inland from the main highway—may plainly see the quarries, sometimes high in the mountains and often looking exactly like patches of snow. There are more than a thousand quarries in all, with many thousands of laborers.

Carrarans are duly proud of the countless churches, palaces and monuments built of the material that the brawn and skills of their forebears quarried. One item of special pride is the huge chunk from which Michelangelo carved his *Moses*, the masterpiece so much admired in Rome's Church of San Pietro in Vincoli.

I found the short trip from the coastal road in to the marble town —there is an aging electric tram—worth while for the evidences, on the approach and within the town itself, of the main industry. The post office is of soft gray marble, with white marble statues flanking its main door. Even the paving of one or two piazze is of the valued and aristocratic stone, though Carrara's population is poor and labor troubles are not infrequent. Seldom in history has a town of such modest size and appearance sent its name so impressively and so widely throughout the world.

CHAPTER 20

PASSES TO THE ADRIATIC

Rival Highways to Ferrara

Two "ribbon roads" of CIAT and other touring companies leading from Florence to Venice separate at the edge of Florence and proceed by two quite different routes over different passes of the Apennines, to converge ultimately at Ferrara, from which point both ribbons use the same highway north to Padua, then east to Venice. CIAT makes the whole run, by either route, in one long day. I have been both ways and can say firmly that "each is better than the other." This chapter, carrying only as far as Ferrara, shall treat minor and major places along the route in the same way that comparable places were treated in the two Rome-Florence routes.

The southerly route shall be outlined first.

Passo del Muraglione (2765 feet altitude) is this highway's pass over the Apennines. The view of valley and mountains, with some snow on the higher peaks at least up to June, is one of great magnificence. Some hundreds of cuckoos will be "cucking" deep down in the valley, if the musical mood is on them. There is a very humble stone albergo at the road's loftiest point and CIAT makes a rest halt of only a few minutes.

Forlì, the second halt, is an important city of the *Romagna*, which was formerly the northeastern portion of the Papal States. Pope Julius II, the vigorous pontiff whose portrait by Raphael is so great a feature of the Uffizi Gallery, "acquired" Forlì for the papacy in 1504. Only a token halt is made here by the busses. The city is not very important now except as an agricultural center.

Ravenna is usually favored with the longest bus halt, two and a half to three hours being allotted to it, though this includes the time for lunch. Ravenna shall be separately discussed below.

Ferrara, where good busses of both routes forgather, when coming from the south, and part, when coming from the north. This large city, with wonderful medieval inheritance, shall likewise be discussed separately below.

Ravenna, Abandoned by the Adriatic

Ravenna and Ferrara each enjoyed a period of splendor, prosperity and fame. Ravenna's heyday was during the three centuries after 402, when it was the capital of the Western World, first under the Roman emperors, then under Theodoric and his Ostrogoths, and finally under the Byzantine Exarchs. Reminding us of Pisa, it was at one time a seaport of great activity and importance, the Bride of the Adriatic, but the Adriatic proved to be no steadier mate to this city than was the Ligurian Sea to the Tuscan port.

Why is it, I wonder, that Italian seas retire so treacherously from the cities that they have served in past ages? Ravenna now lies stranded seven miles from the water. A canal, however, still links it with the Adriatic, and it is an odd sight to see masts and funnels looming up close to the station of this inland city.

Ravenna possesses a three-fold luster quite its own and it seems remarkable that this was infused by three such various regimes as those listed above, one of which is called barbarian. In mosaic work, this city has never been surpassed, even by Palermo, and some students consider that it has never been equaled. Bright mosaics and cylindrical campanili, with graceful double windows on the lower stories and triple windows on the two top stories, set the artistic stamp of those long-ago centuries when the light of civilization had gone out nearly everywhere except here. In Ravenna it burned brightly long after chaos and blight had begun to stalk through the peninsula. In a sense, we may think of Ravenna as the (un)Missing Link between classic civilization and the appearance of Charlemagne. It was less than fifty years after the Lombards finally damped Ravenna's flame that Charlemagne was crowned by Pope Leo III.

If your time in Ravenna is very brief, go straight to the *Church of San Vitale*, built in the sixth century, and you will see some of the finest mosaics in existence. You will see also a pure alabaster altar of rare beauty, the mosaic ceiling above it seeming like a piece of rich brocade. In the mosaics of the apse you will see Christ seated on the globe and you will note, probably with pleasure, that He is a smooth-shaven young man instead of an anemic and sorrowful personage with whiskers and beard.

After you have enjoyed the extraordinary beauties of this queer octagon church, an attendant leads you over a meadow in the rear to the *Tomb of Galla Placidia*, and this is perhaps the very best of all the fine things that Ravenna offers. The *blueness* of the mosaics, possibly accentuated by the strange light that filters in through the alabaster windows, must, I think, be part of the secret of their dazzling effect. If blue is the key to color and the secret of thirteenth-century glass in Gothic cathedrals, as claimed by Viollet-le-Duc, why should it not also be the secret of these fifth-century Byzantine mosaics?

Not the least interesting thing about this tomb is the personality of her who lies in it. Such cannot be said of all great tombs, but it certainly can of this. Galla Placidia was the sister of Emperor Honorius, who transferred his capital to Ravenna in 402, and she was the mother and regent of another emperor, Valentinian III. Tireless in her patronage of new buildings and new works in mosaic, she gave individuality and lasting tang to Ravenna's appearance. But she did not limit her patronage to the adornment of her capital, as we know by recalling that great chancel-arch of St. Paul-without-the-Walls in Rome, which is adorned with mosaics executed to her order fifteen centuries ago. It is quite impossible to cram the whole of Ravenna into one's consciousness in the space of a bus halt, but a good second-class hotel, the *Nuovo San Marco*, is available for lucky stayers-over. Perhaps the easiest way to gain some understanding of the city is to sort out its numerous religious edifices according to the three periods of Ravenna's greatest building activity. Among those dating approximately from the period (1) of *Galla Placidia's regency* are:

San Giovanni Evangelista (near the station)
San Francesco (on Piazza San Francesco)

The former was much altered in the fourteenth century and the latter was terribly damaged by the air bombardments of the Second World

War, so it is only by imagination that we can re-create the original churches.

Under (2) *Theodoric and his Gothic successors*, the following were built:

San Vitale
Sant'Apollinare Nuovo, with Ravenna's finest circular bell tower
Sant'Apollinare in Classe, the largest and best preserved of the basilicas, three miles south of the city
The *Baptistery of the Arians*, an interesting octagonal building

These four structures were consecrated to the Arian faith, to which Theodoric adhered. The Arians, roughly speaking, were the Unitarians of that era. The churches were completed and their decoration extended by the so-called (3) *Exarchs*, who represented the emperors in Byzantium. It was due to their driving force that the brilliant *Byzantine mosaics*, as in San Vitale, were so greatly developed, and the projects of the Ostrogoths so successfully advanced. In mosaic work, the Byzantines devised some special tricks to enhance its brilliance. Hollows and protuberances were injected to reflect the gold beneath, thus furnishing a prismatic radiance that no smooth, flat surface could possibly have given. Some of the best of these Byzantine mosaics were faithfully copied by Italian mosaicists and shipped to London for an exhibition held in the New Burlington Galleries not very long ago, and their success with Londoners made their coming an artistic event of the first importance.

For five or six centuries after the glittering Byzantine period, the city was inconspicuous and of small importance, but before becoming a vassal city of Venice, in 1441, it had one more flash of splendor under the Polenta family. It was then that Dante sought refuge here, but he was broken down by his long exile and shortly died. Near the Piazza San Francesco he lies in a splendid tomb and it is known that his remains actually are here and not, as in the case of so many great men, merely "said to be."

Ravenna is a city of tombs. If you leave it, headed north, either by bus or train, you will see on your right the ten-sided stone *Tomb of Theodoric*, built by himself. It is surmounted by a stone roof in one piece weighing three hundred tons. If you make a sortie to the southeast, your train or car will pass through the *Pineta,* or pine grove (now slowly vanishing), which is a lovely natural tomb for the body of Anita Garibaldi (see Chapter 21).

Ravenna, despite being condemned to be an "inland city," is still continually dampened by tidal seepage. San Vitale, for example, receives a daily baptism of salt water and has continually to be pumped out. When war stringencies halted the electric pumps, the water in this church attained a depth of three feet. The war did a lot of damage to the city, more than a hundred bombs falling upon or near it. The mosaics of Sant'Apollinare Nuovo were removed for storage, and even the revered bones of Dante were taken from their tomb and hidden in a strong refuge chamber. All this adds pathos to a sign I once saw chalked on a damaged building: *Gesu' Benedice La Nostra Città* (Jesus Bless Our City). The slogan was to me a welcome relief from the turgid Communist slogans so often seen chalked on buildings of Emilia and the Romagna.

Ferrara, the Este Citadel

Ferrara's heyday was in the Middle Ages, when the Este Family brought this city to a period of glory. It was, indeed, a full thousand years after Ravenna's period of greatest glory that Ferrara reached the zenith of its importance. During most of the sixteenth century, the court of the Este Family, which had been set up here, was the cynosure of envious eyes and the goal of ambitious spirits. As an art city, Ferrara is far behind Ravenna, but the personages associated with it do, nevertheless, make the name lustrous.

The two outstanding members of the Este Family were Alfonso I and his grandson Alfonso II. The former gave his patronage to *Ariosto* and his heart, after some misgivings, to Lucrezia Borgia. The second Alfonso made himself conspicuous to following generations by patronizing, and then imprisoning, Torquato Tasso. The masterpiece of each poet, *Orlando Furioso* by the former, *Jerusalem Delivered* by the latter, was written in Ferrara, and a part of the actual manuscript of Ariosto's work is still exhibited in the university library.

Alfonso I's patronage of Ariosto was a fortunate thing for humanity. If he did not show himself generous in money matters, he did at least afford the poet a much-needed refuge where he could study and write. The duke's marriage with Lucrezia Borgia was also a fortunate thing, at least for Lucrezia. It took her out of the fetid atmosphere of her family in Rome and made her almost a decent woman. Three times Lucrezia had already been married, by command of her father, the notorious Pope Alexander VI, who hounded Savonarola to martyrdom. Her third husband had been murdered by her brother Cesare. Discarding all the darker gossip (which was probably untrue) about her incestuous relations with her brothers and her father, one must yet look with horror on her family life.

Duke Alfonso did not want to marry this much-handled girl. He fought against it, but dared not refuse the powerful Borgia pope. Having married her, however, he really fell in love with her and cherished her for eighteen years until she died.

Alfonso II was something of a rake, but he maintained the court of Ferrara at a high level of glory. His confinement of Tasso as a madman has been one of the most debated subjects of personal gossip attaching to any great figure of literature. Was Tasso mad or was he not? A clear answer is as impossible as a clear diagnosis of Hamlet's mental condition. Some say Tasso had flirted with Leonora d'Este, Alfonso's sister, and feigned madness to protect her name. Others say Alfonso clapped him into the madhouse for political reasons. In justice to Alfonso it must be stated that he had long endured a behavior on Tasso's part that would have irritated Job himself. Against Alfonso it must be stated that he permitted Tasso's masterpiece, *Jerusalem Delivered*, to be printed without the poet's permission or revision, while the latter was confined in the asylum. Through seven editions the poem went in fewer than seven months, but not one soldo did the author of it ever receive in royalties.

A more unhappy man than Tasso never lived. When finally released from his Ferrara jail—it was the Hospital of Sant'Anna, where his cell is still pointed out—he was lashed hither and yon by a terrible restlessness that would not allow him to bask in any patron's favor. His wanderings became the joke of all Italy. Apparently he was not quite insane but on that miserable border line which is worse than madness.

Ferrara is primarily a city of old palaces, dominated by the colossal four-towered *Castello Estense*, squatting in its moated four-square immensity in the center of the city. A lesser palace, of architectural interest, is called *Palazzo dei Diamanti*, from the diamond-shaped faceted stones, over twelve thousand of them, that compose its façade. The city has also a good cathedral and a picture gallery filled with Ferrarese pictures, but one cannot quite pin one's mind on anything that is not suggestive in some direct way of that glorious, inescapable *Famiglia d'Este*.

High Points of the Northerly Route

The northerly route from Florence to Ferrara, always with a major halt at Bologna, is perhaps scenically superior even to the splendid southerly route, just outlined. The halting points of the CIAT coaches shall be listed here, as on the other route.

As the traveler quits Florence and soon approaches *Pistoia*, he passes mile after mile of shrubs, cultivated flowers, especially roses, and handsome nursery trees, for this section is certainly the Garden of Tuscany. Pistoia itself, hardly more than twenty miles from overshadowing Florence, is almost totally neglected by tourism, including the CIAT busses, which is a minor misfortune of travel, since the city is full of medieval buildings of real importance. Unhappily, the city was a badly hurt war victim and is sometimes called by the local people the Cassino of Tuscany. This sobriquet, however, is a gross exaggeration, for the place was certainly not erased. If you visit Pistoia on your own, you will, of course, make for the wonderful *Piazza del Duomo*, graced by a fine cathedral, complete with soaring campanile and zebra-striped baptistery, and two fourteenth-century palazzi, and when you enter it you will hardly be conscious of any war damage at all. Similarly, you will find the fascinating façade of *San Giovanni Fuorcivitas*, on Via Cavour, almost or quite unscarred by bombs or shells.

Passo della Colline (2796 feet altitude) is the first point where the busses halt, and richly does it deserve a halt for its grand prospect of Apennine hills and valleys. A disturbing bit of bird lore I acquired here. Noting and hearing several skylarks, I exclaimed about them and learned from the guide that in Italy they are considered a *pest* during harvest time. At that season country folk are encouraged to shoot them.

Poretta Terme, where a quarter-hour rest halt is made, is a "little Montecatini," with fine medicinal springs.

The *Gothic Line,* last mountain barrier held by the retreating Germans in 1944, is crossed as the bus passes a series of villages with pretty names but of tragic connotation to Italians: Silla, Vergato, Marzabotto and so forth.

Sasso Marconi, across the provincial line in the Romagna, is the birthplace of wireless telegraphy, of the radio, hence even of television, for here Guglielmo Marconi lived and worked. Here he made his first experiments in sending messages through the air without wires. Near here a pioneer radio station broadcast its first primitive sounds and messages. The house of the great inventor is here, and also his tomb, a rather showy one of granite built during the Fascist era. We read this inscription carved in the stone beneath a cross:

GUGLIELMO MARCONI

XXV APRILE MCCMLXXIV

XX LUGLIO MCMXXXVII-XV

In case this needs a bit of translation, since Italians use a form of Roman numerals that differ from ours, Marconi was born April 25, 1874, and died July 20, 1937, Year of Fascism 15. Marconi's science, be it known, was not an exclusive perquisite of Fascism, but his fame was of course capitalized by Mussolini.

Bologna is to be separately discussed.

Beautiful country lies between Bologna and Ferrara, mulberry country in part, for this is an important region of silk culture. Some apple orchards are also passed, and some rice fields, and so to the junction city of Ferrara, discussed above.

Bologna at the Crossroads

If there were no Bologna one would spring up in exactly this location overnight. Just glance at any map of Italy and note this city's position. That 150-mile line running straight from Piacenza, near Milan, to Rimini, on the Adriatic, is the *Via Emilia*, built in 187 by the Consul Emilius Lepidus and followed by traffic ever since, whether road or rail. Bologna, the historic capital of Emilia, is the central point of this road.

Crossing at right angles, through Bologna, lies the direct historic route from Florence to Venice, so it is inevitable that Bologna should hold the reins of traffic connecting a dozen or more important cities. There are at least eight of them strung at intervals along the Via Emilia itself, like knots in a climbing-rope. Given its hub location and its own intrinsic importance as a great metropolis, this city should serve as a trip center for all who can possibly devote a few days to so rich a region, spiced as it is by the special fillip of the midget republic of San Marino, perching on its triple mountain peak only a few miles inland from Rímini. There is one de luxe hotel in Bologna, the *Hotel Grand e Majestic*, and there are at least twenty-five lesser ones of all categories. Fine restaurants abound in this well-favored city, the most famous one, *Pappagallo*, having been already mentioned, along with Bolognese food specialties, in the Regional Roundup of Chapter 5.

I admire Bologna enormously. The place has an extraordinary distinction, like a scholar who has quietly made money too and can dress to match his fame, yet you cannot stroll through Bologna's delightful arcaded streets and its crowded squares without sensing the perennial verve of the city. It is quite the opposite of the sedate spinster (except at Palio time) that is Siena. Bologna is proud of its business drive but still more so, I think, of its reputation as a distiller of the fragrant essence of learning. Centuries ago it was dubbed *la città dotta* and it has never lost this title. A great many of the most distinguished Italians have been in some way connected with its university, the most venerable in Italy, as teacher, student or special lecturer. The scintillating list includes, to name but a few, Dante, Copernicus, Galvani, Carducci, Marconi.

Today's students in this city are as exuberant a lot as I have ever seen. On the occasion of a matriculation festa I watched them fairly *swamp* the big town. Their sharp-pointed hats were adorned with masses of medals, bangles, jokes and humors of every sort, and their gay horseplay suggested that they were in process of initiating the entire citizenry into a Greek-letter fraternity.

The arcades of the Emilian capital, if laid end to end, would certainly reach to the nearest planet and back. In the beginning they were constructed with wooden posts and beams, painted red. Later the wood was replaced by stone, with massive pilasters supporting rounded arches, and still later, as Gothic swept Romanesque before it, the rounded arches gave way to pointed ones. Whether round or pointed they are charming today in their weathered antiquity. Bologna is one city where the umbrella business is in a state of perpetual stagnation, for one may go almost anywhere in the central parts without deserting the arcades.

In a great triple square the chief sights of Bologna are largely massed. One section of this square is named Piazza Maggiore; another for Neptune, whose stout person, nobly sculptured by Giambologna, surmounts a central fountain; and the third is (sometimes) called Piazza di Re Enzo, though it is actually absorbed by the extremely broad Via Rizzoli. The first two names are obvious enough, but who was King Enzo, or Enzio as he is often spelled, and of what was he king? We learn that he was King of Sardinia, that he was the son of the Hohenstaufen emperor, Frederick II, and the Hohenstaufens were staunchly supported by the Ghibellines and hated by the Guelphs. Bologna, a Guelph city, captured Enzo in a bloody battle, but the citizens were so impressed with his bravery that although they kept him prisoner for twenty-two years they treated him almost like a visiting sovereign. He lived in a sumptuous palace (still intact) on the square that bears his name.

In the Maggiore section of Bologna's triple square, the vast, gaunt edifice of *San Petronio*, the city's most important church though not its cathedral, bears around its main doorway some priceless bas-reliefs by Iacopo della Quercia. These are generally considered the clear heralds of Italy's Renaissance in sculpture, as the frescoes of young Masaccio in the Santa Maria del Carmine Church of Florence are considered heralds of the Renaissance in painting.

As one wanders through Italy one is constantly reminded of some person or some place already seen. If the San Petronio sculptures recall the great Sienese master, certainly Bologna's tall, grim leaning towers, the Torre degli Asinelli and Torre Garisenda, recall the tipsy towers of San Gimignano. In fact, we can see very graphically what would have happened if prosperity had stayed with the little Tuscan town as it did with the Emilian city. Bologna too once boasted *many* towers, but only these two are left. They tip in opposite directions and thus appear to be preposterously out of plumb. Built early in the twelfth century, they have somehow remained through all the vicissitudes of eight and a half centuries. The tower of the Asinelli is 320 feet high and can be ascended by any visitor who feels like climbing five hundred steps!

Do not miss Bologna's curious "eight-ply" *Church of Santo Stefano.* Do not miss *San Domenico,* where you renew acquaintance with Nicolò Pisano and where King Enzo lies buried. Do not miss the *jurists' tombs,* three outside the church of San Francesco and two outside San Domenico. Do not miss, if you have a spare half day, the hilltop sanctuary of *Madonna di San Luca,* reached by funicular. But above all do not miss Bologna itself. Much learning has not made this city mad, but has bestowed upon it an aura of intellectuality which the Bolognese fondly cherish. And because there is money to support this learning there is not a swifter-paced city in all Italy.

CHAPTER 21
TO SAN MARINO, POCKET REPUBLIC ON THE SKYLINE

The Town of Faïence on the Way

Faenza, situated about half way between Bologna and San Marino, is a town of very special significance, for its name has become a proper noun in all the languages and dictionaries of the world. Faenza's EPT puts out a leaflet setting forth its name in twenty-three languages, ranging from the English Faience to the Finnish Fajanssi and from the "modern Latin" Faventina to the Greek, Hebrew and Japanese words which I must leave you to guess at. Do not suppose, however, that this propaganda is all "sound and fury signifying nothing." Faenza still makes lovely faïence in a dozen or more *botteghe di ceramisti* (ceramics factories) and markets its products in many countries. What's more to the point for you and me, it displays ceramics, its own and those of many other cities and nations, in one of the most excitingly *different* museums in all Europe.

The *Museo Internazionale delle Ceramiche* is a marvelous thing, almost wholly unknown to American tourists. It is worth going far to see, worth the canceling of cherished plans, if necessary, in order to make room for it in one's itinerary. Its collections, in a building which was half destroyed by a bombardment in 1944 but has been magnificently rebuilt, include just about everything done in ceramics from late medieval times to the day of your visit, not only in Faenza and throughout Italy but in more than a score of foreign countries in all the continents. I gazed with rapt interest at exhibits from *Brasile, Messico, Cile* (Chile), *Islanda* (Iceland), *India, Pakistan, Il Mondo Islamico* (The Moslem World), *Cina* (China), *Giappone* (Japan) and nearly all the European countries, including *Russia* and its satellites, and of course *England* (Wedgwood, willow ware, etc.)

and our own *America*. Among those American firms and individuals whose work is shown, I noticed Henry Rox of South Hadley, Massachusetts; Lenox, Inc. of Trenton, New Jersey; the Frankoma Pottery Company of Sapulpa, Oklahoma; and Jade Snow Wong of San Francisco, California. I don't know whether Jade is a man or a woman but the bright scarlet plate, with gold-red back, done by him or her, is a thing of striking beauty.

Would you like a few more samples of what I saw and what you may see? Here are five:

An eight-piece "orchestra" of lovely nineteenth-century design, each player being a woman with wings. This puzzled me a bit, for saints don't wear wings and I was under the impression that angels in art are required, by tradition, to be masculine!

A shelf of fine old coppery lusterware from Camborne, Cornovaglia, the last word meaning Cornwall.

A large plate by Eric Owen of London depicting a rector marrying a determined Amazon of a woman to a weak little wisp of a man. The bride has a ham-like hand clamped over the mouth of the frightened groom and *she* says, "HE WILL."

A Swedish dinner set with a design of glistening black leaves on a curious black and white grill pattern.

Two plates from the Paesi Bassi (Nether Lands) with these respective mottoes: HONGER IS DE BESTE KOK and SCHOONHEID IS GEZONDHEID. The first one is self-translating; the second one means "Beauty is Health."

I haven't started to scratch the surface of what there is to see in this world museum of ceramics. There are huge pieces, tiny pieces, animals, portraits on faïence, jokes, religious pieces, delicate fantasies. You could spend all day in the building or could visit it repeatedly and not tire of its wonders, from the grandest conceptions to the merest whimsies. Stop off at Faenza if you can by any means manage it.

Rímini, Port of the Republic

Straight down the Via Emilia—and most travelers use the *ferrovia* (literally ironroad)—lies Rímini, seventy miles from Bologna, forty from Faenza. Rímini is the port of the world's smallest republic, San

Marino, but it is also a city of importance in its own name, having, as a matter of fact, twice the population of the entire republic.

However strongly curiosity tempts one to hurry on to San Marino, every traveler will surely wish to linger in Rímini long enough to scrape acquaintance with the Malatesta family, and especially with Paolo and his beloved Francesca, whose story was immortalized by Dante in the *Inferno* and six centuries later was brought to the theater public by the art of Eleanora Duse. The Italian actress, devoted to d'Annunzio's work, made a great success in his play about this tragic pair.

Paolo Malatesta and his ugly brother John, who murdered the couple with one sword thrust, were sons of the founder of the Malatesta house, a *condottiere* who lived to be a hundred years old and never lost his grip on the territories he controlled. This powerful old noble lives largely in the pages of historians, but a later member of the family, Sigismund, revealed himself clearly to us of today through the amazing church he built, a frankly pagan church erected to glorify his mistress, Isotta.

This Sigismund was the "Compleat Criminal" of the Middle Ages. If there was any crime he failed to commit, this was due merely to an oversight. He was legally accused of "rapine, incendiarism, incest, and murder," but that was only a beginning. In the church nominally dedicated by him to the gentlest of saint, Francis of Assisi, this monster built a magnificent chapel and sarcophagus for Isotta. He dedicated the chapel to St. Michael, but the archangel's sculptured face is that of Sigismund's mistress, and the inscription refers to her as the "Goddess Isotta." His initials and hers are intertwined in this chapel, and throughout the decoration of the church, and they form an almost perfect dollar sign. Sigismund's wife, who was a daughter of the famous Sforza, objected to this sacrilege by her husband, so he felt it wise to strangle her, and did so. Pope Nicholas V then legitimized Sigismund's children by Isotta, the Church of St. Francis was finished and life went buoyantly on, spiced by fresh crimes of every sort. Study this church of the dollar sign, this *Tempio Malatestiana*, to use its official name, and you will glimpse the seamy side of the Middle Ages. The war's bombardment wrought havoc with the church in

1943 and 1944 but restoration has been vigorously and effectively pushed forward.

The Strange Case of San Marino—Postwar

In the Middle Ages San Marino was Ghibelline, which is to say (very roughly) rightist, but times have changed with the centuries. In the political whirlpools and rapids of present-day Italy the republic has shown a strong leaning toward the extreme left. Visitors, generally in escapist mood, pay little or no attention to political moods, nor have they any need to do so here, but the war and postwar history of San Marino is so interesting, as a sort of "sample" of life in this muddled era, that a few notes seem needed.

The republic was officially neutral in the war, but the armies of both sides crossed its territory repeatedly and the planes, chiefly of the Allies, bombed it, sometimes severely. On June 26, 1944, an Allied raid, inflicted upon the mountain capital because it was thought to be a repository for Axis war supplies, caused terrible property damage and sixty-three deaths. The San Marinese government blamed the British and has been seeking full reparations ever since, refusing various offers as inadequate.

San Marino fell under Marxist influence after the war, though it did not become a full-fledged Communist state. There was endless friction with Christian-Democratic Italy, which had long paid the republic a money subsidy, supposedly equal to customs duties collected by Italy on goods entering San Marino. This subsidy, paid always in lire whose value shrank to a small fraction of their prewar worth, became pitifully inadequate. The San Marinese government grew desperate financially, a further contributing feature being that the prewar railway from Rímini, bringer of tourists by the hundred every summer day, had been bombed out of existence. In its plight San Marino tampered with its Marxist conscience, turned to the capitalists and made a deal with Genoese financiers to build a gambling casino that should bring quick profits. This actually was done, the flashy place being opened in a theater in August 1949 and in a truly marvelous new palace of chance in the spring of 1950, where it was maintained until a government order closed it on August 18, 1951.

I visited the republic during the casino era and was frankly appalled to see the incongruous invasion of the Rock by roulette wheels and sleek croupiers, and even by such big money card games as trente-et-quarante, where the *lower* limit was 500,000 lire ($820) and the upper limit was the gambler's sky.

Profits rolled in, but friction with Italy increased and powerful prelates cast a baleful eye at the strange goings-on in San Marino. Crisis piled on crisis. Italy established around the republic what some called a *cordon sanitaire* but what San Marino's officials called a hangman's noose. Police stopped every car that sought to enter the republic and put the occupants through a long and grueling ordeal of questions. They stopped even the busses for tedious grillings of the passengers. By every means they tried to hamper and discourage the casino traffic. The burden of all this became unbearable and finally the republic capitulated and issued the bitter order that closed the gaming house. It stands idle today and the little state is in a parlous condition, fiscally speaking. It racks its collective brain and parleys endlessly with Italy in the attempt to find some way out of its dilemma.

Climbing into the Republic

Recently I have visited San Marino by a crowded city bus from Rímini and again by means of a rented car, both journeys in warm weather, but long ago, before the war, I mounted to its lofty crest for the first time by the aforementioned train in the midst of one of Italy's coldest winters on record. It was a new blue train, as shiny as a nursery toy on Christmas morning, and I hate to think of its being blotted out by bombs. The ride from Rímini by any medium is an inspiring one through the tumbled Romagna, up and up toward the three peaks of Monte Titano. This triple mountain, built by the Titans in their effort to get at Jove and do battle with him, *is* San Marino, given support by a few square miles of hinterland. Each peak is crowned by a stone tower and each tower by a large metal plume, as you can see by getting out your stamp album and studying the postage stamps of the republic.

The manufacture of postage stamps, by the way, is still one of the chief industries of San Marino, though it doesn't bring in anything like enough profit, as it once did, to support the state. The total is now about 75,000,000 lire ($120,000) annually. Issues are frequently changed and much artistic effort is devoted to the designing of each new series. Always the world's philatelists, both amateur and professional, seem ready to purchase these offerings. One of the first buildings inside the Porta San Francesco is occupied by the offices of an international stamp dealer and almost every shop window gives stamps a prominent place in its display. Post cards already stamped with lots of pretty *francobolli* of small denominations to make the correct total for mailing, are on sale at every turn.

In entering within the republic's borders one is not subjected to any feverish business of passports, customs and money changing, for this is one international frontier where these annoyances simply do not exist. You float up to San Marino by bus or car nowadays, as painlessly as you would float across the equator. Passports are not examined nor is baggage opened.

The finding of hotel accommodations is by no means the problem it once was, and I suppose we have the spur of the casino era to thank for this. There used to be only one rather poor place to stay, the unkempt *Albergo Titano*. This still exists and is enormously improved, due to the energies of a new director who calls himself Joe and is always everywhere, on both sides and all levels of his hotel, with a friendly word. The Titano has a *Terrazza Panoramica e Suggestiva* for meal and tea or beverages in summer and it is indeed a gorgeously "suggestive" terrace on the very edge of San Marino two thousand feet above the surrounding region, but don't make the mistake of thinking the Titano your only possible home here. If you walk a few steps higher into the republic you'll find a rather astonishing albergo called the *Diamond*, which *can* be reached—but you'll need the aid of a native—even by your own car, with you at the wheel.

Hotel *Diamond* is a new place that takes its name from a ceiling design in the dining room somewhat in the manner of Ferrara's Palazzo dei Diamanti. The charmingly unconventional plan of the whole thing is the work of an architect named Giuseppe Vaccaro and the wall paintings are by Count Bartolomeo Manzoni Borghesi, whose wife directs the hotel. The dining room is hewn out of the solid rock but it is anything but cavernous. The modernities of it and the interesting lighting make it most cheerful. The bedrooms are as gay as can be, each with bright floor tiles in yellow, or apple green, or blue and white, or pink with white polka dots. The furnishings were surely planned by the countess, for one sees the feminine touch everywhere, and the plumbing in the private bathrooms is the work of someone who knows how to plumb, even on the summit of a rock. Only seven rooms were completed when the hotel opened in 1952, but the upper floors of the building, those with the wonderful view, are to be turned into hotel rooms, each with bath.

On a very lofty spot just back of the Diamond is its *Giardino Pensile*, or *Hanging Garden*, now being developed into its summer restaurant and bar. When you see it, you'll declare that it's not on the edge of San Marino but in the sky above the republic. Hardly ever in my travels have I seen a garden that so thoroughly deserved the adjective "hanging." To look from its parapet to the earth far beneath is like looking down from a poised helicopter. You have to accustom your eyes to this spectacle before you can remember to do anything so routine as eating!

There are two other new hotels in the republic, both of very good name, the *Excelsior* and the *Bellevue*. The former has a superb view from its bedrooms and its restaurant roof, and the latter is also blessed with a fine location, but both are at a little distance from the center of the town and the republic where life is lively.

Romance on Three Levels

The romance of tiny San Marino, clinging so fantastically to its high perch, pervades the visitor's thoughts as he quits his hotel eager to see "what it's all about." How has it happened that thirty-eight square miles of territory embedded in a state three thousand times as large, like a tiny pearl in an oyster (no offense to Italy), have maintained independence for a thousand years? (This is called the oldest state, politically, in all Europe.) I suppose the answer lies partly in the fact that this has not seemed a tempting morsel to conquerors. "San Marino," said one of the popes, "is a tough bread crust; the man who tries to bite it gets his teeth broken." Napoleon, on his victorious sweep through Italy, glanced at this state, smiled indulgently, promised it four new cannons and went his way. It grieves me to report that the cannons have not yet arrived.

There are three levels in San Marino town, with three main squares, and in the middle one, called the *Pianello*, or with more dignity, *Piazza della Libertà*, is the attractive government building, inaugurated in a friendly gesture by Giosuè Carducci in 1894. Ordinarily government buildings are not of absorbing interest to travelers, but we are curious to know the working habits of this one. Shortly after the First World War, San Marino citizens acquired the right of universal suffrage, displacing the old heads-of-families system, but otherwise the government machinery, whether Marxist or not, is as old-fashioned and picturesque as in medieval times. Twice a year, on the Ides of September and the Ides of March, the palace bells announce the hour of electing the two regents or co-presidents, who remind one of the Roman consuls. San Marino flocks to the Pianello while inside the palace the ceremony begins.

First twelve nominators are chosen by lot. These men nominate twelve candidates. The candidates are then voted upon by the white and black ball system and the six receiving the highest number of votes are coupled into three pairs, by personal agreement. A cortège then forms and marches to the cathedral, *La Pieve*, on the upper level of the Rock. After a religious ceremony, including a special prayer by the archpriest to St. Marinus, the three couplets of names are placed in three silver balls and deposited in an urn where they are shaken about. A child then draws out one of the balls and hands it to the outgoing regents, who open it, read the names, but not aloud, and pass the paper to the priest.

Finally, amid tense excitement, the priest announces the results. The band strikes up the national hymn and the procession returns to the palace, where, in a gorgeous state ceremony, the new regents are officially notified of their election. This quaint system certainly reduces corruption to the minimum. A candidate might spend his fortune in securing votes and still he would have only one chance in three. In spite of all vicissitudes, this *free* republic of 14,000 citizens continues on its way.

From any of the three peaks of San Marino, all easy to reach by an interesting path, the outlook is grand, but from a small square at the "prow" of the town there is a view that clings to one's memory as tenaciously as the San Marinese have clung to liberty. It is wild, thrilling, almost terrifying. You get the impression of being in the crow's-nest of a gigantic man-of-war steaming through a violent sea, yet you are comfortably aware that this craft, built by the Titans, will not founder.

Summits of Contrast

St. Marinus was a Christian stonecutter of Dalmatia, says tradition, who fled to the Mountain of the Titans about the year 300 to escape the persecution instigated by Emperor Diocletian. Marinus built a rude chapel on the Rock and sought to convert other downtrodden stonecutters and gather them about him. A saintly fellow-Dalmatian named Leo joined him on the Rock. They carved "beds" for themselves out of the solid stone and these two rude niches all visitors see in the wall behind the altar of the present *Chapel of St. Peter* on the site of the first church built by Marinus. Later, St. Leo left his companion and established his own holy hemitage on a neighboring hilltop, but it did not prosper. The Rock of Marinus, on the other hand, flourished. When the saint died, he bequeathed it to his flock, and in the course of time, certainly before the year 1000, it became a genuine independent state, a republic, and it has remained so ever since. As mentioned above, no conqueror, not even Napoleon, has seen fit to seize it.

One of the "waves" of the turbulent ocean from which the republic rises is the retreat of "the other saint," the *Rock of San Leo*, a peak which got a bad name in the eighteenth century when Cagliostro was exiled there, and there met his ignoble death. This arch-swindler, so smooth that he duped all Europe time after time, died most miserably on that lonely rock. Guilty of every crime and fraud, a dyed-in-the-wool charlatan whom women adored even when they knew him for what he was, the adventurer died only under the ban of "heresy."

If San Leo bows beneath the burden of Cagliostro's infamy, San Marino should—and does—glow with pride to think that it gave shelter to the patriot whom all Italy delights to honor, Giuseppe Garibaldi. After his remarkable "Anabasis" from Rome, the indomitable warrior found shelter on this independent crest. Here he disbanded his army in a single day, but he himself could not bear to submit. In Simoncini's café, still in existence under a different name just within the Porta San Francesco, he plotted with a few of his friends to escape to Venice in order to carry on the struggle with the hated Austrians. At about midnight of the same day of his arrival he suddenly started up from his seat in the café and exclaimed, "Whoever wishes to follow me, I offer him fresh battles, suffering and exile; treaties with the foreigner never." It reminds one inevitably of the stirring rhetoric of Winston Churchill, as war leader.

The San Marinese gatekeeper, who was in the thick of the plot, had "accidentally" left the Porta San Francesco ajar. Out stole Garibaldi and his South American wife Anita and a small band of followers, led by a native peasant. That dash for freedom constitutes one of the epics of history and one of the great tragedies. Anita was all in all to Garibaldi, devoted wife, brave lieutenant, inseparable companion in all his hardships. She was ill now, too ill to go, but she would not stay. A few days later she died in the forest of Ravenna, and Garibaldi, whose iron strength had buoyed up his troops a thousand times, "burst into a flood of prolonged and bitter weeping." He buried Anita in the sand and escaped, ultimately to Piedmont, then to America, where for a while he was a ship chandler in New York. He was made an honorary citizen of San Marino, and even in America he was looked upon in a somewhat similar light until his death many years later.

Winter Sport and a Summer Fete

Presumably you will visit San Marino in mild weather, but if it should be in the middle of winter you will find it hardly less attractive. The February days I spent there were regaled by astonishing facilities for winter sport. I found the entire town coasting on a fast ice path that ended in a trail of sand. Everyone, from the smallest child to the huskiest adult, had his little sled, hardly bigger than a dinner plate, and was enjoying the thrilling sport. A friendly boy, determined that I too should join in the fun, thrust his sled into my hands and down I sped like a shot from a gun. It was marvelous and I accepted another ride and then another. From this distance of time I am sure that there was mischief in this generosity, for the boy must have hoped to see me "spill." Why I did not, is one of the unsolved mysteries of life, for those absurd sleds, on such a slope, invited catastrophe.

There was another winter sport inside the primitive albergo of those prewar days. The bedrooms of the establishment were as cold as only bedrooms can be which have felt no heat since last summer. But—the beds themselves were heated, *brilliantly* heated, each by a brazier of live coals inside a zinc-lined wooden crate that made a great hump in the bedclothes. The temperature of my room could not have been above thirty. Shaking like a man with palsy, I undressed, removed the stove from the bed and fairly plunged in. The tingling sensation of that *warm* plunge was one of the most blissful that has ever come to me. But, alas, each silvery lining has a dark cloud. I could not spend the rest of my life in that bed. As someone has said, "Came the dawn." In order to catch my little blue train back to Rímini it was absolutely necessary to get up, and I report with pride that at the very last second strength was given me to make good!

* * *

One of my two warm-weather visits was timed to coincide with the republic's Great Day, September 3, the Day of St. Marinus. In celebration, San Marino staged its usual very colorful annual pageant, and in the evening the republic's only theater, a building in the suburb called the Borgo, at the base of the three peaks, offered *Lucia di Lammermoor* as its much-touted attraction, the production being given by a wandering opera company of Italy. Lucia was played and sung by a woman with a fine full voice *and* figure. She was simply *enormous*. She must have weighed, conservatively, three hundred pounds. When her Scottish lover sought to embrace her from time to time he literally *could* not get his arm a third of the way around her. But did this arouse laughter from the San Marinese audience? Never. The lady could sing, and that was all that mattered. I could not help comparing the reception this bulky Lucia got in that Borgo theater with the one she would have received in a comparable country theater of America! The comparison, I must admit, was all in San Marino's favor.

CHAPTER 22

A CONSTELLATION OF CENTRAL STARS

Módena for Its Exclamation Point

THE five historic art cities and one "surprise" that make the central but northward-trending constellation of this chapter's plan, namely Módena, Parma, Piacenza, Cremona, Mantua and Montagnana, do not fit into any of the CIAT ribbon tours. The ribbons do not touch the wide area of northern Emilia, bisected by the Via Emilia, nor the transpadane ("across-Po") area of southern Lombardy. The first three cities above named are directly on the Via Emilia, both by road and rail, hence very easy to visit, while the Lombard towns of Cremona and Mantua and the Véneto town of Montagnana call for a bit of cross-country trekking. Modest hotels of the second category exist in the first four towns named, but in Mantua there is as yet nothing above the third class and in Montagnana there is no recommendable place.

Módena—the name is often wrongly accented by travelers—was once the capital of a rich little duchy, and some first-rate monuments of earlier centuries have come down to us. The two outstanding ones are the cathedral and the ducal palace, the latter being now a military school and therefore to be viewed only from the outside. The cathedral is wonderful, and its tall, slim campanile, the *Ghirlandina*, serves as a ready-made exclamation point for the visitor's exuberant comments.

The architecture of the church and its remarkable tower interested me for a special reason. The skillful men who completed the construction of them in the thirteenth and fourteenth centuries were the *Campionese Masters,* and upon learning this I felt a fine glow of smugness enveloping me, for I knew who these worthies were. They were the group of talented architects hailing from the curious village of

Campione, now an Italian enclave on a Swiss flank of Lake Lugano. I recalled seeing a marble commemorative plaque to them not far from the wharf of that village. A major reason why it is still Italian, rather than Swiss, is that these Masters were natives of it and the village clings stubbornly to its pride in them. Arrigo da Campione, perhaps the greatest of the group, was the Master who built the Ghirlandina.

From the purely architectural angle I was fascinated by the many stone lions on whose much-enduring backs pillars of the cathedral rest, both outside and inside. I was interested in the queer outdoor pulpit, in the mixture of Roman and Gothic portals, in the tipsy effect produced by the tower and the adjacent apse, which lean slightly in opposite directions. I was amazed at the sculptural details seen on the divisions of the lofty roof. All of them are bizarre. One of them is downright indecent. Take your stand across the Piazza Grande, look up and see what *you* think. The early carvers in stone and wood were sometimes very earthy fellows, and this is by no means the first bit of ecclesiastical porno-sculpture that I have noticed, but usually such work is camouflaged in some way or slyly tucked into the elaborate designs of choir stalls. Here in Módena it looms up above the town's main square for all to behold.

Inside the edifice, the Campionese Masters did the intricate carving of the reredos, a superb stone construction that gives almost the effect of a rich balcony. Virtually the whole of the interior, except this reredos, is of a strangely soft tone of brick and you will bask in its restfulness. The stone lions, here and there, are as sweet and silly looking as beasties can be, despite the heavy burdens they carry.

Parma for Correggio and the Farnesi

If you drive up the Via Emilia from Módena to Parma you may chance to see, at Réggio Emília, a small sign on a branch road marked Corréggio. That branch road could lead you—but don't bother with it—to the seedy little village where a boy named Antonio Allegri was born in 1489. He lived only forty-five years, but he enriched many a church and convent and museum with masterly frescoes and other paintings. Parma, being especially rich in his works, has a statue of him in its Piazza Garibaldi and the statue is marked simply Antonio

Allegri da Correggio. As in the case of many other masters of the arts in Italy, including da Vinci, his birthplace serves as his surname. If that custom still held, Arturo Toscanini would be called da Parma, or perhaps Parmigiano, for he was born in the city which Correggio had so ably decorated.

Correggio's finest frescoes in Parma, and perhaps the best he ever did anywhere, are in the refectory of an old convent, the room being called *Camera di San Paolo*. To enter it one must apply at the *National Gallery*, situated in the Farnese Palace not far away, and while in the National Gallery itself one may see various famous works by the same artist, including his best-known masterpiece of all, *The Madonna of San Girolamo*.

The *Palace of the Farnesi*, known locally as the *Palazzo della Pilotta*, occupies an enormous area in the heart of the city. The Second World War made very heavy inroads on Parma, and this bulky palace was a conspicuous target. The portion now containing the National Gallery was left a mass of rubble in 1944, as was the portion containing the *Farnese Theater*. The Gallery has been restored, and its contents, which had been carefully stowed away elsewhere during the war years, are back on its walls. The theater, a wooden one of great architectural interest, is being laboriously restored, but this is a very challenging job and may not be fully successful.

If Correggio and the Pilotta are Parma's chief sights they are by no means the sum total of its attractions. The *Duomo* has drawing power because of its fascinating Romanesque façade and because of the *mass* of frescoes adorning every square inch of its interior (those in the cupola by Correggio); and the adjacent *Baptistery* is a queer, lovable, pink-dusty octagon that leaves its image in the memory of everyone who sees it. The church called *Madonna della Steccata* is as chock full of frescoes as the cathedral and these were done by a good, if not great, artist named Francesco Mazzola, called Parmigianino (Little Fellow of Parma).

Music has its important place in the Parma sun. Not only was Toscanini born here but Nicolò Paganini lies buried here, in a grandiose tomb in the Villetta Cemetery; and in the small park in front of the Pilotta there is an exceedingly pretentious monument to Giuseppe Verdi. His presence in September, 1859, roused the citizens to heights of patriotic excitement, for his name, you remember, stood for the popular cry of a new country, and kingdom, a-borning: *Vittorio Emanuele Re d'Italia!*

If Parma's art and its monuments somehow fail to sustain you through long hours of sightseeing, be advised that its *cheese* will come to the rescue! Parmesan cheese does, in fact, enhance the spaghetti of this city and every other city in Italy. In the country and language of its origin it is called *formaggio parmigiano.*

Piacenza for Its Civic Palace

Piacenza is a rather large city which has been going strong for twenty-two centuries. It has an excellent cathedral, a mere youngster seven and a half centuries of age, and some other fine churches, but *the* thing for which travelers visit it is the marvelous *Palazzo del Comune,* or *Civic Palace.*

This building, erected in the thirteenth century, is a very remarkable one for its grace and elegance, in sharp contrast to the usual massive palaces built three centuries later. You can compare the styles very handily, for only a few blocks away is another palace, an enormous, rectangular one built for the same Farnese dukes who required so much space for themselves in Parma. The Palazzo del Comune is in the style called Lombard-Gothic, its lower portion in gray stone, its upper portion in extremely mellow red brick, with marvelous terracotta arches around its windows. You can't quite get away from the Farnese Family even here, for in the large open space in front of the palace two of its dukes, Alexander and Ranuccio, are honored with excellent equestrian statues, both done by a seventeenth-century sculptor named Mochi. Their mounts, it seems, are as much honored as themselves, for the square is called Piazza Cavalli!

Cremona for a Favorite Square—and Violins

Cremona is a city of arcaded charm with a wealth of medieval buildings unusual in a city its size, even in Italy, and this is spiced by inevitable thoughts of the violinmakers who here brought the luthier's art to its highest peaks of resonance and beauty. In this book's Scroll of the Great in Music (Chapter 9), the Amati, the Guarneri and the Stradivari makers have been mentioned and it is a pleasure to report that Cremona does not forget her old masters of so alluring an art and she does not even forget how to make violins. In the *Museo Civico* are some fine examples of the violins of the old master makers, well worth seeing if your way of life includes enjoyment of good music. As for today's makers, it is cheering to find that in spite of the fairly good fiddles now turned out in thousands by machines and in spite of the hydra-headed competition of canned music in every form, Cremona makers still meet a demand for violins slowly and lovingly fashioned by hand. In a number of modest little shops on side streets they still work at their trade, and who knows but that another Antonio Stradivari will one day emerge from the present obscurity of this city?

The medieval buildings I have mentioned are largely in one magnificent group surrounding the *Piazza del Comune*. If you seat yourself at a café table in the arcade of the *Palazzo Comunale*, itself a worthy member of the group, you can gaze out in leisure upon the jumbled wonders across the square. From left to right they are the *Torrazzo*, or campanile, the *Cathedral*, tied to its bell tower by a lovely loggia in Renaissance style, the *Baptistery*, an eight-sided building somewhat reminiscent of the one in Parma, but with marble on two of its sides only. At your right, on the same side of the square as the Palazzo Comunale, is the *Loggia dei Militi*, or *Balcony of the Soldiers*, completed exactly two hundred years before the discovery of America.

The Torrazzo, a tawny brick Gothic campanile surmounted by a double crown and a tapering "cap," is called the highest tower in Italy, and since it rises 364 feet from the pavement, thirty feet more than does the Mangia Tower from Siena's Campo, one feels that this claim must be a mathematical fact and not a booster's fancy. A dial of enormous diameter on the tower's front purports to tell the time of day, month, year, century, millennium, eon and I know not what else. The cathedral, contemporary of Piacenza's Civic Palace, is, like that, of Lombard-Gothic design, but its façade is all of stone, except for two odd brick turrets rising from its flanks. You will be delighted with its central porch and portal, its double gallery, with pillars like two rows of soldiers at attention, its splendid rose window, made in the thirteenth century when, as in the French Gothic, rose windows were at their best. And you will find its lions almost as numerous and quite as harmless as the big kittens seen on and in the cathedrals of Módena and Parma.

Cremona is altogether likeable, perhaps my personal favorite of the group in this chapter. For relaxation it has a modern section, with fine arcades and shops and cafés and tearooms, very near the medieval wonders. Just stroll about aimlessly and you're sure to find it. Your strolling will be enhanced and given point when you come upon such street signs as Corso Stradivari and Via Guarneri.

Mantua for Mantegna

Rarely in Italy have I been disappointed in any community seen for the first time, but Mantua did disappoint me *in one respect*, and for this I must blame the maps of it and not the place itself. The maps always picture three lakes surrounding Mantua, Largo Superiore, Largo di Mezzo and Largo Inferiore and *I* pictured crinkled blue water, dotted with sailboats, sending cool breezes from its surface in whatever direction the wind took, but be warned, as I was not, that the Upper, Middle and Lower Lakes, formed by widenings of the River Míncio, are exactly nothing at all to enjoy or to look at. They are dreary, marshy bodies of seemingly stagnant water and Mantua makes it hard for you to see them even if you would. Nondescript buildings and high walls shut them out, which is no more than they deserve.

Having eased myself of this gripe, I would say, with genuine respect, that the city has a good deal to offer. I do not think, however, that anyone need spend much time in the unkempt *Palazzo del Te*, a sixteenth-century Tea House of the Gonzaga dukes, just outside the walls, though guidebooks usually star it and it does contain, one must admit, lots of remarkable frescoes by Giulio Romano and his pupils. These are remarkable in part for the size of their figures, as where the *Giants Assault Olympus*, and in part for their unblushing boldness, as where *Zeus Embraces Leda*. The god's embrace is total and Zeus is no swan here.

In the center of Mantua the *Sant'Andrea Basilica*, with its lofty coffered ceiling in the form of a "half barrel," is important and the *Piazza delle Erbe* and the *Broletto* are interesting, but the *Ducal Palace of the Gonzagas*, together with the *Castello San Giorgio*, which is a part of the "ducal complex," is by far the most stirring thing in the city. The exterior of the massed palaces and castle will not stir you much, for they are merely big, and in some parts bleak, but the interior, of vast proportions (monumental stairway, huge glittering galleries, 450 rooms, 12 courts and gardens) is imposing and the Castello San Giorgio is really warmed and made human by the art of Andrea Mantegna. His cupids are "working" cupids, quaintly supporting a large commemorative plaque and his *Scenes of the Life of the Gonzagas*, in the *Camera degli Sposi* (Bridal Room) are vigorous anecdotal paintings. The artist here had stories to tell, as Pinturicchio had in the Piccolomini Library in Siena, and he told them well, though never failing, of course, to be duly complimentary to the ducal family that gave him patronage and that held Mantua in a firm dynastic grip for centuries.

Montagnana for Its Surprising Self

Montagnana is an Italian Carcassonne, but with this difference. Everybody has heard of the latter, nobody of the former. Nagel's guide gives it thirteen words. CIT's guide doesn't give it any. The Hotel Annual lists but one albergo, of the fourth class, with eight rooms.

I was driving my miniature Fiat from Mantua to Venice on a Sunday afternoon and was in rather a hurry to get the 134 kilometers behind me when I came full upon this unsung marvel. I was so astonished that I stopped short, for there before my eyes were ancient brick walls that seemed to go completely around a good-sized town, in quadrangular form, with towers at regular intervals and without a single break anywhere. I could hardly believe this wasn't an optical illusion, so I drove completely around Montagnana and then straight through it, entering by the west gate, leaving by the east gate. It was no illusion. The walls are there all right and have been there since Dante's day. They are not only unbroken but even unbruised by

Italy's countless wars, great and small. Nagel, ever on the alert for a work of art, however obscure, devotes eight of his thirteen words to telling us that there is a "Romanesque Gothic Duomo, with a portal by Sansovino," but I am fairly sure that when you see this incredible town, incredibly neglected by tourism, you will ignore Sansovino and concentrate your gaze only on the wonder of its walls.

CHAPTER 23

VENEZIA

No Other "Venice" Can Touch It

A HARMLESS sport of mine has been the collecting of Venices. I have picked them up all over Europe. Annecy is the Venice of Savoy; Amiens is the Venice of Picardy; Bruges is the Venice of Flanders; Stockholm is the Venice of Sweden; and there are many more. Whenever a town has a canal or two its boosters call it the Venice of its region. Many of these places are very beautiful in their own right and they are only stultified by propaganda clothing that doesn't become them. When one visits or revisits the real Venice, the Venice of Italy, one finds that the pseudo-Venices are like reflctions from a cracked mirror. The original Adriatic Venice is something you cannot get over. It smites you; it takes you into camp; it holds you for life. There is only one Grand Canal, the avenue of the world's dreams. There is only one Rialto and news still comes from it as in the Bard's day, for some travelers go there to find the central post office and secure their letters at the *Fermo in Posta* window. There is but one Piazza San Marco, one glittering Church of the Winged Lion, one Palace of the Doges, and one animated Riva degli Schiavoni. Lastly, there is but one Lido, though all the world steals the name for countless beaches and night clubs.

Venice commands universal affection from travelers, inspires perennial excitement, on the tenth visit as on the first. A substantial part of this book, including the present portion, is being written within a three-minute walk of Piazza San Marco. Why? Because I too, like everyone else, "can't get over Venice."

Be it known, incidentally, that Venice, despite the decayed *exterior* appearance of many of its palaces, is *not* dying of old age, as some suppose, destined soon to become a moldering museum piece. It is a vigorous and advancing city of today, with a population approaching the half million mark. Recent port developments and government contracts have added greatly to its importance in the economy of Italy.

Facts for Your Arrival

Tourist helplessness reaches astonishing proportions in Venice. Thousands of first-time visitors each year express amazement that it is possible to *walk* in this city. They consider that *every* venturing forth, however slight, must be by gondola, which conveyance is too often mispronounced by placing the accent on the penult. (The correct pronunciation is, of course, góndola, not gondóla.)

Without fulminating further about this paralysis of the travel will, which is, after all, understandable in those who approach so great a mystery as a large "city afloat," I will try to be specific and helpful.

There are four means by which travelers may arrive in Venice, at four different points. Those few who come by steamer may find their craft anchored in the lagoon directly opposite St. Mark's Square, or, more probably, moored to a quay on the Giudecca Canal. (I have seen such pleasure craft as the famous *Stella Polaris* moored even to the central quay that extends east from the Riva degli Schiavoni.) Those who come by plane (LAI from Rome or Milan) settle to earth at the San Nicolò Airport on the Lido Island and proceed to the city by launch. Those, the vast majority, coming by rail or bus, across viaducts several miles in length, are deposited on the north and south sides, respectively, of the Grand Canal at the most distant point of this S-shaped waterway from St. Mark's. If you come in your own car you will put it up in the huge *autorimessa* adjacent to the bus terminus, and you will find this to be one of the best and most efficiently operated garages in the world!

It is when arriving by rail or road that self-help can take hold. If gondolas are plentiful you will doubtless wish to enter one of them and pay the standard, ample tariff, set forth on a printed card in every gondola, for this "grand entrance" to Venice and to your hotel, though the gondoliers generally avoid the circuitous Grand Canal in favor of a relatively dull short cut, the so-called Rio Nuovo. They often try also to ignore the tariff and charge a few hundred lire extra, but you need only point to the card and insist on your rights. If gondolas are *not* plentiful, for the reason that a lot of people have arrived at once and all are simultaneously clamoring for one of these sea-cabs, you may go by motor boat (*motoscafo*) at a much higher tariff, or you may step aboard a *vaporetto* (little steamer) and be transported to St. Mark's or the Riva for about a tenth of the gondola fare. If your baggage is too bulky to be carried by yourself you will almost surely find a porter eager to go along with you, and even with this service and his steamer fare the cost will be very moderate.

You can't possibly go wrong in boarding a vaporetto, though some take lots of time, chugging the entire length of the Grand Canal, while others, bearing the sign *Diretto,* go by the short cut to the same goals. You only have to watch out that you get off at the desired point. Most of the tourist hotels are near one of two halts, either the important one of *San Marco,* this for several of the large hotels on the Grand Canal (but the *Gritti Palace* and the *Grand* may be reached more easily by gondola or motor boat), or the very next halt, *San Zaccaria,* which is squarely in front of the *Royal Danieli,* in the heart of the hotel sector of the Riva. Traffic schedules, listing all the successive halts, are always conspicuously posted in the vaporetti.

An interpolated word seems needed about these omnipresent steamers, colloquially called waterbusses. They are, of course, the bane of the gondoliers, and many a visitor too has complained that they ruin the Venetian picture, but they are in the picture to stay and what can't be cured must be endured. We must even endure the thought of paying only a nickel to a dime for a ride, depending upon its length. The vaporetti wriggle neatly through the Grand Canal's traffic, the local ones stopping every hundred yards or so at some *pontone.* This mode of travel is not as unromantic as one might think. I personally confess delight in these small craft. They enable one to see the water palaces of this incomparable avenue repeatedly for an outlay of next to nothing.

A few of the hundred and more hotels and pensions of Venice, to return to problems of arrival, shall be mentioned in a separate section immediately below, but the offices that give aid to travelers need mention here. Often they may be friends in court at the very beginning, helping you to get under cover in crowded seasons.

CIT, which of course operates local tours by gondola, has its office in Piazza San Marco, under the arcade on the south side, near Florian's Café. (Pay no attention to street numbers in Venice. The city has a block system all its own, quite incomprehensible to visitors.)
Ente Provinciale for Venice is also in Piazza San Marco, on the same side as CIT. Be sure to equip yourself, early in your stay, with Ente's compact "Carnet di Venezia," an invaluable weekly pamphlet crammed with information about transportation schedules, current gondola tariffs, the latest facts of Venice concerning good food, entertainment, shopping, museum hours and so forth. It is distributed gratis and will very likely be offered to you by the porter of your hotel.

Cook is also in the Piazza (north side, near the clock tower).

American Express is located *just off* the west side of the Piazza, on the lively lane, a large one for Venice, called Bocca di Piazza ("Mouth of the Square").

Hotels, Pensions and Restaurants

The hotels of Venice and the Lido, like wavelets on the lagoon for number, cannot be here discussed in any comprehensive way, but a few notes may be offered on places that I know from having stayed in them.

Riva degli Schiavoni is by all odds my own favorite hotel sector, since a front window there provides a city view as beautiful as it is unique, and since, also, this Riva is "just around the corner" from San Marco.

The *Royal Danieli*, one of the most widely known hotels of all Europe, is the de luxe representative of the Riva group and it is doubly de luxe since it acquired the entire property between its original self and the Doges' Palace and erected here, between 1949 and 1951, a very sumptuous new section, called the *New Excelsior*, with a roof-terrace restaurant-café seating three hundred patrons that is literally the high spot of Venetian dining, dancing, late-evening supping, imbibing and general relaxation, this upper floor of food and fun being supplemented by the smart, air-conditioned *Flamingo Bar* on the pavement level. (Somebody, possibly an over happy patron, had scraped the *o* from the name on the window when I first visited this room, so its label read Flaming Bar!)

The main palazzo of this hotel, flanked now on *both* sides by recently built sections, was the private palace of no less a celebrity than Doge Enrico Dandolo, crusader, conqueror of Constantinople (in 1204), whose tomb is in a gallery of St. Sophia in that city, now Istanbul. His Venice home is a thing to gaze at, in every part, with admiration. Peer into its jewel-box of a writing room, whether or not you wish to write in it. Have yourself a high tea or a drink in its great medieval salon, and while doing so study its huge artistic fireplace, large enough, it seems, to consume a cord of wood at a burning. Ascend to the gallery above the main lobby and just *look*—at everything. No such princely home in any other European city can be *your* home as a transient traveler, and only two or three rural châteaux offering accommodations to visitors can rival it. The Royal Danieli is a name to conjure with, a place "to write home about" whether you lodge in Dandolo's palace, in the more modern part to the east or in the most modern part to the west.

The prospect from the front rooms and from the terrace restaurant, where breakfast too may be delightfully had, is one of the most romantic and fascinating views in all the world, and this goes, whatever the time of day, whatever the weather. Always there is the broad lagoon, backed by the church and campanile of San Giorgio. Always there is life and gaiety on the broad quay below. Always gondolas are wafting past and the little steamboats are continually arriving and starting off, while occasional large ships creep in or out of the Giudecca Canal. Sun or moon or harbor lights always make the lagoon gay, their gleam broken by a million ripples or dancing in jagged, drunken shapes as some passing craft stirs the surface. One evening I watched a tremendous display of fireworks set off from a raft anchored in the lagoon, and how different, how stupendously different, it was from similar lavish displays at, for instance, Coney Island. When the great flares flared, they had something worth lighting up—the circle of a thousand floating gondolas; the quay where Marco Polo landed on returning from the court of Kubla Khan; this palace whence Dandolo set forth to conquer the infidels; the weathered roofs of that great city which was once the Adriatic's "wife," in legal documents, a spouse accomplished, aristocratic, enormously wealthy, lovely beyond all envious rivals. The fabulous wealth has largely fled, but the beauty of Venice has only grown more mellow and compelling, whether seen by the glare of rockets or the searching light of the Italian sun.

On the Riva to the east of the palace hostelry, lie, in this order, the *Londres et Beau Rivage* (first class), the *Savoia e Jolanda* and then the *Metropole*, both second class. I once stayed pleasurably in the Savoia e Jolanda and I am told that the Metropole, also unpretentious by comparison with its elegant neighbor, is equally good. I once sojourned also in the *much* humbler *Casa Paganelli*, a third-class pension directly opposite the Victor Emmanuel monument, only "a bridge and a half" from the Doges' Palace. All these Riva establishments, whatever their category, democratically share the view.

Of the group along or near the Grand Canal, just to the west of Piazza San Marco, the only place in which I have stayed is the *Luna*, an ultra-modern albergo of first, but not de luxe, category. Its cuisine is excellent, its plumbing is a joy to all plumbing-conscious Americans, including myself. The *Gritti Palace* and the *Grand* are the de luxe "entries" of the Grand Canal group, both with a very good reputation for comfort and modernity.

Other first-class places on the Grand Canal, all with the clumsy plural names that seem so dear to Venetian albergatori, are the *Europa e Britannia;* the *Italia Bauer Grünwald;* and the *Monaco e Gran Canale*.

Close to the Rialto, overlooking the Grand Canal, are several very modest but finely located hotels, such as the *Rialto* and the *Marconi e Milano*, both third class; and in the heart of the city, one or two lifts back of Piazza San Marco, are numerous recommendable hotels of the second category, such as the *Saturnia e International*, the *Splendid-Suisse* and the *Cavalletto e Doge Orsolo*, all clinging tenaciously to double names, but no less comfortable for that.

Among pensions, one that I have tried and liked is the second-class *Seguso* on the "unlikely" Zattere Quay facing the broad Giudecca Canal. Its food is good, its atmosphere homelike. Adjacent to it and quite as good, I believe, is the *Calcina*, in a mansion where Ruskin lived for a time. A pension of third category reported favorably by friends of mine is the *Dinesen*, a Danish-run place, on the "far side" of the Grand Canal at the take-off point of the little San Vio Canal, close to the Academy of Fine Arts.

* * *

Among the Lido's forty or more hotels, the luxury leader, beyond any question of competition, is the *Excelsior Palace*, with accommodations for over eight hundred guests. It has a renewed wing, completed in 1952, with 128 front rooms, each having its private bath. Under the same management as the Royal Danieli, this enormous palace of holiday has its own private beach, one kilometer long, with 180 private bathing cabins and with a "garage" for 200 boats, its own sea wharf and of course its own kit of restaurants, special grills and cabarets, the cheerful bamboo-walled "Chez Vous" being the latest and smartest number. Motor boats from Venice come directly to a landing from which stairs lead straight into the lobby.

* * *

Venice is a wonderful city for "eating around," perhaps less for any unusual excellence of its restaurants, though there are many good places, than for the sheer fun of *trying to find* any given place on foot. It can be done, with a good map, and the triumph of discovery sharpens the appetite. On at least half a dozen occasions, commencing when I was a very young thing too many years ago to report, I have eaten around in Venice, first steered by my parents and later by my own urges, and have loved the experience every time. I will offer a few of my trial-and-error findings here, these being all corrected or confirmed during my *present* explorations.

Ristorante La Fenice, close to the *Teatro La Fenice*, Venice's big glittering opera house, is at present the dean of fine restaurants in the city. La Fenice means The Phoenix and this name was first applied to the *theater*, when it burned down about a century ago and immediately rose from its ashes, being rebuilt with great energy under the urging of civic-minded Venetians. The restaurant has long been a great favorite of society and of theatrical folk. With a broad pavement terrace, with interesting inside rooms whose walls are lined in part with autographed photos of actors and actresses, and with a sort of medieval sanctum that is shown to patrons on request, it is a place of remarkable charm to match its remarkable food. It can, of course, be reached by gondola, if the labyrinth of footways proves too challenging, but I think you will enjoy hunting for it. (For a clue, see "How to Get Lost" later in this chapter.) Among the signed photographs on the wall, given to the management by patrons, I noticed one of Tyrone Power, another of Mistinguett, with the words "*Al Signor Zoppi, il mio stomaco riconoscente*" (To Signor Zoppi [the manager], my stomach gratefully acknowledging.)

All'Angelo is a conspicuous restaurant of very good quality just east of Piazza San Marco.

Quadri's, the familiar establishment *in* the Piazza, is more than a café. It is, as well, a pleasant restaurant on two levels, being the only eating place, I believe, from which the patron may look down into this most famous of squares. (*Florian's* also serves meals, but the rooms in which it serves them are cramped, red-plush ones of cabinet size, opening conspicuously on the arcade.)

Alla Colomba (To the Dove) is a Montparnassy sort of place just off the Frezzeria, a busy thoroughfare west and north of St. Mark's Square. It has many rambling rooms, many paintings on their walls. Its plates are decorated with blue doves, but do not expect to find broiled squabs on them. Seafood is The Dove's specialty.

The *Birreria Pilsen*, opened in 1948, is a cheerful-bright, not to say garish, place of modernistic design very close to the Piazza. As the name implies, good beer is favored here, though good wine is also to be had.

The *Ridotto*, on Calle del Ridotto just west of the Piazza (and opposite the side door of Hotel Luna), is perhaps my favorite of the loudly gleaming places. I found its food very good, its service courteous. It offers an attractive lunch or dinner at a moderate *prezzo fisso*, and of course à la carte as well.

Da Noemi is a small restaurant of rather good quality close to the Piazza. I have thought its S.Q. items (*Secondo Qualità*, you remember, meaning "Priced According to Quality") unduly numerous. They included even shrimps, butter, eggs. I don't like to order fish, butter or eggs "according to quality."

Al Peoceto Risorto is last in my list, but very far from least. It needs some special explaining, first about how to find it, second about its name. To find it, walk across the Rialto and keep going straight ahead, perhaps two hundred yards, till you reach a lane on the right called Calle della Donzella. It is on that lane, close to the corner. The name—please grasp something and hold on—means *The Resuscitated Louse*. Upon inquiry, I learned that long ago a favorite hash house existing here was popularly and affectionately called The Louse. It finally folded up or fell into decay and in due course an energetic new owner of the property built a fine new Louse. It prospered. Its food was good and *is* good. The Resuscitated Louse specializes on fish, clams, oysters, mussels, crabs and lobsters. A so-called mussel soup I enjoyed here seemed to me about the most delicious thing that ever came out of the sea and out of a chef's genius. Maybe I had unusually good luck that day, or maybe I was unusually hungry, but in any case I have no fear but that you will enjoy almost any fishy dish prepared in this unusual little place.

St. Mark's Square, the Nucleus of Romance

The central square of Venice, 575 feet long by an average 230 feet wide, is not only the nucleus of romance but also a sort of yardstick, for me at least. When my enthusiasm for the Campo, in Siena, threatened to get the better of me (in Chapter 16) I checked myself by the comment that Siena's central square is "outshone in grandeur *only* by St. Mark's of Venice," and this sort of thing I always do, in all countries. Piazza San Marco is my "absolute." Ruskin called it "the most beautiful room in Europe," and it is indeed a room, a hall, an enormous open-air auditorium, enclosed on three sides by arcaded medieval palaces whose façades are continuous and almost identical, and on the fourth side by the Byzantine *Basilica of St. Mark's*, with its *Campanile*, one of the leading landmarks of world travel, soaring 325 feet from the pavement. At right angles to the Piazza, extending to the lagoon, is the *Piazzetta*, flanked by the Doges' Palace and Sansovino's *Libreria Vecchia* (Old Library). Opposite the campanile is the *Clock Tower*, which doubles as archway-entrance to the *Merceria*, the shopping Main Street of Venice, whose multitude of little dens of trade (glass, beads, tooled leather, textiles, etc.) supplements other multitudes in the Piazza's arcades.

On top of the Clock Tower two giant Moors of bronze pound the count of the hours with bronze hammers. The right-hand Moor pounds it out first, in full, and a half minute later the left-hand Moor repeats it. They've been doing the job since 1497. During Ascension Week and then *only*, a pretty little show takes place every hour on the face of the Clock Tower. Figures representing the Three Wise Men come solemnly trooping out of a door, march in front of the Virgin, bow to Her, and then retire through another door.

The seats in the St. Mark's "auditorium" are chairs, hundreds and hundreds of them, at open café tables, notably those two of such long-standing fame, *Florian* on the south side, *Quadri* on the north, the latter challenged by a newer, jazzier rival, *Laveno*. Each of these major establishments, supplemented by many lesser competitors in the Piazzetta and beyond the Clock Tower, requires what seems like half an acre of the square's space. Each has been doing business right where it is for a century or more. Each numbers its devotees by the thousand. I am usually on the Quadri side, though I've been known to "deviate," so I shall now consider that I am seated at a Quadri table sipping a caffè espresso or a caffè e latte. (If I feel like drinking a glass of plain water too, I won't hesitate, for the water of Venice is piped from pure mountain sources in the Dolomites.) The hour is 6 o'clock of a Saturday or Sunday evening—it doesn't matter which —and the band is awaiting the signal from the leader's baton. The signal is given and the Rakoczy March or the William Tell overture or some other equally popular or hard-worked old favorite fills the square. Everybody, including the sophisticates who usually deplore such chestnuts of music, is humming, and tapping the pavement with rhythmic foot-beats, or laughing and chattering a mile a minute. The cafés are crowded to the gunwales, the arcades are filled with strollers, the whole vast square is seething with life and high spirits. Before the concert is finished darkness comes. The Piazza's lights are turned on, and each brass instrument reflects them. Then, if the night is lucky, the moon appears. His eye jaundiced and his cheeks paled by the brightness of the square, he looks down enviously, wishing that he too could take a table at Florian's or Quadri's.

July 13, 1902, was such a night as this, though I cannot make any sworn deposition concerning the moon. The band was playing martial music when suddenly there was a slight but ominous cracking sound and the campanile was seen by some to shiver. Gendarmes stopped the music, went running about like mice on a hot saucepan, shouting that the square must be cleared. And the square *was* cleared. Have no doubt of that. People trembled in their shoes. Everyone waited for the sickening crash—but nothing happened and Venice finally slept a troubled sleep. The next morning at half past nine the crash came. The bricks of the campanile had survived centuries of stress, including an earthquake of 1591 that had rung the tower's bells and had even brought one stroke from the hammer of one of the Moors on the Clock Tower. They had survived eight lightning bolts since 1548. But now, with a roar that seemed to rock all Italy, they crashed to the Piazza and were crumbled literally to fine red powder. I was in Genoa that morning with my father and mother, who were injecting summer culture into my youthful mind, and I well remember the excitement that filled the city (and got me out of a lesson of some kind). It was as if Genoa itself, instead of her ancient rival, had suffered a catastrophe.

On St. Mark's Day, ten years later, that is April 25, 1912, the glorious new campanile was dedicated with a great ceremony, religious, civil, even national. Twenty-four hundred and seventy-nine carrier pigeons had been brought from every corner of Italy, and to each bird's leg a message was fastened. With the ceremony at its height, trap doors were sprung and twenty-four hundred and seventy-nine messengers started winging their separate ways to the "folks back home," bearing the good news that the beloved Church of the Winged Lion once more had its bell tower.

Venice by Excursion—with Supplements

CIT organizes regular daily excursions, some on foot, more by gondola and motorboat, to the most important tourist sights of Venice and its satellite islands. They are well run, well guided and clearly worth taking as a first-time grounding in the elements of Venice—shopping stops in lace factories and glass works are never overlooked—though every traveler who can eke out a few days for personal explorations will find that his own fumbling efforts are wonderful supplements to the prepared tours.

In general practice, the morning pedestrian tour of CIT takes its patrons through St. *Mark's* and the *Doges' Palace,* both consuming a lot of well-spent time, and thence across the *Bridge of Sighs* (so named in the first instance by Byron) to the gloomy dungeons of the doges. The afternoon gondola tour starts by a comfortable viewing of the Grand Canal and its palaces, but none of these is entered and personal trips should be planned to the famous *Ca' d'Oro* and to *Ca' Rezzonico,* where Browning lived and died. It continues with visits to two famous churches, *Santa Maria della Salute* and *Santa Maria Gloriosa dei Frari.*

Neither of these tours includes the *Accademia di Belle Arte* (Academy of Fine Arts), I suppose because its wealth of great paintings by the Venetian masters would be quite impossible to show to excursionists, even in a breathless dogtrot. This gallery, however, is a "must of musts" to all who have a love for Italian art or even a healthy curiosity about it. Of course you will somehow save a personal morning or afternoon for a visit. You'll be rewarded by seeing the glory of Venice as its masters saw it. Carpaccio shows us the queer old *wooden* Rialto and the gay gondolas of his early day (Daniele Manin, in the nineteenth century, ordered them to be painted black, as they are to this day, as a symbol of mourning for the city's departed glory). Titian is at his mighty best. Tintoretto gives his "furious" brush plenty of play and goes far to prove what some critics assert, that he was "almost another Michelangelo." Veronese gives rein to his passion for pageantry, Tiepolo to his mastery of color. They are all here, from Bellini, the founder of the Venetian school, to Canaletto, one of its latest and lushest flowerings. Don't, by any mischance, miss the Accademia.

To return to the subject of group trips, CIT's morning and afternoon tours, usually by motorboat, are made to the satellite islands in the lagoon. The morning trip chiefly features the *Island of San Giorgio,* with its imposing church that is said by guides to rest upon *one million* piles (a figure you'll accept with some reserve), and the *Island of San Lazzaro degli Armeni,* whose Armenian padres have curious and wonderful things to show, including some relics of "Giorgio Byron." This latter island, lying just within the Lido reef, is strangely neglected by Nagel, as it was by Baedeker before him. I find not a word on San Lazzaro in either tome, but I think you will be glad to supply the lack with some personal paragraphs of pleasant experience.

The afternoon lagoon trip normally devotes its time to three really wonderful and distinctive islands, *Murano,* for its ever-interesting glass factories (and tempting sales rooms), together with a unique *Museum of Glass; Burano,* for its fishy animation and its lace makers; and finally *Torcello,* for its air of progenitorship. This island, a considerable one now largely devoted to the raising of grapes and artichokes, is the withered old mother of Venice, for it was here that the Veneti of old first took refuge from the threatening hordes of the barbarians. It has two remarkable old churches, one of which, with cathedral rank, was first built in 639 and altered *twice* before the Middle Ages.

This tour is surely the one to take, in the lagoon, if your time permits but one. I do not include the Lido in this, for that long strip of celebrated sand is, of course, in a class by itself, but I am inclined to think, and here state, though this be heresy, that I would rather forego even the vacationists' Lido than to miss this trio of special isles, Murano, Burano and Torcello.

I must conclude this counsel, however, with a most unfortunate "but." At the present time, to the dismay of CIT and all tour purveyors, not to mention the touring public, the Mayor of Murano, as I am told, forbids the landing of excursion motorboats on his island. It seems that these excursions rob the gondoliers of some of their trade and they have made a great fuss about it. Glassware shopkeepers in Venice also complain that too many tourists buy glass directly from Murano makers rather than from the shops. Not being a prophet, I cannot give assurances as to how this conflict will come out, but I cannot believe it will long continue to hinder a pleasant traffic that has been going on for many years. Meanwhile, at least one very prominent glassmaker blows glass in an establishment directly on the Grand Canal, nearly opposite the Gritti Palace Hotel. This is

Salvati, samples of whose artistry are on display in the lobbies of the luxury hotels.

How to Get Lost—and Like It

I feel it quite unnecessary to describe the traditional sights of this unique city. It would be absurd to treat them casually, and it is impossible, in a chapter of a book, to treat them with any adequacy. No one can possibly miss these sights, and no one but the most determined eccentric would deny their infinite beauty, charm, importance and romance.

But the obvious is by no means the whole, and many visitors, clinging to the Piazza, the Doges' Palace, the Riva and the Grand Canal, miss one of the finest sports in the world. I mean *getting lost* in Venice. There is nothing quite like it for sheer fun. Of course one can go anywhere in the city, absolutely anywhere (except to the dull Giudecca), on foot. You can walk from the main station or the big garage, at the extreme west, to the remotest point on the Isola di Sant'Elena at the east, and from the Fondamenta delle Zattere, where the Adriatic liners dock, to the Fondamenta Nuova, where the steamers to the satellite islands tie up.

The fun lies in the fact that you can hardly go fifty yards without a sharp right-angle turn. With some misgivings you take this turn, watching for an opportunity to get back on your course, when suddenly you are forced to take another turn in exactly the wrong direction. You pass under the *Sottoportico* Something-or-other and along the *Salizzada* Something-else and are presently facing a blank wall. Clearly that tiny *Rughetto* to the left is a private alleyway, but it is the only possible way out, so you take it, expecting every moment to be collared as a trespasser. When things seem darkest, you suddenly emerge on the loveliest sun-drenched quay you have ever seen. It borders a small canal with a tipsy-towered church and you wander along, not caring where it leads. Presently you have to cross a bridge and then a second bridge. Ah, you remember that second one. You know just where you are now. A turn to the left, another canal-side quay, a stroll through the charming little *Campiello* that you found this morning, and you will be at the Rialto. Triumphantly you step out, whistling a measure or two of a tune that you brought from home. There! That's the Campiello all right. You remember that battered stone lion. The Rialto will be just around the next turn. You can hear the shrill tooting of the vaporetti as they slither up and down the Grand Canal. Oh, it's great to be in Venice when it's—

"What? What on earth? But I thought—"

It's no use, my friend. This broad quay is most certainly the Riva degli Schiavoni and you are a good half mile from the Rialto.

The fun of walking in Venice is enhanced if some definite goal is in view. Suppose, for instance, you quit this Riva on which you have so unexpectedly found yourself and enter some *Calle* or *Rioterra* (an "earth river," that is, a canal filled in), headed for the small square where Bartolommeo Colleoni sits his horse. Horses are rare in Venice, since they exist only in bronze or marble, so this one would be worth hunting up even if it were not one of the greatest bronzes ever cast. It lies due north of the Riva, near the Fondamenta Nuova. Starting briskly from the Riva, I made this goal in sixteen minutes, losing myself in the rough only three times and getting bunkered twice by unexpected canals. Par is ten minutes, but I am not ashamed of my score. I believe I could cut it down to thirteen or fourteen on a second try.

The statue, whether you reach it in par or with a dub's score, will interest you especially by comparison with Donatello's (of Gattamelata) in Padua. Remembering that Verrocchio, who designed this one in Venice, was Donatello's pupil, and taking into account that each artist had a subject of rare power and individuality, which statue do you think is the finer achievement? If you can answer, you will have done rather better than most critics. Of the two *men*, Colleoni was the more respectable. He never broke his word and rarely took anything by force unless he wanted it very much.

I would suggest six other special goals for these Venetian walks, goals not too easily found and therefore not always emphasized, though the first one *is* on the CIT tour agenda.

1. The *Frari Church*. (Par from Piazza San Marco 20 minutes.) It is on the off side of the Grand Canal, reached by a network of tiny streets, and contains the tombs of Titian and Canova, also two of Titian's finest paintings and an enthroned Madonna by Bellini.

Before you leave the Frari Church, note a marker on a pillar on the left aisle indicating that on August 20, 1902, just thirty-seven days after the falling of the campanile of St. Mark's, the tide (*marea*) rose to the point shown. The water was waist deep inside this church, as it was in most other churches of Venice, and must have caused lovers of art agonizing moments as the sea crept up toward masterworks which there was no time to remove. Pious Venetians must have thought, in that year 1902, that St. Mark had deserted his own. Lesser floods, however, are fairly common occurrences in Venice and will become commoner in a few centuries, for the whole city, built entirely on wooden piles, is said to be sinking at the rate of one inch every forty years.

2. The *Fondamenta delle Zattere*, on the Giudecca Canal. (Par 18 minutes.) This, as I have said, is where the big Adriatic steamers come in, a sunny, poverty-stricken quay rarely visited by tourists but showing by several old palaces that it has seen better days. When here, don't fail to take your stand on the bridge called *Ponte Longo*, crossing the *Rio di San Trovaso*, for one of Venice's most romantic canal views. The gondola "shipyard" called *Il Squero* is busily at work (left, on the "Rio,") and the Church of San Trovaso backs the shipyard.

3. *Teatro La Fenice*. (Par 4 minutes.) This opera house of Venice, with a small water square where gondolas back and fill at theater time, has also its small but attractive land square, with the famous restaurant close by. You can find La Fenice on your plan, a little to the west of the Piazza San Marco, and it is to be reached by a narrow lane from Calle Larga 22 Marzo.

4. The *Church of the Madonna dell'Orto*. (Par 30 minutes.) Finding this church, in a northwestern quarter, will test your sense of direction to the limit. Titian lived near here. The church has an interesting Gothic façade and it boasts several good Tintorettos. An attractive variant of this course is the deflection, two canals short of Madonna dell'Orto, to the *Church of San Marcuola* (par 35 minutes from St. Mark's), which has the advantage of being adjacent to a vaporetto station on the Grand Canal, for return to St. Mark's.

5. The *Ca' d'Oro* by foot. (Par 16 minutes.) This greatest of Venetian palaces is virtually *never* visited by means of footwork. Would you like to do some pioneering? It *can* be reached.

6. The *Custom House*. (Par 22 minutes.) This doesn't sound attractive, but it certainly is. Occupying the very tip of Venice's "Left Bank," where the Grand Canal and the Giudecca Canal meet, it commands a splendid view of the San Marco ensemble and the Riva. It can be reached in three or four minutes, for a nickel or so, by gondola-ferry (*traghetto*) or steamboat, but who wants the easy way? The labyrinthine walk is wonderful. I would call this the two-star item on our list.

The Siren Lido

As a young boy I knew the Lido when you could walk the beach for miles, watching occasional groups of fishermen drag in their nets. There were tourists on the same island even then, but not in thousands. There were hotels, but only a few. The huge Excelsior did not exist. A stroller on the beach, at least one of my then age, could even find places to sneak a swim in his birthday suit. Imagine it!

The Lido of today, siren of the multitudes yet shrine of fashion too, is a special tourist phenomenon in a land of phenomena. It has a grandiose marble casino, the *Municipal Casino of Venice*, with "every attraction," including the attraction of losing money at roulette, trente et quarante and baccarat. This institution advertises, in all tourist languages, especially the French of the international playboy set, its *Grandes Soirées de Gala* and its *Spectacles Variés de Fantaisie et d'Art*, "bringing to pinnacles of elegance" the various annual *Manifestations et Fêtes de Venise*. But the gambling, which always supports such ambitious ventures, appears to be itself on a footing of chance. One hears much talk to the effect that Italy may close down all its gambling halls in the near future. The rumor, however, is as often denied.

How has the Lido's fantastic development come about in a few swift decades? The beach, fringing the Adriatic for several miles, is good, but so are countless others in Italy. What has the Lido got that others haven't got? Answer: it has VENEZIA.

The transient visitor who prefers to lodge in Venice itself rather than the Lido may still swim from the Lido's beach, though most certainly not in the Adamic costume of my boyhood. There is a good and modern municipal *stabilimento*, opened in 1950 directly across the island from the steamer pier (frequent service) and thus reachable by trolleybus or by a pleasant walk of ten minutes. The transient visitor may also avail himself of the Casino's pleasures, and mighty welcome too if he has a bit of money to spend. There are fast motorboats that ply from the Riva degli Schiavoni directly to the Casino's private wharf.

The Lido is but one island of a protecting chain of them extending for some twenty miles to *Chióggia*, the fishiest, most unsophisticated, most delightful never-never town in the whole orbit of Venice. If you want a bit of contrast, and if the Lido's siren call grows faint, do take one of the workaday steamers from the Riva of Venice, or from the Lido itself, to this off-beat town of many smells and many native charms, Chióggia. It may astonish you to learn that you can even *leave* Venice by way of Chióggia. At the far end of the fishy port's main street you'll see big busses marked PADOVA. Yes, you may make your exit by bus, across a bridge to a peninsula of the mainland— and so to Padua, city of that colorful saint (Anthony) who preached to eager fishes from the banks of the River Brenta.

Venice Under Moon and Lanterns

You will surely want to float up and down the Grand Canal by moonlight, so, in all seriousness, concentrate your attention on this matter and see what your calendar says on the subject. A moon is one of the essential properties of Venice. You should not even permit clouds to obscure it, but if you have no magic powers, at least do not allow it to play truant altogether.

Venice is at its incomparable best of a warm, moonlit evening. You're strolling the Riva as the last daylight is replaced by lunar light. Half the people you meet are singing; all are strolling, no one is in a hurry. After the stroll will come an hour and a half in a gondola. Wafting up and down the Grand Canal and circling the near lagoon, where guitars really strum and Oriental lanterns vie with the light from the sky, you will pass and repass everybody you have met in Venice and a few thousand whom you have not met. Holiday's reign is complete and unchallenged.

Night spots *do* exist, not only on the Lido but in Venice itself. One may run down such places as the *Antica Pignolo*, not far from the

Clock Tower, and the *Martini Dancing*, on an alley that leads from Calle Larga 22 Marzo, but these seem like rather desperate ventures in Venice, except perhaps on a very rainy evening. One may find dance dens in any large city of the Western World, but one may find Venetian nights only in Venice.

CHAPTER 24

FOUR TOWNS ON THE ROAD TO MILAN

Halts of the Motor Coach Route

THOSE travelers who take the CIAT coaches from Venice to Milan, a distance of about 160 miles covered in ten hours, travel about half of the total distance (Venice-Padua; Brescia-Milan) on broad *autostrade* built at Mussolini's direction. For comfort this has its strong advantages, though picturesqueness is sacrificed.

No real halt is made at Padua, neighbor to Venice, presumably because the Florence-Venice run does provide a halt there, but Padua shall be the opener of this four-town chapter. At the remaining three towns, Vicenza, Verona, Brescia, stops *are* made by CIAT, though the one at Brescia hardly counts, since it is only a hint of a halt.

The trip is very pleasantly spiced between Vicenza and Verona by a lunch stop in the *Castle of the Capulets* (Capuleti), which is more or less matched by a rival *Castle of the Montagues* (Montecchi), both *castelli* looming up on their respective hills near the present small town of Montecchio Maggiore. Of course the former is called Juliet's Castle, the latter Romeo's. "Juliet's" cooking, incidentally, is excellent, and "her" lofty establishment most attractive. The trip is further spiced, between Verona and Brescia, by views of Lake Garda, as the coach rolls along its southern rim, and by a half-hour halt at Gardone Riviera, a big resort part way up the western shore of the same lake.

From Brescia, the coaches streak along on the smooth autostrada, without stopping anywhere, to their terminus-for-the-night, Milan. The superb double town of Bérgamo, approached after passing two rivers named Chério and Sério, is tantalizingly seen, a couple of miles away, but that is as near as the coach comes to it. Bérgamo may be thought of as a distant suburb (about 50 miles) of Milan, and travelers who make the Lombard capital a center for excursions may easily visit it in half a day.

Great Padua, Neighbor to Venice

Padua is the town nobody knows. It is too close to Venice, just as Arezzo is too close to Florence or as Amiens is too close to Paris. If it were in some distant, inaccessible spot travelers would make any necessary effort to get there. Padua is tremendously worth seeing, even though it takes no effort at all—except to save some time for it from one's sojourn in overshadowing Venice. It is a railway halt, so near Venice as to be virtually a major suburb, and I have mentioned that it is reachable by bus from Chióggia. It is reachable from Venice itself by a combination of boat (from the Riva degli Schiavoni) to *Fusina* and a tram from there to Padua. This route is interesting to avoiders of the beaten path.

In the heart of Padua there is a first-category hotel, the *Storione*, and for those who cannot stay over night, there is a very remarkable institution, also in the center, where the visitor may settle himself for a preliminary hour to "study up" before emerging to the town. I refer to Caffè Pedrocchi, one of the most sumptuous and historically significant cafés of Europe.

Designed on neo-classic lines, with impressive Doric columns at its portals and Ionic columns on an upper loggia, it is a thing to see as well as to enjoy. A marble plaque on its main façade commemorates *Antonio Pedrocchi Umile e Grande Creatore di Questo Storico Edificio* (Humble and Great Creator of This Historic Edifice). He was humble at first, as a waiter, and he became great, in a sense, by founding and developing this socio-political center of a large city. The rebirth of Italy, in 1848, owes much to the passionate discussions that went on in this café. Later, it was patronized by many well-known authors and artists. Even today, the leading citizens of Padua and their families "belong" to Pedrocchi's, as to a club, and pay annual dues for special privileges of membership, such as the use of private tearooms and salons upstairs, but anybody, including our traveling selves, may enter and be eagerly welcomed, for the establishment, it seems, has a tendency to fail financially from time to time. One reason is that students from the university, just across the way, flock in here, and Italian students are notoriously *poor*. It is said that a group of students will sometimes wrangle or play cards for an entire afternoon, though purchasing but *one* cup of coffee for the lot of them! Tourists always help to offset this meager trade, for the Pedrocchi's beverages, ices and elaborate pastries are very tempting.

Thought of these impecunious students leads us naturally to look into the *University*, or that part of it which lies almost directly across the street, from the Pedrocchi. Popularly called *Il Bò*, for a like-named primitive eating house that stood here—the sobriquet means "The Bull" —it is known far and wide as one of the most important and colorful universities in all Europe. This central building now houses the administrative offices, the Faculty of Law (other faculties are on land within a bend of the river), and the University Museum.

Everything about this building makes it a museum in itself. In the Court of Honor, on the stairway walls and in the *Aula Magna* upstairs, we see hundreds of coats of arms of masters and students who belonged to the nobility. The main stairway, every stair faced with marble of a different color, leads to the Great Hall, just mentioned in Latin, and it proves to be a room of great magnificence. In the Museum we are shown the "chair"—it looks more like a primitive wooden pulpit—from which Galileo taught his classes, in this very building. We see also an Anatomy Theater dating from 1594, where the leading anatomists of Europe gave demonstrations for centuries, the corpse being laid in the center and the students standing in tiers on an oval "grandstand" about it. I was told that, despite its minuscule proportions, two hundred students at once could peer down, as the professor did his grim business with the corpse, and that this theater continued in regular operation until 1872!

For all its seven and a half centuries of age, the university is perennially young, and it is still great in the educational picture of Europe. Its ten thousand students and many times ten thousand alumni are intricately woven into the life of modern Italy.

Padua bears the genuine stamp of the Middle Ages in several of its squares, it has many charming riverscapes conferred by the Bacchiglione, which meanders through it in several branches, and it has, among its many churches, two that are as individual and as well worth seeing as any in Italy. These are, of course, the *Arena Chapel,* made famous by Giotto's frescoes, and that tremendous domed and minareted pile called by the natives *Il Santo,* as though their Saint Anthony were the only saint in existence.

The Arena Chapel takes its name from the old Roman arena beside which it stands. It was built from Shylock money, as its official name, *Cappella degli Scrovegni,* indicates. The Scrovegni Family made their money from usury and were dearly hated by many a hard-pressed Paduan, but we, of course, feel charitable toward them, for we have this Arena Chapel.

Without the great Florentine, however, this chapel would be dull and undistinguished. Giotto, rising to his loftiest heights, made it one of the supreme shrines of art, "perhaps the greatest miracle in the history of painting," as the critic Elie Faure has said, writing in general of the artist's gift for composition. This is the more remarkable because Giotto, though thirty-eight years of age, was still little known when he "landed the job" of doing these decorations, at a stipulated daily wage. His work in Florence had been on the periphery of art, attracting little attention.

I think it is fair to say that nowhere else can one study this artist so profitably and so comfortably. In the upper church of St. Francis at Assisi his frescoes are perhaps as fine as these, but there a loquacious monk tends to hurry you along. In your effort to understand his torrent of Italian explanations you miss all sense of personal pleasure. Here in the Arena Chapel you may, if you wish, be entirely "on your own," lingering as long as you like. Furthermore, the lighting is excellent and the state of preservation very good.

For more than six centuries these frescoes have brought fame—and visitors—to Padua, and with the visitors has come that curious, ineradicable trait of human nature which one finds everywhere, the combination of vanity and vandalism that induces people to write their names for others to read. Within the very framework of the lowest row of pictures, those painted in *grisaille,* I noticed a veritable network of names, initials and dates. I take pleasure in holding up to shame one Giacomo Bonetti, who wrote his name here in 1823; and a certain Balzolo, who records directly on one of Giotto's pictures that he was here in May 1766. Other visitors are anxious that posterity should know of their coming—in 1820, in 1853, in 1908, and so on. At present, an iron railing, a yard from the walls, prevents further vandalism. The pictures, it seems, must be kept away from us animals.

It is a tragic fact of the times that frescoes cannot be effectively protected from falling bombs. The large and celebrated *Eremitani Church*, near the Scrovegni Chapel, displayed a wonderful series of frescoes by Mantegna for nearly five hundred years, but on March 11, 1944, an air raid wrecked the church almost completely. The edifice is now largely rebuilt, but the frescoes are gone, with the exception of some fragments still to be seen in the *Cappella Ovetari*.

Across the town from the Arena Chapel and the Eremitani Church lies the *Church of Saint Anthony of Padua—Il Santo*. It is enormous, and with its vast collection of domes, seven in all, and its two campanili and smaller minarets, it creates an overpowering effect. The building itself is a huge tomb for Saint Anthony, whom we must by no means confuse with that other Saint Anthony, of Egypt, who struggled against his lascivious dreams a thousand years earlier. St. Anthony of Padua was a Franciscan, a native of Lisbon, who preached all over southern Europe, generally to large and eager audiences. There is a very popular legend, often represented in art, that on one occasion people refused to hear him, so he went to the water's edge and preached to the fishes. A quaint anonymous poem tells us the whole story. Carps, eels, sturgeon, pike, crabs and stockfish made their way to the surface and listened intently. St. Anthony keyed himself to great effort and preached with fiery zeal. His congregation quivered with conviction of sin and determined to live the better life, but perhaps the saint preached too long. Reaction came.

> The sermon now ended,
> Each turned and descended;
> The pikes went on stealing,
> The eels went on eeling,
> The crabs are backsliders,
> The stockfish thick-siders,
> The carps are sharp set;
> All the sermon forget.
> Much delighted were they,
> But preferred the old way.

As an appropriate tribute to Anthony's eloquence, his *tongue* is preserved in the *Treasury Chapel* in the ambulatory. To the faithful this tongue is Anthony's undoubted own, the very tongue that roused a hundred congregations in several lands, and perhaps it actually *is* authentic, for Anthony died only a little over seven centuries ago, in 1231, and he was canonized in a matter of months, quicker even than St. Francis was. The remains of the saint's body are not in this chapel but in a silver casket in the handsome *St. Anthony Chapel* in the left aisle. Crowds are always here praying and touching a Holy Stone that is thought to give special potency to prayers.

Donatello shares honors in the church of Il Santo with the saint himself. The Florentine sculptor made some marvelous bronzes, especially a crucifix, which give distinction to the high altar. This work is fully up to his usual standard of execution. What more can one say?

Outside the church is that masterpiece of Donatello, the equestrian statue of Gattamelata, alluded to on earlier pages. Examine the features of this man and your admiration for Donatello's art grows greater than ever. What indomitable strength to the cut of the jaw! What powerful individuality in the expression! You know positively that the man *looked* like that. If he understood how to tread stealthily and sweeten his speech with honey, he understood also how to ride roughshod over all opposition, lopping off heads when necessary with that great sword that rests so ominously against the left rear flank of his steed.

Take your stand where Via Cappelli enters the square, near the house where Donatello lived while he was working in Padua. Then let your gaze take in the whole grand scene, bit by bit. I think your eyes will rest first, last and longest on that magnificent warrior etched against the eastern sky.

Vicenza of Palládio

Vicenza, only twenty miles west of Padua and straddling the same pleasant river with the hard name, Bacchiglione, is usually given scant attention by hurrying tourists yet, like Padua, it is a town of special character and color.

The color, in this case, comes in large part from the architect Andrea Palladio, a sixteenth-century native of Vicenza who designed that city's most famous public buildings and several private palazzi as well. The pride of the city, and his greatest masterpiece, is the *Basilica Paladiana,* a strongly original building with two colonnades of Greek inspiration, one above the other, the whole enclosing an earlier Palace of Justice in the Gothic style. The ceiling seems to me "Early Marine," for it looks like the inverted hull of an enormous schooner used as a "cover" for the great hall. This is actually a *new* ceiling, for the building was partly wrecked by bombs in the war, but it was, of course, meticulously constructed as an exact replica of the old one. The strangely fascinating ensemble of this Basilica is further dramatized by the soaring twelfth-century tower called *Il Torre di Piazza.*

Two other "Palladian" achievements win attention from all visitors. One is the unfinished but very striking *Loggia del Capitanio,* which stands on the opposite side of the same square that is graced by the big Basilica. This "oblong square," of the first rank even in square-rich Italy, is a remarkable sight, as animated as it is handsome. Two tall, graceful columns, very similar to the two in the Piazzetta of Venice, stand sentinel at the end of the oblong.

Palladio's other special masterpiece is the *Teatro Olimpico.* He designed it in 1580 but died before its completion, leaving the work to a trusted successor. It is called, by local guides at least, the first *covered* theater ever built, but that is not its chief distinction. The really amazing thing is the permanent stage scenery which he designed. Representing a city square and streets of his day, it is worked out with such perfect perspective, as seen from the seats, that one can hardly believe it is a shallow scene on a stage. The innermost part of the set, seeming to represent a considerable distance in this "city," is actually but three inches in depth.

Vicenza is a genuine discovery to all who can stop over and take time really to "find" it. The bus halt lasts only fifteen minutes, but those who merely travel through the city, with a glance here and a glimpse there, are generally so fascinated that they put it down on their "must" list for next time.

Verona of Can Grande

Verona is one of Italy's large cities, with over 200,000 population, and among the cities of metropolitan stature it could well be rated close to Venice and Florence in interest to travelers. It lies within a perfect "S" of the considerable Adige River and has a remarkable legacy of important buildings remaining from its checkered past, especially from its Roman and Scaliger past. The Scaligeri, or, more strictly, the della Scala Family, ruled Verona like a private estate for most of the thirteenth and fourteenth centuries, though it must be said that several of the rulers were very able and enlightened men.

Visitors who are lucky enough to spend a little time in this city will find an attractive first-class hotel in the *Colomba d'Oro*, very close to the Roman Amphitheater; and among the good restaurants of the city they will enjoy the *Dodici Apostoli*. To live in the Golden Dove and to eat a meal in the Twelve Apostles is to add glamor to comfort and good gastronomy.

Can Grande was the patron of Dante, who lived at his court for many years and made the supreme recompense of dedicating to him the third canto of the *Divine Comedy*. The poet sincerely admired the "Greyhound" as a statesman, warrior and wise prince. He was not only the greatest Scaliger, but probably also the greatest of the medieval Italian despots, not even excepting Cosimo the Elder of Florence. He set the colors of Verona and brought the city to its highest peak of power and glory, though it was his successor, Can Grande II, who built the tremendous *Castel Vecchio*, symbol of Scaliger power.

Can Grande's statue and tomb are naturally conspicuous in that celebrated Gothic group of the *Arche degli Scaligeri* (Tombs of the Scaligers) which constitutes the chief goal of all tourists visiting Verona. His name means "Great Khan" and is a steal from the Tartars, but if ever an Italian prince deserved so fulsome a title this man did. He built up the largest state that had yet been seen in northern Italy—Vicenza, Treviso and even Padua came under his sway—and his private income of seven hundred thousand florins was surpassed, in all Europe, only by that of King Charles IV of France. An enthusiastic patron of art and literature, a tireless builder, a man of high integrity, a general of almost Napoleonic genius, this Great Khan towered far above the other princes of his day and brought undying fame to the House of the Ladder (della Scala) and to his native Verona.

It was under the reign of Can Grande's predecessor that Shakespeare placed the story of Romeo and Juliet in this city. Needless to say, that tale was pure fiction, based on the previous fictions of several Italian and French writers, who used approximately the same plot and the same names, and yet, also needless to say, the tomb of Juliet (*la tomba di Giulietta*) was long pointed out to tourists in the Capuchin Cemetery of Verona. When this petty hoax was played out, another tomb was found in the *Convent of San Francesco al Corso,* close to the Ádige. Cynics assert that it is merely an old wash trough and yet tourists eagerly flock to see it, and the convent cloister is undeniably charming, graced as it is by an enormous weeping willow. When I "flocked," I was reminded that in Elsinore a guide once offered to show me the tomb of Ophelia. No doubt the tomb of Madame Butterfly will be found in due course in Japan, but to limit our thought for the moment to Verona, no enterprising researcher has as yet located the sarcophagi of Proteus and Valentine, the "Two Gentlemen of Verona." The "*House of Juliet*" has been located, on Via Cappello near the Scaliger Tombs, and it is the headquarters of Verona's important EPT. Perhaps one may accept this pleasant name without too much caviling (including the "authentic balcony—look up to your right, sir, as you step into the courtyard from our office"), for no doubt the house was the property of the Capulet Family and no doubt somebody in the long line of Capulets was named Giulietta.

Aside from the Scaliger sights and those connected with Romeo and Juliet, Verona offers three special and very great attractions that combine culture and entertainment in settings of noblest distinction.

1. The *Roman Amphitheater,* in the heart of the city, is of huge dimensions (506 feet by 426; seats for 32,000) and wonderful preservation. Even the ancient amphitheaters of southern France cannot match it. In this magnificent arena open-air opera and ballet are presented every year, on summer evenings between mid-August and mid-September.

2. The *Roman Theater,* on the other (left) bank of the Ádige, is small but very appealing in its construction on a hillside whose crest is enhanced by the tiny medieval *Church of Santa Libera.* In this classic theater appropriate plays of Shakespeare are presented, usually in September. Of course *Romeo and Juliet* is a perennial favorite and likewise *I Due Gentiluomini di Verona.*

3. The *Giardino Giusti,* also on the river's left bank, is a garden

of great elegance with a grand outlook, its chief arboreal feature being a perfectly kept avenue of venerable cypresses. In this garden various dramatic attractions are presented in the early summer, before the opening of the Amphitheater Opera Season. Once, when I was there, Sarah Ferrati and others in a company well-known to Italians presented on eight successive evenings *Sogno di Una Notte di Mezza Estate*, whose seven words you recognize as *A Midsummer-Night's Dream*.

Regardless of theaters and their seasons, Verona is always a major attraction in itself. It suffered terrible damage during the war, 43 per cent of its houses being destroyed, but you see little evidence of it today. During the German retreat in 1945, on April 25th, the next to the last day of hostilities, the retiring Nazis gave Verona a final salute by blowing up all of its ten bridges. They were rebuilt with speed and energy, though two of them, one being the famous *Ponte Pietra*, are so far only temporary footbridges. The still more famous *Ponte Scaligero*, leading to the Castelvecchio, has been faithfully replaced with a new bridge like the old one. It is open to motor cars and if you drive into the city from the north it provides an interesting and significant approach. Through Via Roma, on the right bank, you may drive straight into Piazza Bra, beside the vast amphitheater.

That dominating structure of the city, filled to capacity on a gala night of opera, lacks just one thing to complete its glamor, namely, the presence in the central box of Francesco della Scala, known to all the cheering throng as Can Grande!

Brescia, the Lioness

Brescia, once an independent republic but later a part of the Republic of Venice, won for itself a noble nickname in the Italian War for Independence. It fought so uncompromisingly against the Austrians that it was dubbed *La Leonessa d'Italia*, the Lioness of Italy. Its appeal to travelers, however, is more than purely historical, though it would be folly for even its boosters to assert that it is on a par in interest with Verona or Padua.

Its chief architectural curiosity is a *double cathedral*, the *Duomo Vecchio* and the *Duomo Nuovo*, connected by a passage, the Old

Cathedral, from the eleventh and twelfth centuries, being an odd circular affair. The city's finest church, however, is neither portion of this double cathedral. It is the *Church of Santa Maria dei Miracoli,* or perhaps I should say it *was.* I hate to report that Saint Mary of the Miracles suffered bomb hits during the war, and although its exterior was not much hurt, its interior was very heavily damaged. Whenever I come upon "one more" splendid medieval church or monument of Italy that was damaged or quite wrecked in the Second World War I experience an unpleasant feeling of frustration, but presently this tends to wear away in favor of a warm sense of gratitude that so much, so astonishingly much, of Roman and medieval Italy was left intact, and many buildings that were damaged have already been successfully restored. One cannot quite say "all the best," but certainly "most of the best," remains to give pleasure to postwar posterity.

CHAPTER 25

LAKE GARDA AND THE DOLOMITES

Is This the Finest Lake?

LAKE GARDA has been a "hobby" of mine for decades. I have approached it in five ways, as follows: by the port of *Desenzano*, on the direct Venice-Milan rail route and CIAT route, whence steamers ply, via romantic Sirmione, clear to the northern end of the lake; by bus from Verona to the lakeside town called *Garda;* by electric tramway from Brescia to *Salò* on the west coast; by a bus service of SAD (*Società Automobilistica Dolomiti*) from Milan; by SAD also from the north, via Trento and Rovereto to *Riva*, which, before the First World War was an Austrian port but has been solidly Italian ever since. To select the best of these doors is as hard as it would be to select the best of Ghiberti's baptistery panels in Florence or the best of della Robbia's *bambini*. Riva, at the narrow northern tip of the lake, is certainly the grand climax, but there is much to be said for working up to one's climax slowly—from Desenzano.

This crescendo is a perfect "movement" of tourism, whether done by car or lake steamer. If done by private car, there is some advantage in using the less-known *eastern* side of the lake, where there is little traffic, perhaps making a luncheon halt at some small open-air restaurant—consider those of *Torri del Benaco* or *Malcésine*—where the wavelets lap at the wall beside your table. If done by steamer, week ends should be avoided, for the decks may then have standing room only, and not too much of that.

Desenzano is a port and not much else. One presumably hastens to the boat landing to board the steamer moored there. (Failing a convenient steamer departure, one may take a bus to "anywhere.") Then begins the long crescendo that culminates in the stupendous scenic chords of Riva.

Sirmione is the first port of call on the northward trip to Riva. It is a thermal resort on the end of a long and narrow peninsula with sulphur springs that bubble up actually *from* the lake. From Catullus to Tennyson "and after," every poet worthy of the name has produced a verse or two about Sirmione. The place is full of allure, and boasts, incidentally, a *Scaliger Castle*. There are lots of hotels (*Sirmione, Catullo,* etc.), with gardens on the edge of the water, and the chief piazza, beside the steamer landing, is aglow with holiday life.

At the point where the lake begins to narrow, tiny *Garda*, a charming, sleepy fisher-village which yet gave its name to 143 square miles of water, guards the eastern shore; and swank *Gardone*, the western. Gardone is the smartest place on the lake, the center of the Garda Riviera, where warm sunshine makes the tourist comfortable even in late February and early March. It has three imposing first-class hotels and many lesser places, the array making it look almost like a fresh-water San Remo.

One of the attractions of Gardone is Gabriele d'Annunzio, who made his last home (until his death in 1938) in a villa called *Il Vittoriale* in a marvelous lakeside situation just north of the resort. As mentioned in Chapter 9, his battle-cruiser *Puglia*, which figured in his picturesque operations about Fiume, is set up in his gardens. You may board it and walk its decks. His personal plane, a queer little biplane of the cardboard-string-and-glue era, is suspended from the ceiling in a pavilion of honor. His ancient Fiat, from the acetylene-lights-and-outside-gearshift era, is also on display. A new circular mausoleum, now approaching completion on a separate knoll, is one of the most grandiose tombs in Europe.

What an amazing career that poet-adventurer had! I have mentioned that when I first knew anything about him he was the "literary shudder" of many an American community, but that was many years ago. The man whom the world regarded as a sensuous literary aesthete, the poet of the perfumed boudoir, proved to be a soldier of extraordinary courage and resourcefulness. He became a fearless aviator whose exploits were always headline news; and finally, in the Fiume affair, he was able to defy his own country and America's President Wilson for over a year.

Having lived enough for seven lives, d'Annunzio must have been vicariously thrilled when, in the spring of 1933, a fellow aviator of a younger generation, flying over his own Lake Garda, piloted a plane faster than any machine of any kind had ever traveled before. But that too was many years ago. Four hundred miles an hour no longer makes us gasp in astonishment. But the thought of civilian parachutists leaping from planes into his lake in his honor, as is done in a big way every year, does still seem newsworthy, and it must make the hero's bones quiver with pride.

North of Gardone, the lake narrows rapidly and the mountains grow steeper. On both sides, the Gardesana roads, from Brescia and Verona respectively, scratch their marvelous paths along and *through* the cliffs. These twin roads, called the *Gardesana Occidentale* and the *Gardesana Orientale*, driven to completion in 1933, constitute the most spectacular achievement of the kind I have ever seen. The Axenstrasse of Lake Lucerne is a small-scale and primitive thing by comparison. The Grande Corniche and the mountain roads above Nice dwindle to insignificance as engineering achievements. Especially is the Western Gardesana, called also *Il Meandro*, an eighth wonder of the world. For miles and miles it is literally drilled through the cliff, emerging only now and then for a breath of air. On one trip I counted the tunnels and there were 73. Numbers 2, 11 and 37 were long ones. In many stretches, you can tell where the road is (as you gaze at it from the lake boat) only by the regular "windows" cut into the side of the mountain. The paving and entire construction of these roads, which are now in their third decade of public use, seem the last word in modernity, and if you wish the experience of riding over them, inexpensively too, you may do so by the busses of SAD, which make the run several times daily.

Riva, at the northern tip of the lake, is the place I should select from among all Italy's lake *towns*—I do not here include the small resorts—as my personal favorite, and indeed it seems to me to have hardly a rival in Europe. It is a town of unusual quality, and nature has done her bit by furnishing a stage setting of surpassing grandeur. Have you seen lovely Locarno, backed by the Madonna del Sasso? Have you seen Annecy, on the like-named lake, surrounded by the mountains of Savoy? If so, you are ready for the next step. See Riva.

Bolzano as a Scenery Center

Bolzano, chief city of the Upper Ádige province, lies some sixty miles north of Riva at the meeting point of three river valleys, the Talvera, the Isarco and the Ádige, that of the Ádige being the most important. To reach it, either by SAD bus from Lake Garda, or by train from Verona, one goes through *Trento*, the historic town where the Ecumenical Council of Trent met three times in the sixteenth century to debate and fix the standards of Roman Catholic faith.

Trento is an interesting town, full of things to see, and it is a good tripping center too, with a first-class place to serve as headquarters, the *Grand Hotel Trento*, but better centers are "up ahead" and few tourists linger here. One look at the *Duomo*, an imposing and gloomy Romanesque church that must have umpired many heated theological wrangles at the time of the Council, is generally enough to satisfy the traveler bent on pleasure and eager for scenic goals.

Bolzano is one such place. No theological wrangles here, and no moods of gloom to dispel the holiday spirit. Despite some heavy damage in the war, it is a bright and attractive town in its own right, with a lively central square, a wonderful street of arcades, *named* so in two languages (Via dei Portici; Laubenstrasse), a curving market street of unfailing animation and an outdoor theater where summer opera is given; and as a center for trips through mountain scenery, it is rich in possibilities. *Merano*, itself a superb center to be discussed below, is only eighteen miles away, up the Ádige Valley. The *Brenner Pass* to Innsbruck is but fifty miles due north by another road. *Dobbiaco*, near the edge of Austria's Carinthia Province, is but seventy (northeast) by still another. *Cortina d'Ampezzo*, as famous and fine a trip center as any of them, lies sixty-eight miles to the east of Bolzano by way of the *Dolomite Road*, certainly one of the most thrilling mountain highways in the world, a highway that includes, only a few miles on the way, the fantastically photogenic *Lake Carezza*, with its row of pinnacles. To the south and then east of the city lie the mountain resorts of *Cavalese* and *Predazzo*, with the *Rolle Pass* (to *San Martino di Castrozza*), a scenic star of the first magnitude, but nine miles farther on. Southwest of the city runs the wriggling road to the

Pass of La Méndola, and so to Édolo, Sóndrio and Lake Como. The SAD services fan out from Bolzano in all of the six different directions named above and motorists may add many variants to these six, as I know from having driven my "Fiatina" on almost every passable road that is marked on the Touring Club's *Carta Automobilistica*.

This reference to Italy's cartography for motorists, quite as good as the best anywhere, leads me to mention a special English-language booklet called *Touring Routes in the Dolomites*, published by the provincial turismo authorities and available in EPT and Azienda offices. It discusses in detail twenty-seven Dolomite routes, each made easy to follow on a separate accompanying map. Plans of Bolzano, Merano, Riva and other towns are included. If you secure this booklet, and supplement it with a book of 160 photographs entitled *Dolomiten Land*, procurable at Bolzano bookshops or through the EPT office in the city's central square, you have acquired the essentials of a Dolomite library. The photographs, made by three talented men of Bolzano and Merano, are masterpieces, every one. The book will be a treasure for your living-room table when you get home.

Before following any of the spokes or fan ribs from Bolzano, I must repeat from an earlier allusion that Alto Ádige, with Trentino, forms one of three so-called autonomous regions of Italy, the others being the Valley of Aosta and Sicily. Of course the autonomy has its limits, for Italy is one nation, but this status does give real advantages, and it makes for friendly feeling. I must comment too, in personal vein, that it is pleasant to see German-speaking and Italian-speaking people of Alto Ádige, which was the province of South Tyrol until the conclusion of the First World War—Bolzano's name was Bozen—living in at least reasonable amity, whatever currents of feeling may flow beneath the surface. This amity is certainly fostered by the moderate spirit of republican Italy, as compared with the militantly nationalistic spirit and the roughshod methods of Mussolini's Italy. I notice that nowadays there is no stigma whatever attaching to use of the German language in this region. In Bolzano I have heard as much of it as of Italian, and in the small towns and villages of Alto Ádige I have heard little else than Tyrolese German. On country walks I am often greeted by the warmly friendly phrase "*Grüss Gott*," and I notice that street signs and even the names of railway stations, on country or mountain lines, are usually in both languages. On the line, for instance, that toils up by rack and pinion from Bolzano to and along the Renon Plateau, Soprabolzano is also Oberbozen; L'Assunta is Himmelfahrt; Costalovara is Wolfsgruben; Stella is Lichtenstern; and the marvelous terminus, Collalbo, is also Klobenstein.

As a hotel headquarters in Bolzano, I have twice booked at the pleasant *Albergo Città*, a place under the same management as Hotel Quirinale in Rome. It is located in the very heart of the city, on a big main square, which Fascist nationalists renamed Piazza della Madonna but which is now universally called Waltherplatz, for Walther von der Vogelweide, hero of *Die Meistersinger*. At the far end of this square rises the ancient parish church, with a lofty and handsome bell tower, while on the east side is the EPT Information Office (a tobacco shop next door sells American magazines and papers) and on the west side is the conspicuous office of CIT and SAD (combined) whence the Dolomite tourist coaches roll to all points of the compass. The square is wonderfully animated, with shops, cafés and small hotels surrounding it, and with holiday crowds crisscrossing it. The Albergo Città, with its German name, Stadthotel, also set forth conspicuously on its façade, is a rather large hostelry of about a hundred rooms, kept up in the most immaculate fashion by a hotel couple working together. Its bar-café, on the street floor and in the arcade beside its entrance, is by far the most popular one in the city, while its gleaming white dining room is tucked away one flight up. The windows of any bedroom facing the square reveal a fascinating "holidiorama" for sixteen hours out of every twenty-four.

Of *local* mountain trips to be taken from Bolzano four are outstanding.

1. *Guncinà* (1600 feet altitude), reached by funicular from Gries, a suburb of Bolzano served by frequent city busses, has a castle which has become a hotel and restaurant. Its view is enough to make you forget to eat, but presently you'll "come to," for the cooking is very good. The rooms too are good, in case you wish to lodge above Bolzano instead of in it.

2. *La Méndola*, a favorite resort at an altitude of about 4500 feet, may be reached by direct SAD bus in one hour, or by a small electric railway (one hour) to *Sant'António* and from there a funicular railway

(18 minutes) that lifts its passengers 2800 feet. There are a lot of hotels at La Méndola, including two first-class ones (the *Golf* and the *Penegal*), but if you go up for only a short visit, you will find the best of all views right from the terrace where the funicular leaves you. Lago di Caldaro lies placidly in the Ádige Valley and two lesser lakes on a ridge due east of your viewpoint. A little farther to the north, Bolzano, not fully visible from here, fills the bottom of a great geological bowl, and beyond the city tower various Dolomite peaks.

3. *San Genésio*, reached by aerial cableway from a base station just beyond the Talvera River, proves to be a substantial upland village, with a life quite its own. When I first visited it, the local brass band was rehearsing in a small courtyard and some miles of the defenseless air were saturated with the sound. This approach to San Genésio was spiced by a little drama that I shall never forget. I reached the lower funicular station by tram for the 5 P.M. ascent. There were only four passengers, so the guard dourly announced that the car would not run for so few. The next ascent, he said, would be at 6 o'clock. Three of us were annoyed, even a bit angry, but the fourth was *heartbroken*. A little girl of about ten years, the very picture of a Tyrolean Mädl, complete with blond pigtails, burst into an instant flood of tears. She sobbed out her story, in German, that a picnic of all her friends was in progress "*dort oben*," and she pointed up. She had missed the regular 4 o'clock car and if she didn't go up now she would miss the whole picnic "*ganz und gar*." This was too much, quite too much, for the guard. He took the little girl in his arms, dabbed at her eyes with his handkerchief and announced in her language that the car would indeed ascend now—*sofort—immediatemente*. And it did.

I have since been up to San Genésio two or three times and have greatly enjoyed it on each occasion, with or without special drama. There are three or four humble mountain inns, the *Albergo Dolomiten*, having, in my opinion, the best of all the marvelous views.

4. *Renon*, called Ritten by German-speakers, is the grand climax of Bolzano's scenic specialties and the ascent to it is surely one of the grandest of *easy* mountain trips in all the Dolomite Alps. Renon is a partly forested tableland of great extent, beginning just north of the city, and is served by the little Renon Railway, a rack-and-pinion

affair in part, setting out actually from Waltherplatz. The bilingual stations mentioned above are among those reached by this toiling train on the way to its ultimate goal, Collalbo (Klobenstein).

My introduction to Collalbo was a tableau I can't forget, one of the half dozen first-choice pictures of my travel life. The resort stands at the edge of the deep and wide Isarco Valley, beyond which rises one of the most melodramatic of Dolomite groups, two sharp pinnacles soaring up beside the colossal flat-topped Monte Sciliar, which is chopped off at one side, as if with an Olympian cleaver, seemingly to give the others skyroom. A double rainbow of wonderful brilliance filled the valley and threw its arches over the two sharp peaks, which seemed now like a multi-colored stairway for the use of giants in reaching Sciliar. The steps stood out sharply against a black cloud, which served also as a sable backdrop for the rainbow. With a jagged skyline of a type found nowhere else in Europe, other Dolomites strode off toward the east and south. Most of the peaks were naked rock, some of markedly reddish hue, but exactly one, glistening white with snow, peered over the heads of the others, like a tall, white-haired man in the rear row of a group photograph. I made a vow then and there that I would sometime return for at least a brief sojourn in Collalbo and this I have finally done, anchoring in the attractive *Hotel Bemelmans*. On a world's-edge meadow near the tennis courts of this hotel (where a wild ball might roll a mile or so) I have found the perfect viewpoint, and here I am writing these futile lines. Around and below me there are more *greens* than I knew existed. A hamlet and its church are balanced on one of the greens, a ledge a thousand feet down, and beyond the Isarco Valley march the mountains, in three separate ranges.

Merano for Orchards Amid Snow Peaks

Merano, known as Meran when it was a town of Tyrol, is a watering place and health resort of world stature, for some of its twenty or more mineral springs are among the most radioactive to be found in Europe, perhaps surpassing those of Bad Gastein, and the town lies in one of those rarely balmy valleys—a double valley actually, where the Rivers Passírio and Ádige meet—that nature can cause to flourish luxuriantly amid a ring of snow-crowned mountains. The region, fortunately very little marked by war damage, is one of widespreading orchards and vineyards. The orchards produce various luscious fruits, among them an apple specialty called the *Calville* that is grown only in this valley and is considered an epicure's fruit, a true aristocrat of the orchard world. It has a yellow skin, and each apple is encased in paper while still on the tree to prevent its prized golden glow from turning to a sort of faded red.

The vineyards of Merano produce very popular wines, especially the white *Terlaner* and the half-sweet red variety oddly called *Blau Burgunder* (Blue Burgundy). These are but two of *two hundred* different wines of this region and I am happy to report that local wines are not without honor in their own "country." Two or three times a day many a Meraner will drop into one of the numerous wine shops for a "short one" to lighten the grind of work, and I have noticed that when a citizen of this town wishes to show hospitality to a visitor he is likely to say, "Will you have a glass of wine?" instead of offering coffee or tea. The autumn "grape cure," moreover, earnestly administered every year in September and October, is a medical event of some magnitude here. One learns that the world's most celebrated physicians, from Hippocrates to Paracelsus to the eminent specialists of today, have extolled the therapeutic value of grapes. Merano's doctors prescribe for each patient the proper type and weight of grapes to eat and the proper daily schedule for eating them. "And if you've nothing special that needs curing?" I asked one doctor. "Eat grapes anyway," he said. "They're a preventive medicine as well as a cure."

In its role as a pleasure spa, Merano has long been popular. Before the war it had more hotel beds than even Rome or Venice, and its importance seems now to be building up again. Evidence of this is the brand-new *Hotel Bristol*, with four hundred rooms and baths. Owned by the same interests that own the Grand and the Bauer Grünwald of Venice, this Bristol of Merano is establishing itself as one of the most palatial hotels of all Europe. Merano's roster of traditional pleasures, in addition to those stemming from scenery and mountains, is impressive. The race-course is magnificent and the *Gran Premio Merano* is an annual event looked forward to by the horsy world. The local *Lido* has three perfectly kept swimming pools, with the finest equipment and with good restaurant and bar service. One of the pools is huge, about 170 feet by 70, another, of smaller dimensions, is for children. Merano's *Casino* does not have gambling, as it did before Italy began to lift dubious eyebrows at such sport, but it does have a *Pavillon des Fleurs* for social events and dancing, a splendid hall for concerts, a much-sought *Wunder Bar* and a handsome open-air promenade on the bank of the rushing Passírio. I could go on about polo, tennis, winter sports in the hills, cabarets, cinemas, but you know what I mean.

In its role as a health spa Merano offers several types of therapy, in addition to its grape cure, but in the field of radioactive cures it is pre-eminent. The main bath establishment is of the very first rank, and smaller installations are found in the Hotel Excelsior and in the new Bristol. The radioactive waters, descending from the heights of San Vigílio, were discovered as recently as 1934, but they have now drawn world attention. I have watched patients, always under doctor's orders, for this treatment is dangerous to persons with heart ailments or T.B., sitting comfortably in armchairs reading magazines and inhaling radioactive air produced by a constantly dripping fountain and have thought this a mighty pleasant way to get well. There are, of course, baths filled with the same healing waters. I have not, alas, watched *horses* having radioactive treatment, but certainly this happens. Wealthy owners of racing stables in Milan and Rome sometimes bring their horses here for such therapy, supplementing the good mountain air, and I have been told that Senhor Matarazzo, a famous Brazilian industrialist, has even brought his horses from São Paulo to Merano for their health!

As a goal of sightseers, Merano has one item worth quite a galaxy of stars. That is the fifteenth-century Castle of the *Counts of Tyrol*. It is an intimate sort of castle, intelligently shown and explained, but only in German or Italian, by a guardian whose home is in it. Whether or not you understand his words, your eyes will explain most of what he so eagerly shows you. You'll see, in satisfying detail, just how Tyrolese nobility lived five hundred years ago, and if you want to see the very calendar by which they planned their political and social engagements, say for the year 1453, there it is, hanging on the wall of an upstairs room!

In its capacity as a major trip center, Merano is quite as exhilarating as Bolzano. It has four local high spots, of which more presently, and three major motor roads (besides the highway from Bolzano) of surpassing beauty and of thrills-in-crescendo. To the south runs the *Palade Pass* road, continuing through Fondo to other passes and narrow valleys. To the north runs the road to the Austrian Tyrol, passing *"Sandhof"* at *Maso della Rena*, the birthplace of Tyrol's supreme hero, Andreas Hofer, and pushing up and over the *Pass of Monte Giovo*. To the west, up the valley of the baby Adige and then south over the *Stélvio Pass* runs one of the wonder-roads of the Alps.

The Stélvio is usually called, without qualification, the highest pass in Europe. Keeping barely within Italy but sending a branch into Switzerland's Grisons Canton, it climbs to a height of 9050 feet in the lee of the gigantic Ortles (Ortler) Alps. Finally it zigzags down to Bórmio, at a mere 4000 feet, and from there one may go on to Tirano, again just scraping past Switzerland, and so to Sóndrio, in the long Valtellina.

Merano's Heights; the Avelengo Climax

The four special high spots above Merano—I do not yet include a fifth, the lofty *Passo di Nova*, to which a cableway is now being constructed—are Monte Benedetto, Castel Tirolo, San Vigílio and Avelengo, the last-named, to me the clear climax, undebatably equaling in beauty of outlook Bolzano's Collalbo.

Monte Benedetto is a hill of moderate height almost *in* Merano. A chairlift starting from beside the Castle of the Counts will lift you in five minutes to a crest with a stunning panorama and a restaurant that can serve you a superior meal. I shall not soon forget the trout I there enjoyed, freshly caught in one of Merano's mountain streams. The steak that followed it was as good as the fish, and the *fragolini* (wild strawberries) were as good as the steak.

Castel Tirolo, some three or four miles north of Merano, is none other than Schloss Tyrol, long a *mountain* castle (not to be confused with the city castle) of the Tyrolese rulers, including that fabulously ugly lady known as the "Ugly Duchess," called by her enemies Margareta Maultasch ("Pocketmouth").

Tirolo Village, some three miles from Merano, is easy to reach by car or bus, but from that point one must walk—down across a gorge, then up—in about twenty minutes to the castle. It is worth the walk, both for itself and for its view. The outlook from the throne room is provocative of many an exuberant Oh! and Ah!

San Vigílio, a lofty Alpine shoulder (4800 feet) and finally a chapel-crowned crest (5900 feet), is reached by aerial cableway and then a chairlift. The cable cabin lifts you from *Lana di Sopra*, a Merano suburb reached by bus (half-hourly service; 5 miles) from Merano's Theater Square. A couple of unpretentious alberghi, with their restaurants, will be found on San Vigílio's shoulder.

Avelengo, called Hafling in German, is a high spot of such extraordinary appeal that it takes easy precedence, in my personal affections, over all the other wonders among Merano's hills. This appeal is due in very great part to one mountain hotel (though there are several others in Avelengo), where I have twice found the apogee, the zenith, the "nothing-more-beyond," in setting and in holiday relaxation. So special is this place that it warrants special description, as of here and now, for this is my second visit and I am seated on one of its bedroom balconies.

Yesterday I left my car in the small car park of the *funivia* at the base of the hill (but there is a regular bus service from town) and boarded the swinging cabin that was to lift me three thousand feet to Avelengo. My luggage was stowed on a mattress in a sort of net out behind. The cabin was crowded with passengers, so the operator leaped nimbly onto the roof and made the ride up there. In seven minutes, by this aerial cableway, we were at the upper station and a porter wheeled the luggage up through a forest path to the hotel.

Hotel Belvedere, leader of the Avelengo group, is something that bursts upon you with the force of an explosion. A stone terrace and a wooden "deck" extend to the well-railed edge of a precipice, below which, over half a mile nearly straight down, lies the multi-verdant Valley of the Ádige. Merano is on that green floor, a bit to the right, and Alps of various groups, in every shape, many draped with snow, are across the way, spreading in a gigantic half circle. Waving grain fields and thickly forested hills are close by, for Avelengo goes on and up and around and over in the manner of the Renon Plateau. A rough dirt road that leads to a double ski lift two or three thousand feet higher up is traversed by a couple of jeeps.

"But *how*," I asked a hill resident, "did they ever get up here?"

"That was easy," he replied. "They were just hung onto the bottom of the cable cabin and they rode up, dangling in air."

Avelengo is a two-season resort, much loved for its cool summers and likewise for its deep-snow winters, so inviting to skiers, but I know the place only in its summer moods. "Lying-down chairs" (in Italian *sedie a sdraio*) strew the Belvedere's deck every day, each occupied by a worshiper of sun and laziness. If the sun, even here, gets too potent, chairs may be drawn under the shade of white birch trees that rise from the stone portion of the terrace. Groups of café tables are scattered all about, while other tables are in an adjacent pine and beech grove.

At night, a little searchlight attached to the outer wall below the deck flashes down to Merano, four miles distant, but it is not seen from the terrace or the bedrooms. Other lights *are* seen, the fading pink Alpengluh of sunset on the Ortles snow fields, the twinkling of a million stars, the steady silver of the moon on nights when it rides its slow course. At a place so high and so wide open as this, every light in nature's equipment is at its maximum, including the light of fireflies and of lightning. One special firefly lives here in a niche in the terrace. His name is Fritz and everybody likes him and talks to him. And as for lightning! Late yesterday afternoon I watched, from my balcony, the most dramatic lightning storm I've ever seen. It filled the valley, lit the peaks, leaped where it would in zigzag lines and quivering arcs. Hail fell in a wild pelting, its noise filling in the chinks when there was no thunder. Weather is clothed with new interest at Avelengo. In every guise it thrills the people on this lofty perch.

The Cheerful Spokes of SAD

A big briefcase of mine with pebbled leather surface refuses to hold the stickers pasted on it by porters from time to time—with one exception. It will definitely accept the stickers of the *Società Automobilistica Dolomiti*. Two of these, reading simply SAD, are there for the bag's life, and after thousands of miles of travel the briefcase gradually conforms its appearance to the adjective bestowed by the stickers.

Actually SAD is as cheerful a network of bus lines through a mountain wonderland as it would be possible to imagine, and I am happy to record that the tariffs of this system seem pleasantly moderate, considering the arduous tasks of zigzag climbing that must be continually faced by its motors.

Travelers who plan their Dolomite journeys by SAD should know that many of the high passes are not sufficiently clear of snow to permit regular bus service before June 15, while on some routes the service does not start until July 1, and on two or three the starting date is even as late as July 10 or 15.

Similarly, the tour planner should know that a great many of the Dolomite resort hotels do not open until mid-June or even July 1. The exact period of the season, in the case of every individual hotel, is clearly set forth in the annual *Annuario Alberghi d'Italia*. Some resorts, notably Cortina d'Ampezzo, have a double season, the winter-sports months being quite as important as the summer months, but it is obvious that in winter, train services must be depended upon, since busses cannot make their way through snowdrifts, whereas trains can make their way, to certain towns, through tunnels.

The Dolomite Road

To select any one highway through these pinnacled mountains and name it THE Dolomite Road seems arbitrary, but custom—and the travel offices—have done just that, giving this prized title to a wonderful route that connects Bolzano, the chief city of the region, with Cortina d'Ampezzo, the leading resort. In a chain of passes totaling sixty-eight memorable miles, it ties together these two conspicuous goals.

The Dolomite peaks among which the road threads its winding way are unique. They took their name from a French geologist crisply named Déodat Guy Silvain Tancrède Gratet de *Dolomieu*, who first studied them, and they took their form from the rough hands of the elements, which eroded them and wore them into weird shapes because the rock was of too weak a nature to resist. A brochure of remarkable artistry called *Venice, Lake Garda and the Dolomites,* available at EPT offices, quotes a French author-alpinist, Félix Germain, on the subject of Dolomite erosion, as follows: "It is the patient erosion of water which has denuded the peaks, isolated towers and campaniles, sculptured wall faces, [and] opened high chimneys in the splintered and polished stone." The words are good enough, but *no* words can paint the picture.

Lago di Carezza, attained by ascending the almost frightening Ega River Gorge, so narrow in places that the rider in bus or car can hardly see the blue slit of sky far above, is the first special marvel. The lake is fantastically, theatrically photogenic, with a whole row of "campanili," these being the *Latemar Group,* as southern background and with the *Catinaccio Group* (called Rosengarten in German) as eastern "wing." The lake itself is so blue—more from plant life than from the sky—that any possible blue I could name would be an understatement. Even the well-known Blausee near Kandersteg in Switzerland is not in its class, if I'm any judge of blues.

The *Costelunga Pass* (5800 feet) is the first pass of the chain. From it we get the first view of the greatest of Dolomite peaks, *La Marmolada,* rising to a height of 10,961 feet. Don't jump to the conclusion, from that name, that this mighty mountain is a bit soft in the head, or vainly pompous, perhaps a white and feminine counterpart of King Christophe's Duke of Marmalade. It is dignified, massive, grand. No campanili or organ pipes this time, but an enormous glacier, hundreds of yards in length, hundreds of feet in thickness, though this ice river perches on the mountain's northern slope and is not really seen until you mount the next pass.

The *Pordoi Pass* is next. Rising to 7360 feet, it is the highest pass in the Dolomites. There are several hotels here and it serves as a luncheon halt for SAD bus travelers and many motorists. I should state that from this pass itself La Marmolada is hidden, but climb by a path (ask at one of the hotels) only fifteen or twenty minutes and you can see the Dolomite Empress in all her glacial splendor.

I should mention parenthetically that an alternative Dolomite Road to this point, rivaling THE road, runs from Bolzano up the Isarco Valley to *Ponte Gardena, Ortisei, San Cristina,* the *Sella Pass,* then joins the "name road" to climb the Pordoi Saddle. So superb is this rival road, knotting lovely Tyrolese-looking resorts together and then passing between the Sassolungo and Sella Groups, that I would vote it a fraction of 1 per cent better than the usual route *except* for having no Lake of Carezza.

The *Falzárego Pass,* third and last on the highway, is 6960 feet in altitude, with views as good as the others, which is strong talk. From the Falzárego you "unclimb," in ten miles, to Cortina, whose verdant valley seems low by comparison but is still four thousand feet above sea level. These last ten miles actually manage to be a climax. You would never think it possible, but they display more typically Dolomitic fantasies than any other ten along the route.

Cortina d'Ampezzo, a Favorite in Two Roles

Cortina d'Ampezzo, lying just within the edge of the Province of Belluno, has been a darling of the Dolomites for a long time, but she doesn't grow old, as stage favorites have a way of doing. In her winter role she is clad in white. Snow and ice are everywhere. Winter sports of all forms are enormously popular. Each evening dance bands fill the air. Cortina is a gay town of winter carnival. In summer, when she's dressed in green, but with plenty of white trimming too, she is just as gay. It is in this role that I know the resort.

This small community (off-season inhabitants about 2000) has over fifty hotels and pensions in the village and its immediate surroundings. One, the *Majestic-Miramonte,* is de luxe, and three or four others are of the first category.

One of the most popular of them all is the big *Cristallo Palace,* named for the giant *Monte Cristallo* that looms up so hugely northeast of the town. The private park of the Cristallo Palace, with winding, bosky paths, is cool and charming. Two courses for bowling—in the European manner, not the pinfall manner—are on a knoll here. The last-word tennis courts (used in winter for curling) and swimming pool in front of the hotel are lively, and the tea terrace buzzes with chatter. Many of the bedrooms have balconies looking down on all this conviviality, so if you would rather survey it than be a part of it, that choice is yours. The balconies and terrace, which face west, also look at mountains—and what mountains! The name-giver is best seen from the hotel's north and east sides, but the western skyline is hardly less grand, with the three Tofana Peaks, the Cinque Torri (Five Towers), the Croda da Lago, the Becco di Mezzodì (Beak of Noon) and several other queer fantasies. On many a summer night, the early evening hours are mild enough so that one can sit out and enjoy this stage of nature, lit by moon and stars, but later it gets too cool—just right for sleep.

Cortina has a full kit of the resort attractions that give it world caliber. For its two-seasonal activities, it has two aerial cableways and several chairlifts. In summer, it has international golf and tennis tournaments and an automobile race called the Gold Cup of the Dolomites. For winter excitements, it has smooth skating rinks, all varieties of ski runs and jumps, and fast bobsled runs that are kept in top trim for racing.

In winter sports, Cortina has taken on new and very great refulgence since its selection as the scene of the Seventh Olympic Winter Games, to be held in 1956. Enormous preparations are in full swing, including the broadening to normal gauge of the railway line tying the resort to Dobbiaco, so that regular expresses can be routed here from Central Europe, through Austria. An ultra-modern ice stadium, with grandstand for 6000 spectators, is being built, and on the Antelao Curve of the championship bobsled run a three-story grandstand is to be in readiness. All sorts of other things are in the works and to many active citizens no coming event in the world compares in importance with the one that will focus all eyes here for a fortnight. They think, and rightly, that it will make Cortina a name to conjure with wherever people ski and skate and slide.

In all seasons there are things to see and do in Cortina and there are plenty of paths to the heights that challenge strenuous climbers. These will have a special personal interest for any traveler who calls at the Information Office of the *Azienda di Soggiorno* of Cortina, for the active director of it is Federico Terschak, who was long known as one of the topflight alpinists of Italy. Many a steep ascent bears his name, as does at least one awesome cleft, 1400 feet from bottom to top. This is the *Terschak Chimney* which he was the first to climb. A few years ago he broke his left leg in a skiing accident and although the limb mended successfully, this naturally put a halt to his rock climbing.

For easier-going vacationists there are three ascents by electric power that are indeed electric in their effect.

The *Belvedere at Pocol,* with a considerable hotel colony close by, is reached by a cableway from Piazza Roma, in the very center of the town. It is a thousand feet above Cortina, over five thousand above sea level.

Tondi di Falória is ascended by a cableway from the railway station. In three sections, by three separate baskets, you are drawn up, past thrilling rock faces, to a height of almost 7000 feet.

Monte Tofana's Aosta Refuge, at about 6700 feet altitude, is attained in a three-ply chairlift that needs a bit of explaining. The first lift, starting from *Campo Corona* across the Bóite River, carries you high over lush meadows, hillside homes and then pine and larch forests to *Col Fiere.* The second lift hoists you from *Col Fiere,* in a dizzy, almost vertical stretch, up to *Col Druscié,* nearly at the upper limit of the pine tree line, the altitude being a little over 5800 feet. On this "foothill" of the towering *Tofana* there is a café-restaurant, and the view proves so fascinating that some chair-riders say "Enough's enough" and settle down for an hour or so to imbibe the panorama along with coffee or some other beverage. From Col Druscié an easy path winds *down* through the woods on the far side of the hilltop to *Rumerlo,* at a level 500 feet lower, and from Rumerlo the third lift carries up to the *Aosta Refuge* on Tofana, at more than 6600 feet altitude. All in all, this three-part chairlift, to state the case conservatively, is *terrific.*

There are things in, around, above, Cortina that need consideration under the see-and-do department. One, near the Belvedere Rock mentioned above as a cableway goal, is the massive, perhaps over-grandiose, *Monument to the Dead of the First World War.* In a crypt of this monument lie two famous heroes, General Cantore and Lieutenant Barbieri, and buried in niches on the walls are over 7500 soldiers, for the Tofana Mountains were the center of the Alpine carnage of 1915-18. The memorial is enormous beyond your imagining, and if your spirit and body are up to it you may climb hundreds of steps to the summit for its view.

A little north of Cortina is the queer "creeping suburb" of *Staulin*, built on land that slips slowly down every year, because there is a "slough of despond" a hundred feet under the surface. The houses are at the craziest angles you've ever seen and once in a while the municipality has to dynamite a building that gets too dangerous to be inhabited.

A little south of Cortina is the suburban hamlet of *Campo di Sotto*, where Titian was born. Or was he? Pieve di Cadore stoutly claims this master and shows the house where he was born in that town, but the citizens of Campo have not the slightest doubt that he was a native of their community. They assert that Caterina Pompanin, a local domestic who took service with the rich Vecellio family of Pieve di Cadore, was seduced by a licentious priest who was a member of that powerful family, and that Tiziano Vecellio was the fruit of this union. The mother, they say, returned to Campo to have her baby, and supported him for nine years, after which the patrician father, perhaps moved by tardy prickings of conscience and disregarding the scandal involved, claimed the baby as his son, took over the rearing of him and thenceforth brought him up in luxury. He noticed in the youngster a marked gift for painting, and provided the best instructors in art to develop this gift. The Titian birthplace of Campo's claim, bearing the sign CASA NATIVA DI TIZIANO, was unfortunately burned down during the fighting of the First World War. Another house was built on the exact site of it and in this members of the family of Pompanin still live. Close to it is a humble inn of the fourth category called Pensione Tiziano, which has an interesting and delectable specialty. It serves, outdoors, rich "whipped cream with strawberries," when the berries are in season, and to secure this treat, with at least an incidental look at the site of the Casa Nativa, tourists flock in hundreds to Campo every summer. Needless to say, Pieve di Cadore pooh-poohs this folly of the rival birthplace and trumpets *its* claims, which find their easy way into guidebooks and encyclopedias.

In Cortina—to emerge from the Titian controversy to more practical themes—there are some charming and distinctive shops, very notably that of *Verocai*, almost opposite the Municipio, where remarkable silver filigree work, art objects and costume jewelry of local design and inspiration are to be had. This shop is an infallible whetter of shopper appetite, and for your more sheerly physical appetite there is an equally distinctive restaurant, *Al Fogher*, at 12 Via Grohmann, on a descending crossroad not far from Hotel Bellevue. Signora Flora, an artist in preparing viands grilled or spitted, will cook a meal of rare quality to your order, either on the old-fashioned Dolomite hearth or in the modern kitchen.

* * *

Roads from Cortina, a subject of interest both to SAD travelers and to motorists, fan out almost as from Bolzano and Merano. Two different highways work their way north. One follows the Bóite Valley and then the small Val Forame, while the other climbs over the *Tre Croci Pass*, continuing to and beyond the attractive resort and lake named *Misurina*, an excellent place for a luncheon halt. Both roads join at Carbonin and carry on as one to *Dobbiaco*, a double village, Old and New, having as wonderful a Dolomite skyline as any village can boast. Seven miles east of Dobbiaco, through San Cándido, is the frontier of Austria, while nine miles west of the two-part village, mostly by a steep dirt road, which does not, however, discourage busses from climbing it, lies *Lago di Braies*. This is a superlative goal, worth many times nine miles of riding. There is a large first-class hotel, open in summer only, and good boating and bathing facilities are offered. A scenic path circles the entire lake and it takes about an hour to walk the circuit comfortably.

To return to the "road fan" of Cortina, a branch from the Misurina road pushes fifteen miles east to *Auronzo*, then twelve miles south to *Pieve di Cadore*, gateway to the larger cities of Venetia and, as mentioned just above, famous as "one of the birthplaces" of Titian. His house here is richly worth a visit as a medieval home, whatever your views about his birth. Reproductions of many of his masterpieces from many galleries are on the walls and an interesting portrait of his father (original in the Pinacoteca Ambrosiana of Milan) entitles him *Gregorio Vecellio Capitano del Centenaro di Pieve di Cadore*, and portrays him as a knight in shining armor. South by east of Cortina runs a *direct* road (18 miles) to Pieve di Cadore. And, finally, west of our center, runs the Dolomite Road by which this present comment "came."

CHAPTER 26

MILAN, METROPOLIS OF LOMBARDY

Lodging and Living in the Great City

MILAN was the largest city of Italy until the period "between wars," and it still crowds Rome for first place, despite the enormous growth of the capital in the last two or three decades. Milan was terribly battered by frequent bombings during nearly five years of war, but in spite of this its position as the chief industrial and commercial metropolis of Italy remains unchanged.

The city's place in the tourist picture is also unchanged, though it will take years more to fill all the bomb gaps in the central portions with new buildings. We may review the present status of the chief tourist sights.

The *Cathedral* was little hurt, though the west front suffered some bruises that have now been carefully healed.

La Scala, dean of great opera houses, suffered severe damage in 1943, but upon the war's conclusion was quickly and faithfully restored, being reopened as early as the spring of 1946.

The *Cenacolo Vinciano*, in a convent adjacent to the *Church of Santa Maria delle Grazie*, containing Leonardo da Vinci's *Last Supper*, was badly hurt, but the famous wall painting itself was largely saved by a heavy covering, and the room, once the convent's refectory, has been rebuilt.

The *Basilica of Sant'Ambrogio*, masterpiece of the Lombard variety of Romanesque, was considerably damaged but is now also restored.

The *Brera Gallery*, almost rivaling in importance the big Florentine picture galleries, was nearly knocked out by the raids of 1943—such reports as this have a sad sameness—but its pictures were saved, and now the *Palazzo di Brera*, which always housed them, has been laboriously rebuilt.

The *Poldi-Pezzo Museum*, with paintings, sculptures, jewels, carpets, objets d'art of such high rank that the collection is classed with London's Wallace Collection, has been closed, for a variety of reasons, since 1881. It was terribly hurt by bombs in 1943, but was restored, and then triumphantly reopened, with its treasures intact, in 1951.

So Milan lives again, and the ring of wonders circling it, both those built by nature and those built by man, are the same sure magnets that they always were. This ring, meaning chiefly the lake resorts, the triple town of Bérgamo, and the Certosa di Pavia (pronounced Pavía), happily suffered so little from the war that we may almost disregard its impact.

Milan has nearly two hundred hotels and pensions, of which six are in the de luxe rating. Of these six, I have stayed briefly in two, the air-conditioned *Excelsior Gallia*, near the railway station, and the *Continentale*, in the heart of the city, near the cathedral, and found them both to be all that one expects of such tourist palaces, in comfort, in food, and in meticulous upkeep. I have stayed also in the first-class *Regina e Metropole*, recommendable for its location on Via Santa Margherita, so near the vast *Victor Emmanuel Gallery*, the shopping heart of the metropolis, as to be almost a part of it. I have stayed too, in days before the war, in a couple of humble pensions, but these seem to have been bomb victims. Many good pensions, however, still, or again, exist. One that has been favorably mentioned to me is the *Duomo*, at 7 Via Pietro all'Orto, near the cathedral.

Living in Milan may be as expensively luxurious or as inexpensively modest as your budget may suggest. It is easy to spend three or four thousand lire on a meal at the attractive *Biffi*, in the big gallery, in the *Tantolo* just outside it, or at any of a dozen other places. But one can eat well, especially by sticking to places with an advertised prezzo fisso, for *one* thousand, and if you would like to try a *very* humble, but clean and well-run eatery, to see what the hard-pressed Milanese wage-earner can buy for about *two hundred* lire, go to the *Ristorante Giuseppe Verdi*, on the like-named street, near La Scala. To "stoke up" in such a place is purely an adventure in thrift, and the budget would be in a stern mood indeed to counsel regular meals there.

For a further note on transient living in Milan, be advised that the

EPT office, at 5 Via Caserotte, just off Piazza della Scala, is a gold mine of current information on everything Milanese, from bus lines to night clubs. It distributes, as a matter of course, useful brochures and leaflets. Be advised also that "night and day, day and night" the big glass-roofed *Galleria Vittorio Emanuele,* mentioned above by its English equivalent, is a city within a city. It surpasses, by very far, the similar Galleria in Naples and certainly also the inadequate ones in Rome and Genoa. It is bright, clean, cheerful and of enormous dimensions. Shops of every sort, good restaurants (be sure to try *Biffi* once at least), cafés, mouth-watering pastry establishments (try *Motta* in the Gallery's duomo-side arcade), nightspots (the gay *Odeon Roof Garden* is just outside), theater ticket offices, travel offices, including a newly restored one of CIT, all are here in abundance, as are *people* in their thousands, and—a very practical thought—the largest and most flourishing *Albergo Diurno* of all Italy, filling an acre or so of basement space. By all means "drop down," to buy a shoe shine, or a ticket to Hawaii, or to rent an umbrella, or to dictate a letter. A visit to one of Italy's "Day Hotels" at its incredibly active best is an experience.

The Cathedral and La Scala

A really great metropolis is this city of Milan, with the roar and racket of business, with all the facilities for entertaining all comers, whatever their means or cultural level, with a million and a half people eagerly trying to make money—and a good many succeeding in the endeavor.

Contrasting oddly with this spirit, the celebrated cathedral is in the very center of all the hubbub, and a dozen tram and bus lines focus in its piazza, adjoining which is the Galleria.

The *Cathedral of Milan* is roundly condemned by many architects and critics, and one must admit that its sugar-frosting exterior is a little cloying, but its interior is vastly impressive, especially on a hot summer day. To stroll in it is like strolling in the Black Forest or in a grove of California redwoods, and some of its vistas are so long as to defy belief. It is "only one acre smaller" in area than St. Peter's itself, being the largest church in the world except the latter and the Cathedral of Seville.

The various admission fees to special parts of this church contribute what they can to rob it of the air of sacredness it should have. You pay to see the treasury; again to see the Chapel of San Carlo Borromeo beneath the Choir; and again to visit the roof and tower, with an extra disbursement if you use the elevator, which, by the way, goes only half way up. This all seems a trifle venal, but of course it does cost many thousands of dollars a year to keep up a great edifice like this and one must not be too critical of methods.

The view from the roof, as one wanders about among the 2300 marble saints and 130 pinnacles that adorn it, reminds one somewhat of the view from the Frauenkirche towers of Munich. A great, flat city lies below and a marvelous tumble of Alps fills half the horizon, at a distance of about thirty miles, though the atmosphere must be clear in either city to bring the mountains within satisfactory range. My gaze from the Milan Duomo was somewhat distracted on one occasion by a young Italian vandal close to me who was busy carving his name in the ancient yellowed marble of the tower railing and I could not help watching him. It was distracted on a more recent occasion by a Coca-Cola sign and stand, right up there amid the angels. The stand was doing a rattling business, for this drink is exceedingly popular in Italy, and that goes even for the Communists, who are solemnly warned by their Red leaders that it is an American capitalistic drink of very dubious content, an instrument of Wall Street designed to aid in their enslavement.

The *Teatro alla Scala*, close to the cathedral, is unquestionably the greatest of opera houses, capable of frightening aspiring debutantes almost to death. La Scala's verdict, if adverse, is almost insurmountably damning, and if especially favorable, it is almost certain to bring the aspirant glory, honor and riches. The opera houses of Europe and America at once set up a clamor to secure the new star. Toscanini has, of course, been La Scala's most illustrious conductor, but there have been many other conductors and still more singers who have carried this theater's fame to the four corners of the earth. I noted from the placards displayed outside the building these interesting statistics of the personnel:

110 Professori d'Orchestra
112 Coristi e Coriste
24 Ragazzi Cantori (Boy Singers)
30 Bandisti
72 Ballerine
24 Ballerini

The foregoing words translate themselves, and if you have any difficulty with the genders, merely note the endings of the last two words. Who ever heard of any theater in any country where the Ballerine did not outnumber the Ballerini by at least three to one? The baldheaded row must be humored even in grand opera.

The glitter of the theater's interior is wonderfully satisfying to the American visitor, for this is just as he has pictured La Scala. There is a red-plush horseshoe of imposing size, surmounted by six tiers of boxes, also arranged in a horseshoe, the royal box standing sharply out from the others though Italy now has no royalty to occupy it, and it goes without saying that in the center of all these grandeurs, just above the view-line of the gallery gods, is a gigantic crystal chandelier. The color tone of the whole interior is white and gold, plentifully touched up by the crimson of the plush seats, and this too is as it should be. La Scala never lets the tourist down, and—rather more than incidentally —its performances *are* magnificent.

From the Ridiculous to the Sublime

The sights of Milan, for all the city's size, are not too difficult to cope with, though their range is great. They include, in addition to things already named, the faintly ridiculous mourning-in-marble of the famous *Camposanto;* the grandiose *Castello Sforzesco* (Castle of the Sforzas); the scholarly accumulations of the *Palazzo dell'Ambrosiana*, with its *Pinacoteca* of paintings and "da Vinciana" and with its priceless library, of which the man who was to be Pope Pius XI was chief librarian for several years. They include also some grizzly items, of morbid interest only, such as the *Piazzale Loreto* (near the station), where the dead Mussolini and his mistress were savagely kicked about by an infuriated mob and then strung up by their heels.

The *Cimitero Monumentale* of Milan is surpassed in bombastic tomb-sculpture by the similar one in Genoa and certainly by the showy *Recoleta* of Buenos Aires, but even so it gives a good idea of the parade of grief that was so popular in nineteenth-century Italy. In this Camposanto of Milan, visited as a sight of the city by the daily tours of CIT, one sees marble tears, marble anguish, marble nobility and saintliness. The tombs of many rich Milanese of the eighties and nineties are fantastically lavish, competition in advertising the family wealth being what it was. On the tomb of Davide Campari, to mention but a single example, and not a lachrymose one at that, I remember a huge bronze wall piece of *The Last Supper*. It may not have had any special significance in regard to Davide Campari, but at least the work must have cost a lot, so it fulfilled its primary mission.

And since the subject of the bronze brings our attention to the climactic sight of Milan, a badly defaced painting in a convent refectory, we must ask ourselves the why and wherefore of that art work, done by da Vinci in experimental vein on a dry wall rather than a damp one as is used for frescoes. (Critics say he wanted lots of time between brush strokes for contemplation, and fresco work "can't wait.")

Upon first seeing *The Last Supper*, we are startled, puzzled, perhaps even annoyed, to behold the crowd that is inevitably grouped in front of it. Always, in all weathers and all seasons, and even in years when depression casts its shadow on the tourist trade, this picture is literally mobbed. George F. Babbitt is here fresh from his real estate office, the aesthete fresh from classic Athens, the atheist, the hard-boiled businessman and the student on vacation from the Sorbonne or Grenoble or Perúgia. Even the gay fellow who frankly prefers the fleshpots of travel is here studying this very religious painting.

What draws such a motley crowd? It cannot be crude curiosity, alone, for indeed what is there to be so curious about? Italy is rich in masterpieces. Nor can it be solely the fame of Leonardo da Vinci, for Raphael is equally famous and one of his greatest masterpieces is in the Brera Gallery. It must be, I think, in part, the marvelous dramatic character of the picture itself. The Master has just said to his twelve intimate followers, "One of you shall betray me!"

What a terrific bombshell that quiet, sorrowful remark must have been. The reaction on the faces of the twelve is what fascinates all beholders. "Is it I?" the disciples are asking in horror. "Is it I? Is it I?" "Giuda," says the explanatory card, "si rimpicciolisce scostandosi." (Judas shrinks away.) You see the traitor, third from the Master's right. Leonardo of the Tuscan village of Vinci understood how to make this tense moment live for all time and hold the hurrying world's attention.

CHAPTER 27

THE LUSTROUS ORBIT OF MILAN

Il Giro dei Laghi

THE CIRCUIT OF THE LAKES is offered by CIT every day during the spring and summer months and there is a choice between two directions, clockwise and counter-clockwise. The places touched—Stresa, Pallanza, Intra, Ísola Bella, Varese, Como—are approximately the same, whichever the direction, and lunch is taken at the same place, Pallanza, in either case, but there is one real difference, namely that the clockwise tour brings its patrons to the *Villa d'Este*, on Lake Como, for an afternoon tea, whereas the other tour halts for the same enjoyable interlude at Stresa. The Villa d'Este, former palace of Caroline of Brunswick, Princess of Wales, is so outstanding, possibly the finest garden hotel in all Italy, that the tour which includes a satisfying halt here seems to me preferable to the other.

Good as this *giro* is, for the tourist greatly pressed for time, there are necessarily some serious faults of omission in it. In neither direction does it touch Lake Lugano at all and its touching of Lake Como, only at the Como-Cernóbbio "toe" of one foot, is so slight as to be rather tantalizing. The halt at the town of Como, an exceedingly interesting small city, is also tantalizingly brief, but admitting all this, one must admit also that the Circuit of the Lakes does give hurried travelers a lot of glamor in one day. Its covering of Lake Maggiore's glamors—in the lake's Italian portion—is even surprisingly adequate. You really feel you've scraped acquaintance with the Major Lake, as its name, of course, means.

Lake Como on Two Legs

Lake Como is the only one of the three large lakes in Milan's orbit that is wholly Italian. The other two are partly in Italy, partly in

Switzerland's Ticino Canton. To spur lake traffic, the company operating the considerable fleet of lake boats on Como offers, at a very moderate price, a general first-class ticket good on all boats for a period of one to ten days. For the first day's use one pays a little over a dollar, on the second day half a dollar and for any desired number of days beyond this (up to ten) about thirty-five cents. This is lake bargainry at its best.

The *shape* of Lake Como, as seen on any map that is drawn with detailed accuracy, is extraordinary. It is a perfect caricature of a slender ballerina doing a *ballet fantastique*. Head thrown back, body teetering precariously on the tips of her dainty toes, she capers westward. I must not carry this simile too far lest it force me to reveal too much of the lady's anatomy, but perhaps, being in the land of statuary, I may mention that Lecco is the tip of her left foot (east on the map), Como the tip of her right foot and lovely Bellágio, the best-known resort on the lake, the fig leaf that guards her modesty. Most of the other resorts dear to tourism are ranged along her right (west) leg.

Como City is the usual starting point for trips on the lake, and from this port one may take a steamer clear up to its head, at Cólico, a four-hour stretch each way, with numerous halts at lake villages, or one may drive on the very edge of the lake *all* the way around it. I have journeyed along every part of Lake Como's shore except the western part of the Lecco leg, and despite Bellágio's perennial popularity and the special appeal of its well-known *Hotel Villa Serbelloni*, once a honeymoon retreat for royalty, I cast my vote for the well-traveled highway that rims the lake from Como to Menaggio. Every village is an artist's bit, and each has its associations with personages of the past.

The *City of Como*, too often serving as a mere tourist gangplank to a lake steamer, has a Gothic-Renaissance cathedral with a fascinating façade flanked by statues of the two Plinys, the Elder and the Younger, both of whom were born in Como, and surmounted by an odd ornament that resembles nothing so much as an elaborate birthday cake. The city has also an animated lake promenade, from Piazza Cavour to the so-called *Tempio-Voltiano* on a promontory at the water's edge. This Temple to Volta is a memorial to the famous physicist, a native son. The contents of the Temple are of great interest, and the gentle, fringe-whiskered guardian who shows them is worth much more than the price of admission. In a courtly, old-world manner he points out special commemorative floor stones sent from every civilized nation. One of them is a strikingly handsome onyx circle from Mt. Aconcagua, sent by Argentina. He points out, too, the many relics of Volta himself, including the actual frogs, now skeletons, whose legs reacted so famously to scientific experimentation, and the pile of metal discs (alternate silver and lead) by which Volta established the laws of dynamic electricity. The pioneer's first battery is here as well. He commenced the building of it by placing some small green wine glasses, filched from the family cupboard, in a wooden seed box, filched from the family bird cage!

North of Como lies the string of lovely villages and resorts that line the lake for its whole length. Beyond Cernóbbio, with its Villa d'Este, are *Moltrásio Argegno, Tremezzo, Cadenábbia, Menággio.* What music is in Italian place names, and what beauty each Como "note" reveals. The region around Tremezzo is so peculiarly mild in climate that it is a Riviera all by itself, actually known, and not merely to tourist folders, as *La Tremezzina.* Here azaleas bloom in thousands, and the whole shore is one continuous garden. Some of the hotels are worthy of their setting, and this goes in special measure for *Hotel Bazzoni,* lying close to the Tremezzo wharf of the lake steamers. It was built anew after destruction by a tragic bombing that occurred on April 30, 1944, actually a few days *after* the ending of the blackout and, people supposed, the war, and forty-eight hours after the killing of Mussolini and his mistress in the immediate neighborhood (at Mezzegra). Sixteen persons in the hotel were victims of the tardy bombing and Tremezzo's lake front was a shambles. But the Bazzoni rose again, and in better form. A new portion, opened in 1951, is as delightful as any place on Como's shores, though having a second-category rating and therefore much less expensive than some of the "palaces." All the front rooms have private baths, each one amusingly decorated by an artist named Fontana, and, which is quite as important, each room has its private, enclosed balcony, usable in rainy weather as in sunny. The hotel is of unusually ingenious design and decoration, though locally built, without an architect, and its well-shaded lake-front garden, where meals are served on all fair days, is a holiday delight.

Two features of Tremezzo's Riviera warrant very special attention from the traveler, namely Villa Carlotta and the Island of Comacina.

Villa Carlotta, on the shore at the northern edge of the resort, is the sumptuous, jasmine-bowered, eighteenth-century palace of a German princely line (Saxe-Meiningen), and its park is one of the finest in Italy. The art works of the Villa are important, some of the portraits being by Gainsborough and some of the sculptures by Thorwaldsen and Canova. One of Canova's works is the much-photographed *Cupid and Psyche.* This is agreeably amorous, but some of the other nude marbles have been made downright ridiculous, as you will inescapably see, by Vatican-style fig leaves. I know not who was guilty of this absurdity nor when it was perpetrated, but some day, surely, some lover of art will order the shrubbery removed.

The *Island of Comacina,* reached by a small boat from the village of *Sala,* three or four miles south of Tremezzo, is the only island in all the lake, but it is beautiful enough for ten, and it has the added charm of being virtually uninhabited and therefore quite unspoiled. It was once the property of the royal house of Belgium but in 1919, King Albert gave it to Milan's Brera Academy of Fine Arts, which still owns it. In theory, Comacina is supposed to be a retreat for artists, but in practice this has not worked out to any extent. Almost the only regular inhabitants are the family and household of Signor Lino Nessi, but this is quite enough to satisfy you and me, for Lino Nessi and his blond wife run a *locanda,* which is to say an inn, which is to say, in this particular case, a restaurant. Helped by a waiter named Tranquillo and a small daughter and a shaggy dog, they manage to produce meals that are just about as superbly good as any to be had in Italy. I don't mean that they are elegant, for surely they are not. I don't mean that Tranquillo is a tailor's model of a waiter, for he's not. I just mean that you eat extremely well in this locanda and that Signor Nessi and his wife make it a point of honor that you should enjoy the meal. They'll stand by and talk if you like—Nessi says his friends call him Signor Cotoletta (Mr. Cutlet)—or they'll leave you to your own enjoyment of the viands if you want it that way. On days of good weather, you eat outdoors on a verdant knoll, with the lake, corrugated by wavelets, a hundred or so feet below.

I wish I could describe the Comacina meal I had, but it would be much better to eat another one like it. I can only say that from the wondrous antipasto to the final liqueur it was a work of art worthy of the island. Its antipasto included such items as tissue-thin dried beef in an oil dressing and whole green pimentos steeped in oil. The fish course was, I believe, *Agoni alla Contrabandiera*, a Nessi specialty. The wine I know was a delectable white dry Chianti called *Lacrima d'Arno*, and the liqueur was a marvelous firewater called *Kranebet*, a sweet gin made in the Province of Venetia. All in all, I liked my meal, as you may have inferred.

From Tremezzo, Como's lake fleet plies to every part of the lake, some of the boats being local workaday ones that run continually over to Bellágio and Varenna, returning by way of Menággio. From the last-named port, neighbor to Tremezzo, busses run in a short trip over a low pass to *Porlezza*, on Lake Lugano, which thought and port open up a lot of fresh possibilities. A popular circuit, if you have started out from Milan, can bring you back to the Lombardy capital by an international route. You may push on from Porlezza to Lugano in Switzerland, either by bus or boat, continuing thence to Milan by express train or by lake steamer to *Porto Cerésio* and by a minor rail line from that port, via Varese, to Milan's *Porta Nuova Station*. This circuit, with one or two nights spent along the way, can be a marvelous "hand-made" tour.

Lake Lugano and Its Enclave of Chance

Lake Lugano has almost as many legs, it seems, as a starfish, and they are about equally divided between Italian limbs and Swiss limbs. The Porlezza and Porto Cerésio limbs are Italian, the Capolago and Magliaso limbs Swiss, and the Ponte Tresa limb is half-and-half, the effluent River Tresa bisecting this port squarely and serving as frontier between the two nations.

The oddest feature of the contortionist lake frontier is certainly the village of *Campione*, Italy's enclave of chance, surrounded on three sides by Swiss soil and on the fourth by an undeniably Swiss portion of the lake. Campione has long been an escapist retreat where the Swiss and their tourist visitors, held to *very* conservative limits in the gambling rooms of Swiss casinos, could break loose and lose money fast enough to suit any taste. In short, it has flourished as a gambling enclave that has proved extremely profitable. From *Lugano* the steamers and motorboats have shuttled back and forth in an endless weaving of hopes and disappointments, with, I assume, an occasional trip of real triumph, when some lucky player "cleans up" at the casino, and then, by some miracle, stops playing. BUT, the casino closed down in 1951, for a variety of reasons, though not specifically by government action. Whether it will reopen, is at present a much-discussed question.

Fortunately Campione has more than a casino to give it color. It has small but lovely flower gardens, lakeside restaurant cafés, and even a past. Its great cultural pride, and one reason for its retaining allegiance to Italy is, as I have proudly reported in the Módena discussion, its role as home of the *Maestri Campionesi*, a succession of very able architects and sculptors who brought fame to this little community in the fourteenth and fifteenth centuries. A large marble plaque near the quay pays eloquent tribute to these *maestri*.

To sum up Lake Lugano in a few words, it is a holiday haven of the first rank, a series of havens culminating in big, handsome, throbbing Lugano itself, one of the leading lake resorts of all Switzerland. Those who carry American passports can cross from country to country and back again with such utter ease that the frontier is hardly noticeable at all.

Maggiore's Shores and Famous Isles

Italy's longest lake, forty miles in extent from Arona at the southern tip to Switzerland's Locarno at the northern, is also the most celebrated, and this is due chiefly to the romantic *Borromean Isles*, lying opposite the *Stresa-Baveno-Pallanza* complex of fashionable resorts. These islands, whose conspicuous chief is *Ísola Bella*, are so wonderful that many decades of daily visits by hordes of trippers have failed to rob them of their essential beauty and genuine appeal.

"Napoleon slept here," in the *Palazzo Borromeo*, before the Battle of Marengo; and the *Conference of Stresa*, which brewed a pleasant political mirage in 1935, took place here, but if Napoleon's bedchamber and the Hall of Green Blotters leave you cold, you can find many items that have to do with the interesting owners, the Counts of Borromeo, whose scions *still* own the island, still summer on it occasionally, still derive a handsome income from tourist gate receipts. You will even see, in the symbolic decorations of the palace and its gardens, some evidences of the intermingling of those three fabulous families of Milan: Borromeo, Visconti and Sforza. Wherever you see the symbol of *three rings*, it indicates the fusion of these mighty clans, though irreverent American tourists sometimes see the rings as a subtle "plug" for Ballantine Ale. The Borromeo part of the symbolism, featuring a unicorn and the word HUMILITAS, is, of course, especially obvious. One sees it even in the plant designs of the formal garden.

This, by the way, is not "just another garden," as I heard a tourist call it, in justification of his reluctance to climb the rather arduous terraces. It is a vignette of the tropics, lying on the same parallel as Halifax! One sees such exotic items as monkey trees, coffee trees, cassava plants, from whose starch tapioca comes, banana trees and some handsome varieties of orchids. A white peacock, looking deplorably vain, strolls the paths with the visitors. From many points in the garden, and from the palace too, brilliant views are had of the Major Lake, crinkled almost always with minor waves, and of its shores and islands. Three more dots of land in the Borromean group are *Isola dei Pescatori* (Isle of the Fishers), *Isola Madre* and *Isola di San Giovanni*, the last-named having served at times as a retreat for Maestro Toscanini.

By boat or bus from Stresa or Intra one may go most pleasurably to Locarno, but since this is in Switzerland, it is not practicable for the Giro dei Laghi to include it. Those who can go under their own power will love the town, from its gardened lake shore to the hillside convent and church of *Madonna del Sasso*, reached by funicular. This beauty spot has been photographed as persistently as even Ísola Bella but its loveliness, looked at or looked from, seems never to be marred by "posing."

Lake Orta, the Big Lake's Shining Satellite

Lake Orta, a seldom-visited blue jewel almost on the border between Lombardy and Piedmont, is lovely in its own right and is enhanced by two features, the charming peninsular town of *Orta San Giúlio* and the handsome island called *Ísola San Giúlio*, opposite the town. Furthermore, a unique touch adds luster to Orta town, namely the *Sacro Monte*, which rises above it.

This hill, dedicated to Saint Francis, is a great bird sanctuary where nightingales are especially abundant. If the idea of a lovely lost lake familiar to songbirds but off the tourist trails attracts you, then why not play truant and steal a day for Orta? Being on the rail line from Novarra to Domodossola, it is not actually at all difficult to reach.

Bérgamo in Three Layers

The railway station of Milan, largest and most sumptuous in Europe until it was surpassed by Rome's new Stazione Termini, is a vast marble palace of transportation, and there are many alluring goals which may be easily reached from it. In an hour or less one may leave the racket of the metropolis very far behind and find oneself in some placid old-world town or medieval nook of Lombardy.

One town and one shrine of art stand out pre-eminently from among the man-made environs of Milan. The town is *Bérgamo* and the shrine is that matchless Carthusian monastery, the *Certosa di Pavia*. Bérgamo lies thirty miles northeast of Milan, the Certosa di Pavia seventeen miles due south of Milan.

If it is impossible to visit both places, it may prove extremely difficult for the individual to decide between them, since each is a gem of the first quality. And this constantly recurring platitude seems to call for a word on the fine art of deciding, an art which many a tourist never masters. Nothing can wreck a short trip more disastrously than the anguish of continual indecision. We select Trip A, which is obviously the "best bet." And yet Trip B looks extraordinarily fine also. Isn't it perhaps a better bet than A? Or is Trip C better than either? No, we will stick firmly to Trip A, although, come to think of it—

So it goes! I know from experience, as I have sometimes bobbed on the waves for an hour at a time and only pulled myself together by desperate effort. *Any* prompt decision is better than none, and remember this: In Italy, the tourist is always right. With so much that is supremely fine, it is hardly possible to make a serious mistake.

Bérgamo is a "three-layer" town in a much more definite sense than is the little capital of San Marino. The Lower Town, *Bérgamo Bassa,* is modern, with wide boulevards and a remarkable paved promenade called the *Sentierone,* where all the world strolls at twilight. The Upper Town, *Bérgamo Alta,* reached by the funicular, is old and tortuous, with one of the most interesting "church clusters" in Italy. The Topmost Town, reached by another funicular, is a pleasant, rambling belvedere called *Colle San Vigílio,* dotted with suburban villas that command gorgeous views of the two towns below, the wide green Lombard plain and the Bergamasque Alps. There are several lofty restaurants, and one of them, *Ristorante Castello,* is on top of a castle tower on the uttermost summit. If the food isn't too interesting, you won't care, for the glamor of the setting is quite unmatched.

A tram covers the mile or so between the State Railway station and the first funicular—to the Upper Town. A quarter-mile walk straight through the Upper Town brings you to the Porta Sant'Alessandro, outside which is the second funicular for San Vigílio. I can think of no city suburb more romantic than San Vigílio. Imagine returning from work, not by a sooty steam train, but by two funiculars hoisting you nearly a thousand feet above the plain to a tranquil loveliness that seems infinitely far removed from the grind of daily toil. The snow-covered Alps are your neighbors, and villages on a verdant plain your earth-bound subjects.

If I were a San Vigílio commuter I think I should have a great deal of difficulty traversing the Upper Town (which is the *middle* layer) without stopping each day, especially during the ample noon lunch period of Italian business, for an hour or two of refreshment and relaxation in the charming *Piazza Vecchio.* Not being a commuter, I have stopped there several times as a traveler, and have lunched very well, either at the attractive, modern *Biffi* or at the older *Ristorante del Sole,* whose garden hangs over the edge of the town. On briefer visits, I have at least toyed with a cassata or a vermouth in one of the piazza's appealing cafés. Every traveler, on every visit, inevitably takes time to stroll past the *Palazzo della Ragione* (Palace of Law) to the astonishing group of church buildings that lies behind it. There are four buildings in this group: the *Cathedral*, which is the least important; the *Baptistery*, a little eight-sided structure of great elegance; the Romanesque *Church of Santa Maria Maggiore*, extremely rich in tapestries, polished tarsia work (wood mosaics) and marble tombs (including that of Donizetti); and the *Capella Colleoni*.

This last name recalls Venice, and sure enough this magnificent Renaissance building is the tomb of that fabulous general of the Venetian armies, Bartolommeo Colleoni, none other. Giovanni Amadeo, the pride of Lombardy in matters of architectural design, built it, and he also sculptured the marble sarcophagi of Bartolommeo and his daughter Medea inside the building. A guardian shows you (for a *mancia*) the interior of this chapel, which contains several good paintings and some superb inlaid woodwork, but one cannot think of much else except the central figure of it all, Colleoni. If sheer *strength* is good in itself, a dubious premise, then this man was a saint-of-power. He loved Bérgamo, his native town, and was determined to sleep his last sleep in it. He demanded for this purpose the sacristy of Santa Maria Maggiore, and when the authorities refused, he took it anyway and erected this chapel on the spot. There, to this day, sleeps the greatest soldier of fortune that medieval Italy produced, a home-town boy who made good.

Certosa di Pavia for Secluded Splendors

The *Certosa di Pavia* is visited as a sight of the route by all the CIAT busses traversing the stretch between Milan and Genoa, but it is actually so handy to reach from Milan, especially by rail, the Certosa having its own station, that it seems more a suburban feature of that city than a place for a brief halt while touring.

The same grim duke, Gian Galeazzo Visconti, who founded the Milan Cathedral, founded also this Carthusian monastery—Certosa means Carthusian—and like many a powerful leader of his time, he seasoned his bloodthirsty ambition with a genuine love of art and even a sort of religion. Here at Pavia, the thing that he started to create blossomed long after his death into one of the most beautiful religious buildings in Italy, and that is saying much, for half the great artistic creations of this peninsula are of a religious character. One is dazzled by the sumptuousness of the Certosa's marbles and semi-precious stones and fine old carvings and tarsia work, and not least by the sheer beauty of the marble-columned *Chiostro della Fontana* (Fountain Cloister). There is a second *chiostro*, the *Great Cloister*, which gives us clear glimpses of the solitary life of the old Carthusian monks. Each cell, together with its tiny private garden, was completely cut off from the other cells so that the monks could not even see each other. Their food was placed on a revolving shelf set in the door so that the bringer of it would not be seen. Water was drawn by each monk from his own individual well so that there should not be even a chance meeting at a public fountain. Only on Sundays were the contemplative Carthusians allowed to meet and talk to each other. The recurring six-day fasts from fellowship must have challenged the stoutest spirits.

The *Chartreuse liqueur*, by the way, is sold to visitors in the Certosa di Pavia, but do not suppose that monks ever make it nowadays in any of the monasteries of the order. It is prosaically made by a private company today, but if romance has gone out of the product, certainly the wonderful smooth fire of it remains.

There is one great and grievous trouble with any visit to the marvel of architecture which is this Certosa, a difficulty common to many and many a church and palace throughout Europe. One must join a party and plow through this maze of beauty at whatever pace—and it is always far too fast—the guide may think proper. One's only recourse is "to see the show again," like unemployed gentlemen at the afternoon picture show, and thus pick up some of the beauties one has missed on the first hasty tour. It is unsatisfactory, and a little annoying, but travelers learn to be philosophical about such things.

CHAPTER 28

PIEDMONT, WITH AUTONOMOUS AOSTA

Discovering Turin

TURIN, the well-to-do, clean, energetic, up-to-the-minute capital of Piedmont, has two special distinctions. It is the most impressive twentieth-century city of Italy, though of course not the largest, having less than a million inhabitants, and it is certainly the metropolis least visited by us Americans, who like to consider ourselves symbols of the twentieth century.

The reason for this last curious distinction is a bit hard to understand. Turin is handy to reach, since it lies squarely on the Mont-Cenis rail route from Paris and is served by fast trains from most of Italy's large cities. It is marvelously located, since it lies on the banks of Italy's greatest river, the Po, where two tributaries flow into it, and is dramatized on the east by striking hills and on the west, a bit farther away, by magnificent snow peaks. It has all the "past" one could wish. It was the important Augusta Taurinorum of the Romans before the Christian era. It was the capital of the Counts of Savoy, from 1418. (They were also Counts of Piedmont, and, from 1738, through an involved "deal," kings of Sardinia and Princes of Piedmont.) It was the center of Italian national consciousness after Napoleon's downfall, becoming the first capital of Italy (1861-65). And it has, in some degree, rivaled Milan as an industrial city through all the decades of this present century. During the Second World War, its importance was grimly acknowledged in a terrible series of air raids, the city being visited more than a hundred times by ever-increasing fleets of Allied bombers. In spite of this punishing treatment, the central part shows few scars today, and the industrial parts on the periphery have been largely rebuilt, in part with American aid.

I suppose Turin is too modern, too prosperous and imposing to lure from overseas the travelers who want something different, something quaint and queer, and maybe squalid, but more would come if they realized how utterly *not*-American it looks, despite the multitude of shiny modern buildings and one sore-thumb of a skyscraper.

Consider the main stem, *Via Roma*, running for half a mile from the railway station to Piazza Castello. This magnificent artery, rebuilt from the ground up during a six-year Mussolinian drive from 1932 to 1938, is arcaded for its whole length—and what arcades! On either side of the street they are a good twenty feet wide, the buildings over them being upheld by rows of massive pillars, and the shop windows on them forming the brightest array in Italy. They are so spacious, these gleaming arcades, that dozens of cheerful cafés are allowed to set out their tables and chairs in them, and other cafés, almost in the manner of Venice, flourish in all the piazze.

Three of these squares, spaced at intervals along Via Roma, bring touches of repose to the busy broad way. The first is *Piazza Carlo Felice*, surrounded by the most animated shop-and-café arcades of all, but centered by an ample lawn and garden which is as immaculately kept as any I have ever seen. The middle square is *Piazza San Carlo*, architecturally the finest in the city. It has a past as venerable as the city itself, for in its center, where now stands the fine equestrian statue of Emmanuel Philibert, there stood, in Roman times, a pagan altar. The square farthest from the station, *Piazza Castello*, is of enormous size, quite able to absorb in its center the big Palazzo Madama (now housing a Museum of Ancient Art), so named because it was the palace of two Royal Ladies of the House of Savoy, Marie Christine and Jeanne Baptiste. On the far side of the square, and on the *Piazza Reale* beyond it, is the rambling complex of another palace, the huge *Royal Palace of the Kings of Sardinia*. It contains, in one wing, a collection of armor hardly matched in Europe; and attached to the palace, though fronting on a different square, is the cathedral, notable for a dome of unusual design and for its housing of the Holy Shroud. This treasured Shroud, kept in an urn on the altar of a special chapel, is devotedly believed by countless of the faithful to be the very one in which Christ's body was wrapped after its removal from the Cross.

Mention of palaces and royalty brings up thought of one of the city's chief hotels, of luxury class, located just off Via Roma and actually an integral part of the big development concluded in 1938, for its name is *Albergo Principi di Piemonte* (Princes of Piedmont). Built in the spacious style of the whole enterprise and lavish with marble and fine decorations, this hotel is one of the distinguished ones of Italy, though Turin's newly rebuilt *Ligure* has more modernities. I once lodged in a sixth-floor room of the Principi that gave me a window's-eye view of the whole city and its environs. All about me were modern, well-gardened penthouse apartments, and a short distance away rose the contrasting bulk of the palaces and the interesting dome of the cathedral. The central skyline was disfigured by two odd punctuation marks. One of them, a few blocks to the north, was the ugly red-brick skyscraper which Turin bitterly deplores and which its council talks very seriously of cutting down to size, though the cost of such an operation, including indemnities to tenants, would be as high as the building. The other, a few blocks to the northeast, was a queer metal spire stabbing the sky to such a "depth" that it dwarfed its brick neighbor. Inquiry revealed that it was the spire of the *Mole Antonelliana*, a building constructed a century ago by an architect named Antonelli. It was intended to be a synagogue for a Jewish congregation, but was rejected by the Jews, and no wonder, for it is a strange unworshipful thing indeed, or at least its spire is. The iron shaft, as slender as a Titan's spear, rises 550 feet into the blue. The building below it now houses a Museum of Italian History.

Nature's skyline, successfully abetted in one case by an eighteenth-century architect, named Iuvara, I found most alluring. On the edge of the city, to the east, rose the 1500-foot hill called *Superga*, with Iuvara's masterpiece, the *Royal Basilica*, crowning it and raising the height of the hill, while off to the northwest, very much farther away and needing clear weather to bring out the contours to advantage, were the "big boys" of the French-Italian Alps.

Leaving the Alps for later exploration, I hastened to make my way up to Superga. Having my little car, I let its motor haul me up, but without such aid it would still have been easy to make the ascent. A tramway leads from the station to the suburb of Sassi, and a funicular mounts from there to the Basilica. Regular busses also make the zigzag climb.

The *Basilica*, with a terrace that offers a grand panoramic view, is of huge proportions, topped by a great broad dome and two campanili. It serves as a royal resting place, its crypt containing tombs of the Princes of Piedmont. The Basilica itself became a death trap on the fateful day of May 4, 1949, when a championship football team of Italy was being flown back from Lisbon. The plane was supposed to land at Milan, but because of a storm there the pilot was instructed to land at Turin instead. Bad weather prevailed also in the Turin area but landing seemed quite practicable. Preparatory to descending, the plane circled over Superga, but in the thick weather it didn't go *quite* high enough. A wing tip barely brushed against the eastern wall of the Basilica and this was enough to throw the plane out of control and send it crashing in flames on the hilltop. The crew and all of the team were killed, and on the spot where this tragedy occurred a moving monument now stands to commemorate I CAMPIONI D'ITALIA.

A city of such background, importance and varied interests as Turin, has, of course, many sights to see. Its Roman remains are numerous, its *Egyptian Museum* is second in its field only to the Royal Museum in Cairo, its *Galleria Sabauda* (Savoy Gallery) is an art museum of high rank, and several of its churches are agreeably unconventional, especially the improbable "chapel cluster" of the *Consolata*, but I think it is chiefly for easygoing pleasures, for modernities, for outdoor fun, for little excursions, for good food in good settings, that one should come to this city.

Under the head of little excursions one must place Rívoli, eight miles due west by a straight road. A decrepit electric railway to it is now being replaced by modern busses. Tourists who go there find that the name Rívoli means more than a shopping street of Paris, more even than a Napoleonic triumph. It means also a huge castle built by Iuvara, with a romantic view down upon red-tiled roofs and a closer view of the Alps than is afforded by Superga.

Under the head of good food in good settings—but I must gather myself and try to cope with this succulent subject.

The *Cambio Restaurant*, in Piazza Carignano, opposite the striking baroque *Carignano Palace*, where the first Italian Parliament met, is the unchallenged dean of Turin's restaurants and by far the most important in historical associations. Items in the city's archives establish the fact that bills were being paid to the Cambio as early as 1710, for instance 2 lire for three cups of chocolate, and 2 lire for 15 soldi for "*due portugalli*." In 1818, as chroniclers attest, it was a popular social and business rendezvous. In the middle years of the nineteenth century, Count Cavour and other statesmen of dawning Italy often ate here. Cavour's favorite table is still indicated by a plaque. I ate here, at the table next to Cavour's, and loved the place. In this old-fashioned setting the Cambio served me one of the memorable meals of my travel life.

L'Caval d'Brôns, which, I suppose, is Piedmontese for the "Bronze Horse," referring to the near-by equestrian statue, is the name of a restaurant under the arcade of the Square of San Carlo and extending onto the pavement of the square itself. It has been going only since about 1947, but its food is wonderful and its reputation is rising. Give it a couple of hundred years and who knows to what heights the Bronze Horse may climb.

While in Piazza San Carlo, I must insert three surreptitious notes: 1. *Confetteria Stratta*, on the same side of the square as the Bronze Horse, makes very wonderful confectionery, has been making it since 1836. Try its chocolates and see what you think of them. 2. The *Caffé Torino*, on the other side of the square, is an upstart, but is today the city's most fashionable arcade-and-piazza café. 3. In an arcaded building of Piazza Castello—to give the other square its convivial due—a man named A. B. Carpano (accented Cárpano) developed his formula for the famous vermouth that many connoisseurs consider the best in Italy. A tablet sets forth the story and gives the date, 1786, of this pleasant event.

The *Old San Giorgio Restaurant*, in the *Parco del Valentino*, on the Po's left bank, is an eating place of special glamor because of its setting. To reach it you stroll through the beautiful riverside park, pass the Renaissance-style *Castle of Valentino* and enter the *Borgo Medioevale*. The last two words mean *Medieval Village* and here there are faithful and fascinating reproductions of old homes, inns, shops. You'll see, for one item, a replica of Piedmont's first inn, labeled over its door as an "Office of Pity" and promising to passing pilgrims bed, light and fire. In the Medieval Village is a *Medieval Castle*, containing carefully made models of all the castles in Piedmont. On the side of the Borgo that borders the Po you presently find the San Giorgio Restaurant and take your seat at a table close to the broad river—for excellent drinks and viands.

On a summer's day when I enjoyed the San Giorgio, including the little excitements of the river's gay boating life, I topped off the meal by strolling across the Umberto I Bridge and mounting the little rise called *Monte dei Cappuccini* to enter the small church of Santa Maria del Monte on its summit. This has a special flavor as a church in which schoolchildren and older students write their very practical petitionary prayers on the walls, and even on the statuary, despite stern signs that state: *E Vietato Scrivere sui Muri* (It is Forbidden to Write on the Walls). I saw literally thousands of such earnest pleas and deciphered some of them. Five samples I here record in translation, exactly as they appeared.

Carlo: *Jesus, Help me to pass my exams, so I can have my bike.*

Lilliana: *Help me to secure the love of Umberto.*

Vittorio: *St. Anthony, Help me to remain always good and protect my family.*

Carolina: *Let me have my boy.* (This was written with lipstick.)

Giulio: *Jesus, Help me to find my ball, or else Daddy will give me the dickens.*

The Fiat Colossus at Home

For an American traveler to discuss a huge foreign motor car corporation in any detail would be inept, but any picture of Turin without some mention of Fiat, whose very name incorporates the name of the city, would be an absurdity, besides which, the magnitude of this concern, coupled with its practical importance in tourism, makes it an item of travel news.

Fabbrica Italiana Automobili Torino is a world firm, big even by American standards of bigness. In Turin alone, its birthplace and home town, its nine plants and foundries turn out many types of private cars, tractors, busses, even trains and airplanes, in addition to a great variety of motors for land, sea and air locomotion. Diesel engines made by Fiat in Turin alone are today driving some eight hundred large ships of twenty nations through all the Seven Seas. Wherever the tourist goes, outside North America, he may discover that he is being "moved" by Fiat. In Greece last year, for instance, I rode from Athens to Corinth on a fast "automotor" train made at Plant Number 7 in this city, though I didn't know it at the time.

In the *Mirafiori Plant* (Number 1) a completed Fiat car is turned out every three minutes, and later it is tested on the curving *pista,* where test experts tear along scores of times a day in successive cars as though the devil were after them, and there has been not one accident—so far. Could you use a statistic or two? Here are some. The Mirafiori Plant employs nearly 25,000 workers in two shifts. Its glass roofs cover 93 acres of ground. Its main works building is 1640 feet wide, just under half a mile long. There are seven miles and more of railway track in the works, five miles of underground passages. I could go on, but perhaps you've had enough.

Paternalistic care for the workers is carried to very great lengths. In Turin alone there are all sorts of sport and cultural centers, hospitals, sanatoria, day nurseries, and in various parts of Italy there are last-word holiday homes. Whenever you come across an enormous round white tower that looks like a modernistic hotel, it is probably such an establishment for Fiat workers. I happened upon one at the beach of Marina di Massa, near Carrara, and was so amazed by its sixteen stories of gleaming modernity—it proved clearly *not* to be a hotel or public building—that I hunted up a policeman in Massa town to ask what it was. Another such tower is Úlzio, in western Piedmont.

It is quite possible, by making arrangements with the company at least twenty-four hours in advance, to visit the Mirafiori Plant, possible, that is, for *men.* Women, alas, are barred from the roaring monster. I made my application, picturing hours of wearisome trudging, but had a pleasant surprise. I was *driven* through the plant, hither and yon, at a very slow pace, in about three-quarters of an hour.

Outside the plant I saw a newly produced *Campagnola,* a chamois of a jeep that they told me could climb nimbly up cathedral steps, plunge through underbrush, bounce along on rocky river beds and, if necessary, ford streams. Car demonstrations are *not* a part of the sightseeing program, but by wheedling I managed to get myself taken along on a test run of one of these cars. It was an *experience,* and if my bones ache in recollection, I must admit that quite literally "I asked for it." The Campagnola did everything I've just mentioned. It also climbed and unclimbed young precipices that had it seemingly poised first on its derrière, then on its broad nose. In all these operations it never twitched an eyelash nor lamed a muscle. I did both. I was more than glad to return, after the test, to my modest Tina, seat myself gingerly behind the wheel and set off on good paved roads for the mountains of Piedmont.

The Valley of Aosta and the White Roof of Europe

The *Autonomous Valley of Aosta* is 3200 square kilometers of grandeur comprised in one "collector valley," that of Aosta itself, on an east-west axis, with the River Dora Báltea running through it, and a dozen lateral, tributary valleys, six each from north and from south, carved respectively out of the Swiss-Italian Alps and out of the Alpi Graie, with their glacial rampart of the *Gran Paradiso.* Two of the branch valleys manage to keep on going—up and over—crossing famous passes, the *Great St. Bernard* (8170 feet) from Aosta over to Martigny in Switzerland's Rhone Valley, the *Little St. Bernard* from Pré-St.-Didier over to Bourg-St.-Maurice and Albertville in France.

Scores of the peaks that fence in Aosta's lateral valleys rise to heights of 13,000 feet. The *Matterhorn (Monte Cervino), Monte Rosa* and *Mont Blanc* reach heights, in this order, of 14,692, 15,201 and 15,872 feet, the last-named being, as every schoolboy knows, the highest mountain in Europe.

Racially, politically and economically, the Aosta Region is a curious anomaly. Though an integral part of Italy, its language and heritage are French and its people speak French, almost to a man—and woman and child. Its publications, including its handsome travel brochure and *dépliants,* are very frequently in French. Its official correspondence is carried on largely in French. If you write in English to a government official in Aosta, as I did, you will receive an answer in French, as I did.

Italy gives Aosta lots of rope and is smart in doing so, for it thus engenders contentment and a sense almost of independence. The Valley —using this word in its broad sense—has many special privileges, including exemption from various burdensome taxes of Italy. Gasoline, for instance, is not taxed here by Italy, but it *is* taxed, in full measure, by the Aosta government itself. The motorist pays just the same per liter that he pays anywhere else in Italy (though special abatement cards *are* procurable), but the whopping tax, now 86 lire per liter, goes straight into Valley coffers.

Ever so many Italian excise and sumptuary taxes also, perpetual sources of grief and "griping" elsewhere, are not in force in the Valley. This practical application of autonomy, rather than some glittering picture of it, or any mustering of repressive measures, works out well for all concerned. Italy has in its national fold a Happy Valley that speaks an alien tongue.

From a traveler's angle there is nothing in all the richness of Italy that surpasses *Le Pays d'Aoste*, to use the name by which it calls itself. From the moment you enter it, at Pont-St.-Martin, till the various cableways hoist you up to Europe's glistening rooftree, you feel you are in a special compartment of Holiday, one with an A-plus rating. I will try to explain the contours of this compartment, as the average traveler, not the rugged Alpinist, sees them. Perhaps a point-by-point approach will make for clarity. I have made my explorations by car, but they can be done, without too much awkwardness, by train and bus. The SADEM system of Turin runs several busses a day between that city and St.-Vincent, chief resort in the main Valley, and some extra ones between St.-Vincent and Aosta. Trains also run, and with fair frequency, from Turin and Milan to Aosta, a smaller electric line pushing on from there to Pré-St.-Didier.

Pont-St.-Martin provides a wonderful introduction. It has a Roman bridge over the Torrente Lys that is the very picture of what a Roman bridge should be. It is the picturesque *dos-d'âne type*, common in southern France. You may walk up and over its "saddle," though motor cars and busses must use the modern bridge close by. From this introductory town, a branch valley, with infrequent bus service, leads to *Gressoney-St.-Jean* and *Gressoney-la-Trinité*, little resorts at the foot of Monte Rosa that are the climber's delight. An oddity of this one valley is that *German* is spoken instead of French or Italian.

Bard, a bit farther up, has a fortress that creates an overpowering impression of strength. If you are motoring, plan to "stop by" and take a coffee on the terrace of the *Albergo Reale*, letting the colossal bulk of the fortress overpower you. Napoleon brought his army through this defile in 1800 and by clever strategy captured the stronghold.

Verrès introduces you in an elegant manner to the Castles of the Valley, a famous and wonderful race, said by counters of castles to number ninety-eight! To your right is the *Château de Verrès*, a most imposing fastness of the fourteenth century. To your left, across the Dora Báltea, is the *Château d'Issogne*, a bit dull and dour outside but luxurious inside. Push into the courtyard and you'll see an iron well head of such artistry that it was picked for reproduction in Turin's Medieval Village. It represents a growing pomegranate tree. I saw the replica before I saw the original. A branch valley carries seventeen miles north from Verrès to a small resort named *Champoluc*.

St.-Vincent, at the "turn of the Valley," where the east-west axis commences, is the sophisticated member of Valley communities. It is a spa of some importance, with curative waters from a *Fons Salutis*, and it has a grand establishment combining a de luxe hotel (the *Billia*) with a sumptuous *casino*. This casino, complete with several gambling rooms and a cabaret, expects to keep on doing business whatever the Italian government may ultimately decide to do about other casinos. Why? Because this is the *Autonomous* Valley of Aosta. The closing of the place would break open a hornet's nest of resentment, and even far-away Rome might feel the stings.

A special hotel of St.-Vincent seems to me to call for special mention. I refer to *Hotel du Parc*, a second-category house with a first-category atmosphere. It is run by a Valley resident who was born in Baltimore and is proud of carrying an American passport. The food is more than locally famous and deserves its reputation. I have spent but one night here, had but one meal. This brief visit, however, was quite enough to make me an "intending repeater."

Châtillon, only two miles beyond St.-Vincent, is the junction point for the branch valley that leads up to Breuil, and what a goal that is! In seventeen miles, the road climbs up to one of the mightiest settings in Europe.

Breuil, called on Italian maps *Cervinia*, is a resort of top rank, with such excellent first-class hostelries as the *Gran Baita*, the *Gran Cervinia* and the *Monte Cervino*. It is situated at the upper tip of the valley called *Valtournanche*, at the point where it announces to panting motor cars, "Thus far and no farther." Above it tower two of the Alps' most famous giants, the *Matterhorn* and *Monte Rosa*, and to a shoulder of each of these giants we may go the painless way, by aerial cableway. Both of these funivie start from the same station, right in Breuil, and ascend to the first halting point, *Plan Maison*, at an altitude of 8500 feet. From here, one of them proceeds, in two lifts, with a change of cars at a half-way halt, to *Plan Rosa*, 11,600 feet high. The other, opened in 1951, mounts to *Col Furggen*, at about 11,000 feet. Plan Rosa is really less a shoulder than a sort of saddle between the two giants, though much nearer to Monte Rosa. Col Furggen is a rugged ledge only about 3500 feet below the Matterhorn's sharp summit.

Plan Rosa puts you in intimate touch with the eternal snows, for endless smooth fields of whiteness lie all about and below you. Monte Rosa is not a savage of the Alps but a sophisticate, always wearing ermine. No wild head or gesturing fist of rock is thrust up into the sky. Indeed there is hardly the least evidence of any rock at all, but just one clear expanse of unsullied snow. This is said to have a depth of scores of feet, perhaps hundreds in some places. The stone platform where the funivia leaves you is squarely on the frontier between Italy and Switzerland, and markers indicate the line. On the Swiss side, you may look down into the valley where Zermatt rests and almost, but not quite, see Zermatt itself. You do actually see the Gornergrat and the funicular that ascends to it from Zermatt. The hotel at the Gornergrat is considerably below the point where you stand. You may step over to the terrace of the Swiss customs cabin, if you like, and thus be undeniably in Switzerland. I did so, wrote some post cards there and gave them to a friendly Swiss customs guard to mail for me in Zermatt. "I'll be skiing down the valley in three or four days," he said.

The *Castle of Fénis*, across the river from *Nus*, eight miles up the main Aosta Valley from the junction of Châtillon, is often called the finest in the region. Certainly it is also one of the best kept up.

Aosta, a considerable town centering the whole "collector valley" and all its tributaries, is noteworthy for really wonderful Roman remains, for this was *Augusta Praetoria*, an important outpost of the empire founded in 25 B.C. It is still surrounded by the original Roman walls, whose towers are reminders of imperial power, and even the traveler who is most eagerly hastening on to Europe's highest mountain cannot fail to be impressed by the *Arch of Augustus* and the *Porta Praetoria*, through which he rides into town. Just *before* passing through this latter, he may detour very slightly to see a medieval church (*Sant'Orso*), cloister and priory of unusual charm; and just *after* passing through, he will see, and cannot miss, the lofty remaining portion of the *Roman Theater*.

Aosta is a good town for a stopover and there is a pleasant place to stay, *Hotel de la Couronne*, on the central Place Emile Chanoux—how very French it all sounds, and is—but the scenery is less impressive here and few travelers can keep their eagerness on leash. I, for one, could not, so I pushed on, after three or four hours and a good lunch, to higher and narrower valleys. The Great St. Bernard route diverges from the Valley, as I have said, at Aosta, reaching the celebrated Hospiz at the top of the pass (8235 feet) in twenty-five tortuous miles of climbing, but having visited this goal previously from the Swiss side, I hastened on by the main route to Pré-St.-Didier and then three miles more to Courmayeur, at the base of Mont Blanc.

Courmayeur is the only place in the whole Pays d'Aoste that can rival, point for point, the resort of Breuil. Lying at 4000 feet altitude within a magnificent cirque dominated by the White Mountain, monarch of them all, this is one of the choicest places in the world from which to *look*. Having done that to your fill, you may go aloft by a funivia that starts from Entrèves, a hamlet two miles or so up the narrowing valley of the Dora Báltea. Entrèves is interesting in its own right as the Italian terminus of the international highway tunnel now being bored directly through Mont Blanc. Construction of this 26-foot-wide tunnel, a mammoth enterprise, was started in the summer of 1952. It will connect La Dalmaz, near Chamonix (France), with Entrèves and Courmayeur.

To return from future to present wonders, the funivia will lift you smoothly to the *Col du Géant*, at a height of 11,000 feet on the eastern flank of the mountain. Here a fine "refuge," the *Rifugio Torino*, was built in 1952. It is a warming and comforting place that has been much needed, and in size it is surprisingly ample. It has 250 beds and can feed 450 persons at once.

This Rifugio Torino, like Courmayeur, is a supreme place from which to look, in this case *up* at Mont Blanc, *down* at the toy-sized houses so far below, and *over* at the Chamonix Valley of France.

Courmayeur has thirty-four hotels, one of them, the *Royal Bertolini*, being first class. The resort has also a second funivia, this one swinging across the Dora and up to a lovely grassy ledge called *Plan Chécrouit* (7300 feet), where *Le Petit Père*, an extremely humble little restaurant, can serve you food and drinks. The Little Father has no style whatever, but he does have a view!

It may surprise you, as it did me, to find how little it costs to mount to these various heights by aerial cableway. Even the ones that carry you to the highest points, to Plan Rosa and Col du Géant, ask less than three dollars for the whole thing, up and down. It is a mystery how they can be operated at such fares, but all the world likes mysteries, and these of the Valley are as exciting to the senses as any you will ever find.

CHAPTER 29

GREAT GENOA AND ITS TANDEM RIVIERA

The Crescent of the Centuries

THE crescent of central Genoa has a character quite as distinctive, in a setting quite as beautiful, as its perennial maritime rival, Naples. Naples gets the big play in tourist publicity because it has Pompeii, Vesuvius, Capri, Sorrento, Amalfi, but *as a city* Genoa matches Naples point for point in beauty and in charm, while its background far surpasses in splendor and power that of Naples. Genoa is the city of Simon Bocanegra, the vigorous "lifetime doge" (1339-63) who first raised it to a level of distinction. It is also the true birthplace of Columbus, though several other places, in other countries, maintain feeble claims to this honor. It is the city of the Doria Family—the name was long as illustrious as that of Dandolo in Venice—a family that helped to win the city's medieval sobriquet *Genova Superba*. Its vessels roamed the Mediterranean and added conquest to conquest, though finally internal conflicts brought it low and its glory was eclipsed by the newer power and glory of its Adriatic opponent.

Genoa declined sadly, but in time it recovered and became once more a city of wealth and prestige. During the Second World War it suffered enormous damage, especially in its port works (320 ships were at the bottom of its harbor by 1944), but recovery was rapid this time, and today it is certainly the leading port city of Italy, with an immense maritime trade. As an attraction to tourists, at least to those who give it a chance and do not hustle right away to Florence or Milan, it has a charm all its own, for it is strongly individual, with little resemblance to any other city. It is built all up and down against a ring of hills, with a whole battery of funiculars ascending and descending like the angels in Jacob's dream. Its tiny *vicoli*, some of them so narrow that one has to flatten oneself against a wall to let the other fellow pass, are weird and fascinating. Its *Circonvallazione a Monte*, a lofty winding highway that ties the Genoese hills with a band of scenery (take trolleybus #83 from in front of Hotel Savoia-Majestic), is a miracle of lovely tortuosity. Its Via Garibaldi is a chain of medieval palaces, red, white and silver-gray. Its harbor is churned into foam with shipping whose burden, in good years, totals seven or eight million tons. Its two Rivieras, named respectively for the rising and the setting sun, stretch on and on to bright horizons.

The waterfront of Genoa is the city's great magnet for many, and with good reason. If we grant that it is unkempt, disreputable, a seething sector of blatant dance halls catering to sailor sins, we must grant too that it rims a harbor of myriad activities, and we must at least take mental note of one relieving fact. The world's first bank took form here, in the 1400's, in the Palazzo San Giorgio on Piazza Caricamento, a building constructed at Bocanegra's order in the year 1260. The building is now used by the Port Authority, but its dignified old *Hall of the Buyers* and its magnificent *Hall of the Captain of the People*, dating from its civic use before establishment of the bank, may be visited by special request.

Don't be dainty in viewing Genoa's waterfront. If you venture there at all, accept it, smells and all. In reaching it, find, if you can, the Vico dell'Amor Perfetto (Lane of Perfect Love) and stroll through it to the ancient Street of the Jewelers and the Square of the Banks. Then, on the waterfront itself, make your way along the frenetic Sottoripa ("Underbank"), through the hordes of black-market vendors, dodging the tipsy seafaring folk and the knots of dance-hall girls, greedy for customers. You'll see enough queer sights in half an hour to stock your memory cells for life.

Today's Genoa, Its Amenities and Luxuries

Today's Genoa is a relatively easy city for the visitor to understand and he is aided by one of the most effective EPT offices in Italy, at 11 Via Roma. Its tourist literature is copious and easy to use. One booklet, in particular, called merely *Genoa* and prepared for the EPT by the Italian Touring Club, is very handy. It tells the essentials crisply and its maps are extremely clear and simple to use—even in a bus, or on a windy day. As a personal note, I must mention that EPT's buoyant Giulio Tobino, speaking fluent English and even American, gave me unstinted aid in the preparation of this text.

The essentials of Genoa's orientation are easy to grasp, for one need only view it as a city of layers, somewhat as in the case of Bérgamo, though in very different form and color from the Lombard city. The lowest layer here is the bawdy and congested half circle of the port. The middle layer is tourist Genoa, with the big hotels, the bright shops and the places of entertainment. The upper layer is the coronet of hills, reached by zigzag streets, funiculars and outright elevators. For most of the amenities of the metropolis, which now concern us, we look, of course, to the middle layer.

This central level is, in turn, easy to understand, since it is clearly tied to two main squares, about a mile apart as the roads go, and these squares are tied together by a fast and frequent service (line 70) of trolleybusses. The northwestern anchor-square is *Piazza Acquaverde*, where the main railway station (*Porto Principe*) and the big hotels are located (American Express, Cook and CIT are here too); the southeastern anchor-square is *Piazza De Ferrari*, where the opera house, the fine shops, the cinemas and the big restaurants are found. One of the streets through which the trolleybusses race from the former square to the latter is *Via Garibaldi*, beyond a doubt the finest street of medieval palaces in Italy.

The hotels on and near Piazza Acquaverde are a select group indeed. The *Colombia-Excelsior* has a de luxe rating; the *Savoia-Majestic* is one of the half dozen most modern hotels in the country; and besides these leaders there are numerous other hotels of the first and second category in the square and on Via Balbi, which leads from it.

Hotel Savoia-Majestic, whose Italian name, Albergo Savoia-Maestoso, has such an impressively musical sound, is one of my personal favorites in all Italy. After being terribly hurt by bombs in the Second World War, it was rebuilt from the foundation up in 1949 and 1950, and during the next eighteen months a difficult installation of air conditioning was achieved, a feature which is nearly unique in Italian hotels. It is found here not only in the public rooms but in all the bedrooms, though its use there is, of course, *optional.* If you don't like the "claustro-feeling" of being sealed up in coolness you may depend on the breezes of Genoa's "Greenwater Square," which is the meaning of Piazza Acquaverde, to keep your room aired.

Each of the 120 rooms has its private tub-and-shower bath and you won't find anything more modern anywhere in plumbing or appointments or fluorescent lighting. In all these respects it quite matches the new *Vesuvio* of Naples. There's enough marble in this Genoa hotel to qualify it as a Doria or Pallavicini palazzo, but it conveys no hint of formality, for the rugs and furnishings lend warmth and a feeling as of home. Some of the bedroom floors (those on the sixth floor) are of cork, than which nothing has more appeal for slippered feet; and as a special courtesy to your vision, the architect matched the color of the cork with the bathroom floorings of *brown marble*. I am almost surprised that some device does not also brown one's body with a rich and immediate sun tan!

The view over the busy harbor and the tall sixteenth-century *lanterna* (lighthouse) from the upper front rooms, and possibly also from those of the adjacent *Londra e Continentale*, a recommendable place of the second category, is endlessly exciting, and this view is not to be had from the front rooms of the various hotels on the other side, so if the drama and melodrama of a great port count in your planning, consider that point. But in any front room of any hotel on Piazza Acquaverde you should consider also the remarkable acoustics of that square. Every sound comes funneling up to your windows as if a concert-hall architect had planned it that way—only the sounds are rarely of concert quality. Personally I love all this commotion, at whatever hour, but I'm a peculiar type. When I'm in a city I like city noises. You may very well prefer a room that looks out on some other view than the lusty, gusty one of Piazza Acquaverde.

In the neighborhood of Piazza De Ferrari, the center of centers, there is one first-class hotel, the *Bristol e Palazzo*, on Via XX Settembre, a fine arcaded thoroughfare that leads east from the big square. Via Dante, leading southeast from the same square, brings the stroller to Piazza Dante, where he may enter a *grattacielo* (skyscraper), one of two that are the pride of the city, and ascend by elevator thirty-one stories to a famous restaurant and café on the top floor, with open terraces on all sides. This establishment, known to a generation of travelers as the *Capurro,* but now, under different management, named the *Olimpo,* is first class and its good orchestra makes it something of a cabaret in the evening hours. There are, of course, other restaurants of interest in Genoa, for example *Sacco* on Via Roma, *Gino* on Via XX Settembre, *San Pietro alla Foce,* a sort of terrace restaurant on Viale Brigate Partigiane and a character place called *Angela,* close to Piazza Caricamento; and there are some delightful haunts for seafood in the fishy quarter called *Boccadasse* (Monkeymouth), especially that of *Vittorio,* but the mid-air location of the Olimpo, under whatever name, continues to "pack them in" more than its rivals. Seated at an airside table beside the outer railing of the terrace, you feel that you are floating on a space-raft high above the bustle of downtown Genoa, which is, in turn, high above the crescent harbor. By day, by dusk, by evening lights, this place is a tourist's dream.

One other square of Genoa, or circle, should be known to the visitor as an orientation point, namely Piazza Corvetto, near the center but on slightly higher ground than the others stressed. It is reachable by trolleybus #77 from Piazza Acquaverde. Piazza Corvetto is a pleasant and important hub of traffic and on it is a new hotel, by name the *Corvetto Plaza.* On the square too is the smartest tearoom and *pasticceria* in the city, by name *Mangini.*

From an adjacent square, with the fascinating name *Largo Eros Lanfranco,* Genoa's Galleria stretches down a long decline almost to Piazza De Ferrari. It is a glass-covered one, like those of other cities, but with only one un-branching trunk. It bears the name *Galleria Mazzini,* which is appropriate, since that patriot was born in Genoa and is buried in its Staglieno Cemetery. A statue of him graces Piazza Corvetto.

The City Circuit—Predigested

The *Giro della Città,* or Circuit of the City, as purveyed by CIT, American Express and others, is something that I find it easy to forego, for it always concentrates, far too much for my enjoyment, on the dusty statuary of the *Staglieno Cemetery* and races like a bus possessed through most of the glories of central Genoa.

I suppose I am being unfair, since it is an undeniable fact that this city's Camposanto really attracts many visitors and its competitive marbles of mourning *are* a queer and exotic sight for Americans. The dust of ages has so veiled and saturated these marbles that, as I was assured, they literally *cannot* be cleaned properly without chipping off some of the stone itself.

Amid many mawkish expressions of sorrow for the departed, each great family striving, as usual in these cemeteries, to "outgrieve" the other in splendor, one sees some marks of deep feeling. I have not been too much impressed with such efforts as the sumptuous monument representing a pipe organ in black and gray marble, nor with such grandiose memorials as the private funerary chapel built as a miniature of the Milan Cathedral, but I *was* moved when I saw, in sculpture, a young girl emerging from a dark forest (*per una selva oscura*) to a cheerful heaven; and by a still younger girl, of about six, by name Claruccia Isolabella, breaking the chains of her suffering to enter paradise. The *queerest* monument of all the queer ones is surely that of a peanut vendress selling peanuts and sweet bread rings. We see it all in the enduring marble and are assured by the guide that the earnest woman scrimped and saved all her life so as to be able "to hold up her head in death" with as grand a memorial as the rich folks. Her monument was completed three years before she died, so she had that length of time to enjoy gloating over it. The beholder doesn't know whether to laugh at the absurdity of it or weep for the pathos of it.

The predigested tour always halts for a glimpse of the humble (and genuine) childhood home of Columbus, where a Latin inscription advises us that here *Christophorus Columbus Pueritiam Primamque Iuventam Transegit* (spent his childhood and early youth). The tour always pauses also at a church or two, and some of the itineraries, including those of CIT, provide a half hour of relaxation on the terrace of the Olimpo, a welcome halt to all.

Of the churches, the one that deserves and receives the chief attention is the *Cathedral of San Lorenzo,* a remarkable architectural curiosity, for as it grew up, over the centuries, it grew from Romanesque to Gothic and from that to Renaissance. We can see the whole progression; and the zebra stripes, so typical of Genoese churches, though the idea is of Pisan origin, are an enhancement of the picture. Over the main portal, St. Lawrence, to whom the structure is dedicated, writhes on his griddle. Inside the church is the richly ornamented *Chapel of St. John the Baptist*, enshrining the very relics, so the faithful say, of the Precursor. These sacred bones were brought here in the year 1200 from Caesarea. Women are never allowed to enter this chapel and perhaps you have guessed the reason. It was a woman, Salome, who said to Herod the Tetrarch, "Give me John the Baptist's head in a charger," and Herod reluctantly complied.

If you visit San Lorenzo on your own and have time to stroll about the labyrinthine neighborhood between the Ducal Palace above it and the Palace (Bank) of San Giorgio below it, on the waterfront, you will be enthralled by the many evidences of Genoa's past greatness. Striped churches and striped palaces are everywhere, though palaces in this coloring were permitted only to four proud families, Doria, Spinola, Grimaldi and Fieschi. In many of these, perhaps now occupied by cobblers, seamstresses, little drudges of every humble type, you may catch fleeting glimpses of exquisite carvings in stone and wood and of ceilings adorned with bright frescoes. What a city must *La Superba* have been in the centuries of its pomp and circumstance.

To give yourself a good example of the rewards of such a stroll, make your way, with the aid of a detailed map, from San Lorenzo to the *Church of San Matteo*. This is a Doria church, 100 per cent, with inscriptions on the façade glorifying the family that built it and with the splendid tomb of Andrea Doria in the crypt. God seems almost an incidental figure in such an edifice. The little *Piazza San Matteo* on which it fronts is an exclusively Doria square, with a big old palace of that illustrious family dominating it. The palace is now a workaday building of little businesses, but you may easily see the splendors of it, including some glimpses of the interior. I have been told that an ancient dame of the Doria tribe, in relatively straitened circumstances, *still* inhabits an upper floor. From Piazza San Matteo pursue your way along the *Campetto*, a palace street, or long square, that was the center of Genoa in very early times, to reach the interesting *Church of Santa Maria delle Vigne* (Saint Mary of the Vineyards), whence it is but a short walk to Piazza Caricamento. This sample stroll, stimulating as it proves to be, could be matched by almost any walk in almost any direction from the Church of San Lorenzo.

Via Garibaldi, Italy's Finest Street of Palaces

As a Palace Highway, Via Garibaldi bears the same relation to Genoa that the Grand Canal bears to Venice, but in every other way it is as different as can possibly be. The Grand Canal is so conspicuous that no visitor can miss it. Via Garibaldi is so hidden that many visitors never find it, even though they may remain in the city for several days. By "hidden" I do not mean that this magnificent street is remote, or actually barred from vision. It is, as I have said, so central that when you take a bus from Piazza Acquaverde to Piazza De Ferrari you go roaring right through the whole length of it, which seems a terrible sacrilege to the Ghosts of Grandeur. Via Garibaldi is hidden because it is such a canyon of palaces, both sides solid with them, wall to wall, for three hundred yards, that unless you *walk* through it, flattening yourself against massive façades whenever traffic comes too close for comfort, you simply do not see it at all. So, by all that's wonderful in travel, hearken to my urging and traverse Garibaldi Street on foot, however iniquitous and unfragrant the motor traffic.

One man, the Perúgia-born architect Galeazzo Alessi (1512-72), of the school of Michelangelo, is mainly responsible for the whole *design* of Via Garibaldi (though he built few of the palaces), and indeed for the monumental look of sixteenth- and seventeenth-century Genoa in general, and this is worth knowing when you come upon a square and a street of this city that bear his name.

The "name palaces" of importance on Via Garibaldi—perhaps I should include here also the large *Royal Palace* on Via Balbi, which is of some interest—number about a dozen (there are more than sixty in the whole city), but I think only three need be viewed in the interior, the so-called *Palazzo Bianco* (White Palace), the *Palazzo Rosso* (Red Palace) and the *Palazzo Municipale,* or Town Hall, and before looking into the matter at all I urge that you arm yourself with a leaflet published by the EPT called *The Palaces and Museums of Genoa*. Supplementing the pocket guide *Genoa*, already mentioned, it presents thumbnail commentaries about each palace (and museum), including hours of admission. For fuller comment one may buy at some bookstore the illustrated booklet *I Palazzi di Genova*, with English and French text as well as Italian.

The *Palazzo Bianco*, at Number 11, was built in the sixteenth century, redesigned in the eighteenth, bombed to 60 per cent destruction in the Second World War and rebuilt since its close in faithful reproduction, the rebuilders even using no cement. In its latest form, this palace is a most amazing thing, an art gallery more modern in its appointments—I believe you will agree—than even the Mellen Gallery of Washington. In homelike comforts its planners have thought of everything—fine carpets, luxurious leather armchairs from which to survey the collections, Venetian blinds to control the entrance of daylight, latest and cleverest indirect lighting in every room. In displaying the works of art they have been equally thoughtful and even more ingenious. Fine plate glass cases enclose certain treasures which need to be seen both front and back. Electric devices raise and lower other treasures at will. The paintings and carvings in this most modern of galleries are not of supreme importance, though there are excellent Italian, French, Flemish and Oriental items. The gallery itself *is* important, a sight straight out of tomorrow.

The *Palazzo Rosso*, at Number 18, was built in the seventeenth century by Pietro Antonio Corradi. Like its neighbor across the way it was terribly hurt by bombing in the war (on October 22, 1942), but it is now in process of being reopened and its lovely old third-floor rooms, meticulously restored, house many fine paintings, chiefly by Italian masters.

A very interesting oddity attaches to the Palazzo Rosso. It was owned by a noble lady named Maria Brignole Sale De Ferrari, Duchessa di Gallieri. This lady lived much of her life in Paris, and loved that city, so before her death she drew up a strange will stipulating that no changes whatsoever could be made in her Genoa property, the building or its contents, without the official permission of the City of Paris, on penalty of the whole estate reverting to

Paris. That stipulation still holds. If the directors wish to make any alteration, however slight, they have to "clear" the matter with the Parisian authorities.

The *Palazzo Municipale*, sometimes called the *Doria Tursi Palace*, at Number 9, was designed in the middle of the sixteenth century by a follower of Alessi named Rocco Lurago and the skill with which he solved the problems of terrain—the back of the palace runs squarely into the Castelletto Hill—stamped him as a man of genius. This is the largest of Via Garibaldi's palaces and in many ways the most interesting, not only for its ingenious construction on several levels, with a courtyard part way up the slope, but for its rich decorations and its special contents. In the Committee Room is a bronze Roman tablet of 187 B.C. that fixed the boundaries of the Genoese, and, of more recent date, there are some remains of a famous son, Columbus, kept reverently in a special case. In another room a favorite violin of Nicolò Paganini is displayed, a Guarneri del Gesu. It has been played, in public, four times in recent years (all since the Second World War) by trusted artists, three of these times by a well-known violinist named De Barbieri.

In connection with visiting this palace, take note of an interesting thing about the "geography" of Via Garibaldi, and incidentally about political psychology. Directly opposite the palace's main entrance is an alley called Vico del Duca that plunges down into the old town. It is really picturesque and adds a strong touch of contrast to the Street of Palaces. But had you been here in Mussolini's day and had you emerged from the Palazzo Municipale you would not have seen the Vico del Duca. In Fascist thinking it was untidy, disreputable, so the upper end of it was completely blocked from sight.

Electric Ladders to the Heights

The only way to appreciate Genoa's infinite variety of charms is to allow time enough for personal explorations, not only of the early and later medieval sectors, the waterfront and the city of today but certainly also of the heights. By taking the prepared tour one rolls along the Circonvallazione a Monte, perhaps with a halt at some marvelous viewpoint like Piazzale San Francesco, but this is hardly more than a tantalizing hint of what the hills offer. I will list, in order, from northwest to southeast, six of the heights reached by "electric ladders" of one sort or another.

1. *Granarolo*, a lofty hamlet with church, is reached by an ancient funicular that ascends from Via Pagano Doria, behind the main railway station of Porto Principe (Piazza Acquaverde).

2. *Montegalletto* (together with the Circonvallazione a Monte) is reached by an elevator from Via Balbi, close to Hotel Savoia-Majestic.

3. The so-called *Righi*, whose name seems a needless "plagiarism" in the lovely heights of this ultra-Italian city, is a full thousand feet above the harbor, but is swiftly reached by a funicular (making several intermediate stops) from Piazza Corridoni. Its lofty position on a saddle affords a magnificent double view, one outlook toward the city and the sea, the other toward Genoa's hinterland, a dramatic tumble of hills and vales, some of the nearer low spots packed solid with factories or with humble dwelling quarters. There is a terrace restaurant called *Ristorante Righi*, with a prospect that used to be very remarkable but is nowadays somewhat hindered by persistently growing trees in front of it.

4. *Il Castelletto* (The Little Castle), a convenient viewpoint on the Circonvallazione a Monte, is reached by means of an ordinary elevator from Piazza Portello, one block north of Via Garibaldi.

5. *Sant'Anna*, reached by another of the city's serried funiculars, this one starting from the same Piazza del Portello, is another goal of views almost as good as the best, but not quite, I think. The Righi, if you climb up a bit from the funicular station and the restaurant, is my personal best.

6. *Casella*, terminus of a tiny mountain railway whose Genoa station is just above Piazza Manin, hardly qualifies as a high spot of the big city but it is a goal of some interest to those who enjoy taking such a toy railway "to see where it goes." This one goes to little lost towns of no conceivable importance, but exploration can be fun.

Riviera of the Rising Sun

Little counsel is needed for the enjoyment of Genoa's two Rivieras, except the gratuitous advice to visit them and have fun. They are called the *Riviera di Levante* (of the Rising Sun) and *Riviera di Ponente* (of the Setting Sun) and lie to the east and west respectively of Genoa.

The Rising Riviera is much nearer, in its best portions, than the other, and countless busses, including those of CIT, make the trip daily, for the benefit of turismo, to *Camogli, Santa Margherita Ligure, Portofino a Mare* (halt) and *Rapallo* (halt). It is a glorious littoral all the way, and the National Road hugs the sea except when it is forced to climb over a particularly rugged hill. The fishing hamlet of Portofino a Mare is a special magnet to holiday seekers and their eager cameras. The tourist babel at a few hundred café tables along the quays is a bit damaging to its innate charm, but does not succeed in destroying it. In this respect, though in no other, one is reminded of Cornwall's Clovelly, which is also able to withstand unceasing tourist invasions. Rapallo, the most famous of this Riviera's resorts, is usually the climax of the tours, but if you are driving or riding in a private car, you may roll your own climax, for you will find a score of wholly unsung wonders all along the coast, as well as such amply trumpeted marvels as *Portofino Vetta*, high above the sea, with its own *Grand Hotel* and an esplanade from which *both* Rivieras are seen stretching to hazy infinity.

Riviera of the Setting Sun

The *Setting Riviera* is industrially important, industrially dull for the first fifty or sixty miles west of Genoa. At *Albenga* and *Alássio* it picks up interest and at *San Remo* (85 miles) it is, of course, supremely beautiful and important, for this is a greater Rapallo. In fact, it is by far the largest and most flourishing resort on either Riviera. It has three de luxe hotels and hordes of lesser ones. Its *Municipal Casino*, though at present under a cloud of apprehension lest, perchance, the government shall decide to close it up, is Italy's great rival to the Casino of Monte Carlo, and the avenue of palms called Corso dell'Imperatrice is quite the equal in splendor, if not in length, of Nice's Promenade des Anglais.

I personally feel somewhat overborne by resorts of such grandiose proportions and ambitions, so I am always content to look briefly at

San Remo and then move along to some lesser place of equal loveliness, like *Ospedaletti* or *Bordighera*.

The sheltered nature of this whole Riviera di Ponente is almost a natural phenomenon. So thoroughly do the mountains protect it from the raw north winds that its climate is genuinely sub-tropical. The international CIAT route that connects Genoa and Nice, via San Remo, is really in order in calling itself *Nastro dei Fiori*, Ribbon of Flowers. There is nothing far-fetched about this fanciful tag, for the flowers are indeed as profuse and brilliant as in any favored spot of the whole Mediterranean. If you leave Italy by this route, I think the colors of it will be color-photographed in your mind for life.

CHAPTER 30

MEANDERINGS OF MEMORY

THE traveler's path of memory, after a trip packed to its limits with varied sights and experiences, is more unpredictable than the wind and its blowing. It bobs about "where it listeth," without seeming pattern, and that is one of its delights. Many travelers, certainly including this one, enjoy giving memory free play, letting it meander through the recent past, the past that is saturated with marvelous scenes of nature, with exotic sights and people, with interesting personal contacts, with small happenings, sometimes exciting, sometimes odd and funny to look back upon.

In the case that now concerns us, the traveler's memory will weave an intricate design from his store of *Italiana*, and there are no richer, more various, more absorbing materials of experience in the whole range of journeyings than those that are found in the long peninsula and the islands of Italy.

To illustrate the personal pleasure to be had from reminiscence, I shall here and now let my own memory meander for a bit wherever it will amid Italian scenes, without leash, without conscious direction. I shall be more interested than anyone else to see what places, people, sights, occurrences, it selects for its successive halts, as, for instance . . .

The 124 steps, a bit "skewgee," that lead to Rome's Church of Santa Maria in Aracoeli, on the Campidoglio. On my first visit, I found the main doors closed, but after all, I had only to descend the 124 steps and mount by *another* flight, about as high, to reach a side door. Nothing to it really, a mere 496 steps up and down.

The 28,000 shades of color—count 'em—seen in the mosaics of St. Peter's.

An ingenious scissor-grinder encountered on Via di Porta Angelica, outside St. Peter's. Whenever he was given a grinding job he would detach the chain from his bike, then fasten another one to the sprocket wheel and to a portable emery wheel that was affixed to his handle bars. He would then pedal energetically until the grinding was done, after which he would re-attach the regular chain and ride on, looking for his next customer.

An ingenious marketing custom, seen at its best in the "skyscraper slums" of old Naples. Housewives in these cliff-like buildings of crowded flats often shop by the basket-on-a-string method, lowering money to various vendors, chaffering in lusty shouts, and then drawing up the produce, along with their change.

The chains that hang by the hundred from barrels and buoys in Naples Bay for a special kind of "produce." Mussels in their thousands attach themselves to these chains and are ultimately drawn up, to make succulent tidbits and stews for many a restaurant of Italy.

A Neapolitan wine called Nasti—but it really wasn't!

A heartening sign seen chalked on a Palermo wall: W GLI STATI UNITI DI AMERICA. W is the short form of VIVA, and I rejoiced in this stray tribute to the USA, among so many crude slogans chalked by faithful Reds in tribute to Russia.

A quaint "carillon wheel" displayed in Monreale's cathedral, near Palermo. In olden times it was used to conclude the benediction.

The chromatic carts seen on Sicilian roads. At their best, they are rolling art works.

The carp of Arethusa's Fountain, in Syracuse. I wondered if their ancestors came here from Greece by the magic of Diana, as did the nymph herself.

The *domes* of solid white formed by magnificent Shasta daisies in the garden of Taormina's San Domenico Palace Hotel.

The "Door of Paradise"—so called by Carducci—opening onto a balcony behind the altar of Perúgia's Church of San Pietro. When thrown open by the sacristan, this reveals a valley view as sudden and almost as "shockingly lovely" as that from the cloister garden of Monreale.

A quite different view seen *in* Perúgia. It was the amazing skyscraper effect of Piazza Piccinino. The ancient buildings of flats on the upper side of this piazza, opening only on a lofty street quite hidden from the square, seem to soar like residential mountains of New York City—but, oh, so different.

A castle that nobody knows, seen on the mountain road from Perúgia to Gúbbio. It rises from Monte Biscina like a strange but wonderful dream.

The curious "false front" of the Pieve di Santa Maria, in Arezzo. This great church façade, "pasted on" as it were, is a sublime cousin of the ridiculous store fronts of our western prairie towns.

Pedoni a Sinistra (Pedestrians to the Left), a familiar sign in Italian cities. This regulation, usually a pious myth, becomes a stern reality in Little Old Siena, whose narrow main street is often so packed with *pedoni*, wall to wall, that movement would hardly be possible without a system.

A new side door opened in Siena's medieval cathedral with ceremonial solemnity in 1946—by General Mark Clark. The general is a towering figure in Italy's modern history.

The burnt sienna pigment in the big frescoes in the town hall of Siena. The color is from Sienese earth (from oxides of iron) and the extra *n* that we gratuitously add to its spelling does not alter it. The reddish brown hue is beautifully mellow.

A *Natività* by **Lorenzo** Lotto seen and vastly admired in Siena's Pinocoteca. In this small masterpiece of the Sienese school, the Holy

Child in the manger sheds a luminous glow on those who bend over Him.

The shaft of sunlight pouring through the tiny hole purposely left by Brunelleschi in his great dome of the Cathedral of Florence. On June 21, this shaft falls squarely upon a brass plate set into the floor of the church. If, in any year, it *fails* to hit the brass plate full and true, it means danger. The deviation, however slight, indicates that there has been a shifting of the structure.

The "Little Bacchus" statue in the Boboli Gardens of Florence seen enduring a manicure administered solemnly by a statuary cleaner. The wine godling was frightfully bored by the silly business and wanted nothing so much as another draught of Chianti.

The purely "decorative stairway" seen above the choir of the Cathedral of Pisa. It leads from nowhere up to nowhere and down the other side! Just beneath it is the emblem of the Medici pills, the usual six, in indication of the long dominance of that family in Tuscany.

The font of the baptistery of the same cathedral, of such superior marble, from Carrara's finest quarries, that you would swear it is of ivory.

Some blocks of masonry with inscriptions from classic Rome embedded in the cathedral's outer walls. They were put in, and remain, *upside down,* as a mark of dishonor to the pagan gods and those who worshiped them. One of the inverted inscriptions was originally a tribute to IMP. CAESAR.

The sweetly beaming stone lions that support hundreds of pillars, all told, in the churches of east central Italy. So gentle and friendly are these charming "cats" that you can practically hear them purr.

The statue of *Evangelista Torricelli* in his native city of Faenza, habitat of faïence. What did *he* do? He discovered the principle of the barometer.

The consulate of tiny Monaco, noticed in tiny San Marino. It is a case of one miniature state, grown rich from gambling, making a friendly gesture to another that longs to do likewise.

The tombstone of Antenor, pointed out to tourists in Padua. Who was Antenor? Paduans say he was the brother of Aeneas, hero of Troy, and that he founded Padua about 1000 B.C.!

Il Milione, the home of Marco Polo, seen in Venice. Its name, meaning "The Million," is in reference to the explorer's nickname, Marco Milioni, bestowed upon him because of his penchant for talking in big round numbers.

Three old men seen repairing three old umbrellas in a sunny courtyard of Venice named Court of the Old Bakehouse (Corte del Forno Vecchio).

The milkmen of Venice making their early-dawn rounds in big, workaday milk gondolas.

A marker in the huge Roman amphitheater of Verona showing that the River Ádige filled the big bowl to a depth of about ten feet in a flood on September 17, 1882.

The Lion of St. Mark's painted on Gabriele d'Annunzio's plane, on view at Il Vittoriale. Beneath the lion is the motto: ITERUM RUDIT LEO, meaning "The Lion Roars Again."

The railway stationmistress of Collalbo, Dolomite village on the Renon Plateau, courteously insisting that I, a total stranger, should borrow her umbrella because rain threatened. "You may bring it back when you leave," she said easily. Such trusting friendliness is worth a dozen sermons on international amity.

The office of the Garage Centrale in Cortina d'Ampezzo, so full of art works and precious bibelots that it actually looks like a collector's private gallery—which is just what it is. The mayor of Cortina owns the garage, but collecting *oggetti d'arte* is his passion.

Hotel Corona, another of his business properties, that is a veritable picture gallery.

Gabriel blowing a lusty trumpet atop the campanile of the parish church in Borca di Cadore, a hamlet near Cortina. You won't find anything about this insignificant community in guidebooks of the Nagel type, yet its bell tower and winged archangel make one of the loveliest vignettes in Italy.

Lawns under larches, seen everywhere in the Dolomites. Beneath most trees lawns won't flourish, but the type of shade provided by larches seems built to their special order.

The white fields of wool-grass near Lago di Braies. In July, they look as if blanketed by a summer snowstorm.

Boots for beer, at the sumptuously decorated and gardened Pedavena Brewery, near Feltre. The vast beer tankards, veritable jeroboams, are in the form of tall glass boots.

A little sight of big Milan. A tiny child was flying an odd "living kite." The kite was an unhappy flying beetle that had been attached to a thread clutched in the baby hands. One trusts the kite finally escaped and flew free.

A full-grown man of Bérgamo in a home-made cab being drawn at a good clip by a powerful great Dane.

An artist's bit on the shore of Lake Como, the hamlet of Nesso, on the lake's Bellágio "wedge." Nesso seems to be quite unsung, yet in leaping the Gorge of the Órrido by several quaint bridges, it makes an unforgettable "action picture," with a fine cascade for background.

Sesto Calende, straddling the broad River Ticino, here an effluent of Lake Maggiore. Crossing the long bridge on foot, I once got caught by a sudden cloudburst and became the wettest tourist in Europe.

A wine tun near Alba (Piedmont), of such huge dimensions that a small car can drive around in circles in it. A brass band once secretly ensconced itself in the big cask and gave a concert to mystified listeners, some of whom believed it "miracle music."

The original Rue de Rivoli—without shops. It is a highway leading west from Piedmont's Rívoli toward France.

The stone pillars, in tens of thousands, that support the hillside vineyards of Piedmont in the neighborhood of Ivrea. They alter the entire landscape for miles.

The babbling of the baby river called Dora Báltea, heard from the balconies of a pension at Courmayeur. The stream is attempting to "empty the snow" of Mont Blanc into the Po.

A river race of motorboats called by Italians the longest held anywhere in the world. The competing craft traverse the Po from Pavia, near Milan, clear to its mouth in the Adriatic, and so to Venice.

The three ships of Columbus, the *Santa Maria*, the *Pinta* and the *Niña*, cleverly pictured in plants at the upper end of Piazza della Vittoria, in the discoverer's native city, Genoa.

Genoa's densest jungle of traffic and humanity, Piazza Caricamento, where Antonio Paganini once kept a wine shop. In leisure hours he played the violin, and also taught his little boy Nicolò to play!

The pulling power, in opposite directions, of Genoa's two Rivieras. The Riviera of the Setting Sun, pulling toward the west and home, wins out in the tug-of-holiday, when finally "time's up."

INDEX

Abbey of Monte Cassino, 200
Abetone (snow resort), 85
Abruzzi, 260
Accademia di Belle Arti, 277, 335
Acqualagna, Italy, 263
Acquapendente, Italy, 237, 238
Ádige River, 350, 351, 361, 422
Ádige Valley, war damage, 23
Adriatic Sea, 295
Aeneas, 95, 210
Aeolian Islands, see Lípari Islands
Aerolinee Italiane Internazionali, 3
Aeschylus, 18
Africanus, Scipio, 101
Agnes, St., 110-111
Agricola, 102
Agrigento, Sicily, 25, 96, 226-227, 231-232
Agrippa, Emperor, 210
Agrippina, 102, 210
Air France, 3, 4-5, 145
Air lines, 3
Alaric, 103
Alássio, Italy, 416
Alba, Italy, 424
Alba Longa, 188
Alban Hills, 61, 179, 189, 190, 191
Albano, Italy, 190
Albano, Lake, 188, 189
Albenga, Italy, 416
Alberobello, Italy, 224
Albert, King, 384
Albergo Diurno, 78
Alessi, Galeazzo, 412
Alexander, Duke, 319
Alexander VI, Pope, 299
Alexander Severus, Emperor, 102
Alfieri, Vittorio, 280
Alfonso I, 117, 120, 298, 299

Alfonso II, 120, 298, 299
Alfredo, 153, 175
Alitalia, see Aerolinee Italiane Internazionali
Alps, 5, 14, 19, 85, 365, 389, 395, 402
Alto Ádige, 99, 358
Amadeo, Giovanni, 390
Amalfi, Italy, 209, 215, 217
  restaurants, 65
Amalfi Drive, 215
Amati, Niccolò, 120
Amati, The, 120-121, 320
Ambrose, St., 111
American Embassy, 50
American Export Lines, 6
American Express Company, 36, 41, 42, 69, 71, 150, 273, 327, 407, 409
Anacapri, 220
Ancona, Italy, 60
Andrea Doria, S.S., 7
Angelico, Fra, 129, 130, 278
Anio River, 192
Annual of Hotels of Italy, 44
Annuario Alberghi d'Italia, 367
Annunziata, Dr., 27
Annunzio, Gabriele d', 106, 116-117, 307, 355-356, 422
Antenor, 422
Anthony, St., of Padua, 111, 346, 347-348
Antignano, Italy, 292
Antonelli (architect), 394, 395
Antoninus Pius, Emperor, 102
Ánzio, Italy, 195-196
  war damage, 22
Aosta, Italy, 399, 403
  hotels, 403
Aosta, Valley of, 19, 399-404
Aosta Refuge, on Tofana, 371

425

Apennines, 14, 19, 261, 294
Apértifs, 61
Appian Way, 187
Appius Claudius, 187
Apples (Calville), 362
Aprília, Italy, 195
Apulia, 20, 224
Aqua Claudia, 6
Aqua Felix, 6
Aquarium of Naples, 205-206
Aquinas, St. Thomas, 113
Archeological Institute of America, 212
Ardenza, Italy, 292
Arezzo, Italy, 17, 26, 96, 135, 237, 252, 344, 420
  restaurants, 252
Argentina, S.S., 7
Arians, The, 297
Aríccia, Italy, 190
Ariosto, Ludovico, 117, 298
Arno, River, 252, 288, 290, 291
Arnold of Bréscia, 111
Arona, Italy, 112, 386
Assergi, Italy, 261
Assisi, Italy, 26, 28, 237, 249, 250, 251, 252-256
  hotels, 255
Associazione Paracadutisti del Vittoriale, 117
Atrani, Italy, 215
Augusta Praetoria, 403
Augustine, St., 111, 196
Augustus, Emperor, 210, 258
Aurelian, Emperor, 146
Auronza, Italy, 373
Automobiles, see Car, travel by
Avelengo, Italy, 364, 365-366
Averno, Lake, 210
Azalea Week, 151
Azienda di Cura, Soggiorno e Turismo, 37

"Babylonian Exile," 104
Bacchiglione, River, 345, 348
Bach, Johann Sebastian, 131
Bácoli, Italy, 210
Báia, Italy, 209-210
Baker, Josephine, 157

Ballantine Ale, 387
Ballet, 78, 80, 283
Barbarelli family, 139
Barbieri, Lieutenant, 371
Bard, Italy, 401
Bari, Italy, 223
Bars, 66-67, 77
Basilicata, 20
Baths of Caracalla, 79, 149, 178
Baths of Diocletian, 178
BEA, see British European Airways
Beauharnais, Eugène, 105
Beer, 62
Bellágio, Italy, 382, 385
Bellini, Gentile, 319
Bellini, Giovanni, 138-139, 335, 338
Bellini, Iacopo, 138
Bellini, Vincenzo, 121, 227
Bellosguardo, Italy, 127
Bellotto, Bernardo, 141
Benedict, St., 200
Benedict XIV, 163
Benedict XV, 126
Benevento, Italy, 62
Benincasa, Giacomo di, 111
Benjamin, Dorothy Park, 121
Bérgamo, Italy, 24, 113, 121, 343-344, 375, 388-390, 407, 423
Bergman, Ingrid, 20
Bernard, St., of Clairvaux, 111
Bernini, Giovanni Lorenzo, 138, 165, 169, 179, 180, 181, 184
Bernini, Pietro, 179
Blue Grotto, 219
BOAC, see British Overseas Airways
Boats, see Steamship lines
Boboli Gardens, 277
Bocanegra, Simon, 405, 406, 410, 414, 424
Boccaccio, Giovanni, 86, 117-118, 216, 266
Bóite River, 371
Bologna, Italy, 104, 112, 118, 119, 123, 300, 301-304
  food, 59
  hotels, 302
  opera house, 79
Bolsena, Italy, 238
Bolsena, Lake of, 237, 238

INDEX

Bolzano, Italy, 99, 357, 358, 359, 360, 367, 368
   hotels, 359
Bonaparte, Charlotte Napoléon, 280
Bonaparte, Joseph, 105
Bonetti, Giacomo, 346
Borca di Cadore, Italy, 423
Bordighera, Italy, 85, 417
Borghese, Pauline, 142
Borghese Gardens, 182
Borghesi, Count Bartolomeo Manzoni, 310
Borgia, Cesare, 299
Borgia, Lucrezia, 298, 299
Borgo Marinaro, 201
Bórmio, Italy, 364
Borromean Isles, 386
Borromeo, Saint Charles, 112
Borromini, Francesco, 180
Bosch, Hieronymus, 184
Boston's Metropolitan Travel Service, 235
Botticelli, Sandro, 130, 281
Bramante, Donato, 137, 172, 173
Brenner Pass, 357
Bréscia, Italy, 111, 343, 352-353, 354, 356
Bresciano, Próspero, 179
Bressanone, Italy, 99
Breuil, Italy, 401-402
Briga, France, 19
Bríndisi, Italy, 187
British European Airways, 3, 49, 145
British Overseas Airways, 3, 49, 145
Brooklyn, New York, 216
Browning, Elizabeth Barrett, 125-126, 162
Browning, Robert, 125-126, 335
Brumante, 105
Brunelleschi, Filippo, 131, 276, 421
Brutus, 101
Buonarroti, Michelangelo, *see* Michelangelo
Buonconvento, Italy, 238
Buoninsegna, Duccio de, 245
Burano Island, 336
Busseto, Italy, 124
Bute, Lucrezia, 130
Byron, Lord, 126, 279, 335
Byzantines, The, 97, 98, 227, 297

Cabarets, 83
Cabs, *see also* Taxis,
   horse-drawn, 75
Cadenábbia, Italy, 383
Cadore, Italy, 140
Caesar, Julius, 101
Caesar Augustus, 221
Cagliostro, Count Alessandro di, 313
Cagney, James, 157
Calabria, 20
Calendar of Italian Events, 17, 82
Caligula, Emperor, 102, 190, 195
Cambio dens, 41, 42
Camogli, Italy, 416
Campari, Davide, 379
Campi Flegrei, 209
Campidoglio, 160
Campione, Arrigo da, 317
Campione, Italy, 317, 385-386
Campionesi, Maestri, 386
Campo, Italy, 372
Campo Imperatore, 261
Campo di Sotto, Italy, 372
Can Grande, 350, 352
Can Grande II, 350
Canale, Antonio, 141
Canaletto, 141-142, 335
Canova, Antonio, 142, 338, 384
Cantore, General, 371
Capitoline, the, 149, 160, 185-186
Caprarola, Italy, 26
Caprera, 114
Caprese, Italy, 132
Capri, 20, 202, 208, 209, 214, 217-221
   restaurants, 65
Capua, Italy, 187
Car, travel by, 12-15
Caracalla, Emperor, 102
Carbonin, Italy, 373
Carducci, Giosuè, 302, 312, 420
Carezza, Lake, 84, 357, 368
Caroline of Brunswick, 381
Carpaccio, Vittore, 139, 141, 335
Carpano, A. B., 396
Carrani Travel Service, 150
Carrara, Italy, 293
Carta Stradale d'Italia, 21
Carthaginians, The, 97, 227
Caruso, Enrico, 121, 124

428 INDEX

Casamícciola, Ischia, 222
Caserta, Italy, 100, 200
Cassino, Italy, 195, 199-200
  war damage, 22
Castel dell'Ovo, 201, 202
Castel Fusano, 196
Castel Gandolfo, Italy, 127, 188-189
Castel Sant'Angelo, 149, 184
Castel Sant'Elmo, 207
Castel Tirolo, 364-365
Castelli Romani, 189
Castello, 222
Castle of Fénis, 402
Castle of Frederick II of Swabia, 223
Castle of the Capulets, 343
Castle of the Montagues, 343
Catacombs, 187-188
Catánia, Sicily, 121, 225, 227, 231
Cathedrals,
  Amalfi, 215
  Ferrara, 300
  Florence, 421
  Milan, 23, 374, 376-377
  Palermo, 228-229
  Pisa, 286, 287, 421
  Pistoia, 300
  Ravello, 216
  St. John Lateran, 165-166
  St. Mark's, 115
  St. Peter's, 6, 17, 81, 105, 123, 126, 132, 137, 147, 149, 164-165, 168-170, 184, 185, 418
  San Lorenzo, 410-411
  Siena, 243-245
Catherine, St., 111-112, 245, 246
Catholic Action, 108
Cato the Elder, 101
Catullus, 355
Cava, Italy, 214
Cavalese, Italy, 357
Cavour, Count di Camillo, 106, 113, 280
Cecilia, St., 112
Cellini, Benvenuto, 133, 277
Cellini, Costanza, 133
Cernóbbio, Italy, 383
Certaldo, Italy, 266
Certosa di Pavia, 388, 390-391
Cetara, Italy, 215
Champoluc, Italy, 401

Charlemagne, Emperor, 98, 99, 103, 295
Charles IV, King, of France, 350
Châtillon, Italy, 401
Chério, River, 343
Cherubini, Maria Luigi Carlo Zenobio Salvatore, 121, 280
Chesterton, Gilbert, 274
Chigi, Agostino, 135
Chigi, Count, 245
Chigi Palace, 183
Chióggia, Italy, 65, 341, 344
Christ, Jesus, 101, 102, 165, 188, 211
Christina, Queen of Sweden, 126
Church of St. Paul-without-the-Walls, 149, 166
Churches, see also Cathedrals, 17, 21, 26, 98
  Florence, 279-280
  Genoa, 410-412
  L'Aquila, 261
  Lucca, 285-286
  Padua, 345-348
  Palermo, 97, 98, 229
  Pisa, 289-290
  Rome, 163-167, 418
  Siena, 245
Churchill, Winston, 314
Ciampino Airport (Rome), 6, 37, 145
CIAT, see Compagnia Italiana Autoservizi Turistici
Cicero, 195
Cimabue, Giovanni, 128, 253, 281, 287
Circumvesuviana, 211, 214
Circus Maximus, 161
CIT, see Compagnia Italiana Turismo
Civitacastellana, Italy, 26, 250
Clark, Eleanor, 38
Clark, General Mark, 271, 420
Claudius, Emperor, 102, 195
Clothing, 72-74
Coathangers, 74
Cobianchi, Cleopatro, 78
Coca-Cola, 108, 377
Col du Géant, 404
Col Furggen, 402
Cólico, Italy, 382
Collalbo, Italy, 359, 361, 422
Colleoni, Bartolommeo, 113, 132, 338, 390

INDEX

Colleoni, Medea, 113, 390
Colonna, Vittoria, 190-191, 222
Colonna Family, 190
Colosseum, 149, 160, 161-163, 207
Columbus, Christopher, 113, 167, 286, 405
Comacina, Island of, 384-385
Commodus, Emperor, 102
Communism, 107-108
Como, Italy, 381, 382
Como, Lake, 16, 65, 84, 358, 381-385, 423
Compagnia Italiana Autoservizi Turistici, 10-12, 28, 49, 123, 145, 199, 200, 230, 235, 236, 237, 250, 251, 285, 292, 294, 300, 316, 343, 354, 390
Compagnia Italiana Turismo, 12, 28-29, 32-33, 37, 49, 145, 149, 150, 159, 189, 207, 208, 228, 237, 248, 272, 273, 327, 334, 335, 336, 338, 359, 376, 379, 381, 407, 409, 416
Conca dei Marini, Italy, 216
Conrad, Joseph, 221
Constance, 228
Constantine the Great, 102-103, 165, 182, 185
Constitution, S.S., 6
Consuma, Italy, 267
Conte Biancamano, S.S., 7
convents, 17
 accommodations in, 48
Cook's Travel Service, 36, 69, 71, 150, 327, 407
Cooper, Gordon, 38, 51
Cooper, Lord, 115
Copernicus, Nicolas, 126, 302
Corelli, Arcangelo, 121
Coriolanus, 195
Corno Grande, 251
Corradi, Pietro Antonio, 413
Corregio, Antonio Allegri da, 137-138, 182, 317-318
Corrégio, Italy, 138, 317
Corte, Dr. M. Della, 212
Cortina d'Ampezzo, Italy, 85, 357, 367, 369-373, 422
Cortona, Italy, 96, 135, 240, 241, 252
Cortone, Italy, 26
Cosimo the Elder, 115, 350
Costalovara, Italy, 359

Costelunga Pass, 368
Courmayeur, Italy, 19, 85, 403, 404, 424
Cremona, Italy, 120, 121, 124, 316, 319-321
Croce, Benedetto, 118
Cuma, Italy, 210
Cumaean Sibyl, 210

Dacron, 72, 73
Daily American, The, 38, 66
Daisy Products, 72
Dandolo, Enrico, 114, 328
d'Annunzio, *see* Annunzio
Dante Alighieri, 83, 86, 117, 118, 152, 248, 249, 265, 266, 276, 297, 298, 302, 307, 322, 350
Dante's Tomb, 118
David, 277-278, 280, 281
"Day Hotels," 78, 276
Day of St. Marinus, 315
d'Azeglio, Massimo, 110
De Barbieri (violinist), 414
Della Robbia, Andrea, 131, 279, 354
Della Robbia, Luca, 131, 279
Della Scala, Francesco, 352
Della Scala Family, 350
Desenzano, Italy, 354
d'Este, Cardinal Ippolito, 192-193
d'Este, Leonora, 299
Diocletian, Emperor, 102, 112, 313
Dobbiaco, Italy, 357, 370, 373
Dolomieu, Déodat Guy Silvain Tancrède Gratet de, 367
Dolomite Road, 357, 367-369
Dolomiten Land, 358
Dolomites, 14, 19, 84, 357-373, 423
Dominic, St., 112
Domitian, Emperor, 102, 161
Donatello di Betto Bardi, 110, 114, 129, 131, 132, 244, 250, 277, 279, 280, 281, 338, 348
Donizetti, Gaetano, 121, 390
Dora Báltea, River, 399, 424
Doria, Andrea, 114, 411
Doria Family, 405, 411
Double Riviera Road, 12, 19
Douglas, Norman, 221
Duccio di Buoninsegna, 133-134
Duse, Eleanora, 116, 307

INDEX

East Goths, 98
Eating the Italian Way, 57
Economic Cooperation Administration, 39
Edolo, Italy, 358
Ega River Gorge, 368
Elba, 20, 273
Emissarium, 188
Ente Nazionale Industrie Turistiche, 27-28, 37, 44, 57
Ente Provinciale per il Turismo, 147, 154, 208, 272, 305, 327, 351, 358, 359, 368, 376, 406, 407, 413
Entrèves, Italy, 403
Enzo, King, 303, 304
Ercolano, Italy, 189, 211
ERP, *see* European Recovery Program
Esposizione Universale Roma, 145, 149, 175-177
Este Family, 298
Etna, Mt., 226, 231, 234
Etruria, Kingdom of, 105
Etruscan Gate, 258
Etruscan Museum, 266
Etruscans, The, 96
Eugubine Tablets, 96, 262
EUR, *see* Esposizione Universale Roma
Euripides, 18
Europabus system, 12, 28
European Recovery Program, *see also* Marshall Plan, 23, 30, 107
Exarchs, 297
Excambion, S.S., 6

Faenza, Italy, 305, 421
Fairbanks, Douglas, 153
Falzárego Pass, 369
Farnese Family, 319
Farouk, ex-King, 14, 226
Fascism, 109
Fattorusso, Giuseppe, 38, 39, 128, 134, 141
Faure, Elie, 346
Federigo, Duke, di Montefeltro, 264
Feltre, Italy, 423
Ferdinand of Bourbon, 229
Ferrara, Italy, 104, 117, 120, 126, 294, 295, 298-300
  cathedrals, 300

Ferrari, Maria Beignole Sale De, Duchessa di Gallieri, 413
Ferrati, Sarah, 352
Festivals, 81-82, 241, 246-247, 263
Festivals, folk, 17, 29, 81
Fiat Motor Company, 11, 13-15, 28, 260, 397-399
Fields, Gracie, 221
Fieschi Family, 411
Fiésole, Italy, 65, 272, 278
  hotels, 272
Filipopi, Alessandro, *see* Botticelli, Sandro
Fiume, 106, 116, 117, 355
Flaminius, 251
Flora, Signora, 373
Florence, Italy, 15, 17, 24, 96, 104, 105, 115-116, 118, 119, 121, 123, 125, 238, 249, 252, 270-284, 286, 290
  art, 18
  artists, 128-133, 136, 137
  Blowing Up of the Chariot, 81
  cafés, 66
  cathedrals, 421
  churches, 279-280
  food, 58
  guided tours, 29
  hotels, 270-272
  Il Giuoco del Calcio, 81
  Musical May of, 80, 81, 280, 283-284
  night life, 272-273, 275
  opera house, 79
  restaurants, 273-275
  shops, 68, 270
  symphony orchestra, 80
  war damage, 271, 283
Foligno, Italy, 251
Folk festivals, 17, 29, 81
Fondo, Italy, 364
Fontana, Carlo, 126, 238
Fontana, Domenico, 179
Fonte del Clitunno, 250
Food, *see also* Cafés; Restaurants
  air-lines, 4-5
  Florence, 273
  Italian, 16, 52-59
  railways, 10, 34-35
  steamships, 7, 8

INDEX 431

Footloose in Italy (Sutton), 38
Forio, Ischia, 222
Forli, Italy, 294
Fórmia, Italy, 146, 199
Foro Italico, 149, 173, 174
Forum, 183
Fountain of Arethusa, 227
Fountains, 178-181, 192-193, 200
Francis, St., of Assisi, 26, 112, 253-254, 255, 307, 348, 388
Frangipani Family, 163
Frankoma Pottery Company, 306
Franks, The, 98
Frascati, Italy, 191
Frederick II, Emperor, 303
Frederick Barbarossa, Emperor, 103, 238
Freighter Life, 7
Freighters, 7
Fugger, Johannes, 61
Furlo Gorge, 263
Furore, Italy, 216
Fusaro, Lake, 210
Fusina, Italy, 344

Gaddi, Taddeo, 129
Gaeta, Gulf of, 199
Gainsborough, Thomas, 384
Galileo Galilei, 118-119, 126, 280, 287, 288, 345
Galla Placidia, 166
Galleni, Giovanni, 29
Galvani, Luigi, 119, 302
Game of the Bridge, 290-291
Gander, Newfoundland, 4
Garda, Italy, 354, 355
Garda, Lake, 16, 65, 59, 99, 117, 127, 343, 354, 355, 356, 357
Gardone, Italy, 117, 355
Gardone Riviera, Italy, 343
Garducci, Giosuè, 118
Garibaldi, Anita, 182, 298, 314
Garibaldi, Giuseppe, 106, 113, 114, 115, 182, 261, 313-314
Gasoline, 13, 14, 15, 400
Gastronomy in Rome, 154
Gattamelata, 110, 114-115, 132, 250, 338, 348
Gaynor, Mitzi, 157
Genoa (booklet), 406

Genoa, Italy, 5, 24, 104, 105, 113, 114, 115, 122, 290, 334, 405-417, 424
   churches, 410-412
   food, 58
   guided tours, 29
   heights, 414-415
   hotels, 407-409
   opera house, 79
   palaces, 412-414
   restaurants, 65, 407, 408-409
   Rivieras, 415-417, 424
   shops, 407
   war damage, 23, 405, 407, 413
Genseric, 103
Genzano, Italy, 190
Germain, Félix, 368
Gherardesca, Count Ugolino della, 289
Ghibellines, The, 104
Ghiberti, Lorenzo, 131, 276, 354
Ghirlandaio, Domenico, 130, 249, 280
Giacalucci, Signor Silvio, 235
Giambologna, 303
Gibbon's Rome, 101
Gide, André, 274
Giorgione, 138, 139
Giotto di Bondone, 128-129, 139, 253, 276, 281, 288, 346
Giotto's Tower, 276
Giovane, Palma, 139
Goethe, Johann Wolfgang von, 126-127
Goldoni, Carlo, 119
Golf, 84
Goodman, Benny, 157
Gorge of the Órrido, 423
Göring, Hermann, 22
Gothic Line, The, 301
Goths, 227
Gozzoli, Benozzo, 249, 286
Gran Sasso d'Italia, 261
Great St. Bernard Pass, 399
Greek Theater of Syracuse, 18
Greeks, The, 96
Gregory VII, Pope, 103
Gregory XI, Pope, 104, 111
Gregory the Great, 103
Gressoney-la-Trinité, Italy, 400
Gressoney-St.-Jean, Italy, 400
Gries, Italy, 359
Grimaldi Family, 411

Grossa Quércia, Italy, 134
Grottaferrata, Italy, 191
Group tours, 35-36, 189
Guareschi, Giovanni, 108
Guarneri, Giuseppe Antonio, 122, 320
Guarneri, The, 121-122
Gúbbio, Italy, 17, 26, 96, 262-263, 266
  Feast of the Candles, 82
Guelphs, The, 104
Guicciardini, Francesco, 119
Guiccioli, Countess Teresa, 126
Guide of Rome, 147
Guide to Italy, 237
Guidebooks, 29, 37-39
Guidobaldo, 265
Guncinà, Italy, 359
  hotels, 359
  restaurants, 359
Gustaf V, King, 219
Gustavus Adolphus, 126
Gypping of tourists, 76-77

Habsburgs, The, 99
Hadrian, Emperor, 102
Hadrian's Villa, 191
Hamilton, Lady, 201
Hannibal, 101, 251
Harian Publications, 7
Haussmann, Baron, 160
Hauteville, Roger de, 227
Helena, Saint, 165
Henry IV, Emperor, 103
Henry the Navigator, 61
Herculaneum, 205, 208, 210-211
Hercules, 210
Herod, 411
Herulians, The, 98
Hippocrates, 362
History, 95-109
Hitler, Adolf, 107, 196
Hofer, Andreas, 364
Holy Roman Empire, 99, 104
Holy Week, 81
Home Lines, 6, 7
Homeland, S.S., 7
Honorius, Emperor, 296
Horse-drawn cabs, 75
Hospital of Sant'Anna, 299
Hostels, 49

Hotels, 39, 44-51, 316
  Aosta, 403
  Assisi, 255
  Avelengo, 365
  Bellágio, 382
  Bologna, 302
  Bolzano, 359
  Breuil, 402
  Capri, 220
  Collalbo, 361
  Cortina d'Ampezzo, 369-370
  Courmayeur, 404
  "Day," 78, 276
  Fiésole, 272
  Florence, 270-272
  Fórmia, 199
  Gardone, 355
  Genoa, 407-409
  Guncinà, 359
  Ischia, 222
  La Méndola, 360
  L'Aquila, 261
  Merano, 362-363
  Milan, 375
  Montecatini Terme, 268
  Naples, 201-202, 204, 408
  Orvieto, 239
  Padua, 344
  Perúgia, 256
  Pisa, 289
  prices, 44-51
  Ravenna, 296
  Rome, 49-51, 148
  St.-Vincent, 401
  Saltino, 268
  San Marino, 310-311
  San Remo, 416
  Siena, 241
  Sirmione, 355
  Sorrento, 216-217
  Tremezzo, 383
  Trento, 357
  Turin, 394
  Urbino, 263
  Venice, 326, 327-330
  Verona, 350
House of St. Catherine, 111
House of the Vestal Virgins, 184

INDEX 433

Hume, Major General Edgar Erskine, 246

Ibañez, Vicente Blasco, 206
Ibsen, Henrik, 222
Il Palio, 241, 246-247
Il Guglia, 117
Illumination of the Arno's Banks, 290, 291
Impruneta, Italy, 267
Independence, S.S., 6
Intra, Italy, 381
Ionian Sea, 226
Irredentists, The, 99
Isa, Italy, 104
Isarco Valley, 361
Ischia, 20, 208, 209, 221
 hotels, 222
 restaurants, 65
Island of San Giorgio, 335
Island of San Lazzaro degli Armeni, 335
Islands, *see also* names of islands, 20
Ísola Bella, 112, 381, 386
Ísola dei Pescatori, 387
Ísola di San Giovanni, 387
Ísola Madre, 387
Istituto Geografico Visceglia, 21
Istria, 105, 106
Italian language, 86-91
Italian Line, 6, 7
Italian State Railways, 20, 30
Italian State Tourist Office, 17, 27, 44
Italian Touring Club, 406
Italy (Baedeker), 247
Italy (Nagel), 37
Italy (Ogrizek), 38
Iuvara (architect), 394, 395
Ivrea, Italy, 424

Janiculum Hill, 149, 182
Januarius, St., 112
Joan of Arc, 129
Johnson, Van, 157
Jubilee Year Plan of Rome, 148
Juliet, 343, 350, 351
Julius II, Pope, 171, 172, 294

Keats, John, 127
Kerr, Deborah, 187

Kesselring, Albert, 195
Keyserling, Hermann, 274
KLM Royal Dutch Airlines, 3-4, 145
Knights of St. Stephen, 289
Krupp, Friederich, 220

La Marmolada, 368
La Méndola, Italy, 359-360
 hotels, 360
La Scala, 78-79, 374, 376-377
Lacco Ameno, Ischia, 222
Lago di Braies, 373, 423
LAI, *see* Linee Aeree Italiane
Lakes, *see also* names of lakes, 16, 19
Lana di Sopra, Italy, 365
Landini (artist), 180
Landor, Walter Savage, 125
Language, Italian, 86-91
Lanza, Mario, 121
L'Áquila, Italy, 26, 260
 churches, 261
 hotels, 261
L'Assunta, Italy, 359
Last Supper, The, 379
Lateran Treaty, 107, 108
Latina, Italy, 193-195, 196
Laughlin, Clara, 38
Laundry, 72, 73, 74
Lawrence, D. H., 221
Lawrence, St., 411
League of Nations, 106, 107
Leaning Tower of Pisa, 22, 24, 119, 286, 287-288
Lecco, Italy, 120, 382
Leghorn, Italy, 5, 122, 292
 war damage, 292
Lenox, Inc., 306
Leo III, Pope, 103, 295
Leo X, Pope, 171
Leo, St., 313
Leonardo da Vinci, 132, 136, 153, 267-268, 280, 282, 318, 374, 379-380
Leoncavallo, Ruggiero, 122
Lepidus, Consul Emilius, 302
Lido, The, 19, 65, 330, 340
Lido Castel Fusano, 85, 196
Life (magazine), 140, 173
Ligurian Sea, 292, 295
Limerick, Ireland, 5

Linee Aeree Italiane, 3, 225, 325
Linzi, Comm. Enrico, 28
Lípari Islands, 20
Lippi, Filippino, 130
Lippi, Fra Filippo, 129-130, 281
Liqueurs, 62
Liszt, Franz, 246
Little St. Bernard Pass, 399
Little World of Don Camillo, The (Guareschi), 108
Locande, 49
Locarno, Switzerland, 386
Locatelli, Pietro, 122
Lombard League, 98
Lombards, The, 98, 295
Lombardy, 98, 105, 106
Lorenzetti, Ambrogio, 134
Lorenzo the Magnificent, 104, 115, 116, 130
Lotto, Lorenzo, 420
Louis XIV, King, 200
Lozzi Editore, 148
Lucca, Italy, 123, 285-286
  churches, 285-286
Lucrino, Lake, 210
Lugano, Lake, 16, 317, 381, 385
Lugano, Switzerland, 385, 386
Luggage, 34, 72
Lurago, Rocco, 414

Machiavelli, Nicolò di Bernardo, 115, 119, 280
Mackenzie, Compton, 221
Marcus Vinicius, 187
Maderna, Carlo, 181, 188
Maggiore, Lake, 16, 65, 112, 381, 386-387
Magna Graecia, 224
Mail, 69-71
Maiori, Italy, 215
Maitani, Lorenzo, 134, 239, 240
Malatesta, John, 307
Malatesta, Paolo, 307
Malatesta, Sigismund, 307
Malcésine, Italy, 127
Manin, Daniele, 115, 335
Mantegna, Andrea, 137, 138, 322, 347
Mantua, Italy, 104, 137, 316, 321-322
Manzoni, Alessandro, 120

Maps, 20-21, 146
March, Frederic, 133
Marco Polo, 116, 139, 328, 422
Marconi, Guglielmo, 301, 302
Marcus Aurelius, Emperor, 102
Margaret, St., 252
Marina, Italy, 215
Marina di Pisa, Italy, 292
Marino, Italy, 190
Marinus, St., 312, 313
Marshall Plan, *see also* European Recovery Program, 10, 17, 30
Marzabotto, Italy, 301
Masaccio, Tommaso, 129, 134, 139, 281
Mascagni, Pietro, 122
Masolino, 129
Massaciúccoli, Lake, 123, 292
Matarazzo, Senhor, 363
Matterhorn, the, 19, 399, 402
Mausoleum of Augustus, 161, 184
Mausoleum of Hadrian, 184
Maxentius, Emperor, 103, 182
Mazzarò, Sicily, 85
Mazzini, Giuseppe, 106, 115, 409
Mazzola, Francesco, 318
Meadow of Miracles, 286
Medici, Catherine de', 279
Medici, Cosimo de', 277
Medici, Giovanni de', 115
Medici, The, 104, 115-116
Medici Art Series, 128
Medici Chapels, 279
Mellen Gallery (Washington), 413
Memmi, Lippo, 249
Menaggio, Italy, 382, 383, 385
Merano, Italy, 99, 357, 358, 361-364, 365
  hotels, 362-363
Meredith, George, 221
Messalina, 102
Messina, Strait of, 225
Metaponto, Italy, 224
Metáuro, River, 264
Metropolitan Travel Service (Boston), 35
Mezzegra, Italy, 383
Michelangelo, 104, 105, 112, 129, 131, 132-133, 135, 136, 137, 138, 164, 169,

INDEX

170, 172-173, 179, 191, 222, 240, 271, 276, 277, 279, 280, 281, 282, 293, 412
Milan, Italy, 5, 98, 111, 112, 120, 124, 132, 133, 137, 290, 343, 374-380, 388, 423
  Cathedral, 23, 374, 376-377
  food, 58
  guided tours, 29
  hotels, 375
  La Scala, 78, 79
  restaurants, 65, 375, 376
  shops, 68, 376
  symphony orchestra, 80
  war damage, 23, 78, 374-375
Milazzo, Sicily, 20
Milton, John, 127, 268
Míncio, River, 321
Mineral waters, 62
Minori, Italy, 215
Miseno, Italy, 210
Misenum, Italy, 210
Mistinguett, 331
Misurina, Italy, 373
Mochi (sculptor), 319
Módena, Italy, 106, 120, 316, 322-323
Mola, Sicily, 233
Moltrásio Argegno, Italy, 383
Monaco, 422
Monaco, Guido, 252
Monasteries, accommodations in, 48
Monastery of St. Francis, 250
Money, 39-42
Monica, Santa, 196
Mont Blanc, 5, 19, 300, 403, 404, 424
Montagnana, Italy, 316
Montaigne, Michel de, 83, 153
Monte Benedetto, 364
Monte Biscina, 420
Monte Cristallo, 369-370
Monte Mário, 149, 174
Monte Oliveto Maggiore, Italy, 267
Monte Rosa, 19, 399, 400, 402
Monte Sciliar, 361
Monte Tofana, 371
Montecatini Alto, Italy, 268, 269
Montecatini Terme, Italy, 268
  hotels, 268
Montecatini Valdenievole, Italy, 269
Montecchio Maggiore, Italy, 343

Montefalco, Italy, 26, 251
Montefeltro, Duke of, 136
Montefiasco, Italy, 26
Montefiascone, Italy, 61, 237-238
Monteluco Hill, 250
Montepiano, Italy, 267
Montepulciano, Italy, 267
Monteriggioni, Italy, 265-266
Morosini, Francesco, 116
Moses, 164, 179, 293
Mount Etna, 85
Movie houses, 157
MSA, *see* Mutual Security Agency
Munthe, Axel, 218, 219, 221
Murano Island, 336
Murat, Marshal, 105
Muratori, Ludovico Antonio, 120
Music, 17, 78-80, 83, 120-125, 245-246, 257, 283, 292, 318
Mussolini, Benito, 106, 107, 109, 146, 149, 150, 151, 159, 160, 161, 168, 173, 174, 176, 184, 194, 261, 301, 343, 358, 379, 383, 393
Mutual Security Agency, 23, 39, 107

Naples, Italy, 24, 105, 106, 112, 121, 138, 201-208, 405, 419
  Bay of, 20
  food, 57
  guided tours, 29
  hotels, 201-202, 204, 408
  Miracle of San Gennaro, 81
  money racket, 41
  opera house, 79
  Piedigrotta Festival, 82
  restaurants, 65
  shops, 68
  symphony orchestra, 80
  war damage, 22
Naples and Surroundings, 208
Napoleon Bonaparte, 99, 105, 311, 313, 386, 401
Napoleon III, 105
Nardini, Pietro, 122
Narni, Erasmo da, *see* Gattamelata
Narni, Italy, 250
Narriman, Queen, 226
National Geographic Magazine, 223, 246
National Institute of Ancient Drama, 17

National Organization for Tourist Industries, see Ente Nazionale Industrie Turistiche
Nelson, Horatio, 201
Nemi, Lake, 190
Neptune, 303
Nera, River, 250
Neri, St. Philip, 112-113
Nero, Emperor, 102, 154, 161, 184, 195, 210
Nerva, Emperor, 102
Nessi, Lino, 384
Nesso, Italy, 423
Nettuno, Italy, 195-196
New Appian Way, 6, 187
New York City Ballet, 284
New Yorker, The, 288
Newton, Sir Isaac, 288
Nice, France, 5, 105, 106, 114
Nicholas V, Pope, 307
Night clubs, 83, 156, 157
Night life, 83-84, 150, 156-158
  Florence, 272-273, 275
  Venice, 341-342
Nightingale, Florence, 127
Nocera, Italy, 214
Nola, Italy, 82
Normans, The, 97, 227, 228
Noves, Laura de, 120
Nus, 402
Nylon, 72, 73

Ocean travel, see Steamship lines
Octavian, 101
Odoacer, 97-98, 103
O'Faolain, Sean, 38
Ogrizek, Doré, 38
Oltremare, 36
Opera, 78, 79, 121-124, 248, 283, 315, 352
Opera houses, 78-80
Orario Generale, 20, 30
Orario Generale degli Autoservizi, 30
Orcagna, Andrea, 280
Orchestras, 80
Orcto, valley of the, 230
Orlon, 72, 73
Orly airport (Paris), 6
Orsini Family, 161
Orta, Lake, 387-388

Orta San Giúlio, Italy, 388
Ortisei, Italy, 369
Ortles (Ortler) Alps, 364
Ortygia Island, 232
Orvieto, Italy, 26, 60, 134, 135, 237, 238-241
  hotels, 239
Ospedaletti, Italy, 417
Ostia, Italy, 85, 196
Ostrogoths, the, 98, 103, 295, 297
Otto I, Emperor, 99
Owen, Eric, 306

Padua, Italy, 98, 111, 115, 118, 126, 250, 294, 338, 341, 344-348, 350, 422
  artists, 133, 137
  churches, 345-348
  hotels, 344
  war damage, 347
Paestum, Italy, 96, 215, 231
Paganini, Antonio, 424
Paganini, Niccolò, 122, 318, 414, 424
Palaces, 183-184
  Genoa, 412-414
  Siena, 245
Palaces and Museums of Genoa, The (leaflet), 413
Palazzo Barberini, 184
Palazzo Madama, 183
Palazzo Montecitorio, 183
Palazzo Rufolo, 216
Palazzo Venezia, 183
Palermo, Sicily, 24-25, 97, 225, 226, 227-230, 295, 419
  Cathedral, 228-229
  churches, 97, 98
  Feast of Santa Rosa, 82
  opera house, 79
Palestrina, Giovanni Pierluigi da, 122-123
Palestrina, Italy, 122
Palio festival, 25
Palladio, Andrea, 348-349
Pallanza, Italy, 381
Pantheon, 149, 164, 184
Pan American World Airways, 3, 145
Papal States, 98, 103, 105, 106, 265, 294
Paracelsus, 362
Paris, France, 4, 6, 132

INDEX

Parma, Italy, 105, 106, 124, 133, 316, 317-319
  artists, 137-138
  war damage, 318
Parmigianino, 318
Parthenope, 204, 221
Pass of La Méndola, 358
Pass of Monte Giovo, 364
Passírio River, 361
Passo del Muraglione, 294
Passo della Colline, 300
Passo di Nova, 364
Passports, 42-43
Patti, Adelina, 123
Paul, St., 111, 166
Pavia, Italy, 98, 111, 390, 424
PAWA, see Pan American World Airways
Peace of Campo Formio, 105
Pedavena Brewery, 423
Pedrocchi, Antonio, 344-345
Pensioni, 44, 50, 202, 272
  Venice, 329
Perera and Company, 41
Perugia, Italy, 25, 28, 60, 96, 118, 119, 125, 136, 237, 241, 249, 250, 251, 253, 256-259, 266, 420
  hotels, 256
  restaurants, 258
Perugino, Pietro Vannucci, 136, 256, 258, 281, 282
Perusia, Augusta, 182
Pésaro, Italy, 123
Pescasséroli, Italy, 118
Peter, St., 103, 187
Petrarch, 86, 117, 120, 252
Petrucci, Pandolfo, 245
Phlegraean Fields, 209
Phoenicians, 96, 227
Piacenza, Italy, 316, 319
Píccola Marina, 220
Piccolomini, Aeneas Silvius, 244
Piccolomini, Cardinal Francesco, 244
Pickford, Mary, 153
Piedmont, 105, 392-405, 424
  western, 19
Pier Busseti, 36
Piero della Francesca, 135, 136, 252
Pienza, Italy, 265

Pieve di Cadore, Italy, 372, 373
Pincian, 181
Pinturicchio, Bernardino, 136, 244, 251, 265, 322
Pisa, Italy, 5, 17, 24, 118, 244, 273, 285-291, 295
  artists, 133, 137
  cathedral, 286, 287, 421
  churches, 289-290
  Giuoco del Ponte, 81
  hotels, 289
  Leaning Tower of, 22, 24, 119, 286, 287-288
  restaurants, 291
  war damage, 22, 286-287, 290
Pisano, Giovanni, 137, 287, 288-289
Pisano, Nicolò, 137, 285, 287, 288, 304
Piscina Mirabile, 210
Pistoia, Italy, 300
Pitti Gallery, 281, 282-283
Pitti Palace, 131, 277
Pius II, Pope, 130, 136, 265
Pius IV, Pope, 112
Pius VII, Pope, 165
Pius X, 126, 165
Pius XI, Pope, 171, 378
Pius XII, Pope, 171
Placidia, Galla, 296
Plan Chécrouit, 404
Plan Maison, 402
Plan Rosa, 402
Plane travel, see Air lines
Pliny, the Elder, 382
Pliny, the Younger, 382
Ploetz' Epitome, 101
Po, River, 392, 424
Poggibonsi, Italy, 60, 248
Poldi-Pezzo Museum, 375
Pomézia, Italy, 195
Pompanin, Caterina, 372
Pompei Scavi, Italy, 211
Pompeii, 205, 208, 210-214
Pone Gardena, Italy, 369
Ponte delle Torri, 250
Ponte Giovanni, Italy, 251
Pontinia, Italy, 195
Pontifical Palace, 188
Pontino, Agro, 194-195
Pont-St.-Martin, Italy, 400

Pordoi Pass, 368
Poretta Terme, Italy, 301
Porlezza, Italy, 385
Porta, Giocomo della, 180
Porta, Giovanni Battista della, 179
Portinari, Beatrice, 118, 249
Porto Cerésio, Italy, 385
Portofino a Mare, Italy, 416
Portofino Vetta, Italy, 416
Posíllipo, Italy, 146, 201
Positano, Italy, 209, 216
Power, Tyrone, 331
Pozzo Brothers, 30-31, 34
Pozzuoli, Italy, 208, 209
Praiano, Italy, 216
Prato, Italy, 130, 267
Predazzo, Italy, 357
Pré-St.-Didier, Italy, 400
Pro Loco, 37
Processions of Penitents, 81
Prócida, 209, 221
Prostitution, 83-84
Puccini, Giacomo, 123, 292-293
Puglia, 355
Pugliano, Italy, 211, 214
Pugnani, Gaetano, 122
Punic Wars, 101
Punta della Penna, 224
Punta Carena, 218
Puteoli, Italy, 209
Pyramid of Caius Cestius, 149
Pythagoras, 224

Quercia, Iacopo della, 131, 134, 242, 243, 244, 276, 285, 303
Quirinal, The, 183
Quirinal Palace, 183
Quo Vadis, 187

Rabelais, François, 83, 153
Radicófani, Italy, 238
Railways, 8-10, 29-35
Raimondi, Ing. di, 30
Ranuccio, Duke, 319
Rapallo, Italy, 65, 416
Raphael Sanzio, 26, 104, 129, 136, 164, 170, 171, 172, 182, 238, 263, 264, 280, 282, 294, 379

Rasini di Castelcampo, Count Giovanni, 267, 268
Ravello, Italy, 209, 216, 217
Ravenna, Italy, 24, 97, 98, 103, 118, 126, 166, 228, 229, 249, 294, 295-298, 314
  hotels, 296
  war damage, 23, 296-297, 298
Réggio Emília, Italy, 317
Religion, *see also* Churches, 17
Remus, 95, 101, 161, 188
Renon, Italy, 360
Renon Plateau, 359
Resina, Italy, 211
Respighi, Ottorino, 123, 178
Restaurants, 39, 52-53, 54, 56, 77
  Arezzo, 252
  Comacina, 384
  Florence, 273-275
  Fórmia, 199
  Genoa, 65, 407, 408-409
  Guncinà, 359
  Milan, 65, 375, 376
  Monte Benedetto, 364
  Naples, 65
  outdoor, 64-65, 155, 192, 196, 354
  Perúgia, 258
  Pisa, 291
  prices, 62-64
  Rome, 64, 65, 152-156
  Siena, 242
  Tivoli, 192
  Todi, 262
  Turin, 395-397
  Venice, 328, 330-332
  Verona, 350
Rieti, Italy, 96
Rifugio Torino, 404
Rímini, Italy, 104, 302
Riva, Italy, 99, 354, 355, 356, 358
Rívoli, Italy, 395
Rocca di Papa, Italy, 191
Roger I, King, 97
Roger II, King, 228, 229
Rolle Pass, 357
Roman Catholic Church, 17, 107
Roman Polyphonic Society, 80
Romagna Riviera, 19
Romano, Giulio, 321

INDEX 439

Rome, Italy, 120, 133, 145-186
  air lines, 3-6
  ancient, 160-163
  art, 18
  artists, 137, 138
  bars, 66-67
  bridges, 182
  churches, 163-167, 418
  Ciampino Airport, 6, 37, 145
  concerts, 80
  Easter Sunday in, 81
  food, 57
  fountains, 178-181
  guided tours, 29, 149-150, 159, 178
  hills, 181-182
  history, 101
  hotels, 49-51, 148
  maps, 146-148, 178
  modern, 173-175
  monuments, 119, 151
  night life, 150, 156-158
  Opera House, 79
  restaurants, 64, 65, 152-156, 175
  Seven Hills of, 147
  shops, 68, 148-149, 175
  statues, 115
  subway, 175
  symphony orchestra, 80
  Termini Station, 10, 37, 50, 145, 388
  war damage, 22
Rome (Medici Art Series), 38
Rome and a Villa (Clark), 38
Rome and its Environs (Nagel), 37
Rome Today (Rothery), 38
Romeo, 343, 350
Romulus, 95, 101, 161, 188
Romulus Augustulus, 97
Rosalia, Santa, 229
Rossellini, Roberto, 20
Rossellino (architect), 265
Rossini, Gioacchino Antonio, 123, 280, 284
Rothery, Agnes, 38
Rovereto, Italy, 354
Rox, Henry, 306
Ruegg, Ernest, 35, 235
Rumerlo, Italy, 371
Ruskin, John, 329, 332
Rutelli (artist), 178

Sabáudia, Italy, 195
Sabines, The, 95-96
Sacro Monte, 388
SAD, *see Società Automobilistica Dolomiti*
Sade, Hugo de, 120
SADEM, 28
St. John Lateran Cathedral, 165-166
St. Mark's Cathedral, 115
St. Mark's Church (Venice), 98
St. Peter's Cathedral, 6, 17, 81, 105, 123, 126, 132, 137, 147, 149, 164-165, 168-170, 184, 185, 418
St.-Germain, Treaty of, 99
St.-Vincent, Italy, 401
Sala, Italy, 384
Sala Goldoni, 258
Salerno, Gulf of, 209, 214
Salerno, Italy, 195
  war damage, 22
Salome, 411
Saltino, Italy, 268
  hotels, 268
Salvati, 337
San Cristina, Italy, 369
San Genésio, Italy, 360
San Gimignano, Italy, 26, 60, 118, 238, 247-249, 273, 304
San Marco d'Alúnzio, Sicily, 26
San Marino, 302, 306-315, 422
  hotels, 310-311
  war damage, 22, 308
San Martino, 207-208
San Miniato, 278
San Quérico d'Orcia, Italy, 238, 267
San Remo, Italy, 85, 416-417
San Vigílio, Italy, 364, 365, 389
Sangallo, Antonio, 167, 239
Sanguinetti, Italy, 252
Sansovino, 323, 332
Santa Lucia, 201
Santa Margherita Ligure, Italy, 416
Sant'António, Italy, 359
Santi, Giovanni, 264
Saracens, The, 97, 195, 227, 228, 287
Sardinia, 20
Sarto, Andrea del, 287
Sassi, Italy, 394
Sasso Marconi, Italy, 301

SATI, see *Società Autoservizi Turistici Italiani*
Saturday Review of Literature, The, 38
Saturnia, S.S., 6
Savonarola, Girolamo, 105, 277, 299
Savoy, 105, 106
Scafati, Italy, 214
Scala Santa, 165-166
Scarlatti, Domenico Girolamo, 123-124
Schéggia, Italy, 263
Scotti, Antonio, 124
Scrovegni Family, 346
Sea travel, see Steamship lines
SEAG, see Società Editoriale Anno Giubilare
Seeing Europe Today Without Red Tape as Nearly as Possible on a Shoestring (Tyarks), 7
Segesta, Sicily, 231
Self-ironing fabrics, 72-73
Selinunte, Sicily, 231
Sella Pass, 369
Septimius Severus, Emperor, 102
Sério, River, 343
Serrara Fontana, Ischia, 222
Servius Tullius, 163
Sestrières (snow resort), 85
Seven Hills of Rome, 149
Sforza, 307
Shakespeare, William, 350, 351
Shannon, Ireland, 4, 5
Shelley, Percy Bysshe, 127, 293
Shoonmaker, Frank, 139
Shops, 68-69
  Florence, 270
  Genoa, 407
  midday closing hours, 74
  Milan, 376
  Rome, 148-149
  Sicily, 233
  Sorrento, 216
Sibylline Books, 210
Sicily, 20, 225-234, 419
  food, 57-58
  hotels, 225-227
  shops, 233
  war damage, 22
Sicilian Vespers, The, 104, 228

Siena, Italy, 17, 25, 28, 104, 111, 112, 237, 238, 241-247, 257, 273, 286, 302, 320, 332, 420
  artists, 133-135
  cathedrals, 243-245
  churches, 245
  hotels, 241
  Il Palio, 82
  palaces, 245
  restaurants, 242
Signorelli, Luca, 135, 136, 240-241, 252, 267, 282
Silla, Italy, 301
Simplon Tunnel, 9
Sirmione, Italy, 354, 355
Sixtus V, Pope, 179
Skiing, 85
Skylarks, 300
So You're Going to Italy (Laughlin), 38
Società Automobilistica Dolomiti, 28, 354, 356, 357, 358, 359, 366-367, 368
Società Autoservizi Turistici Italiani, 28
Società Editoriale Anno Giubilare, 148
Sodoma, Il, 135, 245, 267
Sóndrio, Italy, 358, 364
Soprabolzano, Italy, 359
Sorrento, Italy, 120, 209, 214, 216-217
  restaurants, 65
South Tyrol, 105, 106
Spartacus, 206
Spello, Italy, 251
Spinola Family, 411
Spoleto, Italy, 26, 237, 250
Sports, 17, 29, 84-85, 117, 174, 314-315, 369, 370
Stadium of the Marbles, 174
Staulin, Italy, 372
Strauss, Richard, 274
Steamship lines, 6-8
Stella, Italy, 359
Stella Polaris, 325
Stélvio Pass, 364
Stoppini, Giulio, 255
Stradivari, Antonio, 121, 124, 320
Stresa, Italy, 381
Strómboli Island, 200
Summer in Italy, A (O'Faolain), 38
Superga, Italy, 394, 395

INDEX

Sutton, Horace, 38
Sweeney, Betty Laughlin, 38
Symonds, John Addington, 98, 138
Symphony orchestras, 80
Syracuse, Sicily, 18, 25, 225, 227, 231, 232-233, 419
   Greek Theater, 96-97
   Mid-May Fortnight of Greek Drama, 82

Talvera River, 360
Taormina, Sicily, 65, 68, 225, 226, 229, 231, 233-234, 419
   Greek Theater, 97
Táranto, Italy, 223, 224
Tarkington, Booth, 221
Tarpeian Rock, 160-161, 182
Tartini, Giuseppe, 122
Tasso, Torquato, 120, 298, 299
Taxis, 74-75, 76-77
Taylor, Robert, 187
Temple of Divus Romulus, 184
Temple of Vesta, 184
Tenda, France, 19
Tennyson, Alfred, 355
Termini Station (Rome), 10, 37, 50, 145, 388
Terminillo (snow resort), 85
Terni, Italy, 237, 250, 260
Terschak, Federico, 370
Terschak Chimney, 370
Theater of Marcellus, 161
Theodoric the Great, 98, 295, 297
Thetis (ship), 206
This Week in Rome, 38, 156, 158
Thorwaldsen, Bertel, 384
Tiber, River, 251
Tiberius, Emperor, 102, 190, 218
Ticino, River, 423
Tiepolo, Giovanni Battista, 141, 142, 335
Tintoretto, 140-141, 335, 339
Tipping, 46-47
Tirano, Italy, 364
Tirolo Village, Italy, 365
Tirrénia, Italy, 292
Titan, The, 133
Titian, 138, 139-140, 182, 335, 338, 339, 372, 373
Titus, Emperor, 102, 161, 211

Tivoli, Italy, 191-192
Tobacco, 71-72
Tobino, Giulio, 407
Todi, Italy, 261-262
   restaurants, 262
Tomb of Galla Placidia, 296
Tomb of the Unknown Soldier, 185
Tor Sanguigna, 151
Torcello Island, 336
Torre Annunziata, Italy, 212
Torre del Greco, Italy, 211-212
Torre del Lago—Puccini, Italy, 123, 292
Torrenova, Sicily, 26
Torricelli, Evangelista, 421
Toscanini, Arturo, 17, 19, 79, 124, 293, 318, 387
Touring Club Italiano, 20, 21
Touring Routes in the Dolomites, 358
Tourist Guide to Florence, 272
Tourist News, 17
Tourist News from Italy, 82
Trajan, Emperor, 102
Trajan's Market, 161
Trams, 75
Trans World Airlines, Inc., 3, 145
Transportation, *see also* Air lines; Railways; Steamship lines
   local, 74-76
Trasimeno, Lake, 237, 251
Travel Routes Around the World, 7
Tre Croci Pass, 373
Treaty of St.-Germain, 99
Trelawny, Captain Edward John, 127
Tremezzo, Italy, 383, 385
   hotels, 383
Trentino, Italy, 99, 106, 358
Trento, Italy, 354, 357
Tresa, River, 835
Trevi, Italy, 26, 250
Treviso, Italy, 350
Trieste, 99, 106
Trollybusses, 75, 76, 152
Turin, Italy, 28, 392
   food, 58-59
   hotels, 394
   opera house, 79
   restaurants, 395-397
   war damage, 23, 392

Tuscany, 105, 106, 291
  food, 58
TWA, see Trans World Airlines, Inc.
Tyarks, Frederic E., 7
Tyrolese of Alto Ádige, 99

Uccello, Paolo, 129, 280, 281
Uffizi Gallery, 22, 277, 281, 282, 294
Ulysses, 204, 221
Umbria, Italy, artists, 133, 135-137
Umbrians, The, 96
Unità, 108
United States Information Service, 39
Urban VIII, Pope, 105, 265
Urbino, Italy, 26, 136, 137, 263-265
  hotels, 263
USIS, see United States Information Service

Vaccaro, Giuseppe, 310
Valentinian III, 296
Valette, Marc de, 86
Valicella, Italy, 113
Valley of Aosta, 19, 399-404
Vallombrosa, Italy, 127, 268
Vallombrosian Order, 268
Vandals, The, 103
Varenna, Italy, 385
Varese, Italy, 381
Vasari, Giorgio, 130, 131, 135, 240, 252, 289
Vatican, 17, 99, 136, 147, 149, 167-173
Vatican City, 17, 99, 107, 167-173
Vecchio, Palma, 138, 139
Velletri, Italy, 190
Venetia, 105
Venice, Italy, 24, 113, 114, 115, 116, 119, 125, 126, 132, 137, 141, 294, 297, 314, 324-342, 344, 421
  artists, 138-142
  cafés, 66
  food, 59
  guided tours, 29
  history, 100, 104, 105, 106
  hotels, 326, 327-330
  night life, 341-342
  opera house, 79
  restaurants, 65, 328, 330-332
  shops, 68

Venice, Italy (Cont.)
  symphony orchestra, 80
  war damage, 23
Verdi, Giuseppe, 79, 120, 124-125, 241, 280, 292, 318
Vergato, Italy, 301
Verona, Italy, 104, 118, 141, 249, 290, 343, 349-352, 354, 356, 421
  hotels, 350
  restaurants, 350
Veronese, Paolo, 141, 335
Verrès, Italy, 401
Verrocchio, Andrea del, 113, 132, 277, 280, 338
Vespasian, Emperor, 102, 161
Vestal Virgins, 162
Vesuvius, 206-207, 210, 212, 214
Via Emilia, 302, 316, 317
Via Flaminia, 263
Via Travel Service, 150
Viaréggio, Italy, 127, 293
Vicenza, Italy, 193, 343, 348-349, 350
Victor Emmanuel II, 105, 106, 151, 160, 185
Victor Emmanuel III, 107, 173
Vietri, Italy, 215
Villa d'Este, 191, 192-193, 200, 381
Villa San Michele, 219
Vinci, Italy, 132, 267
Vincoli, Italy, 293
Viollet-le-Duc, 296
Visconti, Gian Galeazzo, 390
Visigoths, The, 103
Vitali, Giovanni, 122
Viterbo, Italy, 26, 61, 237
Vivaldi, Antonio, 125, 257
Vogelweide, Walther von der, 359
Volsci, 195
Volta, Alessandro, 119, 382-383
Volterra, Daniele, 172
Volterra, Italy, 26, 266
Vulcan, 209
Vulcania, S.S., 6
Vulcano Island, 20

Wagner, Richard, 216
War damage, 21-23, 78, 190, 199-200, 215, 237, 252

War damage (Cont.)
  Bolzano, 357
  Brescia, 353
  Faenza, 305
  Florence, 271, 283
  Genoa, 405, 407, 413
  Leghorn, 292
  Milan, 374-375
  Padua, 347
  Parma, 318
  Pisa, 286-287, 290
  Pistoia, 300
  Ravenna, 296-297, 298
  Rimini, 307, 308
  San Marino, 308
  Tremezzo, 383
  Turin, 392
  Verona, 352
Well of San Patrizio, 239

White Mountain, 403
Wilhelm II, 221
William, the Conqueror, 227
Wilson, Woodrow, 355
Wilstach, Paul, 224
Wines, 16-17, 26, 29, 59-62, 189, 212, 237, 331, 362, 419
Witty Brothers, 73
Wonders of Italy (Fattorusso), 38-39, 128
Wong, Jade Snow, 306

Young, Francis Brett, 221
Young, Loretta, 157
Your Holiday in Italy (Cooper), 38

Zermatt, Switzerland, 402
Zoppi, Signor, 331
Zweig, Stefan, 274

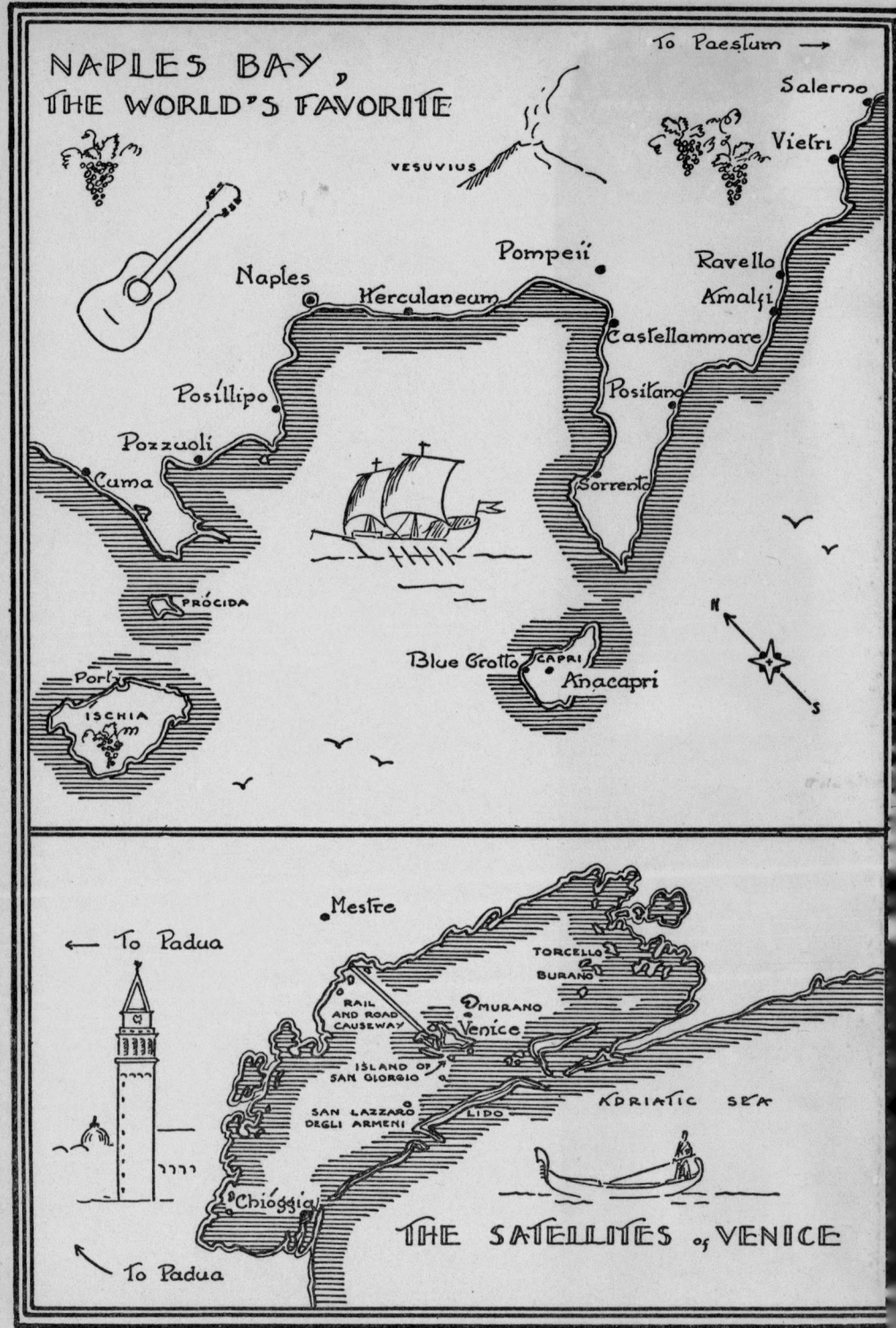